SHAKESPEAREAN CRITICISM

Volume 2

HENRY THE FOURTH
PARTS I AND II

HENRY THE FOURTH
PARTS I AND II
Critical Essays

Edited by
DAVID BEVINGTON

Routledge
Taylor & Francis Group
LONDON AND NEW YORK

First published in 1986

This edition first published in 2015
by Routledge
2 Park Square, Milton Park, Abingdon, Oxon, OX14 4RN

and by Routledge
711 Third Avenue, New York, NY 10017

Routledge is an imprint of the Taylor & Francis Group, an informa business

British Library Cataloguing in Publication Data
A catalogue record for this book is available from the British Library

ISBN: 978-1-138-84955-6 (Set)
eISBN: 978-1-315-72488-1 (Set)
ISBN: 978-1-138-84960-0 (Volume 2)
eISBN: 978-1-315-72545-1 (Volume 2)
Pb ISBN: 978-1-138-85077-4 (Volume 2)

Publisher's Note
The publisher has gone to great lengths to ensure the quality of this book but points out that some imperfections from the original may be apparent.

Disclaimer
The publisher has made every effort to trace copyright holders and would welcome correspondence from those they have been unable to trace.

HENRY THE FOURTH PARTS I AND II
Critical Essays

David Bevington

GARLAND PUBLISHING, INC. • NEW YORK & LONDON
1986

Library of Congress Cataloging-in-Publication
Data
Main entry under title:

Henry the Fourth, parts I and II.

   (Shakespearean criticism; vol. 5)
   Bibliography: p.
   1. Shakespeare, William, 1564–1616.   King
Henry IV—Addresses, essays, lectures.
   2. Kings and rulers in literature—
Addresses, essays, lectures.
   I. Bevington, David M.   II. Series.
PR2809.H46   1986   822.3′3   85-45117
ISBN 0-8240-8706-2 (alk. paper)

Printed on acid-free, 250-year-life paper
Manufactured in the United States of America

Contents

General Editor's Preface

The Garland series is designed to bring together the best that has been written about Shakespeare's plays, both as dramatic literature and theatrical performance. With the exception of some early plays which are treated in related combinations, each volume is devoted to a single play to include the most influential historical criticism, the significant modern interpretations, and reviews of the most illuminating productions. The collections are intended as resource companions to the texts. The scholar, the student, the reader, the director, the actor, the audience, will find here the full range of critical opinion, scholarly debate, and popular taste. Much of the material reproduced has been extremely difficult for the casual reader to locate. Original volumes have long since been out of print; definitive articles have been buried in journals and editions now obscure; theatrical reviews are discarded with each day's newspaper.

"The best that has been written" about each play is the criterion for selection, and the volumes represent the collective wisdom of foremost Shakespearean scholars throughout the world. Each editor has had the freedom and responsibility to make accessible the most insightful criticism to date for his or her play. I express my gratitude to the team of international scholars who have accepted this challenge. One would like to say with Keats "that is all/Ye know on earth, and all ye need to know," but the universality of Shakespeare will stimulate new responses, yield fresh meanings, and lead new generations to richer understandings of human nature.

Generally the essays have been reproduced as they appeared originally. Some concessions in punctuation, spelling, and documentation have been made for the sake of conformity. In the case of excerpts, notes have been renumbered to clarify the references. A principle of the series, however, is to reproduce the full text, rather than excerpts, except for digressive material having no bearing on the subject.

Joseph Price

Editor's Preface

No single volume can do justice to criticism of the *Henry IV* plays. I have tried to represent the best and most characteristic thought of the neoclassical age, of character criticism in the latter eighteenth and the nineteenth centuries, of historical and New Criticism in the twentieth century, of myth criticism, psychoanalytic criticism, speech act theory, theatrical interpretation, and others. These labels are themselves inadequate; the finest criticism refuses to be pigeonholed, and we read Samuel Johnson, W. H. Auden, C. L. Barber, or Jonas Barish on *Henry IV* to widen our own imaginations rather than to understand the past. A volume like this can only hope to indicate in a partial way the rich variety of critical responses to the *Henry IV* plays and even more the infinite complexity in those plays themselves.

Such an undertaking inevitably produces its regrets. I am sorry not to have included more of the historical criticism of E. E. Stoll and Levin Schücking, alluded to in my Introduction and bibliography but omitted from the collection. "Prince Hal's Conflict" (*Psychoanalytic Quarterly* 17 (1948), 487–506) by Ernst Kris deserves a place in this volume; I have left it out primarily because Robert Watson's more recent study incorporates much of it. William Empson's *Some Version of Pastoral* (1935) says some wonderfully insightful things about *Henry IV* but is hard to excerpt. Harold Jenkins' *The Structural Problem in Shakespeare's "Henry the Fourth"* (1956), baldly summarized in my Introduction, is influential but is rather long and technical for a collection of this sort. I fear that metadramatic criticism is underrepresented, and I would have liked to include James L. Calderwood's "*1 Henry IV*: Art's Gilded Lie" (*English Literary Renaissance* 3 (1973), 131–44), but have had to rely on the earlier metadramatic discussion of Sigurd Burckhardt to which Calderwood is indebted. E. M. W. Tillyard's schematization of honor and justice has been importantly amplified by Sherman H. Hawkins' "*Henry IV*: The Structural Problem Revisited" (*Shakespeare Quarterly* 33 (1982), 278–301), and I recommend this essay to the reader. At one point my manuscript included a fine essay by Gordon Zeeveld in *The Temper of Shakespeare's Thought* (1974), Sheldon Zitner's "Anon, Anon: or, a Mirror for a Magistrate" (*Shakespeare Quarterly* 3 (1952), 249–53), Wyndham Lewis' *The Lion and the Fox* (1927), Joseph Porter's *The Drama of Speech Acts* (1979), Alvin Kernan's "The Henriad: Shakespeare's Major History Plays" (*Yale Review* 59 (1969), 3–32), and still more. I hope that my collection will encourage the reader to go beyond it to the essays named here and to many others.

In the making of choices and other matters, I have been assisted by Leeds Barroll, David Kastan, Richard Strier, Eugene Waith, and the general editor of this series, Joseph Price. I greatly appreciate their wise counsel and cherish their support and friendship. The custodians of the rare book room at Regenstein Library, University of Chicago, have been unfailingly resourceful and courteous.

David Bevington
Chicago, May 1985

Introduction

Although criticism in the seventeenth and eighteenth centuries generally brought to the study of drama a classical perspective, it made a grand exception for Shakespeare as one whose native genius transcends the usual requirements of classical unity and decorum. The point is often made in terms of an instructive contrast between Shakespeare and his more classically correct contemporary, Ben Jonson. Jonson himself complains that Shakespeare lacks "art" when he provides the landlocked country of Bohemia with a seacoast or allows whole decades of time to elapse in the course of a single play or wafts his characters overseas between scenes, though Jonson is as quick to grant that Shakespeare has "an excellent phantasy." Milton's *L'Allegro* contrasts Jonson's "learned sock" with "sweetest Shakespeare, fancy's child," warbling "his native wood-notes wild."

The *Henry IV* plays, and especially Falstaff, illustrate the point. Part I in particular was enormously popular in the seventeenth century, going through more editions in Shakespeare's lifetime than any other of his plays and surviving as a kind of "droll" or skit about Falstaff even when the theaters were closed in the 1640s and 1650s. Falstaff struck eighteenth-century critics as a quintessentially Shakespearean character, indeed his finest comic creation. Corbyn Morris (1744), for example, to prove his thesis that true humour (in which English comedy excels) is at its best a foible or remarkable oddity of character giving more delight than satirical wit, extols Falstaff as one in whom humour "is the groundwork and chief substance" while wit "quickens the whole with embellishments." Sir John is a creature of "generosity, cheerfulness, alacrity, invention, frolic, and fancy superior to all other men," so that it is impossible to hate him despite his manifest failings. He is unlike anything created by Jonson, in whose characters, accurate and truthful though they be, "there is something very justly to be hated or despised." Dr. Samuel Johnson (1765), more aware than Morris of vices in Falstaff that may have seemed too much like Jonson's own (corpulence, sloth, overindulgence, delight in repartee), nonetheless apostrophizes Falstaff as "unimitated" and "unimitable."

Elizabeth Montagu (1769) views Shakespeare as "little under the discipline of art," and accordingly takes Shakespeare to task for some indecent passages (especially involving Doll Tearsheet) that are "not only indefensible but inexcusable" and that not even the supposed barbarity or corruption of Shakespeare's age could excuse, and yet concedes of Falstaff's character that "we must certainly admire it and own it to be perfectly original." Henry Mackenzie and Richard Cumberland, writing in 1786, both address their remarks to "the Character of Falstaff," agreeing that in this remarkable creation Shakespeare shows himself of all poets "to have possessed a fancy the most prolific, an imagination the most luxuriantly fertile." Falstaff outdistances anything achieved even by Homer, says Mackenzie, "in the mere creation of fancy." Cumberland insists on Shakespeare's superiority not only to Ben Jonson but to Congreve and other practitioners of classically decorous comedy of manners. This is high praise indeed from a classical age. With a single voice the seventeenth and eighteenth centuries commended Shakespeare as the supreme poet of fancy and imagination, and turned again and again to Falstaff as an unsurpassed instance of Shakespeare's creative genius.

Despite this unanimity of critical favor, later eighteenth century critics do not agree as to the nature of our sympathies with the Prince's fat companion. Dr. Johnson finds Falstaff corrupt and despicable, a thief and glutton and cowardly boaster, all the more dangerous to the Prince because of his seductive power to please. Mrs. Montagu agrees that "gluttony, corpulency, and cowardice are the peculiarities of Falstaff's composition," rendering him "ridiculous" though without folly, and skillfully made ridiculous and contemptible by Shakespeare in order to offset his entertaining wit and thus prevent us (and the Prince) from too great an attraction to one who is a tempter to vice. Maurice Morgann (1777), on the other hand, takes issue with the very terms in which Falstaff is regarded as a threat to the future king of England. Morgann wishes to argue above all that Falstaff is no real coward. He points to Falstaff's reputation among his acquaintances for a swordsman and commander of men in battle, one who has indeed led his soldiers where they have been heavily fired upon. He distinguishes between Falstaff's resourceful evasion of death at the hands of Douglas and the natural cowardice of Bardolph or Peto. In the Gad's Hill episode, Morgann similarly argues on behalf of an old fat man who undertakes a robbery with no apparent signs of fear and who then, after a blow or two, refuses to engage two bold and vigorous assailants who are plainly too much for him.

Morgann's defense of Falstaff as a soldier and man of courage has not found many adherents, but it does illustrate certain features of criticism in the age for which it was written. Most important is the focus on character. All the critics mentioned so far judge Falstaff as though he were a man who once lived and whom one might have known; they wonder what he would have been like as a companion, they evaluate him morally as an influence on behavior, they want to know more about his earlier years. They also view Hal as a realistic human figure, one who did in fact rule England as Henry V. In character criticism, Falstaff and Hal live independently from the play in which they are located. As Robert Langbaum observes (1957), sympathy of this sort for Shakespeare's characters appears, not coincidentally, in the latter eighteenth century when humanitarian attitudes were on the rise. Falstaff appeals to an age of sensibility, liberal politics, and mistrust of prudence. The notion of a constitutional courage, explicitly divorced from actions that appear cowardly to our outward understanding, is an appeal to what Falstaff in himself seems to be. Falstaff is admired because he is no hypocrite, and conversely because he is one in whom self-expression is supreme. In Langbaum's terms, the latter eighteenth-century Falstaff is the central figure of a dramatic monologue accentuating character at the expense of dramatic function. Not surprisingly, we find in Morgann a mistrust of his contemporary stage, especially the "low buffoonery" of those actors who play up Falstaff's cowardice and allow him to be humbled by the Prince and Poins at Gad's Hill until "he is goaded off the stage like a fat ox for slaughter." The psychological criticism of the latter eighteenth century is a literary response to the play and a repudiation of the Shakespearean acting styles of the times.

Nineteenth-century criticism retains a psychological focus and skepticism toward theatrical interpretation. Samuel Taylor Coleridge (c. 1811) speaks of Falstaff as "no coward," a first rate wit and talent who can only feel a profound contempt for those by whom he is usually surrounded—including, we must suppose, the Prince of Wales. William Hazlitt (1817) is more explicit in his preference for a life of sensual freedom to one of Machiavellianism at court. Falstaff is a philosopher on the field of battle, pulling out his bottle "to show his contempt for glory accompanied with danger," and systematically adhering to his Epicurean philosophy even "in the most trying circumstances." We can never forgive the Prince's heartless treatment of Falstaff. Hal is too like his father, prudent and cautious in keeping what he has got. Between Hal and Falstaff the moral choice is clear: "Falstaff is the better man of the two." George Bernard Shaw (1907), though well ahead of his time in his theatrical sensitivity and in his refusal to sentimentalize Falstaff ("a besotted and disgusting old wretch"), agrees with Hazlitt in denouncing Prince Henry as a "Jingo hero" in whom are unattractively combined conventional propriety and brute masterfulness in things political, and "low-lived blackguardism" in his private tastes. Hal's self-indulgent good fellowship with the Boar's Head crew is, in Shaw's view, "consciously and deliberately treacherous."

A. C. Bradley admirably sums up (in 1902) the prevailing nineteenth-century view of Falstaff, just as in his essays on Shakespearean tragedy Bradley gives most eloquent and finished expression to the study of Shakespeare's characters. Rejecting out of hand the hoodwinked and humiliated Falstaff of *Merry Wives* as not "the real" Falstaff, Bradley sees in the *Henry IV* plays a comic figure whom we hugely enjoy, one who is no mere reprobate and cowardly sensualist but a genius of mirth and a devoted companion of the Prince. Falstaff rides all day and night to greet the newly crowned Henry V, in Bradley's view, thinking "of nothing else but to see Henry." The rejection overwhelms him, and we hear in *Henry V* that "the King has killed his heart." The Prince, on the other hand, disappoints us severely by his "ungenerous" and "dishonest" conduct in lecturing Falstaff as the misleader of his youth. Henry is a hero king, to be sure, but he displays a characteristic hardness and regard for policy that should warn us of what is to come. And since Shakespeare surely intended his *Henry* plays to end "pleasantly," it follows (1) that Shakespeare must have intended our sympathy with Falstaff to weaken progressively, and (2) that Shakespeare missed his aim in this crucial regard. Shakespeare "overshot his mark," creating in Falstaff "so extraordinary a being" and so firmly fixed on his intellectual throne that "when he sought to dethrone him he could not." *Henry IV* is in this sense a noble and generous failure, for however imperfect the ending of the second play, we are given an immortal creation of "humorous superiority to everything serious" whose "freedom of soul" can teach us to enjoy those things the Prince must reject.

Even by the time of Bradley's defense of Falstaff, however, we perceive a reaction in Shakespeare criticism against the study of psychological character and in favor of historical understanding. Edward Dowden, writing in 1875, surveys the development of Shakespeare's mind and art in a chronological frame made newly possible by increasingly accurate dating of Shakespeare's plays, some of it accomplished by German scholars. The experiment leads Dowden to wonder if there may not have been "passages in Shakespeare's own experience" which prompted him to explore a conflict between two states of being in the inner self, one temporary and provisional, the other absolute and final. The focus is on Hal, not Falstaff, as Dowden's Prince enters "without reserve into the fun and frolic of his Eastcheap life" while at the same time keeping himself "from subjugation to what was truly base." Dowden's interest is in the historical figure of young Henry, one who goes beyond his father's troubled and partial success to become Shakespeare's "ideal of manhood." Such a young king must unfalteringly estrange himself from Falstaff.

The Falstaff of twentieth-century historical critics is almost invariably one who must be rejected. Historically, Falstaff is discovered to possess a remarkable ancestry in literature and on the stage, and this complex ancestry seldom does him credit. He resembles the braggart cowardly soldier of Roman and Elizabethan comedy, Gluttony among the seven Deadly Sins, the Folly of Erasmus' *Encomium Moriae*, Apuleius' Golden Ass, the Lord of Misrule, the Pedant as a stage type, the famous Elizabethan comic actor Richard Tarleton, the professional soldier and the highwayman as portrayed (often satirically) in contemporary pamphlets, the martyred Lollard Sir John Oldcastle whose name Falstaff evidently bore in the earliest version of *1 Henry IV*, the Picaresque rogue, the Centaur of Greek mythology, and still others. Bernard Spivack (1958) invokes the tradition of the morality Vice to explain the way in which "the shadow of a serious moral judgment" hovers about Falstaff, presenting him as "an inextricable mixture of farce and high moral seriousness, the source of both the gaiety and gravity of the play." Historical critics like E. E. Stoll (1927) and Levin Schücking (1922) attack what they view as the sentimentality of character criticism and its deplorable tendency to search for a "real" Falstaff outside the play; cowardly behavior is a literary and stage convention, to be historically traced and defined, and according to such definition the cowardice of Falstaff at Gad's Hill is perfectly clear. Falling flat and roaring are old tricks of clowns. Hal's first-act soliloquy is not to be explored psychologically but viewed as explanatory and chorus-like in its function. The rejection of Falstaff must not be judged by modern and subjective standards; the Prince's actions are those of a renaissance monarch and must be understood in that context.

Among the historical critics represented in this collection, John Dover Wilson (1943) and E. M. W. Tillyard (1944) are perhaps the most influential. Wilson is openly skeptical of Maurice Morgann's brave Falstaff or Bradley's apostle of free soul. He adroitly insists that what emerges from Bradley's pages is not Falstaff at all but the effect of Falstaff on that hypersensitive and donnish reader of English poetry at Oxford. Instead, Wilson urges a return to the unsentimentalized Falstaff of Dr. Johnson, a Falstaff at once endlessly entertaining and all the more dangerous for being so. Wilson buttresses this Johnsonian position with an array of historical insights. Falstaff must be seen as related to Vanity or Riot in the old morality play, escaping from tight corners with dexterity, jesting about the gallows, and prevailing upon Youth with his counsel of irresponsibility. Shakespeare's chronicle and dramatic sources show us where Shakespeare got his idea of Hal as prodigal and Falstaff as an old white-bearded Satan. The main theme, for Wilson, of Shakespeare's "morality play" is "the growing-up of a madcap prince into the ideal king, who was Henry V." It is a story of conversion, and inevitably directs its characters toward that end. The signs of Falstaff's debauchery are to be found everywhere in the *Henry IV* plays, and owe much to the Eastcheap taverns and shops of Shakespeare's London. The very similes used by and about Falstaff constitute an inventory of ribs, tallow, chops, and other combustibles. Falstaff's mocking role of Repentance similarly draws on Puritan habits of speech familiar to Shakespeare's audience.

Like Wilson, Tillyard sees *Henry IV* as a morality play written in two parts but best understood as a single play. The struggle between Prince Henry and Hotspur is only part of a larger plan, evident in the structural similarity of the two parts. In both, Hal must choose between antithetically contrasted companions or role models. The choice in Part I is between "the excess and the defect of the military spirit," between "honour exaggerated and dishonour"; in Part II, Hal must choose between order or justice and disorder or misrule. The Prince is both Magnificence in a morality play and Aristotle's "middle quality between two extremes." Though entertained by Falstaff, Hal is from the start Olympian, powerful, and sophisticated. He is Shakespeare's "studied picture of the kingly type." When we see the plays in the context of Thomas Elyot's *Governor* and Castiglione's *Cortegiano* we realize that the Prince is Shakespeare's embodiment of *sprezzatura* or princely nonchalance. The argument for a single two-part structure is carried further by Harold Jenkins' *The Structural Problem in Shakespeare's "Henry the Fourth"* (1956), in which Jenkins argues that Shakespeare originally intended a single play but changed his mind as he wrote. Justice is a theme from the very start, along with honor, and the parallels between Falstaff and Hotspur are closely pursued until Act IV, when the writing becomes less compressed; having more material than he could encompass in one play, Shakespeare improvised a second part with subplots on the theme of justice.

Much recent criticism in the twentieth century can be viewed as a response to or divergence from the historical emphases of Tillyard, Wilson, and others. Mark Van Doren (1939) offers a close reading of the *Henry IV* plays based not on historical perspective or ideas of convention but on a sensitivity to the idiom of Falstaff's talk about vocation and his expertise in miming, or to the explosive rhythms of Hotspur in which Shakespeare has "learned at last to make poetry as natural as the human voice." Van Doren is less attracted to Hal than to Falstaff, who "understands everything and so is never serious," whose mind "is at home everywhere" and "never darkened with self-thought." R. J. Dorius' essay, "A Little More Than a Little" (1960), nicely demonstrates what the so-called New Criticism can do with imagistic and thematic patterns of prudence and economy versus carelessness, excess, disease, and the wasting of time. Far from threatening the structure of the histories, as some writers have argued, Falstaff here becomes "one of their central organizing symbols." D. J. Palmer (1970) pays close attention to Biblical quotation in the *Henry IV* plays, to Falstaff's "damnable iteration" of Scripture, to Prince Henry's echoes of St. Paul on redeeming time, and to the Pauline injunction to cast off "the old man" or unregenerate Adam. Paul Gottschalk (1974) provides a thematic focus on a single episode, the "play extempore," in which two kinds of role-playing come into conflict: Falstaff's impulse to "reduce all things to play" and hence convert reality into a timeless fiction, and Hal's embracement of his own future political reality. Jonas Barish (1965) brings to his close reading of the *Henry IV* plays an awareness of genre and the competing claims of history and comedy, in which context Prince Hal displays an element of self-rejection and even self-mutilation as he turns away from his former self. History defeats those who (like Falstaff) would defy it by trying to live in a changeless youth.

A more frontal assault on historical criticism is that of Sigurd Burckhardt (1968), who insists that the "calculated symmetries of dialectics" so neatly laid out in Tillyard's Aristotelian schema are not as victorious over disorder as one might complacently suppose. In the end it is Falstaff, the creature of Shakespeare's imagination rather than of history, who asserts himself as "the reality principle incarnate," rising at Shrewsbury field to destroy all sorts of reassuring symmetries including that of stage and world. *2 Henry IV* is a still more disillusioning play than Part I: it promises to repeat the design of the first play but then frustrates our expectation and with it the comforting truisms of Tudor doctrine condemning rebellion as wicked and ungodly. Prince John of Lancaster's treachery at Gaultree forest, shocking in itself, is accepted without comment. The piety is more offensive than the treachery. Monarchical order has become secular, resting on pragmatic rather than divine sanction; the age of holy wars is past. Tillyard's symmetries fail to account for the play's sense of debility and decline, its "unexpressed, stifled grief." Shakespeare is of course aware of the "Elizabethan world picture" so extolled by Tillyard, but he opposes it dramatically and complementarily with the harsher realities of *de facto* rule and human action in time.

Burckhardt's argument finds support from Henry Ansgar Kelly (1970), who argues that Tillyard's monolithic "Tudor myth" is in fact several conflicting myths set down in the chronicles to suit the arguments of various political sides in late medieval and Tudor England, and used dramatically by Shakespeare to represent political conflict among self-interested parties. Ronald Macdonald (1984) carries the argument into the realm of speech act theory by studying a transition in the *Henry IV* plays between a feudal language of sacred kingship as ineffectually practiced by Richard II and the pragmatic idiom of Falstaff, to whom the locutionary act of swearing an oath no longer means what it once signified. Even in Richard's day the claim of royal divinity bespeaks an awareness that the king is fragile and vulnerable, whereas the newer world of the Henrys clings nostalgically to the idiom of the old order as something precious and forever lost. Yet "the changes of history demand changes of language"; to speak effectively in the new world created by usurpation "requires the exploitation of all the figurative resources of language, of irony, of understatement, of wary hyperbole and deft paronomasia." Simple grandiloquence gives way to equivocation, thereby illustrating through language the uneasy conflict in these plays that Burckhardt insists upon and Tillyard tends to explain away.

Myth criticism offers another glimpse of the disorder that Tillyard and Wilson seek to contain and rationalize. Following up on Northrop Frye's suggestion that Falstaff is "a mock king, a lord of misrule, and his tavern is a Saturnalia" (1949), C. L. Barber (1959) argues that Shakespeare dramatizes "not only holiday but also the need for holiday and the need to limit holiday." Analogies to the temporary king and scapegoat in folk rituals highlight both the likeness of comedy to ritual and the differences. The antithesis of holiday and everyday is as important to Hal as to Falstaff, for Hal must choose between Misrule and Good Government. Falstaff's comic resurrection at Shrewsbury reminds us of those in the St. George plays, and his apology for counterfeiting applies not merely to himself but (as William Empson also shows, 1935) to the counterfeiting of the king. We need not assume Shakespeare's awareness of ritual analogies to see a strategy at work fundamentally like that of carrying off bad luck by the scapegoat of saturnalian ritual. Barber gives a particularly useful insight into magical notions of royal power, whether in Falstaff's burlesques or in the tragic ironies of Richard II's hyperbolic appeals to heavenly assistance. In *2 Henry IV* Carnival is put on trial and is run out of town, thereby completing the folk custom of "limiting, by ritual, the attitudes and impulses set loose by ritual," though Falstaff of course proves more difficult to bring to book than any ordinary mummery king. Burlesque does not severely threaten social values in a monolithic culture, but Shakespeare's culture is no longer monolithic; hence our perception of the relation between order and disorder must be problematic.

G. K. Hunter (1959) similarly invokes anthropology to understand how a king or governor may sometimes have to sacrifice his own private good for the public welfare: "the scapegoat reigns in honour, even adoration, but then he is slaughtered mercilessly and his death rejoiced over as taking away the sins of the nation." Robert G. Hunter (1978) defines Carnival as "an attempt to regain occasionally and temporarily the bliss of living within appetitive time," a period society sets aside for "sanctioned play" and role-playing, a necessary holiday and yet one that is riddled with conflict because of the Protestant ethic of Shakespeare's day, with which Falstaff is unwilling and unable to come to terms.

The insights of psychoanalytic criticism, though sometimes obscured by technical terms and by a disposition to view characters as if they were patients with whole lives of their own, are often supportive of myth criticism. Franz Alexander (1933) sees Falstaff as "the deep infantile layers of the personality, the simple innocent wish to live and enjoy life." Prince Hal must overcome this self-centered narcissistic libido of the child, and in killing Hotspur must destroy his own self-destructive likeness and his aggression toward his parent. As W. H. Auden (1948) puts it, "Once upon a time we were all Falstaffs: then we became social beings with super-egos." Falstaff's happiness is almost an impregnable tower, but not quite; he is also "the prince's dog," to be condemned as a blasphemer and Lord of Misrule and Bad Companion for mankind. To Ernst Kris (1948), Prince Hal's conflict with his father is repeatedly reflected elsewhere in *1 Henry IV*, for Hal has in effect two fathers (King Henry and Falstaff) while the King has two sons (Hal and Hotspur), and Hotspur in turn stands between a weak father and a scheming uncle. The inconsistencies in Hal's character are not unlike those of Hamlet; only one side of the Oedipal conflict is presented, since Hal's mother remains invisible, but we are still presented with Hal's difficulty in forming a superego and with the need for a displacement of filial attachment onto a father substitute. Hal goes to the tavern rather than acquiesce in a regicide. Later, at Shrewsbury, he saves the threatened life of his father and kills his alter ego (Hotspur) instead.

Robert N. Watson (1984) offers a pre-Oedipal interpretation of *Henry IV* in which Shakespeare's ambitious figures are versions of primal criminals such as Oedipus and Cronus, whose myths associate father-son rivalry with political ambition. Prince Hal's difficult task is to come to terms with his father without succumbing to the self-destroying impulses seen in Hotspur of claiming autochthonous birth. Hal must also somehow tame the hydra monster of rebellion unleashed by his father's usurpation. Hal destroys and incorporates the opponent (Hotspur) who is both rebel and noble son, appropriating a loyal filial posture and subsuming his father's identity when he seizes Hotspur's glories. Conversely, he must come to terms with the pleasure-seeking principle or id in Falstaff, and refashion his identity without surrendering to the Oedipal desires put forward by the id. "In forbidding Falstaff (and therefore his own id) from using royal power to gratify his appetites at the expense of others, Hal is reenacting society's first triumph over the force that threatened to destroy it."

Theatrical criticism offers one final and invaluable perspective on the continuing debate over the *Henry IV* plays. Theatrical critics are generally wary of thematic readings dependent on the idea of *Henry IV* as a two-part single play, for audiences usually see the plays apart from one another and have to deal with the wholeness of each as an independent theater-going experience. Equally, theatrical critics mistrust the literary responses of nineteenth-century writers such as Morgann and Bradley with their discovery of such "latent" meanings as Falstaff's bravery. Arthur Colby Sprague (1953) confronts this parting of the ways between critics and theater-goers with a historical account of famous actors' handling of the Falstaffian role, concluding that in the theater we are inevitably given "a Falstaff of dexterous evasions and miraculous escapes, lawless in his exaggerations, redoubtable only in repute, and the funnier for being fat and old and a coward." Reviews of recent productions by R. L. Smallwood and T. F. Wharton (1983) give us a sense of the enormous range of possible interpretations in every major role of the *Henry IV* plays, and of the crucial importance of visual imagery to Shakespeare's imagination. Without living productions of Shakespeare, we would be not only less well entertained but significantly impoverished in our critical understanding of the world's greatest dramatist.

HENRY IV
PARTS I AND II

Corbyn Morris

An Essay Towards Fixing the True Standards of Wit, Humor, Raillery, Satire, and Ridicule (1744)

Humor, extensively and fully understood, is any remarkable oddity or foible belonging to a person in real life, whether this foible be constitutional, habitual, or only affected, whether partial in one or two circumstances or tinging the whole temper and conduct of the person.

It has from hence been observed that there is more humor in the English comedies than in others, as we have more various odd characters in real life than any other nation, or perhaps than all other nations together.

That humor gives more delight, and leaves a more pleasurable impression behind it than wit, is universally felt and established, though the reasons for this have not yet been assigned. I shall therefore beg leave to submit the following:

1. Humor is more interesting than wit in general, as the oddities and foibles of persons in real life are more apt to affect our passions than any oppositions or relations between inanimate objects.

2. Humor is nature, or what really appears in the subject, without any embellishments; wit only a stroke of art where the original subject, being insufficient of itself, is garnished and decked with auxiliary objects.

3. Humor, or the foible of a character in real life, is usually insisted upon for some length of time, from whence, and from the common knowledge of the character, it is universally felt and understood; whereas the strokes of wit are like sudden flashes,

vanishing in an instant, and usually flying too fast to be sufficiently marked and pursued by the audience.

4. Humor, if the representation of it be just, is complete and
perfect in its kind, and entirely fair and unstrained; whereas in
the allusions of wit the affinity is generally imperfect and defec-
tive in one part or other, and even in those points where the
affinity may be allowed to subsist some nicety and strain is
usually required to make it appear.

5. Humor generally appears in such foibles as each of the
company thinks himself superior to; whereas wit shows the quickness and abilities of the person who discovers it, and places him
superior to the rest of the company.

6. Humor, in the representation of the foibles of persons in
real life, frequently exhibits very generous benevolent sentiments
of heart, and these, though exerted in a particular odd manner,
justly command our fondness and love; whereas in the allusions
of wit, severity, bitterness, and satire are frequently exhibited,
and where these are avoided, not worthy amiable sentiments of
the heart but quick unexpected efforts of the fancy are presented.

7. The odd adventures and embarrassments which persons in
real life are drawn into by their foibles are fit subjects of mirth;
whereas in pure wit the allusions are rather surprising than
mirthful, and the agreements or contrasts which are started
between objects, without any relation to the foibles of persons in
real life, are more fit to be admired for their happiness and
propriety than to excite our laughter. Besides, wit, in the frequent
repetition of it, tires the imagination with its precipitate sallies
and flights, and teases the judgment; whereas humor, in the
representation of it, puts no fatigue upon the imagination and
gives exquisite pleasure to the judgment.

These seem to me to be the different powers and effects of
humor and wit. However, the most agreeable representations or
compositions of all others appear not where they separately exist
but where they are united together in the same fabric, where
humor is the groundwork and chief substance and wit, happily
spread, quickens the whole with embellishments.

This is the excellency of the character of Sir John Falstaff. The
groundwork is humor, or the representation and detection of a
bragging and vaunting coward in real life. However, this alone

would only have exposed the knight as a mere Noll Bluff, to the derision of the company, and after they had once been gratified with his chastisement he would have sunk into infamy, and become quite odious and intolerable. But here the inimitable wit of Sir John comes in to his support, and gives a new rise and luster to his character. For the sake of his wit you forgive his cowardice, or rather are fond of his cowardice for the occasions it gives to his wit. In short, the humor furnishes a subject and spur to the wit, and the wit again supports and embellishes the humor.

At the first entrance of the knight, your good humor and tendency to mirth are irresistibly excited by his jolly appearance and corpulency; you feel and acknowledge him to be the fittest subject imaginable for yielding diversion and merriment. But when you see him immediately set up for enterprise and activity with his evident weight and unwieldiness, your attention is all called forth, and you are eager to watch him to the end of his adventures, your imagination pointing out with a full scope his future embarrassments. All the while, as you accompany him forwards, he heightens your relish for his future disasters by his happy opinion of his own sufficiency, and the gay vaunts which he makes of his talents and accomplishments, so that at last, when he falls into a scrape, your expectation is exquisitely gratified, and you have the full pleasure of seeing all his trumpeted honor laid in the dust. When, in the midst of his misfortunes, instead of being utterly demolished and sunk he rises again by the superior force of his wit, and begins a new course with fresh spirit and alacrity, this excites you the more to renew the chase, in full view of his second defeat, out of which he recovers again and triumphs with new pretentions and boastings. After this he immediately starts upon a third race, and so on, continually detected and caught, and yet constantly extricating himself by his inimitable wit and invention, thus yielding a perpetual round of sport and diversion.

Again, the genteel quality of Sir John is of great use in supporting his character; it prevents his sinking too low after several of his misfortunes. Besides, you allow him, in consequence of his rank and seniority, the privilege to dictate and take the lead, and to rebuke others upon many occasions. By this he is saved from appearing too nauseous and impudent. The good sense which he possesses comes also to his aid, and saves him from being despicable by forcing your esteem for his real abilities. Again, the privilege you allow him of rebuking and checking others, when he assumes it with proper firmness and superiority, helps to settle anew and compose his character after an embarrassment, and reduces in some measure the spirit of the company to a proper level before he sets out again upon a fresh adventure. Without this, they would be kept continually strained and wound up to the highest pitch without sufficient relief and diversity.

It may also deserve to be remarked of Falstaff that the figure of his person is admirably suited to the turn of his mind, so that there arises before you a perpetual allusion from one to the other, which forms an incessant series of wit whether they are in contrast or agreement together. When he pretends to activity there is wit in the contrast between his mind and his person, and wit in their agreement when he triumphs in jollity.

To complete the whole, you have in this character of Falstaff not only a free course of humor, supported and embellished with admirable wit, but this humor is of a species the most jovial and gay in all nature. Sir John Falstaff possesses generosity, cheerfulness, alacrity, invention, frolic, and fancy superior to all other men. The figure of his person is the picture of jollity, mirth, and good nature, and banishes at once all other ideas from your breast; he is happy himself, and makes you happy. If you examine him further, he has no fierceness, reserve, malice, or peevishness lurking in his heart; his intentions are all pointed at innocent riot and merriment; nor has the knight any inveterate design, except against sack, and that too he loves. If, besides this, he desires to pass for a man of activity and valor, you can easily excuse so harmless a foible which yields you the highest pleasure in its constant detection.

If you put all these together, it is impossible to hate honest Jack Falstaff. If you observe them again, it is impossible to avoid loving him. He is the gay, the witty, the frolicsome, happy, and fat Jack Falstaff, the most delightful swaggerer in all nature. You must love him for your own sake; at the same time you cannot but love him for his own talents. And when you have enjoyed them you cannot but love him in gratitude; he has nothing to disgust you, and everything to give you joy. His sense and his foibles are equally directed to advance your pleasure, and it is impossible to be tired or unhappy in his company.

This jovial and gay humor, without anything envious, malicious, mischievous, or despicable, and continually quickened and adorned with wit, yields that peculiar delight, without any alloy, which we all feel and acknowledge in Falstaff's company. Ben Jonson has humor in his characters, drawn with the most masterly skill and judgment. In accuracy, depth, propriety, and truth he has no superior or equal amongst ancients or moderns. But the characters he exhibits are of a satirical and deceitful, or of a peevish or despicable, species, as Volpone, Subtle, Morose, and Abel Drugger, in all of which there is something very justly to be hated or despised. And you feel the same sentiments of dislike for every other character of Jonson's, so that after you have been gratified with their detection and punishment you are quite tired and disgusted with their company. Whereas Shakespeare, besides the peculiar gaiety in the humor of Falstaff, has guarded him from disgusting you with his forward advances by giving him rank and quality; from being despicable, by his real good sense and excellent abilities; from being odious, by his harmless plots and designs; and from being tiresome, by his inimitable wit and his new and incessant sallies of highest fancy and frolic.

This discovers the secret of carrying comedy to the highest pitch of delight, which lies in drawing the persons exhibited with such cheerful and amiable oddities and foibles as you would choose in your own companions in real life. Otherwise, though you may be diverted at first with the novelty of a character and with a proper detection and ridicule of it, yet its peevishness, meanness, or immorality will begin to disgust you after a little reflection, and become soon tiresome and odious—it being certain that whoever cannot be endured as an accidental companion in real life will never become, for the very same reasons, a favorite comic character in the theater.

Samuel Johnson

Notes from The Plays of William Shakespeare (1765)

[End-note to 2 *Henry IV*]

I fancy every reader, when he ends this play, cries out with Desdemona, "O most lame and impotent conclusion!" As this play was not, to our knowledge, divided into acts by the author, I could be content to conclude it with the death of Henry the Fourth: "In that Jerusalem shall Harry die." These scenes which now make the fifth act of *Henry the Fourth* might then be the first of *Henry the Fifth*; but the truth is that they do unite very commodiously to either play. When these plays were represented I believe they ended as they are now ended in the books; but Shakespeare seems to have designed that the whole series of action, from the beginning of *Richard the Second* to the end of *Henry the Fifth*, should be considered by the reader as one work, upon one plan, only broken into parts by the necessity of exhibition.

None of Shakespeare's plays are more read than the *First* and *Second Parts* of *Henry the Fourth*. Perhaps no author has ever in two plays afforded so much delight. The great events are interesting, for the fate of kingdoms depends upon them; the slighter occurrences are diverting, and, except one or two, sufficiently probable; the incidents are multiplied with wonderful fertility of invention, and the characters diversified with the utmost nicety of discernment, and the profoundest skill in the nature of man.

The Prince, who is the hero both of the comic and tragic part, is a young man of great abilities and violent passions, whose sentiments are right, though his actions are wrong, whose virtues are obscured by negligence, and whose understanding is dissipated by levity. In his idle hours he is rather loose than wicked, and when the occasion forces out his latent qualities he is great without effort and brave without tumult. The trifler is roused into a hero, and the hero again reposes in the trifler. This character is great, original, and just.

Percy is a rugged soldier, choleric and quarrelsome, and has only the soldier's virtues, generosity and courage.

But Falstaff unimitated, unimitable Falstaff, how shall I describe thee? Thou compound of sense and vice; of sense which may be admired but not esteemed, of vice which may be despised but hardly detested. Falstaff is a character loaded with faults, and with those faults which naturally produce contempt. He is a thief and a glutton, a coward and a boaster, always ready to cheat the weak and prey upon the poor, to terrify the timorous and insult the defenseless. At once obsequious and malignant, he satirizes in their absence those whom he lives by flattering. He is familiar with the Prince only as an agent of vice, but of this familiarity he is so proud as not only to be supercilious and haughty with common men, but to think his interest of importance to the Duke of Lancaster. Yet the man thus corrupt, thus despicable, makes himself necessary to the Prince that despises him by the most pleasing of all qualities, perpetual gaiety, by an unfailing power of exciting laughter, which is the more freely indulged as his wit is not of the splendid or ambitious kind, but consists in easy escapes and sallies of levity, which make sport but raise no envy. It must be observed that he is stained with no enormous or sanguinary crimes, so that his licentiousness is not so offensive but that it may be borne for his mirth.

The moral to be drawn from this representation is that no man is more dangerous than he that, with a will to corrupt, hath the power to please; and that neither wit nor honesty ought to think themselves safe with such a companion when they see Henry seduced by Falstaff.

Elizabeth Montagu

An Essay on the Writings and Genius of Shakespeare, Compared with the Greek and French Dramatic Poets (1769)

[From *The First Part of Henry IV*]

Our author is so little under the discipline of art that we are apt to ascribe his happiest successes, as well as his most unfortunate failings, to chance. But I cannot help thinking there is more of contrivance and care in his execution of this play than in almost any he has written. It is a more regular drama than his other historical plays, less charged with absurdities, and less involved in confusion. It is indeed liable to those objections which are made to tragicomedy. But if the pedantry of learning could ever recede from its dogmatical rules I think that this play, instead of being condemned for being of that species, would obtain favor for the species itself, though perhaps correct taste may be offended with the transitions from grave and important to light and ludicrous subjects, and more still with those from great and illustrious, to low and mean persons. Foreigners unused to these compositions will be much disgusted at them. The vulgar call all animals that are not native of their own country monsters, however beautiful they may be in their form or wisely adapted to their climate and natural destination. The prejudices of pride are as violent and unreasonable as the superstitions of ignorance. On the French Parnassus, a tragicomedy of this kind will be deemed a monster fitter to be shown to the people at a fair than exhibited to circles of the learned and polite. From some peculiar circumstances relating to the characters in this piece, we may perhaps find a sort of

apology for the motley mixture thrown into it. We cannot but
suppose that at the time it was written many stories yet subsisted
of the wild adventures of this Prince of Wales and his idle companions. His subsequent reformation and his conquests in France
rendered him a very popular character. It was a delicate affair to
expose the follies of Henry V before a people proud of his victories and tender of his fame, at the same time so informed of the
extravagancies and excesses of his youth that he could not appear
divested of them with any degree of historical probability. Their
enormity would have been greatly heightened if they had appeared in a piece entirely serious and full of dignity and decorum.
How happily therefore was the character of Falstaff introduced,
whose wit and festivity in some measure excuse the Prince for
admitting him into his familiarity and suffering himself to be led
by him into some irregularities. There is hardly a young hero full
of gaiety and spirits who, if he had once fallen into the society of
so pleasant a companion, could have the severity to discard him or
would not say, as the Prince does, "He could better spare a better
man."

How skillfully does our author follow the tradition of the
Prince's having been engaged in a robbery, yet make his part in it
a mere frolic to play on the cowardly and braggart temper of
Falstaff! The whole conduct of that incident is very artful: he
rejects the proposal of the robbery, and only complies with playing a trick on the robbers; and care is taken to inform you that the
money is returned to its owners. The Prince seems always diverted rather than seduced by Falstaff; he despises his vices while
he is entertained by his humor, and though Falstaff is for a while
a stain upon his character yet it is of a kind with those colors
which are used for a disguise in sport, being of such a nature as
are easily washed out without leaving any bad tincture. And we
see Henry, as soon as he is called to the high and serious duties of
a king, come forth at once with unblemished majesty. The disposition of the hero is made to pierce through the idle frolics of the
boy throughout the whole play, for his reformation is not effected in the last scene of the last act, as is usual in our comedies,
but is prepared from the beginning of the play. The scene between the Prince and Francis is low and ridiculous, and seems one
of the greatest indecorums in the piece; at the same time the

attentive spectator will find the purpose of it is to show him that Henry was studying human nature in all her variety of tempers and faculties. I am now, says he, acquainted with all humors (meaning dispositions) since the days of goodman Adam to the present hour. In the play of *Henry V* you are told that in his youth he had been sedulously observing mankind; and from an apprehension, perhaps, how difficult it was to acquire an intimate knowledge of men whilst he kept up the forms his rank prescribed, he waived the ceremonies and decorums of his situation, and familiarly conversed with all orders of society. The jealousy his father had conceived of him would probably have been increased if he had affected such a sort of popularity as would have gained the esteem and love of the multitude.

Whether Henry in the early part of his life was indulging a humor that inclined him to low and wild company, or endeavoring to acquire a deeper and more extensive knowledge of human nature by a general acquaintance with mankind, it is the business of his historians to determine. But a critic must surely applaud the dexterity of Shakespeare for throwing this color over that part of his conduct, whether he seized on some intimations historians had given of that sort, or of himself imagined so respectable a motive for the Prince's deviations from the dignity of his birth. This piece must have delighted the people at the time it was written, as the follies of their favorite character were so managed that they rather seemed foils to set off its virtues than stains which obscured them.

Whether we consider the character of Falstaff as adapted to encourage and excuse the extravagancies of the Prince, or by itself, we must certainly admire it and own it to be perfectly original.

The professed wit, either in life or on the stage, is usually severe and satirical. But mirth is the source of Falstaff's wit. He seems rather to invite you to partake of his merriment than to attend to his jest; a person must be ill-natured as well as dull who does not join in the mirth of this jovial companion, who is in all respects the best calculated to raise laughter of any that ever appeared on a stage.

He joins the finesse of wit with the drollery of humor. Humor is a kind of grotesque wit, shaped and colored by the disposition of the person in whom it resides, or by the subject to which it is applied. It is oftenest found in odd and irregular minds; but this peculiar turn distorts wit, and, though it gives it a burlesque air which excites momentary mirth, renders it less just and consequently less agreeable to our judgments. Gluttony, corpulency, and cowardice are the peculiarities of Falstaff's composition; they render him ridiculous without folly, throw an air of jest and festivity about him, and make his manners suit with his sentiments without giving to his understanding any particular bias. As the contempt attendant on these vices and defects is the best antidote against any infection that might be caught in his society, so it was very skillful to make him as ridiculous as witty and as contemptible as entertaining. The admirable speech upon honor would have been both indecent and dangerous from any other person. We must everywhere allow his wit is just, his humor genuine, and his character perfectly original and sustained through every scene in every play in which it appears.

As Falstaff, whom the author certainly intended to be perfectly witty, is less addicted to quibble and play on words than any of his comic characters, I think we may fairly conclude our author was sensible it was but a false kind of wit, which he practiced from the hard necessity of the times; for in that age the professor quibbled in his chair, the judge quibbled on the bench, the prelate quibbled in the pulpit, the statesman quibbled at the council-board; nay, even majesty quibbled on the throne.

[From *The Second Part of Henry IV*]

I have before observed that Shakespeare had the talents of an orator as much as of a poet; and I believe it will be allowed the speeches of Westmoreland and Lancaster are as proper on this occasion [the meeting of their armies in Act IV] and the particular circumstances are as happily touched, as they could have been by the most judicious orator. I know not that any poet, ancient or modern, has shown so perfect a judgment in rhetoric as our countryman. I wish he had employed his eloquence too in arraigning the baseness and treachery of John of Lancaster's conduct in breaking his covenant with the rebels.

Pistol is an odd kind of personage, intended I suppose to ridicule some fashionable affectation of bombast language. When such characters exist no longer anywhere but in the writings in which they have been ridiculed, they seem to have been monsters of the poet's brain. The originals lost and the mode forgot, one can neither praise the imitation nor laugh at the ridicule. Comic writers should therefore always exhibit some characteristic distinctions as well as temporary modes. Justice Shallow will forever rank with a certain species of men; he is like a well painted portrait in the dress of his age. Pistol appears a mere antiquated habit, so uncouthly fashioned we can hardly believe it was made for anything but a masquerade frolic. The poets who mean to please posterity should therefore work as painters, not as tailors, and give us peculiar features rather than fantastic habits. But where there is such a prodigious variety of well-drawn portraits as in this play we may excuse one piece of mere drapery, especially when exhibited to expose an absurd and troublesome fashion.

Mine hostess Quickly is of a species not extinct. It may be said the author there sinks from comedy to farce, but she helps to complete the character of Falstaff, and some of the dialogues in which she is engaged are diverting. Every scene in which Doll Tearsheet appears is indecent, and therefore not only indefensible but inexcusable. There are delicacies of decorum in one age unknown to another age, but whatever is immoral is equally blamable in all ages, and every approach to obscenity is an offense for which wit cannot atone, nor the barbarity or the corruption of the times excuse.

Maurice Morgann

An Essay on the Dramatic Character of Sir John Falstaff (1777)

The ideas which I have formed concerning the courage and military character of the dramatic Sir John Falstaff are so different from those which I find generally to prevail in the world that I shall take the liberty of stating my sentiments on the subject, in hope that some person as unengaged as myself will either correct and reform my error in this respect or, joining himself to my opinion, redeem me from what I may call the reproach of singularity.

I am to avow, then, that I do not clearly discern that Sir John Falstaff deserves to bear the character so generally given him of an absolute coward; or, in other words, that I do not conceive Shakespeare ever meant to make cowardice an essential part of his constitution.

I know how universally the contrary opinion prevails, and I know what respect and deference are due to the public voice. But if to the avowal of this singularity I add all the reasons that have led me to it, and acknowledge myself to be wholly in the judgment of the public, I shall hope to avoid the censure of too much forwardness or indecorum.

It must, in the first place, be admitted that the appearances in this case are singularly strong and striking; and so they had need be, to become the ground of so general a censure. We see this extraordinary character, almost in the first moment of our acquaintance with him, involved in circumstances of apparent dishonor, and we hear him familiarly called coward by his most intimate companions. We see him, on occasion of the robbery at

Gads Hill, in the very act of running away from the Prince and
Poins; and we behold him, on another of more honorable obligation, in open daylight, in battle, and acting in his profession as a
soldier, escaping from Douglas even out of the world as it were,
counterfeiting death and deserting his very existence; and we find
him on the former occasion betrayed into those lies and braggadocioes which are the usual concomitants of cowardice in military
men and pretenders to valor. These are not only in themselves
strong circumstances, but they are moreover thrust forward,
pressed upon our notice as the subject of our mirth, as the great
business of the scene. No wonder therefore that the word should
go forth that Falstaff is exhibited as a character of cowardice and
dishonor.

What there is to the contrary of this, it is my business to
discover. Much, I think, will presently appear; but it lies so
dispersed, is so latent, and so purposely obscured that the reader
must have some patience whilst I collect it into one body and
make it the object of a steady and regular contemplation.

But what have we to do, may my readers exclaim, with principles so latent, so obscured? In dramatic composition the impression is the fact; and the writer who, meaning to impress one
thing, has impressed another, is unworthy of observation.

It is a very unpleasant thing to have, in the first setting out, so
many and so strong prejudices to contend with. All that one can
do in such a case is to pray the reader to have a little patience in
the commencement, and to reserve his censure, if it must pass,
for the conclusion. Under his gracious allowance, therefore, I
presume to declare it as my opinion that cowardice is not the
impression which the whole character of Falstaff is calculated to
make on the minds of an unprejudiced audience, though there be,
I confess, a great deal of something in the composition likely
enough to puzzle and consequently to mislead the understanding.
The reader will perceive that I distinguish between mental impressions and the understanding. I wish to avoid everything that
looks like subtlety and refinement, but this is a distinction which
we all comprehend. There are none of us unconscious of certain
feelings or sensations of mind which do not seem to have passed
through the understanding—the effects, I suppose, of some secret influences from without, acting upon a certain mental sense,

and producing feelings and passions in just correspondence to the force and variety of those influences on the one hand, and to the quickness of our sensibility on the other. Be the cause however what it may, the fact is undoubtedly so, which is all I am concerned in. And it is equally a fact, which every man's experience may avouch, that the understanding and those feelings are frequently at variance. The latter often arise from the most minute circumstances, and frequently from such as the understanding cannot estimate or even recognize, whereas the understanding delights in abstraction and in general propositions which, however true considered as such, are very seldom (I had like to have said never) perfectly applicable to any particular case. And hence, among other causes, it is that we often condemn or applaud characters and actions on the credit of some logical process, while our hearts revolt and would fain lead us to a very different conclusion.

. . . .

We will begin then, if the reader pleases, by inquiring what impression the very vulgar had taken of Falstaff. If it is not that of cowardice, be it what else it may, that of a man of violence or a ruffian in years (as Harry calls him) or anything else, it answers my purpose, how insignificant soever the characters or incidents to be first produced may otherwise appear; for these impressions must have been taken either from personal knowledge and observation or, what will do better for my purpose, from common fame. Although I must admit some part of this evidence will appear so weak and trifling that it certainly ought not to be produced but in proof impression only.

The Hostess Quickly employs two officers to arrest Falstaff. On the mention of his name, one of them immediately observes "that it may chance to cost some of them their lives, for that he will stab." "Alas a day," says the Hostess, "take heed of him, he cares not what mischief he doth; if his weapon be out, he will foin like any devil; he will spare neither man, woman, or child." Accordingly, we find that when they lay hold on him he resists to the utmost of his power, and calls upon Bardolph, whose arms are at liberty, to draw. "Away, varlets, draw, Bardolph, cut me off the villain's head, throw the quean in the kennel." The officers cry, "a rescue, a rescue!" But the Chief Justice comes in and the scuffle ceases. In another scene, his wench Doll Tearsheet asks him "when he will leave fighting . . . and patch up his old body for heaven." This is occasioned by his drawing his rapier on great provocation, and driving Pistol, who is drawn likewise, downstairs and hurting him in the shoulder. To drive Pistol was no great feat, nor do I mention it as such; but upon this occasion it was necessary. "A rascal bragging slave," says he, "the rogue fled from me like quicksilver"—expressions which, as they remember the cowardice of Pistol, seem to prove that Falstaff did not value himself on the adventure. Even something may be drawn from Davy, Shallow's serving man, who calls Falstaff, in ignorant admiration, the man of war. I must observe here, and I beg the reader will notice it, that there is not a single expression dropped by these people or either of Falstaff's followers from which may be inferred the least suspicion of cowardice in his character, and this is I think such an implied negation as deserves considerable weight.

But to go a little higher, if indeed to consider Shallow's opinion be to go higher: it is from him, however, that we get the earliest account of Falstaff. He remembers him a page to Thomas Mowbray, Duke of Norfolk: "He broke," says he, "Schoggan's head at the court gate when he was but a crack thus high." Shallow throughout considers him as a great leader and soldier, and relates this fact as an early indication only of his future prowess. Shallow it is true is a very ridiculous character, but he picked up these impressions somewhere, and he picked up none of a contrary tendency. I want at present only to prove that Falstaff stood well in the report of common fame as to this point; and he was now near seventy years of age, and had passed in a military line through the active part of his life. At this period common fame may be well considered as the seal of his character—a seal which ought not perhaps to be broke open on the evidence of any future transaction.

But to proceed. Lord Bardolph was a man of the world, and of sense and observation. He informs Northumberland, erroneously indeed, that Percy had beaten the King at Shrewsbury. "The King," according to him, "was wounded; the Prince of Wales and the two Blunts slain, certain nobles (whom he names) had es-

caped by flight; and the brawn Sir John Falstaff was taken prisoner." But how came Falstaff into this list? Common fame had
put him there. He is singularly obliged to common fame. But if he
had not been a soldier of repute, if he had not been brave as well
as fat, if he had been mere brawn, it would have been more
germane to the matter if this lord had put him down among the
baggage or the provender. The fact seems to be that there is a real
consequence about Sir John Falstaff which is not brought forward. We see him only in his familiar hours; we enter the tavern
with Hal and Poins; we join in the laugh and take a pride to gird at
him. But there may be a great deal of truth in what he himself
writes to the Prince, that though he be "Jack Falstaff with his
familiars, he is Sir John with the rest of Europe." It has been
remarked, and very truly I believe, that no man is a hero in the
eye of his valet-de-chambre, and thus it is we are witnesses only
of Falstaff's weakness and buffoonery; our acquaintance is with
Jack Falstaff, Plump Jack, and Sir John Paunch; but if we would
look for Sir John Falstaff we must put on, as Bunyan would have
expressed it, the spectacles of observation. With respect, for instance, to his military command at Shrewsbury, nothing appears
on the surface but the Prince's familiarly saying, in the tone
usually assumed when speaking of Falstaff, "I will procure this fat
rogue a charge of foot," and in another place, "I will procure thee
Jack a charge of foot; meet me tomorrow in the Temple Hall."
Indeed we might venture to infer from this that a Prince of so
great ability, whose wildness was only external and assumed,
would not have procured, in so nice and critical a conjuncture, a
charge of foot for a known coward. But there was more it seems
in the case: we now find from this report, to which Lord Bardolph
had given full credit, that the world had its eye upon Falstaff as an
officer of merit, whom it expected to find in the field, and whose
fate in the battle was an object of public concern. His life was, it
seems, very material indeed, a thread of so much dependence that
fiction, weaving the fates of Princes, did not think it unworthy,
how coarse soever, of being made a part of the tissue.

We shall next produce the evidence of the Chief Justice of
England. He inquires of his attendant "if the man who was then
passing him was Falstaff; he who was in question for the
robbery." The attendant answers affirmatively, but reminds his

lord "that he had since done good service at Shrewsbury"; and the Chief Justice, on this occasion rating him for his debaucheries, tells him "that his day's service at Shrewsbury had gilded over his night's exploit at Gads Hill." This is surely more than common fame. The Chief Justice must have known his whole character taken together, and must have received the most authentic information, and in the truest colors, of his behavior in that action.

But perhaps after all the military men may be esteemed the best judges in points of this nature. Let us hear then Coleville of the Dale, a soldier, in degree a knight, a famous rebel, and "whose betters, had they been ruled by him, would have sold themselves dearer"—a man who is of consequence enough to be guarded by Blunt and led to present execution. This man yields himself up even to the very name and reputation of Falstaff. "I think," says he, "you are Sir John Falstaff, and in that thought yield me." But this is but one only among the men of the sword; they shall be produced then by dozens, if that will satisfy. Upon the return of the King and Prince Henry from Wales, the Prince seeks out and finds Falstaff debauching in a tavern, where Peto presently brings an account of ill news from the North, and adds "that as he came along he met or overtook a dozen captains, bare-headed, sweating, knocking at the taverns, and asking every one for Sir John Falstaff." He is followed by Bardolph, who informs Falstaff that "He must away to the court immediately; a dozen captains stay at door for him." Here is military evidence in abundance, and court evidence too, for what are we to infer from Falstaff's being sent for to court on this ill news but that his opinion was to be asked, as a military man of skill and experience, concerning the defenses necessary to be taken. Nor is Shakespeare content here with leaving us to gather up Falstaff's better character from inference and deduction. He comments on the fact by making Falstaff observe that "Men of merit are sought after: The undeserver may sleep when the man of action is called on." I do not wish to draw Falstaff's character out of his own mouth, but this observation refers to the fact and is founded in reason. Nor ought we to reject what in another place he says to the Chief Justice, as it is in the nature of an appeal to his knowledge. "There is not a dangerous action," says he, "can peep out his head but I am thrust upon it." The Chief Justice seems by his answer to admit the fact. "Well, be honest, be honest, and heaven bless your expedition." But the whole passage may deserve transcribing.

> *Ch. Just.* Well, the King has severed you and Prince Henry. I hear you are going with Lord John of Lancaster, against the Archbishop and the Earl of Northumberland.
>
> *Fals.* Yes, I thank your pretty sweet wit for it; but look you pray, all you that kiss my lady peace at home, that our armies join not in a hot day; for I take but two shirts out with me, and I mean not to sweat extraordinarily. If it be a hot day, if I brandish anything but a bottle, would I might never spit white again. There is not a dangerous action can peep out his head but I am thrust upon it. Well, I cannot last for ever. But it was always the trick of our English nation, if they have a good thing to make it too common. If you will needs say I am an old man, you should give me rest. I would to God my name were not so terrible to the enemy as it is. I were better to be eaten to death with a rust than to be scoured to nothing with perpetual motion.
>
> *Ch. Just.* Well be honest, be honest, and heaven bless your expedition.

Falstaff indulges himself here in humorous exaggeration—these passages are not meant to be taken, nor are we to suppose that they were taken, literally—but if there was not a ground of truth, if Falstaff had not had such a degree of military reputation as was capable of being thus humorously amplified and exaggerated, the whole dialogue would have been highly preposterous and absurd and the acquiescing answer of the Lord Chief Justice singularly improper. But upon the supposition of Falstaff's being considered upon the whole as a good and gallant officer, the answer is just, and corresponds with the acknowledgment which had a little before been made, "that his day's service at Shrewsbury had gilded over his night's exploit at Gads Hill.—You may thank the unquiet time," says the Chief Justice, "for your quiet o'erposting of that action," agreeing with what Falstaff says in another place: "Well God be thanked for these rebels, they offend none but the virtuous; I laud them, I praise them." Whether this be said in the true spirit of a soldier or not I do not determine; it is surely not in that of a mere coward and poltroon.

. . . .

Thus the deeper we look into Falstaff's character, the stronger is our conviction that he was not intended to be shown as a constitutional coward. Censure cannot lay sufficient hold on him, and even malice turns away and more than half pronounces his acquittal.

But as yet we have dealt principally in parole and circumstantial evidence, and have referred to fact only incidentally. But facts have a much more operative influence: they may be produced not as arguments only, but records; not to dispute alone, but to decide. It is time then to behold Falstaff in actual service as a soldier, in danger, and in battle. We have already displayed one fact in his defense against the censure of Lancaster, a fact extremely unequivocal and decisive. But the reader knows I have others, and doubtless goes before me to the action at Shrewsbury. In the midst and in the heat of battle we see him come forwards; what are his words? "I have led my rag-o-muffians where they are peppered; there's not three of my hundred and fifty left alive." But to whom does he say this? To himself only; he speaks in soliloquy. There is no questioning the fact he had led them; they were peppered, there were not three left alive. He was in luck, being in bulk equal to any two of them, to escape unhurt. Let the author answer for that, I have nothing to do with it; he was the poetic maker of the whole corps, and he might dispose of them as he pleased. Well might the Chief Justice, as we now find, acknowledge Falstaff's services in this day's battle—an acknowledgment which amply confirms the fact. A modern officer who had performed a feat of this kind would expect not only the praise of having done his duty but the appellation of a hero. But poor Falstaff has too much wit to thrive. In spite of probability, in spite of inference, in spite of fact, he must be a coward still. He happens unfortunately to have more wit than courage, and therefore we are maliciously determined that he shall have no courage at all. But let us suppose that his modes of expression, even in soliloquy, will admit of some abatement; how much shall we abate? Say that he brought off fifty instead of three; yet a modern captain would be apt to look big after an action with two thirds of his men, as it were, in his belly. Surely Shakespeare never meant to exhibit this man as a constitutional coward; if he did, his means were sadly destructive of his end. We see him, after he had expended his rag-o-muffians, with sword and target in the midst of battle, in perfect possession of himself, and replete with humor and jocularity. He was, I presume, in some immediate personal danger, in danger also of a general defeat, too corpulent for flight; and to be led a prisoner was probably to be led to execution; yet we see him laughing and easy, offering a bottle of sack to the Prince instead of a pistol, punning, and telling him, "there was that which would sack a city."—"What, is it a time (says the Prince) to jest and dally now?" No, a sober character would not jest on such an occasion, but a coward could not; he would neither have the inclination or the power. And what could support Falstaff in such a situation? Not principle; he is not suspected of the point of honor; he seems indeed fairly to renounce it. "Honor cannot set a leg or an arm; it has no skill in surgery. What is it? a word only; mere air. It is insensible to the dead; and detraction will not let it live with the living." What then but a strong natural constitutional courage which nothing could extinguish or dismay? In the following passages the true character of Falstaff as to courage and principle is finely touched, and the different colors at once nicely blended and distinguished. "If Percy be alive, I'll pierce him. If he do come in my way, so. If he do not, if I come in his willingly, let him make a carbonado of me. I like not such grinning honor as Sir Walter hath; give me life, which, if I can save, so; if not, honor comes unlooked for, and there's an end." One cannot say which prevails most here, profligacy or courage; they are both tinged alike by the same humor, and mingled in one common mass; yet when we consider the superior force of Percy, as we must presently also that of Douglas, we shall be apt, I believe, in our secret heart to forgive him. These passages are spoken in soliloquy and in battle. If every soliloquy made under similar circumstances were as audible as Falstaff's, the imputation might perhaps be found too general for censure. These are among the passages that have impressed on the world an idea of cowardice in Falstaff; yet why? He is resolute to take his fate. If Percy do come in his way, so; if not, he will not seek inevitable destruction. He is willing to save his life, but if that cannot be, why, "honor comes unlooked for, and there's an end." This surely is not the language of cowardice.

It contains neither the bounce or whine of the character. He derides, it is true, and seems to renounce that grinning idol of military zealots, honor. But Falstaff was a kind of military free-thinker, and has accordingly incurred the obloquy of his condition. He stands upon the ground of natural courage only and common sense, and has, it seems, too much wit for a hero. But let me be well understood. I do not justify Falstaff for renouncing the point of honor; it proceeded doubtless from a general relaxation of mind, and profligacy of temper. Honor is calculated to aid and strengthen natural courage and lift it up to heroism; but natural courage, which can act as such without honor, is natural courage still—the very quality I wish to maintain to Falstaff. And if without the aid of honor he can act with firmness, his portion is only the more eminent and distinguished. In such a character, it is to his actions, not his sentiments, that we are to look for conviction. But it may be still further urged in behalf of Falstaff that there may be false honor as well as false religion. It is true; yet even in that case candor obliges me to confess that the best men are most disposed to conform, and most likely to become the dupes of their own virtue. But it may however be more reasonably urged that there are particular tenets both in honor and religion which it is the grossness of folly not to question. To seek out, to court assured destruction without leaving a single benefit behind may be well reckoned in the number. And this is precisely the very folly which Falstaff seems to abjure; nor are we perhaps entitled to say more, in the way of censure, than that he had not virtue enough to become the dupe of honor, nor prudence enough to hold his tongue. I am willing however, if the reader pleases, to compound this matter, and acknowledge on my part that Falstaff was in all respects the old soldier, that he had put himself under the sober discipline of discretion, and renounced in a great degree at least what he might call the vanities and superstitions of honor, if the reader will on his part admit that this might well be, without his renouncing at the same time the natural firmness and resolution he was born to.

But there is a formidable objection behind. Falstaff counterfeits basely on being attacked by Douglas; he assumes, in a cowardly spirit, the appearance of death to avoid the reality. But there was no equality of force; not the least chance for victory, or life. And is it the duty then, think we still, of true courage, to meet, without benefit to society, certain death? Or is it only the phantasy of honor? But such a fiction is highly disgraceful; true, and a man of nice honor might perhaps have grinned for it. But we must remember that Falstaff had a double character. He was a wit as well as a soldier, and his courage, however eminent, was but the accessary; his wit was the principal, and the part which, if they should come in competition, he had the greatest interest in maintaining. Vain indeed were the licentiousness of his principles if he should seek death like a bigot yet without the meed of honor, when he might live by wit and increase the reputation of that wit by living. But why do I labor this point? It has been already anticipated, and our improved acquaintance with Falstaff will now require no more than a short narrative of the fact.

Whilst in the battle of Shrewsbury he is exhorting and encouraging the Prince who is engaged with the Spirit Percy—"Well said, Hal, to him, Hal"—he is himself attacked by the Fiend Douglas. There was no match; nothing remained but death or stratagem, grinning honor or laughing life. But an expedient offers, a mirthful one: take your choice, Falstaff, a point of honor or a point of drollery. It could not be a question. Falstaff falls, Douglas is cheated, and the world laughs. But does he fall like a coward? No, like a buffoon only; the superior principle prevails, and Falstaff lives by a stratagem growing out of his character to prove himself no counterfeit, to jest, to be employed, and to fight again. That Falstaff valued himself, and expected to be valued by others, upon this piece of saving wit is plain. It was a stratagem, it is true; it argued presence of mind; but it was moreover (what he most liked) a very laughable joke, and as such he considers it, for he continues to counterfeit after the danger is over that he may also deceive the Prince and improve the event into more laughter. He might, for ought that appears, have concealed the transaction; the Prince was too earnestly engaged for observation; he might have formed a thousand excuses for his fall; but he lies still and listens to the pronouncing of his epitaph by the Prince with all the waggish glee and levity of his character. The circumstance of his wounding Percy in the thigh, and carrying the dead body on his back like luggage, is indecent but not cowardly. The declaring, though in jest, that he killed Percy seems to me idle, but it is not

meant or calculated for imposition; it is spoken to the Prince
himself, the man in the world who could not be, or be supposed to
be, imposed on. But we must hear, whether to the purpose or not,
what it is that Harry has to say over the remains of his old friend.

> *P. Hen.* What, old acquaintance! could not all this flesh
> Keep in a little life? Poor Jack, farewell!
> I could have better spared a better man.
> Oh! I should have a heavy miss of thee,
> If I were much in love with vanity.
> Death hath not struck so fat a deer today,
> Though many a dearer in this bloody fray;
> Imbowelled will I see thee by and by;
> Till then, in blood by noble Percy lie.

This is wonderfully proper for the occasion; it is affectionate, it
is pathetic, yet it remembers his vanities, and, with a faint gleam
of recollected mirth, even his plumpness and corpulency; but it is
a pleasantry softened and rendered even vapid by tenderness, and
it goes off in the sickly effort of a miserable pun. But to our
immediate purpose: why is not his cowardice remembered too?
What, no surprise that Falstaff should lie by the side of the noble
Percy in the bed of honor! No reflection that flight, though
unfettered by disease, could not avail; that fear could not find a
subterfuge from death? Shall his corpulency and his vanities be
recorded, and his more characteristic quality of cowardice, even in
the moment that it particularly demanded notice and reflection,
be forgotten? If by sparing a better man be here meant a better
soldier, there is no doubt but there were better soldiers in the
army, more active, more young, more principled, more knowing;
but none, it seems, taken for all in all, more acceptable. The
comparative *better* used here leaves to Falstaff the praise at least of
good; and to be a good soldier is to be a great way from coward. But
Falstaff's goodness in this sort appears to have been not only
enough to redeem him from disgrace, but to mark him with
reputation; if I was to add with eminence and distinction, the
funeral honors which are intended his obsequies, and his being
bid till then to lie in blood by the noble Percy, would fairly bear me
out.

Upon the whole of the passages yet before us, why may I not
reasonably hope that the good natured reader (and I write to no
other) not offended at the levity of this exercise may join with me

in thinking that the character of Falstaff as to valor may be fairly and honestly summed up in the very words which he himself uses to Harry, and which seem, as to this point, to be intended by Shakespeare as a compendium of his character. "What," says the Prince, "a coward, Sir John Paunch!" Falstaff replies, "Indeed I am not John of Gaunt your grandfather, but yet no coward, Hal."

. . . .

Though the robbery at Gads Hill, and the supposed cowardice of Falstaff on that occasion, are next to be considered, yet I must previously declare that I think the discussion of this matter to be now unessential to the reestablishment of Falstaff's reputation as a man of courage. For suppose we should grant, in form, that Falstaff was surprised with fear in this single instance, that he was off his guard, and even acted like a coward; what will follow but that Falstaff, like greater heroes, had his weak moment and was not exempted from panic and surprise? If a single exception can destroy a general character, Hector was a coward, and Anthony a poltroon. But for these seeming contradictions of character we shall seldom be at a loss to account, if we carefully refer to circumstance and situation. In the present instance, Falstaff had done an illegal act; the exertion was over, and he had unbent his mind in security. The spirit of enterprise and the animating principle of hope were withdrawn. In this situation, he is unexpectedly attacked; he has no time to recall his thoughts or bend his mind to action. He is not now acting in the profession and in the habits of a soldier; he is associated with known cowards; his assailants are vigorous, sudden, and bold; he is conscious of guilt; he has dangers to dread of every form, present and future, prisons and gibbets as well as sword and fire; he is surrounded with darkness, and the sheriff, the hangman, and the whole Posse Comitatus may be at his heels. Without a moment for reflection, is it wonderful that, under these circumstances, "he should run and roar, and carry his guts away with as much dexterity as possible"?

But though I might well rest the question on this ground, yet as there remains many good topics of vindication, and as I think a more minute inquiry into this matter will only bring out more evidence in support of Falstaff's constitutional courage, I will not

decline the discussion. I beg permission therefore to state fully, as
well as fairly, the whole of this obnoxious transaction, this unfortunate robbery at Gads Hill.

In the scene wherein we become first acquainted with Falstaff,
his character is opened in a manner worthy of Shakespeare. We
see him in a green old age, mellow, frank, gay, easy, corpulent,
loose, unprincipled, and luxurious; a robber, as he says, by his
vocation, yet not altogether so. There was much, it seems, of
mirth and recreation in the case. "The poor abuses of the times,"
he wantonly and humorously tells the Prince, "want countenance;
and he hates to see resolution fobbed off, as it is, by the rusty
curb of old father antic, the law." When he quits the scene, we are
acquainted that he is only passing to the tavern. "Farewell," says
he, with an air of careless jollity and gay content, "You will find
me in Eastcheap." "Farewell," says the Prince, "thou latter spring;
farewell, all-hallown summer." But though all this is excellent for
Shakespeare's purposes, we find, as yet at least, no hint of Falstaff's cowardice, no appearance of braggadocio, or any preparation whatever for laughter under this head. The instant Falstaff is
withdrawn, Poins opens to the Prince his meditated scheme of a
double robbery; and here then we may reasonably expect to be let
into these parts of Falstaff's character. We shall see.

> *Poins.* Now my good sweet lord, ride with us tomorrow; I
> have a jest to execute that I cannot manage alone. Falstaff,
> Bardolph, Peto, and Gadshill shall rob those men that we
> have already waylaid; yourself and I will not be there; and
> when they have the booty, if you and I do not rob them,
> cut this head from off my shoulders.

This is giving strong surety for his words; perhaps he thought
the case required it. "But how," says the Prince, "shall we part
with them in setting forth?" Poins is ready with his answer; he
had matured the thought, and could solve every difficulty: "They
could set out before, or after; their horses might be tied in the
wood; they could change their visors; and he had already procured
cases of buckram to inmask their outward garments." This was
going far; it was doing business in good earnest. But if we look
into the play we shall be better able to account for this activity; we
shall find that there was at least as much malice as jest in Poins's

intention. The rival situations of Poins and Falstaff had produced on both sides much jealousy and ill will, which occasionally appears, in Shakespeare's manner, by sidelights, without confounding the main action; and by the little we see of this Poins he appears to be an unamiable, if not a very brutish and bad, character. But to pass this. The Prince next says, with a deliberate and wholesome caution, "I doubt they will be too hard for us." Poins's reply is remarkable: "Well, for two of them, I know them to be as true bred cowards as ever turned back; and for the third, if he fights longer than he sees cause, I will forswear arms." There is in this reply a great deal of management. There were four persons in all, as Poins well knew, and he had himself, but a little before, named them: Falstaff, Bardolph, Peto, and Gadshill. But now he omits one of the number, which must be either Falstaff, as not subject to any imputation in point of courage, and in that case Peto will be the third; or, as I rather think, in order to diminish the force of the Prince's objection he artfully drops Gadshill, who was then out of town and might therefore be supposed to be less in the Prince's notice; and upon this supposition Falstaff will be the third, who will not fight longer than he sees reason. But on either supposition, what evidence is there of a presupposed cowardice in Falstaff? On the contrary, what stronger evidence can we require that the courage of Falstaff had to this hour, through various trials, stood wholly unimpeached, than that Poins—the ill-disposed Poins, who ventures for his own purposes to steal as it were one of the four from the notice and memory of the Prince, and who shows himself, from worse motives, as skillful in diminishing as Falstaff appears afterwards to be in increasing of numbers—than that this very Poins should not venture to put down Falstaff in the list of cowards, though the occasion so strongly required that he should be degraded. What Poins dares do however in this sort, he does. "As to the third" (for so he describes Falstaff, as if the name of this veteran would have excited too strongly the ideas of courage and resistance), "if he fights longer than he sees reason I will forswear arms." This is the old trick of cautious and artful malice. The turn of expression or the tone of voice does all, for as to the words themselves, simply considered, they might be now truly spoken of almost any man who ever lived, except the iron-headed hero of Sweden. But Poins however adds something, which may appear more decisive: "The virtue of this jest will be the incomprehensible lies which this fat rogue will tell when we meet at supper; how thirty at least he fought with; and what wards, what blows, what extremities, he endured; and in the reproof of this lies the jest." Yes, and the malice too. This prediction was unfortunately fulfilled, even beyond the letter of it—a completion more incident, perhaps, to the predictions of malice than of affection. But we shall presently see how far either the prediction, or the event, will go to the impeachment of Falstaff's courage. The Prince, who is never duped, comprehends the whole of Poins's views. But let that pass.

In the next scene we behold all the parties at Gads Hill in preparation for the robbery. Let us carefully examine if it contains any intimation of cowardice in Falstaff. He is shown under a very ridiculous vexation about his horse, which is hid from him, but this is nothing to the purpose, or only proves that Falstaff knew no terror equal to that of walking eight yards of uneven ground. But on occasion of Gadshill's being asked concerning the number of the travelers, and having reported that they were eight or ten, Falstaff exclaims, "Zounds! will they not rob us!" If he had said more seriously, "I doubt they will be too hard for us," he would then have only used the Prince's own words upon a less alarming occasion. This cannot need defense. But the Prince, in his usual style of mirth, replies, "What, a coward, Sir John Paunch!" To this one would naturally expect from Falstaff some light answer, but we are surprised with a very serious one: "I am not indeed John of Gaunt your grandfather, but yet no coward, Hal." This is singular. It contains, I think, the true character of Falstaff, and it seems to be thrown out here, at a very critical conjuncture, as a caution to the audience not to take too sadly what was intended only (to use the Prince's words) "as argument for a week, laughter for a month, and a good jest for ever after." The whole of Falstaff's past life could not, it should seem, furnish the Prince with a reply, and he is therefore obliged to draw upon the coming hope. "Well," says he, mysteriously, "let the event try," meaning the event of the concerted attack on Falstaff, an event so probable that he might indeed venture to rely on it. But the travelers approach. The Prince hastily proposes a division of strength, that he with Poins should take a station separate from the rest, so that if the travelers should escape one party they might light on the other. Falstaff does not object, though he supposes the travelers to be eight or ten in number. We next see Falstaff attack these travelers with alacrity, using the accustomed words of threat and terror. They make no resistance, and he binds and robs them.

Hitherto I think there has not appeared the least trait either of boast or fear in Falstaff. But now comes on the concerted transaction which has been the source of so much dishonor. *As they are sharing the booty* (says the stage direction), *the Prince and Poins set upon them, they all run away; and Falstaff after a blow or two runs away too, leaving the booty behind them.* "Got with much ease," says the Prince, as an event beyond expectation, "Now merrily to horse." Poins adds, as they are going off, "How the rogue roared!" This observation is afterwards remembered by the Prince who, urging the jest to Falstaff, says, doubtless with all the license of exaggeration, "And you, Falstaff, carried your guts away as nimbly, with as quick dexterity, and roared for mercy, and still ran and roared, as I ever heard bull-calf." If he did roar for mercy, it must have been a very inarticulate sort of roaring, for there is not a single word set down for Falstaff from which this roaring may be inferred, or any stage direction to the actor for that purpose. But in the spirit of mirth and derision the lightest exclamation might be easily converted into the roar of a bull-calf.

We have now gone through this transaction considered simply on its own circumstances, and without reference to any future boast or imputation. It is upon these circumstances the case must be tried, and every color subsequently thrown on it, either by wit or folly, ought to be discharged. Take it then as it stands hitherto, with reference only to its own preceding and concomitant circumstances, and to the unbounded ability of Shakespeare to obtain his own ends, and we must I think be compelled to confess that this transaction was never intended by Shakespeare to detect and expose the false pretenses of a real coward, but on the contrary to involve a man of allowed courage, though in other respects of a very peculiar character, in such circumstances and suspicions of cowardice as might, by the operation of those peculiarities, produce afterwards much temporary mirth among his familiar and intimate companions. Of this we cannot require a stronger proof than the great attention which is paid to the decorum and truth of character in the stage direction already quoted. It appears from thence that it was not thought decent that Falstaff should run at all until he had been deserted by his companions and had even afterwards exchanged blows with his assailants; and thus a just distinction is kept up between the natural cowardice of the three associates and the accidental terror of Falstaff.

Hitherto, then, I think it is very clear that no laughter either is, or is intended to be, raised upon the score of Falstaff's cowardice. For after all it is not singularly ridiculous that an old inactive man, of no boast (as far as appears) or extraordinary pretensions to valor, should endeavor to save himself by flight from the assault of two bold and vigorous assailants. The very players, who are, I think, the very worst judges of Shakespeare, have been made sensible (I suppose from long experience) that there is nothing in this transaction to excite any extraordinary laughter; but this they take to be a defect in the management of their author, and therefore I imagine it is that they hold themselves obliged to supply the vacancy and fill it up with some low buffoonery of their own. Instead of the dispatch necessary on this occasion, they bring Falstaff, stuffing and all, to the very front of the stage, where with much mummery and grimace he seats himself down with a canvas money-bag in his hand to divide the spoil. In this situation he is attacked by the Prince and Poins, whose tin swords hang idly in the air and delay to strike till the player Falstaff, who seems more troubled with flatulence than fear, is able to rise, which is not till after some ineffectual efforts, and with the assistance (to the best of my memory) of one of the thieves, who lingers behind, in spite of terror, for this friendly purpose; after which, without any resistance on his part, he is goaded off the stage like a fat ox for slaughter by these stony-hearted drivers in buckram. I think he does not roar; perhaps the player had never perfected himself in the tones of a bull-calf. This whole transaction should be shown between the interstices of a back scene. The less we see in such cases the better we conceive. Something of resistance and afterwards of celerity in flight we should be made witnesses of; the roar we should take on the credit of Poins. Nor is there any occasion for all that bolstering with which they fill up the figure of Falstaff; they do not distinguish betwixt humorous exaggeration and necessary truth. The Prince is called starveling, dried neat's tongue, stock fish, and other names of the same nature. They might with almost as good reason search the glass-houses for some exhausted stoker to furnish out a Prince of Wales of sufficient correspondence to this picture.

We next come to the scene of Falstaff's braggadocioes. I have already wandered too much into details, yet I must, however, bring Falstaff forward to this last scene of trial in all his proper coloring and proportions. The progressive discovery of Falstaff's character is excellently managed. In the first scene we become acquainted with his figure, which we must in some degree consider as a part of his character; we hear of his gluttony and his debaucheries, and become witnesses of that indistinguishable mixture of humor and licentiousness which runs through his whole character. But what we are principally struck with is the ease of his manners and deportment, and the unaffected freedom and wonderful pregnancy of his wit and humor. We see him, in the next scene, agitated with vexation. His horse is concealed from him, and he gives on this occasion so striking a description of his distress, and his words so labor and are so loaded with heat and vapor, that, but for laughing, we should pity him. Laugh however we must at the extreme incongruity of a man at once corpulent and old, associating with youth in an enterprise demanding the utmost extravagance of spirit and all the wildness of activity. And this it is which makes his complaints so truly ridiculous. "Give me my horse!" says he, in another spirit than that of Richard. "Eight yards of uneven ground," adds this Forester of Diana, this enterprising gentleman of the shade, "is threescore and ten miles afoot with me." In the heat and agitation of the robbery, out come more and more extravagant instances of incongruity. Though he is most probably older and much fatter than either of the travelers, yet he calls them bacons, bacon-fed, and gorbellied knaves. "Hang them," says he, "fat chuffs, they hate us youth. What! young men must live. You are grand jurors, are ye? We'll jure ye, i'faith." But as yet we do not see the whole length and breadth of him. This is reserved for the braggadocio scene. We expect entertainment, but we don't well know of what kind. Poins, by his prediction, has given us a hint. But we do not see or feel Falstaff to be a coward, much less a boaster, without which even cowardice is not suffi-

ciently ridiculous, and therefore it is that on the stage we find
them always connected. In this uncertainty on our part he is, with
much artful preparation, produced. His entrance is delayed to
stimulate our expectation, and at last, to take off the dullness of
anticipation and to add surprise to pleasure, he is called in as if for
another purpose of mirth than what we are furnished with. We
now behold him fluctuating with fiction and laboring with dis-
sembled passion and chagrin. Too full for utterance, Poins provokes him by a few simple words, containing a fine contrast of
affected ease. "Welcome, Jack, where hast thou been?" But when
we hear him burst forth, "A plague on all cowards! Give me a cup
of sack. Is there no virtue extant!" we are at once in possession of
the whole man, and are ready to hug him, guts, lies and all, as an
inexhaustible fund of pleasantry and humor. Cowardice, I apprehend, is out of our thought; it does not, I think, mingle in our
mirth. As to this point, I have presumed to say already, and I
repeat it, that we are in my opinion the dupes of our own wisdom,
of systematic reasoning, of second thought and after reflection.
The first spectators, I believe, thought of nothing but the laughable scrape which so singular a character was falling into, and
were delighted to see a humorous and unprincipled wit so happily
taken in his own inventions, precluded from all rational defense,
and driven to the necessity of crying out, after a few ludicrous
evasions, "No more of that, Hal, if thou lov'st me."

I do not conceive myself obliged to enter into a consideration
of Falstaff's lies concerning the transaction at Gad's Hill. I have
considered his conduct as independent of those lies; I have examined the whole of it apart, and found it free of cowardice or fear,
except in one instance which I have endeavored to account for
and excuse. I have therefore a right to infer that those lies are to
be derived not from cowardice but from some other part of his
character, which it does not concern me to examine. But I have
not contented myself hitherto with this sort of negative defense,
and the reader I believe is aware that I am resolute (though I
confess not untired) to carry this fat rogue out of the reach of
every imputation which affects, or may seem to affect, his natural
courage.

The first observation then which strikes us as to his braggadocioes is that they are braggadocioes after the fact. In other cases

we see the coward of the play bluster and boast for a time, talk of distant wars and private duels out of the reach of knowledge and of evidence, of storms and stratagems and of falling in upon the enemy pell-mell and putting thousands to the sword, till at length, on the proof of some present and apparent fact, he is brought to open and lasting shame—to shame I mean as a coward, for as to what there is of liar in the case, it is considered only as accessory and scarcely reckoned into the account of dishonor. But in the instance before us everything is reversed. The play opens with the fact—a fact, from its circumstances as well as from the age and inactivity of the man, very excusable and capable of much apology, if not of defense. This fact is preceded by no bluster or pretense whatever. The lies and braggadocioes follow, but they are not general; they are confined, and have reference to this one fact only; the detection is immediate, and after some accompanying mirth and laughter the shame of that detection ends. It has no duration, as in other cases, and for the rest of the play the character stands just where it did before without any punishment or degradation whatever.

To account for all this, let us only suppose that Falstaff was a man of natural courage, though in all respects unprincipled, but that he was surprised in one single instance into an act of real terror—which, instead of excusing upon circumstances, he endeavors to cover by lies and braggadocio; and that these lies become thereupon the subject, in this place, of detection. Upon these suppositions the whole difficulty will vanish at once and everything be natural, common, and plain. The fact itself will be of course excusable—that is, it will arise out of a combination of such circumstances as, being applicable to one case only, will not destroy the general character. It will not be preceded by any braggadocio, containing any fair indication of cowardice, as real cowardice is not supposed to exist in the character. But the first act of real or apparent cowardice would naturally throw a vain unprincipled man into the use of lies and braggadocio; but these would have reference only to the fact in question, and not apply to other cases or infect his general character, which is not supposed to stand in need of imposition. Again, the detection of cowardice as such is more diverting after a long and various course of pretense, where the lie of character is preserved as it were whole and brought into sufficient magnitude for a burst of discovery; yet mere occasional lies, such as Falstaff is hereby supposed to utter, are, for the purpose of sport, best detected in the telling, because indeed they cannot be preserved for a future time; the exigence and the humor will be past. But the shame arising to Falstaff from the detection of mere lies would be temporary only, his character as to this point being already known and tolerated for the humor. Nothing therefore could follow but mirth and laughter and the temporary triumph of baffling a wit at his own weapons and reducing him to an absolute surrender, after which we ought not to be surprised if we see him rise again like a boy from play and run another race with as little dishonor as before.

What then can we say but that it is clearly the lies only, not the cowardice, of Falstaff which are here detected—lies to which what there may be of cowardice is incidental only, improving indeed the jest but by no means the real business of the scene. And now also we may more clearly discern the true force and meaning of Poins's prediction. "The jest will be," says he, "the incomprehensible lies that this fat rogue will tell us, how thirty at least he fought with, and in the reproof of this lies the jest"—that is, in the detection of these lies simply, for as to courage he had never ventured to insinuate more than that Falstaff would not fight longer than he saw cause. Poins was in expectation indeed that Falstaff would fall into some dishonor on this occasion—an event highly probable. But this was not, it seems, the principal ground of their mirth, but the detection of those incomprehensible lies which he boldly predicts, upon his knowledge of Falstaff's character, this fat rogue, not coward, would tell them. This prediction therefore, and the completion of it, go only to the impeachment of Falstaff's veracity and not of his courage. "These lies," says the Prince, "are like the father of them, gross as a mountain, open, palpable. Why thou clay-brained guts, thou knotty-pated fool, how couldst thou know these men in Kendal Green, when it was so dark thou couldst not see thy hand? Come, tell us your reason."

"*Poins.* Come, your reason, Jack, your reason."

Again, says the Prince, "Hear how a plain tale shall put you down. What trick, what device, what starting hole canst thou now find out to hide thee from this open and apparent shame?"

"*Poins.* Come, let's hear, Jack, what trick hast thou now?"

All this clearly refers to Falstaff's lies only as such, and the objection seems to be that he had not told them well and with sufficient skill and probability. Indeed nothing seems to have been required of Falstaff at any period of time but a good evasion. The truth is that there is so much mirth and so little of malice or imposition in his fictions that they may for the most part be considered as mere strains of humor and exercises of wit, impeachable only for defect, when that happens, of the quality from which they are principally derived. Upon this occasion Falstaff's evasions fail him; he is at the end of his invention, and it seems fair that, in defect of wit, the law should pass upon him and that he should undergo the temporary censure of that cowardice which he could not pass off by any evasion whatever. The best he could think of was instinct: He was indeed a coward upon instinct, in that respect like a valiant lion, who would not touch the true Prince. It would have been a vain attempt, the reader will easily perceive, in Falstaff to have gone upon other ground and to have aimed at justifying his courage by a serious vindication. This would have been to have mistaken the true point of argument. It was his lies, not his courage, which was really in question. There was besides no getting out of the toils in which he had entangled himself. If he was not, he ought at least by his own showing to have been at half-sword with a dozen of them two hours together, whereas it unfortunately appears, and that too evidently to be evaded, that he had run with singular celerity from two after the exchange of a few blows only. This precluded Falstaff from all rational defense in his own person; but it has not precluded me, who am not the advocate of his lies but of his courage.

But there are other singularities in Falstaff's lies which go more directly to his vindication. That they are confined to one scene and one occasion only, we are not now at a loss to account for; but what shall we say to their extravagance? The lies of Parolles and Bobadill are brought into some shape, but the fictions of Falstaff are so preposterous and incomprehensible that one may fairly doubt if they ever were intended for credit and therefore if they ought to be called lies and not rather humor—or, to compound the matter, humorous rhodomontades. Certain it is that they destroy their own purpose and are clearly not the effect in this respect of a regulated practice and habit of imposition. The real truth seems to be that had Falstaff, loose and unprincipled as he is, been born a coward and bred a soldier, he must naturally have been a great braggadocio, a true *miles gloriosus*. But in such case he should have been exhibited active and young, for it is plain that age and corpulency are an excuse for cowardice which ought not to be afforded him. In the present case, wherein he was not only involved in suspicious circumstances but wherein he seems to have felt some conscious touch of infirmity, and having no candid construction to expect from his laughing companions, he bursts at once and with all his might into the most unweighed and preposterous fictions, determined to put to proof on this occasion his boasted talent of swearing truth out of England. He tried it here to its utmost extent and was unfortunately routed on his own ground, which indeed, with such a mine beneath his feet, could not be otherwise. But without this he had mingled in his deceits so much whimsical humor and fantastic exaggeration that he must have been detected. And herein appears the admirable address of Shakespeare, who can show us Falstaff in the various light not only of what he is but what he would have been under one single variation of character—the want of natural courage— whilst with an art not enough understood he most effectually preserves the real character of Falstaff even in the moment he seems to depart from it, by making his lies too extravagant for practiced imposition, by grounding them more upon humor than deceit and turning them (as we shall see) into a fair and honest proof of general courage, by appropriating them to the conceal- ment only of a single exception. And hence it is that we see him draw so deeply and so confidently upon his former credit for courage and achievement. "I never dealt better in my life—thou know'st my old ward, Hal," are expressions which clearly refer to some known feats and defenses of his former life. His exclama- tions against cowardice, his reference to his own manhood—"Die when thou wilt old Jack, if manhood, good manhood, be not forgot upon the face of the earth, then am I a shotten herring"— these and various expressions such as these would be absurdities, not impositions, farce, not comedy, if not calculated to conceal some defect supposed unknown to the hearers, and these hearers were, in the present case, his constant companions and the daily witnesses of his conduct. If before this period he had been a known and detected coward and was conscious that he had no credit to lose, I see no reason why he should fly so violently from a familiar ignominy which had often before attached him, or why falsehoods, seemingly in such a case neither calculated for or expecting credit, should be censured or detected as lies or imposition.

That the whole transaction was considered as a mere jest and as carrying with it no serious imputation on the courage of Falstaff is manifest not only from his being allowed, when the laugh was past, to call himself, without contradiction in the personated character of Hal himself, "valiant Jack Falstaff, and the more valiant being, as he is, old Jack Falstaff," but from various other particulars, and above all from the declaration which the Prince makes on that very night of his intention of procuring this fat rogue a charge of foot—a circumstance doubtless contrived by Shakespeare to wipe off the seeming dishonor of the day. And from this time forward we hear of no imputation arising from this transaction; it is born and dies in a convivial hour; it leaves no trace behind, nor do we see any longer in the character of Falstaff the boasting or braggadocio of a coward.

Though I have considered Falstaff's character as relative only to one single quality, yet so much has been said that it cannot escape the reader's notice that he is a character made up by Shakespeare wholly of incongruities—a man at once young and old, enterprising and fat, a dupe and a wit, harmless and wicked, weak in principle and resolute by constitution, cowardly in appearance and brave in reality, a knave without malice, a liar without deceit, and a knight, a gentleman, and a soldier without either dignity, decency, or honor. This is a character which, though it may be de-compounded, could not I believe have been formed, nor the ingredients of it duly mingled, upon any receipt whatever. It required the hand of Shakespeare himself to give to every particular part a relish of the whole, and of the whole to every particular part—alike the same incongruous, identical Falstaff, whether to the grave Chief Justice he vainly talks of his youth and offers to caper for a thousand, or cries to Mrs. Doll, "I am old, I am old," though she is seated on his lap and he is courting her for busses. How Shakespeare could furnish out sentiment of so extraordinary a composition, and supply it with such appropriated and characteristic language, humor and wit, I cannot tell; but I may however venture to infer, and that confidently, that he who so well understood the uses of incongruity, and that laughter was to be raised by the opposition of qualities in the same man and not by their agreement or conformity, would never have attempted to raise mirth by showing us cowardice in a coward unattended by pretense and softened by every excuse of age, corpulence, and infirmity. And of this we cannot have more striking proof than his furnishing this very character, on one instance of real terror, however excusable, with boast, braggadocio, and pretense exceeding that of all other stage cowards the whole length of his superior wit, humor, and invention.

Henry MacKenzie

Remarks on the Character of Falstaff (1786)

That "Poet and creator are the same" is equally allowed in criticism as in etymology, and that without the powers of invention and imagination nothing great or highly delightful in poetry can be achieved.

I have often thought that the same thing holds true in some measure with regard to the reader as well as the writer of poetry. Without somewhat of a congenial imagination in the former, the work of the latter will afford a very inferior degree of pleasure. The mind of him who reads should be able to imagine what the productive fancy of the poet creates and presents to his view, to look on the world of fancy set before him with a native's eye, and to hear its language with a native's ear, to acknowledge its manners, to feel its passion, and to trace with somewhat of an instinctive glance those characters with which the poet has peopled it.

If in the perusal of any poet this is required, Shakespeare of all poets seems to claim it the most. Of all poets Shakespeare appears to have possessed a fancy the most prolific, an imagination the most luxuriantly fertile. In this particular he has been frequently compared to Homer, though those who have drawn the parallel have done it, I know not why, with a sort of distrust of their assertion. Did we not look at the Greek with that reverential awe which his antiquity impresses, I think we might venture to affirm that in this respect the other is more than his equal. In invention of incident, in diversity of character, in assemblage of images we can scarcely indeed conceive Homer to be surpassed; but in the mere creation of fancy I can discover nothing in the *Iliad* that equals the *Tempest* or the *Macbeth* of Shakespeare. The machinery of Homer is indeed stupendous, but of that machinery the materials were known; or, though it should be allowed that he added something to the mythology he found, yet still the language and the manners of his deities are merely the language and the manners of men. Of Shakespeare the machinery may be said to be produced as well as combined by himself. Some of the beings of whom it is composed, neither tradition nor romance afforded him; and of those whom he borrowed thence, he invented the language and the manners; language and manners peculiar to themselves, for which he could draw no analogy from mankind. Though formed by fancy, however, his personages are true to nature, and a reader of that pregnant imagination which I have mentioned above can immediately decide on the justness of his conceptions; as he who beholds the masterly expression of certain portraits pronounces with confidence on their likeness, though unacquainted with the persons from whom they were drawn.

But it is not only in those untried regions of magic or of witchery that the creative power of Shakespeare has exerted itself. By a very singular felicity of invention he has produced in the beaten field of ordinary life characters of such perfect originality that we look on them with no less wonder at his invention than on those preternatural beings which "are not of this earth;" and yet they speak a language so purely that of common society that we have but to step abroad into the world to hear every expression of which it is composed. Of this sort is the character of Falstaff.

On the subject of this character I was lately discoursing with a friend, who is very much endowed with that critical imagination of which I have suggested the use in the beginning of this paper. The general import of his observations may form neither a useless nor unamusing field for speculation to my readers.

Though the character of Falstaff, said my friend, is of so striking a kind as to engross almost the whole attention of the audience in the representation of the play in which it is first introduced, yet it was probably only a secondary and incidental object with Shakespeare in composing that play. He was writing a series of historical dramas on the most remarkable events of the English history from the time of King John downwards. When he arrived at the reign of Henry IV, the dissipated youth and extravagant pranks of the Prince of Wales could not fail to excite his attention as affording at once a source of moral reflection in the serious department and a fund of infinite humor in the comic part of the drama. In providing him with associates for his hours of folly and of riot, he probably borrowed, as was his custom, from some old play, interlude, or story the names and incidents which he has used in the *First Part of Henry IV*. Oldcastle, we know, was the name of a character in such a play, inserted there, it is probable (in those days of the Church's omnipotence in every aspect of writing), in odium of Sir John Oldcastle, chief of the Lollards, though Shakespeare afterwards, in a Protestant reign, changed it into Falstaff. This leader of the gang, which the wanton extravagance of the Prince was to cherish and protect, it was necessary to endow with qualities sufficient to make the young Henry, in his society, "doff the world aside,/And bid it pass." Shakespeare therefore has endowed him with infinite wit and humor, as well as an admirable degree of sagacity and acuteness in observing the characters of men, but has joined those qualities with a grossness of mind which his youthful master could not but see, nor seeing but despise. With talents less conspicuous Falstaff could not have attracted Henry; with profligacy less gross and less contemptible he would have attached him too much. Falstaff's was just "that unyoked humor of idleness" which the Prince could "a while uphold," and then cast off for ever. The audience to which this strange compound was to be exhibited were to be in the same predicament with the Prince; to laugh and to admire while they despised; to feel the power of his humor, the attraction of his wit, the justice of his reflections, while their contempt and their hatred attended the lowness of his manners, the grossness of his pleasures, and the unworthiness of his vice.

Falstaff is truly and literally *"ex Epicuri grege porcus,"* placed here within the pale of this world to fatten at his leisure, neither disturbed by feeling nor restrained by virtue. He is not, however, positively much a villain, though he never starts aside in the pursuit of interest or of pleasure when knavery comes in his way. We feel contempt, therefore, and not indignation at his crimes, which rather promotes than hinders our enjoying the ridicule of the situation and the admirable wit with which he expresses himself in it. As a man of this world he is endowed with the most superior degree of good sense and discernment of character; his conceptions, equally acute and just, he delivers with the expression of a clear and vigorous understanding; and we see that he thinks like a wise man even when he is not at the pains to talk wisely.

Perhaps, indeed, there is no quality more conspicuous throughout the writings of Shakespeare than that of good sense, that intuitive sagacity with which he looks on the manners, the characters, and the pursuits of mankind. The bursts of passion, the strokes of nature, the sublimity of his terrors, and the wonderful creation of his fancy are those excellencies which strike spectators the most, and are therefore most commonly enlarged on; but to an attentive peruser of his writings, his acute perception and accurate discernment of ordinary character and conduct, that skill, if I may so express it, with which he delineates the plan of common life, will, I think, appear no less striking, and perhaps rather more wonderful; more wonderful because we cannot so easily conceive that power of genius by which it tells us what actually exists, though it has never seen it, than that by which it creates what never existed. This power, when we read the works and consider the situation of Shakespeare, we shall allow him in a most extraordinary degree. The delineation of manners found in the Greek tragedians is excellent and just; but it consists chiefly of those general maxims which the wisdom of the schools might inculcate, which a borrowed experience might teach. That of Shakespeare marks the knowledge of intimacy with mankind. It reaches the elevation of the great, and penetrates the obscurity of the low; detects the cunning, and overtakes the bold; in short, presents that abstract of life in all its modes, and indeed in every time, which everyone without experience must believe and everyone with experience must know to be true.

With this sagacity and penetration into the characters and motives of mankind, Shakespeare has invested Falstaff in a remarkable degree. He never utters it, however, out of character, or at a season where it might better be spared. Indeed, his good sense is rather in his thoughts than in his speech; for so we may call those soliloquies in which he generally utters it. He knew what coin was most current with those he dealt withal, and fashioned his discourse according to the disposition of his hearers;

and he sometimes lends himself to the ridicule of his companions when he has a chance of getting any interest on the loan.

But we oftener laugh with than at him, for his humor is infinite and his wit admirable. This quality, however, still partakes in him of that Epicurean grossness which I have remarked to be the ruling characteristic of his disposition. He has neither the vanity of a wit nor the singularity of a humorist, but indulges both talents, like any other natural propensity, without exertion of mind or warmth of enjoyment. A late excellent actor, whose loss the stage will long regret, used to represent the character of Falstaff in a manner different from what had been uniformly adopted from the time of Quinn downwards. He exchanged the comic gravity of the old school for those bursts of laughter in which sympathetic audiences have so often accompanied him. From accompanying him it was indeed impossible to refrain; yet, though the execution was masterly, I cannot agree in that idea of the character. He who laughs is a man of feeling in merriment. Falstaff was of a very different constitution. He turned wit, as he says he did "disease, into commodity."—"Oh! it is much that a lie with a slight oath, and a jest with a sad brow, will do with a fellow that never had the ache in his shoulders."

No. 69: *Continuation of the Remarks on the Character of Falstaff.*

To a man of pleasure of such a constitution as Falstaff, temper and good humor were necessarily consequent. We find him therefore but once I think angry, and then not provoked beyond measure. He conducts himself with equal moderation towards others; his wit lightens, but does not burn; and he is not more inoffensive when the joker than unoffended when joked upon: "I am not only witty myself, but the cause that wit is in other men." In the evenness of his humor he bears himself thus (to use his own expression), and takes in the points of all assailants without being hurt. The language of contempt, of rebuke, or of conviction neither puts him out of liking with himself or with others. None of his passions rise beyond this control of reason, of self-interest, or of indulgence.

Queen Elizabeth, with a curiosity natural to a woman, desired Shakespeare to exhibit Falstaff as a lover. He obeyed her, and wrote the *Merry Wives of Windsor*; but Falstaff's love is only factor for his interest, and he wishes to make his mistress "his Exchequer, his East and West Indies, to both of which he will trade." Though I will not go so far as a paradoxical critic has done, and ascribe valor to Falstaff, yet if his cowardice is fairly examined it will be found to be not so much a weakness as a principle. In his very cowardice there is much of the sagacity I have remarked in him; he has the sense of danger but not the discomposure of fear. His presence of mind saves him from the sword of Douglas where the danger was real; but he shows no sort of dread of the sheriff's visit, when he knew the Prince's company would probably bear him out. When Bardolph runs in frightened, and tells that the sheriff with a monstrous watch is at the door, "Out, you rogue! (answers he) play out the play; I have much to say in behalf of that Falstaff." Falstaff's cowardice is only proportionate to the danger; and so would every wise man's be, did not other feelings make him valiant.

Such feelings it is the very characteristic of Falstaff to want. The dread of disgrace, the sense of honor, and the love of fame he neither feels nor pretends to feel. "Like the fat weed / That roots itself at ease on Lethe's wharf" [*Hamlet*, 1.5.32–33], he is contented to repose on that earthy corner of sensual indulgence in which his fate has placed him, and enjoys the pleasures of the moment without once regarding those finer objects of delight which the children of fancy and of feeling so warmly pursue.

The greatest refinement of morals, as well as of mind, is produced by the culture and exercise of the imagination, which derives or is taught to derive its objects of pursuit and its motives of action not from the senses merely but from future considerations which fancy anticipates and realizes. Of this, either as the prompter or the restraint of conduct, Falstaff is utterly devoid; yet his imagination is wonderfully quick and creative in the pictures of humor and the associations of wit. But the "pregnancy of his wit," according to his own phrase, "is made a tapster," and his fancy, how vivid soever, still subjects itself to the grossness of those sensual conceptions which are familiar to his mind. We are astonished at that art by which Shakespeare leads the powers of genius, imagination, and wisdom in captivity to this son of earth; 'tis as if, transported into the enchanted island in the *Tempest*, we saw the rebellion of Caliban successful and the airy spirits of Prospero ministering to the brutality of his slave.

Hence perhaps may be derived great part of that infinite amusement which succeeding audiences have always found from the representation of Falstaff. We have not only the enjoyment of those combinations, and of that contrast to which philosophers have ascribed the pleasure we derive from wit in general, but we have that singular combination and contrast which the gross, the sensual, and the brutish mind of Falstaff exhibits when joined and compared with that admirable power of invention, of wit, and of humor which his conversation perpetually displays.

In the immortal work of Cervantes we find a character with a remarkable mixture of wisdom and absurdity, which in one page excites our highest ridicule and in the next is entitled to our highest respect. Don Quixote, like Falstaff, is endowed with excellent discernment, sagacity, and genius; but his good sense holds fief of his diseased imagination, of his overruling madness for the achievements of knight-errantry, for heroic valor and heroic love. The ridicule in the character of Don Quixote consists in raising low and vulgar incidents, through the medium of his disordered fancy, to a rank of importance, dignity, and solemnity to which in their nature they are the most opposite that can be imagined. With Falstaff it is nearly the reverse: the ridicule is produced by subjecting wisdom, honor, and other the most grave and dignified principles to the control of grossness, buffoonery, and folly. 'Tis like the pastime of a family-masquerade, where laughter is equally excited by dressing clowns as gentlemen or gentlemen as clowns. In Falstaff the heroic attributes of our nature are made to wear the garb of meanness and absurdity. In Don Quixote the common and the servile are clothed in the dresses of the dignified and the majestic, while to heighten the ridicule, Sancho, in the half deceived simplicity and half discerning shrewdness of his character, is every now and then employed to pull off the mask.

If you would not think me whimsical in the parallel, continued my friend, I should say that Shakespeare has drawn, in one of his immediately subsequent plays, a tragic character very much resembling the comic one of Falstaff, I mean that of Richard III. Both are men of the world, both possess the sagacity and understanding which is fitted for its purposes, both despise those refined feelings, those motives of delicacy, those restraints of virtue which might obstruct the course they have marked out for themselves. The hypocrisy of both costs them nothing, and they never feel that detection of it to themselves which rankles in the conscience of less determined hypocrites. Both use the weaknesses of others as skillful players at a game do the ignorance of their opponents; they enjoy the advantage not only without self-reproach but with the pride of superiority. Richard indeed aspires to the crown of England, because Richard is wicked and ambitious; Falstaff is contented with a thousand pounds of Justice Shallow's, because he is only luxurious and dissipated. Richard courts Lady Anne and the Princess Elizabeth for his purposes: Falstaff makes love to Mrs Ford and Mrs Page for his. Richard is witty like Falstaff, and talks of his own figure with the same sarcastic indifference. Indeed, so much does Richard, in the higher walk of villainy, resemble Falstaff in the lower region of roguery and dissipation, that it were not difficult to show in the dialogue of the two characters, however dissimilar in situation, many passages and expressions in a style of remarkable resemblance.

. . . .

Falstaff is the work of Circe and her swinish associates who, in some favored hour of revelry and riot, molded this compound of gross debauchery, acute discernment, admirable invention, and nimble wit, and sent him for a comfort to England's madcap Prince, to stamp currency on idleness and vice, and to wave the flag of folly and dissipation over the seats of gravity, of wisdom, and of virtue.

Richard Cumberland

Remarks Upon the Characters of Falstaff and His Group (1786)

When it had entered into the mind of Shakespeare to form an historical play upon certain events in the reign of Henry the Fourth of England, the character of the Prince of Wales recommended itself to his fancy as likely to supply him with a fund of dramatic incidents. For what could invention have more happily suggested than this character, which history presented ready to his hands? a riotous disorderly young libertine, in whose nature lay hidden those seeds of heroism and ambition which were to burst forth at once to the astonishment of the world and to achieve the conquest of France. This prince, whose character was destined to exhibit a revolution of so brilliant a sort, was not only in himself a very tempting hero for the dramatic poet, who delights in incidents of novelty and surprise, but also offered to his inspiration a train of attendant characters, in the persons of his wild comrades and associates, which would be of themselves a drama. Here was a field for invention wide enough even for the genius of Shakespeare to range in. All the humors, passions, and extravagancies of human life might be brought into the composition, and when he had grouped and personified them to his taste and liking he had a leader ready to place at the head of the train, and the truth of history to give life and interest to his drama.

With these materials ready for creation the great artist sat down to his work; the canvas was spread before him, ample and capacious as the expanse of his own fancy; nature put her pencil into his hand, and he began to sketch. His first concern was to give a chief or captain to this gang of rioters; this would naturally be the first outline he drew. To fill up the drawing of this person-

49

age he conceived a voluptuary in whose figure and character there should be an assemblage of comic qualities. In his person he should be bloated and blown up to the size of a Silenus, lazy, luxurious, in sensuality a satyr, in intemperance a bacchanalian. As he was to stand in the post of a ringleader amongst thieves and cutpurses he made him a notorious liar, a swaggering coward, vainglorious, arbitrary, knavish, crafty, voracious of plunder, lavish of his gains, without credit, honor, or honesty, and in debt to everybody about him. As he was to be the chief seducer and misleader of the heir apparent of the crown, it was incumbent on the poet to qualify him for that part in such a manner as should give probability and even a plea to the temptation. This was only to be done by the strongest touches and the highest colorings of a master; by hitting off a humor of so happy, so facetious, and so alluring a cast as should tempt even royalty to forget itself and virtue to turn reveller in his company. His lies, his vanity, and his cowardice, too gross to deceive, were to be so ingenious as to give delight; his cunning evasions, his witty resources, his mock solemnity, his vaporing self-consequence were to furnish a continual feast of laughter to his royal companion. He was not only to be witty himself but the cause of wit in other people, a whetstone for raillery, a buffoon whose very person was a jest. Compounded of these humors, Shakespeare produced the character of Sir John Falstaff, a character which neither ancient nor modern comedy has ever equalled, which was so much the favorite of its author as to be introduced in three several plays, and which is likely to be the idol of the English stage as long as it shall speak the language of Shakespeare.

This character almost singly supports the whole comic plot of the first part of *Henry the Fourth*; the poet has indeed thrown in some auxiliary humors in the persons of Gadshill, Peto, and Bardolph, and Hostess Quickly; the two first serve for little else except to fill up the action, but Bardolph as a butt to Falstaff's raillery, and the Hostess in the wrangling scene with him when his pockets had been emptied as he was asleep in the tavern, give occasion to scenes of infinite pleasantry. Poins is contrasted from the rest of the gang, and, as he is made the companion of the Prince, is very properly represented as a man of better qualities and morals than Falstaff's more immediate hangers-on and dependents.

The humor of Falstaff opens into full display upon his very first introduction with the Prince. The incident of the robbery on the highway, the scene in Eastcheap in consequence of that ridiculous encounter, and the whole of his conduct during the action with Percy are so exquisitely pleasant that upon the renovation of his dramatic life in the second part of *Henry the Fourth* I question if the humor does not in part evaporate by continuation. At least I am persuaded that it flattens a little in the outset, and though his wit may not flow less copiously yet it comes with more labor and is farther-fetched. The poet seems to have been sensible how difficult it was to preserve the vein as rich as at first, and has therefore strengthened his comic plot in the second play with several new recruits who may take a share with Falstaff, to whom he no longer entrusts the whole burden of the humor. In the front of these auxiliaries stands Pistol, a character so new, whimsical, and extravagant that if it were not for a commentator now living, whose very extraordinary researches amongst our old authors have supplied us with passages to illuminate the strange rhapsodies which Shakespeare has put into his mouth, I should for one have thought Ancient Pistol as wild and imaginary a being as Caliban. But I now perceive, by the help of these discoveries, that the character is made up in great part of absurd and fustian passages from many plays, in which Shakespeare was versed and perhaps had been a performer. Pistol's dialogue is a tissue of old tags of bombast, like the middle comedy of the Greeks, which dealt in parody. I abate of my astonishment at the invention and originality of the poet, but it does not lessen my respect for his ingenuity. Shakespeare founded his bully in parody, Jonson copied his from nature, and the palm seems due to Bobadil upon a comparison with Pistol. Congreve copied a very happy likeness from Jonson, and by the fairest and most laudable imitation produced his Noll Bluff, one of the pleasantest humorists on the comic stage.

Shallow and Silence are two very strong auxiliaries to this second part of Falstaff's humors, and though they do not absolutely belong to his family they are nevertheless near of kin and derivatives from his stock. Surely two pleasanter fellows never trod the stage; they not only contrast and play upon each other, but Silence sober and Silence tipsy make the most comical reverse in nature; never was drunkenness so well introduced or so happily employed in any drama. The dialogue between Shallow and Falstaff, and the description given by the latter of Shallow's youthful frolics, are as true nature and as true comedy as man's invention ever produced. The recruits are also in the literal sense the recruits of the drama. These personages have the further merit of throwing Falstaff's character into a new cast, and giving it the seasonable relief of variety.

Dame Quickly also in this second part resumes her role with great comic spirit, but with some variation of character, for the purpose of introducing a new member into the troop in the person of Doll Tearsheet, the common trull of the times. Though this part is very strongly colored, and though the scene with her and Falstaff is of a loose as well as ludicrous nature, yet if we compare Shakespeare's conduct of this incident with that of the dramatic writers of his time, and even since his time, we must confess he has managed it with more than common care, and exhibited his comic hero in a very ridiculous light, without any of those gross indecencies which the poets of his age indulged themselves in without restraint.

The humor of the Prince of Wales is not so free and unconstrained as in the first part. Though he still demeans himself in the course of his revels, yet it is with frequent marks of repugnance and self-consideration, as becomes the conqueror of Percy, and we see his character approaching fast towards a thorough reformation. But though we are thus prepared for the change that is to happen when this young hero throws off the reveller and assumes the king, yet we are not fortified against the weakness of pity when the disappointment and banishment of Falstaff takes place and the poet executes justice upon his inimitable delinquent with all the rigor of an unrelenting moralist. The reader or spectator who has accompanied Falstaff through his dramatic story is in debt to him for so many pleasant moments that all his failings, which should have raised contempt, have only provoked laughter, and he begins to think they are not natural to his character but assumed for his amusement. With these impressions we see him delivered over to mortification and disgrace, and bewail his punishment with a sensibility that is only due to the sufferings of the virtuous.

Samuel Taylor Coleridge

Henry IV: The Character of Falstaff (1811)

"Falstaff was no coward, but pretended to be one merely for the sake of trying experiments on the credulity of mankind: he was a liar with the same object, and not because he loved falsehood for itself. He was a man of such preeminent abilities as to give him a profound contempt for all those by whom he was usually surrounded, and to lead to a determination on his part, in spite of their fancied superiority, to make them his tools and dupes. He knew, however low he descended, that his own talents would raise him, and extricate him from any difficulty. While he was thought to be the greatest rogue, thief and liar, he still had that about him which could render him not only respectable, but absolutely necessary to his companions. It was in characters of complete moral depravity, but of first-rate wit and talents, that Shakespeare delighted."

(*Coleridge in conversation, as reported by J. P. Collier.*)

William Hazlitt

Henry IV in Two Parts (1817)

If Shakespeare's fondness for the ludicrous sometimes led to faults in his tragedies (which was not often the case) he has made us amends by the character of Falstaff. This is perhaps the most substantial comic character that ever was invented. Sir John carries a most portly presence in the mind's eye; and in him, not to speak it profanely, "we behold the fulness of the spirit of wit and humor bodily." We are as well acquainted with his person as his mind, and his jokes come upon us with double force and relish from the quantity of flesh through which they make their way, as he shakes his fat sides with laughter, or "lards the lean earth as he walks along." Other comic characters seem, if we approach and handle them, to resolve themselves into air, "into thin air," but this is embodied and palpable to the grossest apprehension; it lies "three fingers deep upon the ribs," it plays about the lungs and the diaphragm with all the force of animal enjoyment. His body is like a good estate to his mind, from which he receives rents and revenues of profit and pleasure in kind, according to its extent and the richness of the soil. Wit is often a meager substitute for pleasurable sensation, an effusion of spleen and petty spite at the comforts of others from feeling none in itself. Falstaff's wit is an emanation of a fine constitution, an exuberance of good-humor and good-nature, an overflowing of his love of laughter and good-fellowship, a giving vent to his heart's ease and over-contentment with himself and others. He would not be in character if he were not so fat as he is; for there is the greatest keeping in the boundless luxury of his imagination and the pampered self-indulgence of his physical appetites. He manures and nourishes his mind with jests, as he does his body with sack and sugar. He carves out his jokes, as he would a capon or a haunch of venison, where there is *cut and come again;* and pours out upon them the oil of gladness. His tongue drops fatness, and in the chambers of his brain "it snows of meat and drink." He keeps up perpetual holiday and open house, and we live with him in a round of invitations to a rump and dozen.—Yet we are not to suppose that he was a mere sensualist. All this is as much in imagination as in reality. His sensuality does not engross and stupefy his other faculties, but "ascends me into the brain, clears away all the dull, crude vapors that environ it, and makes it full of nimble, fiery, and delectable shapes." His imagination keeps up the ball after his senses have done with it. He seems to have even a greater enjoyment of the freedom from restraint, of good cheer, of his ease, of his vanity, in the ideal exaggerated description which he gives of them, than in fact. He never fails to enrich his discourse with allusions to eating and drinking, but we never see him at table. He carries his own larder about with him, and he is himself "a tun of man." His pulling out the bottle in the field of battle is a joke to show his contempt for glory accompanied with danger, his systematic adherence to his Epicurean philosophy in the most trying circumstances. Again, such is his deliberate exaggeration of his own vices that it does not seem quite certain whether the account of his hostess's bill found in his pocket, with such an out-of-the-way charge for capons and sack with only one halfpenny-worth of bread, was not put there by himself as a trick to humor the jest upon his favorite propensities and as a conscious caricature of himself. He is represented as a liar, a braggart, a coward, a glutton, etc., and yet we are not offended but delighted with him, for he is all these as much to amuse others as to gratify himself. He openly assumes all these characters to show the humorous part of them. The unrestrained indulgence of his own ease, appetites, and convenience has neither malice nor hypocrisy in it. In a word, he is an actor in himself almost as much as upon the stage, and we no more object to the character of Falstaff in a moral point of view than we should think of bringing an excellent comedian, who should represent him to the life, before one of the police offices. We only consider the number of pleasant lights in which he puts certain foibles (the more pleasant as they are opposed to the received rules and necessary restraints of society), and do not trouble ourselves about the consequences resulting from them, for no mischievous consequences do result. Sir John is old as well as fat, which gives a melancholy retrospective tinge to the character, and by the disparity between his inclinations and his capacity for enjoyment makes it still more ludicrous and fantastical.

The secret of Falstaff's wit is for the most part a masterly presence of mind, an absolute self-possession, which nothing can disturb. His repartees are involuntary suggestions of his self-love, instinctive evasions of everything that threatens to interrupt the career of his triumphant jollity and self-complacency. His very size floats him out of all his difficulties in a sea of rich conceits, and he turns round on the pivot of his convenience with every occasion and at a moment's warning. His natural repugnance to every unpleasant thought or circumstance of itself makes light of objections, and provokes the most extravagant and licentious answers in his own justification. His indifference to truth puts no check upon his invention, and the more improbable and unexpected his contrivances are, the more happily does he seem to be delivered of them, the anticipation of their effect acting as a stimulus to the gaiety of his fancy. The success of one adventurous sally gives him spirits to undertake another; he deals always in round numbers, and his exaggerations and excuses are "open, palpable, monstrous as the father that begets them." His dissolute carelessness of what he says discovers itself in the first dialogue with the Prince:

> *Falstaff.* By the Lord, thou say'st true, lad; and is not mine
> hostess of the tavern a most sweet wench?
> *P. Henry.* As the honey of Hibla, my old lad of the castle; and
> is not a buff-jerkin a most sweet robe of durance?
> *Falstaff.* How now, how now, mad wag, what in thy quips
> and thy quiddities? what a plague have I to do with a buff-
> jerkin?
> *P. Henry.* Why, what a pox have I to do with mine hostess of
> the tavern?

In the same scene he afterwards affects melancholy, from pure satisfaction of heart, and professes reform because it is the farthest thing in the world from his thoughts. He has no qualms of conscience, and therefore would as soon talk of them as of anything else when the humour takes him.

Falstaff. But, Hal, I pr'ithee trouble me no more with vanity. I would to God thou and I knew where a commodity of good names were to be bought. An old lord of council rated me the other day in the street about you, sir; but I mark'd him not, and yet he talked very wisely, and in the street too.

P. Henry. Thou didst well, for wisdom cries out in the street, and no man regards it.

Falstaff. O, thou hast damnable iteration, and art indeed able to corrupt a saint. Thou hast done much harm unto me, Hal; God forgive thee for it. Before I knew thee, Hal, I knew nothing, and now I am, if a man should speak truly, little better than one of the wicked. I must give over this life, and I will give it over, by the Lord; an I do not, I am a villain. I'll be damned for never a king's son in Christendom.

P. Henry. Where shall we take a purse tomorrow, Jack?

Falstaff. Where thou wilt, lad, I'll make one; an I do not, call me villain, and baffle me.

P. Henry. I see good amendment of life in thee, from praying to purse-taking.

Falstaff. Why, Hal, 'tis my vocation, Hal. 'Tis no sin for a man to labor in his vocation.

Of the other prominent passages, his account of his pretended resistance to the robbers, "who grew from four men in buckram into eleven" as the imagination of his own valor increased with his relating it, his getting off when the truth is discovered by pretending he knew the Prince, the scene in which in the person of the old king he lectures the Prince and gives himself a good character, the soliloquy on honor, and description of his new-raised recruits, his meeting with the chief justice, his abuse of the Prince and Poins, who overhear him, to Doll Tearsheet, his reconciliation with Mrs. Quickly who has arrested him for an old debt, and whom he persuades to pawn her plate to lend him ten pounds more, and the scenes with Shallow and Silence, are all inimitable. Of all of them, the scene in which Falstaff plays the part, first, of the King, and then of Prince Henry, is the one that has been the most often quoted. We must quote it once more in illustration of our remarks.

Falstaff. Harry, I do not only marvel where thou spendest thy time, but also how thou art accompanied; for though the camomile, the more it is trodden on, the faster it grows, yet youth, the more it is wasted, the sooner it wears. That thou art my son, I have partly thy mother's word, partly my own opinion, but chiefly a villainous trick of thine eye, and a foolish hanging of thy nether lip, that doth warrant me. If then thou be son to me, here lies the point;—Why, being son to me, art thou so pointed at? Shall the blessed sun of heaven prove a micher, and eat blackberries? A question not to be ask'd. Shall the son of England prove a thief, and take purses? a question to be ask'd. There is a thing, Harry, which thou hast often heard of, and it is known to many in our land by the name of pitch. This pitch, as ancient writers do report, doth defile; so doth the company thou keepest. For, Harry, now I do not speak to thee in drink, but in tears; not in pleasure, but in passion; not in words only, but in woes also.—And yet there is a virtuous man, whom I have often noted in thy company, but I know not his name.

P. Henry. What manner of man, an it like your majesty?

Falstaff. A goodly portly man, i'faith, and a corpulent; of a cheerful look, a pleasing eye, and a most noble carriage; and, as I think, his age some fifty, or, by'r-lady, inclining to threescore; and now I do remember me, his name is Falstaff. If that man should be lewdly given, he deceiveth me; for, Harry, I see virtue in his looks. If then the fruit may be known by the tree, as the tree by the fruit, then peremptorily I speak it, there is virtue in that Falstaff. Him keep with, the rest banish. And tell me now, thou naughty varlet, tell me, where hast thou been this month?

P. Henry. Dost thou speak like a king? Do thou stand for me, and I'll play my father.

Falstaff. Depose me? if thou dost it half so gravely, so majestically, both in word and matter, hang me up by the heels for a rabbit-sucker or a poulterer's hare.

P. Henry. Well, here I am set.

Falstaff. And here I stand—Judge, my masters.

P. Henry. Now, Harry, whence come you?

Falstaff. My noble lord, from Eastcheap.

P. Henry. The complaints I hear of thee are grievous.

Falstaff. S'blood, my lord, they are false.—Nay, I'll tickle ye
for a young prince, i'faith.

P. Henry. Swearest thou, ungracious boy? henceforth ne'er
look on me. Thou art violently carried away from grace.
There is a devil haunts thee, in the likeness of a fat old
man; a tun of man is thy companion. Why dost thou
converse with that trunk of humors, that bolting-hutch of
beastliness, that swoln parcel of dropsies, that huge bombard of sack, that stuffed cloak-bag of guts, that roasted
Manning-tree ox with the pudding in his belly, that reverend vice, that grey iniquity, that father ruffian, that vanity
in years? wherein is he good, but to taste sack and drink it?
wherein neat and cleanly, but to carve a capon and eat it?
wherein cunning, but in craft? wherein crafty, but in villainy? wherein villainous, but in all things? wherein
worthy, but in nothing?

Falstaff. I would your grace would take me with you. Whom
means your grace?

P. Henry. That villainous, abominable misleader of youth,
Falstaff, that old white-bearded Satan.

Falstaff. My lord, the man I know.

P. Henry. I know thou dost.

Falstaff. But to say I know more harm in him than in myself
were to say more than I know. That he is old (the more
the pity) his white hairs do witness it; but that he is
(saving your reverence) a whore-master, that I utterly
deny. If sack and sugar be a fault, God help the wicked! if
to be old and merry be a sin, then many an old host that I
know is damned. If to be fat be to be hated, then Pharaoh's lean kine are to be loved. No, my good lord, banish
Peto, banish Bardolph, banish Poins; but for sweet Jack
Falstaff, kind Jack Falstaff, true Jack Falstaff, valiant Jack
Falstaff, and therefore more valiant, being as he is, old
Jack Falstaff, banish not him thy Harry's company; banish
plump Jack, and banish all the world.

P. Henry. I do, I will.

[*Knocking; and Hostess and Bardolph go out.*
Re-enter Bardolph, running.]

Bardolph. O, my lord, my lord; the sheriff, with a most monstrous watch, is at the door.

Falstaff. Out, you rogue! play out the play. I have much to say
in the behalf of that Falstaff.

One of the most characteristic descriptions of Sir John is that which Mrs. Quickly gives of him when he asks her "What is the gross sum that I owe thee?"

> *Hostess.* Marry, if thou wert an honest man, thyself, and the money too. Thou didst swear to me upon a parcel-gilt goblet, sitting in my Dolphin-chamber, at the round table, by a sea-coal fire on Wednesday in Whitsunweek, when the Prince broke thy head for likening his father to a singing man of Windsor; thou didst swear to me then, as I was washing thy wound, to marry me, and make me my lady thy wife. Canst thou deny it? Did not goodwife Keech, the butcher's wife, come in then, and call me gossip Quickly? coming in to borrow a mess of vinegar; telling us she had a good dish of prawns; whereby thou didst desire to eat some; whereby I told thee they were ill of a green wound? And didst thou not, when she was gone down stairs, desire me to be no more so familiarity with such poor people; saying, that ere long they should call me madam? And didst thou not kiss me, and bid me fetch thee thirty shillings? I put thee now to thy book-oath; deny it, if thou canst.

This scene is to us the most convincing proof of Falstaff's power of gaining over the good will of those he was familiar with, except indeed Bardolph's somewhat profane exclamation on hearing the account of his death, "Would I were with him, wheresoe'er he is, whether in heaven or hell."

One of the topics of exulting superiority over others most common in Sir John's mouth is his corpulence and the exterior marks of good living which he carries about him, thus "turning his vices into commodity." He accounts for the friendship between the Prince and Poins, from "their legs being both of a bigness," and compares Justice Shallow to "a man made after supper of a cheese-paring." There cannot be a more striking gradation of character than that between Falstaff and Shallow, and Shallow and Silence. It seems difficult at first to fall lower than the squire; but this fool, great as he is, finds an admirer and humble foil in his cousin Silence. Vain of his acquaintance with Sir John, who makes a butt of him, he exclaims, "Would, cousin Silence, that thou had'st seen that which this knight and I have

seen!"—"Aye, Master Shallow, we have heard the chimes at midnight," says Sir John. To Falstaff's observation, "I did not think
Master Silence had been a man of this mettle," Silence answers,
"Who, I? I have been merry twice and once ere now." What an
idea is here conveyed of a prodigality of living! What good husbandry and economical self-denial in his pleasures! What a stock
of lively recollections! It is curious that Shakespeare has ridiculed
in Justice Shallow, who was "in some authority under the king,"
that disposition to unmeaning tautology which is the regal infirmity of later times, and which, it may be supposed, he acquired
from talking to his cousin Silence, and receiving no answers.

> *Falstaff.* You have here a goodly dwelling, and a rich.
> *Shallow.* Barren, barren, barren; beggars all, beggars all, Sir
> John; marry, good air. Spread Davy, spread Davy. Well
> said, Davy.
> *Falstaff.* This Davy serves you for good uses.
> *Shallow.* A good varlet, a good varlet, a very good varlet. By
> the mass, I have drank too much sack at supper. A good
> varlet. Now sit down, now sit down. Come, cousin.

The true spirit of humanity, the thorough knowledge of the
stuff we are made of, the practical wisdom with the seeming
fooleries in the whole of the garden-scene at Shallow's country-
seat, and just before in the exquisite dialogue between him and
Silence on the death of old Double, have no parallel anywhere
else. In one point of view, they are laughable in the extreme; in
another they are equally affecting, if it is affecting to show *what a
little thing is human life*, what a poor forked creature man is!

The heroic and serious part of these two plays founded on the
story of Henry IV is not inferior to the comic and farcical. The
characters of Hotspur and Prince Henry are two of the most
beautiful and dramatic, both in themselves and from contrast,
that ever were drawn. They are the essence of chivalry. We like
Hotspur the best upon the whole, perhaps because he was unfortunate. The characters of their fathers, Henry IV and old
Northumberland, are kept up equally well. Henry naturally succeeds by his prudence and caution in keeping what he has got;
Northumberland fails in his enterprise from an excess of the
same quality, and is caught in the web of his own cold, dilatory

policy. Owen Glendower is a masterly character. It is as bold and original as it is intelligible and thoroughly natural. The disputes between him and Hotspur are managed with infinite address and insight into nature. We cannot help pointing out here some very beautiful lines, where Hotspur describes the fight between Glendower and Mortimer.

> —When on the gentle Severn's sedgy bank,
> In single opposition hand to hand,
> He did confound the best part of an hour
> In changing hardiment with great Glendower.
> Three times they breath'd, and three times did they drink,
> Upon agreement, of swift Severn's flood;
> Who then affrighted with their bloody looks,
> Ran fearfully among the trembling reeds,
> And hid his crisp head in the hollow bank,
> Blood-stained with these valiant combatants.

The peculiarity and the excellence of Shakespeare's poetry is that it seems as if he made his imagination the hand-maid of nature, and nature the plaything of his imagination. He appears to have been all the characters, and in all the situations he describes. It is as if either he had had all their feelings, or had lent them all his genius to express themselves. There cannot be stronger instances of this than Hotspur's rage when Henry IV forbids him to speak of Mortimer, his insensibility to all that his father and uncle urge to calm him, and his fine abstracted apostrophe to honor, "By heaven, methinks it were an easy leap to pluck bright honor from the moon," etc. After all, notwithstanding the gallantry, generosity, good temper, and idle freaks of the madcap Prince of Wales, we should not have been sorry if Northumberland's force had come up in time to decide the fate of the battle at Shrewsbury; at least, we always heartily sympathize with Lady Percy's grief, when she exclaims,

> Had my sweet Harry had but half their numbers,
> To-day might I (hanging on Hotspur's neck)
> Have talked of Monmouth's grave.

The truth is that we never could forgive the Prince's treatment of Falstaff; though perhaps Shakespeare knew what was best, according to the history, the nature of the times, and of the man. We speak only as dramatic critics. Whatever terror the French in those days might have of Henry V, yet, to the readers of poetry at present, Falstaff is the better man of the two. We think of him and quote him oftener.

Edward Dowden

The English Historical Plays (1875)

Shakespeare has judged Henry IV and pronounced that his life was not a failure; still, it was at best a partial success. Shakespeare saw, and he proceeded to show to others, that all which Bolingbroke had attained, and almost incalculably greater possession of good things could be attained more joyously, by nobler means. The unmistakable enthusiasm of the poet about his Henry V has induced critics to believe that in him we find Shakespeare's ideal of manhood. He must certainly be regarded as Shakespeare's ideal of manhood in the sphere of practical achievement—the hero and central figure therefore of the historical plays.

The fact has been noticed that, with respect to Henry's youthful follies, Shakespeare deviated from all authorities known to have been accessible to him. "An extraordinary conversion was generally thought to have fallen upon the Prince on coming to the crown, insomuch that the old chroniclers could only account for the change by some miracle of grace or touch of supernatural benediction."[1] Shakespeare, it would seem, engaged now upon historical matter and not the fantastic substance of a comedy, found something incredible in the sudden transformation of a reckless libertine (the Henry described by Caxton, by Fabyan and others) into a character of majestic force and large practical wisdom. Rather than reproduce this incredible popular tradition concerning Henry, Shakespeare preferred to attempt the difficult task of exhibiting the Prince as a sharer in the wild frolic of youth, while at the same time he was holding himself prepared for the splendid entrance upon his manhood, and stood really aloof in his inmost being from the unworthy life of his associates.

The change which effected itself in the Prince, as represented by Shakespeare, was no miraculous conversion, but merely the transition from boyhood to adult years, and from unchartered freedom to the solemn responsibilities of a great ruler. We must not suppose that Henry formed a deliberate plan for concealing the strength and splendor of his character, in order afterwards to flash forth upon men's sight and overwhelm and dazzle them. When he soliloquizes (1 Henry IV, *Act* i, *Scene* 2), having bid farewell to Poins and Falstaff,

> I know you all, and will awhile uphold
> The unyoked humor of your idleness;
> Yet herein will I imitate the sun,
> Who doth permit the base contagious clouds
> To smother up his beauty from the world,
> That, when he please again to be himself,
> Being wanted, he may be more wonder'd at,
> By breaking through the foul and ugly mists
> Of vapors that did seem to strangle him.

—when Henry soliloquizes thus, we are not to suppose that he was quite as wise and diplomatical as he pleased to represent himself, for the time being, to his own heart and conscience.[2] The Prince entered heartily and without reserve into the fun and frolic of his Eastcheap life; the vigor and the folly of it were delightful; to be clapped on the back, and shouted for as "Hal," was far better than the doffing of caps and crooking of knees, and delicate, unreal phraseology of the court. But Henry, at the same time, kept himself from subjugation to what was really base. He could truthfully stand before his father (1 Henry IV, *Act* iii, *Scene* 2), and maintain that his nature was substantially sound and untainted, capable of redeeming itself from all past, superficial dishonor.

Has Shakespeare erred? Or is it not possible to take energetic part in a provisional life, which is known to be provisional, while at the same time a man holds his truest self in reserve for the life that is best, and highest, and most real? May not the very consciousness, indeed, that such a life is provisional, enable one to give oneself away to it, satisfying its demands with scrupulous care, or with full and free enjoyment, as a man could not if it were a life which had any chance of engaging his whole personality, and that finally? Is it possible to adjust two states of being, one temporary and provisional, the other absolute and final, and to pass freely out of one into the other? Precisely because the one is perfect and indestructible, it does not fear the counter-life. May there not have been passages in Shakespeare's own experience which authorized him in his attempt to exhibit the successful adjustment of two apparently incoherent lives?[3]

The central element in the character of Henry is his noble realization of fact. To Richard II life was a graceful and shadowy ceremony, containing beautiful and pathetic situations. Henry IV saw in the world a substantial reality, and he resolved to obtain mastery over it by courage and by craft. But while Bolingbroke with his caution and his policy, his address and his ambition, penetrated only a little way among the facts of life, his son, with a true genius for the discovery of the noblest facts, and of all facts, came into relation with the central and vital forces of the universe, so that, instead of constructing a strong but careful life for himself, life breathed through him, and blossomed into a glorious enthusiasm of existence. And therefore from all that was unreal, and from all exaggerated egoism, Henry was absolutely delivered. A man who firmly holds, or rather is held by the beneficent forces of the world, whose feet are upon a rock, and whose goings are established, may with confidence abandon much of the prudence, and many of the artificial proprieties of the world. For every unreality Henry exhibits a sovereign disregard—for unreal manners, unreal glory, unreal heroism, unreal piety, unreal warfare, unreal love. The plain fact is so precious it needs no ornament.

From the coldness, the caution, the convention of his father's court (an atmosphere which suited well the temperament of John of Lancaster), Henry escapes to the teeming vitality of the London streets, and the tavern where Falstaff is monarch. There, among ostlers, and carriers, and drawers, and merchants, and pilgrims, and loud robustious women, he at least has freedom and frolic. "If it be a sin to covet honor," Henry declares, "I am the most offending soul alive." But the honor that Henry covets is not that which Hotspur is ambitious after:

> By heaven, methinks it were an easy leap
> To pluck bright honor from the pale-faced moon.[4]

The honor that Henry covets is the achievement of great deeds, not the words of men which vibrate around such deeds. Falstaff, the despiser of honor, labors across the field bearing the body of the fallen Hotspur, the impassioned pursuer of glory, and in his fashion of splendid imposture or stupendous joke the fat knight claims credit for the achievement of the day's victory. Henry is not concerned on this occasion to put the old sinner to shame. To have added to the deeds of the world a glorious deed is itself the only honor that Henry seeks. Nor is his heroic greatness inconsistent with the admission of very humble incidents of humanity:

> *Prince.* Doth it not show vilely in me to desire small beer?
> *Poins.* Why, a prince should not be so loosely studied as to remember so weak a composition.
> *Prince.* Belike, then, my appetite was not princely got; for by my troth I do now remember the poor creature, small beer. But indeed these humble considerations make me out of love with my greatness.[5]

Henry with his lank frame, and vigorous muscle (the opposite of the Danish Prince who is "fat and scant of breath"), is actually wearied to excess and thirsty, and he is by no means afraid to confess the fact; his appetite at least has not been pampered. "Before God, Kate," such is Henry's fashion of wooing, "I cannot look greenly, nor gasp out my eloquence, nor I have no cunning in protestation; only downright oaths, which I never use till urged, nor never break for urging . . . I speak to thee plain soldier; if thou canst love me for this take me; if not, to say to thee that I shall die is true; but for thy love, by the Lord, no; yet I love thee too."

And as in his love there is a certain substantial homeliness and heartiness, so is there also in his piety. He is not harassed like his son, the saintly Henry, with refinements of scrupulosity, the disease of an irritable conscience, which is delivered from its irritability by no active pursuit of noble ends. Henry has done what is right; he has tried to repair his father's faults; he has built "two chantries, where the sad and solemn priests still sing for Richard's soul." He has done his part by God and man, will not God in like manner stand by him and perform what belongs to God? Henry's freedom from egoism, his modesty, his integrity,

his joyous humor, his practical piety, his habit of judging things
by natural and not artificial standards—all these are various de-
velopments of the central element of his character, his noble
realization of fact.

But his realization of fact produces something more than this
integrity, this homely honesty of nature. It breathes through him
an enthusiasm which would be intense if it were not so massive.
Through his union with the vital strength of the world, he becomes one of the world's most glorious and beneficent forces.
From the plain and mirth-creating comrade of his fellow-soldiers
he rises into the genius of impassioned battle. From the modest
and quiet adviser with his counselors and prelates, he is transformed, when the occasion requires it, into the terrible adminis-
trator of justice. When Henry takes from his father's pillow the
crown, and places it upon his own head, the deed is done with no
fluttering rapture of attainment. He has entered gravely upon his
manhood. He has made very real to himself the long, careful, and
joyless life of the father who had won for him this "golden care."
His heart is full of tenderness for this sad father, to whom he had
been able to bring so little happiness. But now he takes his due,
the crown, and the world's whole force shall not wrest it from
him:

> Thy due from me
> Is tears and heavy sorrows of the blood,
> Which nature, love, and filial tenderness,
> Shall, O dear father, pay thee plenteously;
> My due from thee is this imperial crown,
> Which, as immediate from thy place and blood,
> Derives itself to me. Lo, here it sits,
> Which God shall guard; and put the world's whole strength
> Into one giant arm, it shall not force
> This lineal honor from me.

Here is no aesthetic feeling for the "situation," only the profoundest and noblest entrance into the fact.

The same noble and disinterested loyalty to the truth of
things renders it easy, natural, and indeed inevitable that Henry
should confirm in his office the Chief Justice who had formerly
executed the law against himself, and equally inevitable that he
should disengage himself absolutely from Falstaff and the asso-

ciates of his provisional life of careless frolic. To such a life an end must come; and as no terms of half-acquaintance are possible with the fat Knight, exorbitant in good fellowship as he is, and inexhaustible in resources, Henry must become to Falstaff an absolute stranger:

> I know thee not, old man: fall to thy prayers.
> How ill white hairs become a fool and jester.

Henry has been stern to his former self, and turned him away for ever; therefore he can be stern to Falstaff. There is no faltering. But at an enforced distance of ten miles from his person (for the fascination of Falstaff can hardly weave a bridge across that interval) Falstaff shall be sufficiently provided for:

> For competence of life I will allow you
> That lack of means enforce you not to evil:
> And as we hear you do reform yourselves,
> We will, according to your strengths and qualities,
> Give you advancement.°

NOTES

1. Hudson, "Shakespeare: his Life, Art, and Characters," vol. ii., p. 78. See also C. Knight's Studies of Shakespeare, B, iv., chap. ii., p. 164.
2. Kreyssig. Vorlesungen über Shakespeare (ed. 1874), vol. i., p. 212. R. Genée: Shakespeare, sein Leben und seine Werke, p. 202.
3. Rümelin, who argues that Shakespeare wrote to please the *jeunesse dorée* of the period, suggests that the character of the Prince was drawn from that of the Earl of Southampton. The originals of many of Shakespeare's historical personages, Rümelin supposes, sat upon the side-seats of the stage, and are, alas! irrecoverably lost. (With such conjectures must "realist" criticism buttress up its case!) Shakespeare-Studien (ed. 1874), p. 127.
4. 1 Henry IV, *Act* i., *Scene* 3. Kreyssig contrasts Hotspur's passion for honour with Falstaff's indifference to it. "Can honour set to a leg or an arm? no: or take away the grief of a wound? no." Henry in this matter is equally remote from Falstaff and from Hotspur. Vorlesungen über Shakespeare, vol. i., pp. 244, 245.
5. Jack Cade, in his aspiration after greatness, announces—"I will make it felony to drink small beer. . . . when I am king, as king I will be." Henry's desire would seem then to be inexpressibly humiliating.

6. It is noteworthy that although we meet Sir John so often in 2 Henry IV., we find the Prince only on a single occasion in his company; and it would be beyond human nature to deny himself the delight and edification of such a spectacle as the fat Knight cuddling and kissing Doll Tearsheet. Henry *must* go.

George Bernard Shaw

Dramatic Opinions and Essays (1907)

I am cured now. It is all a delusion: there is no profession, no art, no skill about the business [of acting] at all. We have no actors: we have only authors, and not many of them. When Mendelssohn composed "Son and Stranger" for an amateur performance, he found that the bass could only sing one note. So he wrote the bass part all on that one note; and when it came to the fateful night, the bass failed even at that. Our authors do as Mendelssohn did. They find that the actors have only one note, or perhaps, if they are very clever, half a dozen. So their parts are confined to these notes, often with the same result as in Mendelssohn's case. If you doubt me, go and see "Henry IV" at the Haymarket. It is as good work as our stage can do; but the man who says that it is skilled work has neither eyes nor ears; the man who mistakes it for intelligent work has no brains; the man who finds it even good fun may be capable of Christy Minstrelsy but not of Shakespeare. Everything that charm of style, rich humor, and vivid and natural characterization can do for a play are badly wanted by "Henry IV," which has neither the romantic beauty of Shakespeare's earlier plays nor the tragic greatness of the later ones. One can hardly forgive Shakespeare quite for the worldly phase in which he tried to thrust such a Jingo hero as his Harry V down our throats. The combination of conventional propriety and brute masterfulness in his public capacity with a low-lived blackguardism in his private tastes is not a pleasant one. No doubt he is true to nature as a picture of what is by no means uncommon in English society, an able young Philistine inheriting high position and authority, which he holds on to and goes through with by keeping a tight grip on his conventional and legal advantages, but who would have been quite in his place if he had been born a gamekeeper or a farmer. We do not in the first part of "Henry IV" see Harry sending Mrs. Quickly and Doll Tearsheet to the whipping-post, or handing over Falstaff to the Lord Chief Justice with a sanctimonious lecture; but he repeatedly makes it clear that he will turn on them later on, and that his self-indulgent good-fellowship with them is consciously and deliberately treacherous. His popularity, therefore, is like that of a prizefighter: nobody feels for him as for Romeo or Hamlet. Hotspur, too, though he is stimulating as ginger cordial is stimulating, is hardly better than his horse; and King Bolingbroke, preoccupied with his crown exactly as a miser is preoccupied with his money, is equally useless as a refuge for our affections, which are thus thrown back undivided on Falstaff, the most human person in the play, but none the less a besotted and disgusting old wretch. And there is neither any subtlety nor (for Shakespeare) much poetry in the presentation of all these characters. They are labelled and described and insisted upon with the roughest directness; and their reality and their humor can alone save them from the unpopularity of their unlovableness and the tedium of their obviousness. Fortunately, they offer capital opportunities for interesting acting. Bolingbroke's long discourse to his son on the means by which he struck the imagination and enlisted the snobbery of the English people gives the actor a chance comparable to the crafty early scenes in "Richelieu." Prince Hal's humor is seasoned with sportsmanlike cruelty and the insolence of conscious mastery and contempt to the point of occasionally making one shudder. Hotspur is full of energy; and Falstaff is, of course, an unrivalled part for the right sort of comedian. Well acted, then, the play is a good one in spite of there not being a single tear in it. Ill acted—O heavens!

Of the four leading parts, the easiest—Hotspur—becomes pre-eminent at the Haymarket, not so much by Mr. Lewis Waller's superiority to the rest as by their inferiority to him. Some of the things he did were astonishing in an actor of his rank. At the end of each of his first vehement speeches, he strode right down the stage and across to the prompt side of the proscenium on the frankest barnstorming principles, repeating this absurd "cross"—a well-known convention of the booth for catching applause—three times, step for step, without a pretense of any dramatic motive. In the camp scene before the battle of Shrewsbury, he did just what I blamed Miss Violet Vanbrugh for trying to do in "Monsieur de Paris": that is, to carry through a long crescendo of excitement by main force after beginning fortissimo. Would it be too farfetched to recommend Mr. Waller to study how Mozart, in rushing an operatic movement to a spirited conclusion, knew how to make it, when apparently already at its utmost, seem to bound forward by a sudden pianissimo and lightsome change of step, the speed and force of the execution being actually reduced instead of intensified by the change? Such skilled, resourceful husbandry is the secret of all effects of this kind; and it is in the entire absence of such husbandry that Mr. Waller showed how our miserable theater has left him still a novice for the purposes of a part which he is fully equipped by nature to play with most brilliant success, and which he did play very strikingly, considering he was not in the least sure how to set about it, and hardly dared to stop blazing away at full pitch for an instant lest the part should drop flat on the boards. Mr. Mollison presented us with an assortment of effects, and tones, and poses which had no reference, as far as I could discover, to the part of Bolingbroke at any single point. I did not catch a glimpse of the character from one end of his performance to the other, and so must conclude that Shakespeare has failed to convey his intention to him. Mr. Gillmore's way of playing Hal was as bad as the traditional way of playing Sheridan. He rattled and swaggered and roystered, and followed every sentence with a forced explosion of mirthless laughter, evidently believing that, as Prince Hal was reputed to be a humorous character, it was his business to laugh at him. Like most of his colleagues, he became more tolerable in the plain sailing of the battle scene, where the parts lose their individuality in the general warlike excitement, and an energetic display of the commonest sort of emotion suffices. Mr. Tree only wants one thing to make him an excellent Falstaff, and that is to get born over again as unlike himself as possible. No doubt, in the course of a month or two, when he begins to pick up a few of the lines of the part, he will improve on his first effort; but he will never be even a moderately good Falstaff. The basket-work figure, as expressionless as that of a Jack in the Green; the face, with the pathetic wandering eye of Captain Swift belying such suggestion of character as the lifeless mask of paint and hair can give; the voice, coarsened, vulgarized, and falsified without being enriched or colored; the hopeless efforts of the romantic imaginative actor, touching only in unhappy parts, to play the comedian by dint of mechanical horseplay: all that is hopeless, irremediable. Mr. Tree might as well try to play Juliet; and if he were wise he would hand over his part and his breadbasket to Mr. Lionel Brough, whose Bardolph has the true comic force which Mr. Tree never attains for a moment.

A. C. Bradley

The Rejection of Falstaff[1] (1902)

Of the two persons principally concerned in the rejection of Falstaff, Henry, both as Prince and as King, has received, on the whole, full justice from readers and critics. Falstaff, on the other hand, has been in one respect the most unfortunate of Shakespeare's famous characters. All of them, in passing from the mind of their creator into other minds, suffer change; they tend to lose their harmony through the disproportionate attention bestowed on some one feature, or to lose their uniqueness by being conventionalised into types already familiar. But Falstaff was degraded by Shakespeare himself. The original character is to be found alive in the two parts of *Henry IV.*, dead in *Henry V.*, and nowhere else. But not very long after these plays were composed, Shakespeare wrote, and he afterwards revised, the very entertaining piece called *The Merry Wives of Windsor*. Perhaps his company wanted a new play on a sudden; or perhaps, as one would rather believe, the tradition may be true that Queen Elizabeth, delighted with the Falstaff scenes of *Henry IV.*, expressed a wish to see the hero of them again, and to see him in love. Now it was no more possible for Shakespeare to show his own Falstaff in love than to turn twice two into five. But he could write in haste—the tradition says, in a fortnight—a comedy or farce differing from all his other plays in this, that its scene is laid in English middle-class life, and that it is prosaic almost to the end. And among the characters he could introduce a disreputable fat old knight with attendants, and could call them Falstaff, Bardolph, Pistol, and Nym. And he could represent this knight assailing, for financial purposes, the virtue of two matrons, and in the event baffled, duped, treated like dirty linen, beaten, burnt, pricked, mocked, insulted, and, worst of all, repentant and didactic. It is horrible. It is almost enough to convince one that Shakespeare himself could sanction the parody of Ophelia in the *Two Noble Kinsmen*. But it no more touches the real Falstaff than Ophelia is degraded by that parody. To picture the real Falstaff befooled like the Falstaff of the *Merry Wives* is like imagining Iago the gull of Roderigo, or Becky Sharp the dupe of Amelia Osborne. Before he had been served the least of these tricks he would have had his brains taken out and buttered, and have given them to a dog for a New Year's gift. I quote the words of the impostor, for after all Shakespeare made him and gave to him a few sentences worthy of Falstaff himself. But they are only a few—one side of a sheet of notepaper would contain them. And yet critics have solemnly debated at what period in his life Sir John endured the gibes of Master Ford, and whether we should put this comedy between the two parts of *Henry IV.*, or between the second of them and *Henry V.* And the Falstaff of the general reader, it is to be feared, is an impossible conglomerate of two distinct characters, while the Falstaff of the mere playgoer is certainly much more like the impostor than the true man.

The separation of these two has long ago been effected by criticism, and is insisted on in almost all competent estimates of the character of Falstaff. I do not propose to attempt a full account either of this character or of that of Prince Henry, but shall connect the remarks I have to make on them with a question which does not appear to have been satisfactorily discussed—the question of the rejection of Falstaff by the Prince on his accession to the throne. What do we feel, and what are we meant to feel, as we witness this rejection? And what does our feeling imply as to the characters of Falstaff and the new King?

1.

Sir John, you remember, is in Gloucestershire, engaged in borrowing a thousand pounds from Justice Shallow; and here Pistol, riding helter-skelter from London, brings him the great news that the old King is as dead as nail in door, and that Harry the Fifth is the man. Sir John, in wild excitement, taking any man's horses, rushes to London; and he carries Shallow with him, for he longs to reward all his friends. We find him standing with his companions just outside Westminster Abbey, in the crowd that is waiting for the King to come out after his coronation. He himself is stained with travel, and has had no time to spend any of the thousand pounds in buying new liveries for his men. But what of that? This poor show only proves his earnestness of affection, his devotion, how he could not deliberate or remember or have patience to shift himself, but rode day and night, thought of nothing else but to see Henry, and put all affairs else in oblivion, as if there were nothing else to be done but to see him. And now he stands sweating with desire to see him, and repeating and repeating this one desire of his heart—"to see him." The moment comes. There is a shout within the Abbey like the roaring of the sea, and a clangour of trumpets, and the doors open and the procession streams out.

> *Fal.* God save thy grace, King Hal! my royal Hal!
> *Pist.* The heavens thee guard and keep, most royal imp of
>   fame!
> *Fal.* God save thee, my sweet boy!
> *King.* My Lord Chief Justice, speak to that vain man.
> *Ch. Just.* Have you your wits? Know you what 'tis you
>   speak?
> *Fal.* My King! my Jove! I speak to thee, my heart!
> *King.* I know thee not, old man: fall to thy prayers:
>   How ill white hairs become a fool and jester!
>   I have long dream'd of such a kind of man,
>   So surfeit-swell'd, so old and so profane;
>   But being awaked I do despise my dream.
>   Make less thy body hence, and more thy grace;
>   Leave gormandizing; know the grave doth gape
>   For thee thrice wider than for other men.
>   Reply not to me with a fool-born jest:
>   Presume not that I am the thing I was;
>   For God doth know, so shall the world perceive,
>   That I have turn'd away my former self;
>   So will I those that kept me company.
>   When thou dost hear I am as I have been,
>   Approach me, and thou shalt be as thou wast,
>   The tutor and the feeder of my riots:

> Till then, I banish thee, on pain of death,
> As I have done the rest of my misleaders,
> Not to come near our person by ten mile.
> For competence of life I will allow you,
> That lack of means enforce you not to evil:
> And, as we hear you do reform yourselves,
> We will, according to your strengths and qualities,
> Give you advancement. Be it your charge, my lord,
> To see perform'd the tenour of our word.
> Set on.

The procession passes out of sight, but Falstaff and his friends remain. He shows no resentment. He comforts himself, or tries to comfort himself—first, with the thought that he has Shallow's thousand pounds, and then, more seriously, I believe, with another thought. The King, he sees, must look thus to the world; but he will be sent for in private when night comes, and will yet make the fortunes of his friends. But even as he speaks, the Chief Justice, accompanied by Prince John, returns, and gives the order to his officers:

> Go, carry Sir John Falstaff to the Fleet;
> Take all his company along with him.

Falstaff breaks out, "My lord, my lord," but he is cut short and hurried away; and after a few words between the Prince and the Chief Justice the scene closes, and with it the drama.

What are our feelings during this scene? They will depend on our feelings about Falstaff. If we have not keenly enjoyed the Falstaff scenes of the two plays, if we regard Sir John chiefly as an old reprobate, not only a sensualist, a liar, and a coward, but a cruel and dangerous ruffian, I suppose we enjoy his discomfiture and consider that the King has behaved magnificently. But if we *have* keenly enjoyed the Falstaff scenes, if we have enjoyed them as Shakespeare surely meant them to be enjoyed, and if, accordingly, Falstaff is not to us solely or even chiefly a reprobate and ruffian, we feel, I think, during the King's speech, a good deal of pain and some resentment; and when, without any further offence on Sir John's part, the Chief Justice returns and sends him to prison, we stare in astonishment. These, I believe, are, in greater or less degree, the feelings of most of those who really

enjoy the Falstaff scenes (as many readers do not). Nor are these
feelings diminished when we remember the end of the whole
story, as we find it in *Henry V.*, where we learn that Falstaff
quickly died, and, according to the testimony of persons not very
sentimental, died of a broken heart.[2] Suppose this merely to mean
that he sank under the shame of his public disgrace, and it is
pitiful enough: but the words of Mrs. Quickly, "The king has
killed his heart"; of Nym, "The king hath run bad humours on the
knight; that's the even of it"; of Pistol,

> Nym, thou hast spoke the right,
> His heart is fracted and corroborate,

assuredly point to something more than wounded pride; they
point to wounded affection, and remind us of Falstaff's own
answer to Prince Hal's question, "Sirrah, do I owe you a thousand
pound?" "A thousand pound, Hal? a million: thy love is worth a
million: thou owest me thy love."

Now why did Shakespeare end his drama with a scene which,
though undoubtedly striking, leaves an impression so unpleasant? I will venture to put aside without discussion the idea that he
meant us throughout the two plays to regard Falstaff with disgust or indignation, so that we naturally feel nothing but pleasure
at his fall; for this idea implies that kind of inability to understand
Shakespeare with which it is idle to argue. And there is another
and a much more ingenious suggestion which must equally be
rejected as impossible. According to it, Falstaff, having listened to
the King's speech, did not seriously hope to be sent for by him in
private; he fully realised the situation at once, and was only
making game of Shallow; and in his immediate turn upon Shallow
when the King goes out, "Master Shallow, I owe you a thousand
pound," we are meant to see his humorous superiority to any
rebuff, so that we end the play with the delightful feeling that,
while Henry has done the right thing, Falstaff, in his outward
overthrow, has still proved himself inwardly invincible. This suggestion comes from a critic who understands Falstaff, and in the
suggestion itself shows that he understands him.[3] But it provides
no solution, because it wholly ignores, and could not account for,
that which follows the short conversation with Shallow. Falstaff's
dismissal to the Fleet, and his subsequent death, prove beyond

doubt that his rejection was meant by Shakespeare to be taken as a catastrophe which not even his humour could enable him to surmount.

Moreover, these interpretations, even if otherwise admissible, would still leave our problem only partly solved. For what troubles us is not only the disappointment of Falstaff, it is the conduct of Henry. It was inevitable that on his accession he should separate himself from Sir John, and we wish nothing else. It is satisfactory that Sir John should have a competence, with the hope of promotion in the highly improbable case of his reforming himself. And if Henry could not trust himself within ten miles of so fascinating a companion, by all means let him be banished that distance: we do not complain. These arrangements would not have prevented a satisfactory ending: the King could have communicated his decision, and Falstaff could have accepted it, in a private interview rich in humour and merely touched with pathos. But Shakespeare has so contrived matters that Henry could not send a private warning to Falstaff even if he wished to, and in their public meeting Falstaff is made to behave in so infatuated and outrageous a manner that great sternness on the King's part was unavoidable. And the curious thing is that Shakespeare did not stop here. If this had been all we should have felt pain for Falstaff, but not, perhaps, resentment against Henry. But two things we do resent. Why, when this painful incident seems to be over, should the Chief Justice return and send Falstaff to prison? Can this possibly be meant for an act of private vengeance on the part of the Chief Justice, unknown to the King? No; for in that case Shakespeare would have shown at once that the King disapproved and cancelled it. It must have been the King's own act. This is one thing we resent; the other is the King's sermon. He had a right to turn away his former self, and his old companions with it, but he had no right to talk all of a sudden like a clergyman; and surely it was both ungenerous and insincere to speak of them as his "misleaders," as though in the days of Eastcheap and Gadshill he had been a weak and silly lad. We have seen his former self, and we know that it was nothing of the kind. He had shown himself, for all his follies, a very strong and independent young man, deliberately amusing himself among men over whom he had just as much ascendency as he chose to exert. Nay, he amused himself not only among them, but at their expense. In his first soliloquy—and first soliloquies are usually significant—he declares that he associates with them in order that, when at some future time he shows his true character, he may be the more wondered at for his previous aberrations. You may think he deceives himself here; you may believe that he frequented Sir John's company out of delight in it and not merely with this cold-blooded design; but at any rate he *thought* the design was his one motive. And, that being so, two results follow. He ought in honour long ago to have given Sir John clearly to understand that they must say good-bye on the day of his accession. And, having neglected to do this, he ought not to have lectured him as his misleader. It was not only ungenerous, it was dishonest. It looks disagreeably like an attempt to buy the praise of the respectable at the cost of honour and truth. And it succeeded. Henry *always* succeeded.

You will see what I am suggesting, for the moment, as a solution of our problem. I am suggesting that our fault lies not in our resentment at Henry's conduct, but in our surprise at it; that if we had read his character truly in the light that Shakespeare gave us, we should have been prepared for a display both of hardness and of policy at this point in his career. And although this suggestion does not suffice to solve the problem before us, I am convinced that in itself it is true. Nor is it rendered at all improbable by the fact that Shakespeare has made Henry, on the whole, a fine and very attractive character, and that here he makes no one express any disapprobation of the treatment of Falstaff. For in similar cases Shakespeare is constantly misunder-stood. His readers expect him to mark in some distinct way his approval or disapproval of that which he represents; and hence where *they* disapprove and *he* says nothing, they fancy that he does *not* disapprove, and they blame his indifference, like Dr. Johnson, or at the least are puzzled. But the truth is that he shows the fact and leaves the judgment to them. And again, when he makes us like a character we expect the character to have no faults that are not expressly pointed out, and when other faults appear we either ignore them or try to explain them away. This is one of our methods of conventionalising Shakespeare. We want the world's population to be neatly divided into sheep and goats, and we want an angel by us to say, "Look, that is a goat and this is a sheep," and we try to turn Shakespeare into this angel. His impartiality makes us uncomfortable: we cannot bear to see him, like the sun, lighting up everything and judging nothing. And this is perhaps especially the case in his historical plays, where we are always trying to turn him into a partisan. He shows us that Richard II. was unworthy to be king, and we at once conclude that he thought Bolingbroke's usurpation justified; whereas he shows merely, what under the conditions was bound to exist, an inextricable tangle of right and unright. |Or, Bolingbroke being evidently wronged, we suppose Bolingbroke's statements to be true, and are quite surprised when, after attaining his end through them, he mentions casually on his death-bed that they were lies. Shakespeare makes us admire Hotspur heartily; and accordingly, when we see Hotspur discussing with others how large his particular slice of his mother-country is to be, we either fail to recognise the monstrosity of the proceeding, or, recognising it, we complain that Shakespeare is inconsistent. Prince John breaks a tottering rebellion by practising a detestable fraud on the rebels. We are against the rebels, and have heard high praise of Prince John, but we cannot help seeing that his fraud is detestable; so we say indignantly to Shakespeare, "Why, you told us he was a sheep"; whereas, in fact, if we had used our eyes we should have known beforehand that he was the brave, determined, loyal, cold-blooded, pitiless, unscrupulous son of a usurper whose throne was in danger.

To come, then, to Henry. Both as prince and as king he is deservedly a favourite, and particularly so with English readers, being, as he is, perhaps the most distinctively English of all Shakespeare's men. In *Henry V.* he is treated as a national hero. In this play he has lost much of the wit which in him seems to have depended on contact with Falstaff, but he has also laid aside the most serious faults of his youth. He inspires in a high degree fear, enthusiasm, and affection; thanks to his beautiful modesty he has the charm which is lacking to another mighty warrior, Coriolanus; his youthful escapades have given him an understanding of simple folk, and sympathy with them; he is the author of the saying, "There is some soul of goodness in things evil"; and he is much more obviously religious than most of Shakespeare's heroes. Having these and other fine qualities, and being without certain dangerous tendencies which mark the tragic heroes, he is, perhaps, the most *efficient* character drawn by Shakespeare, unless Ulysses, in *Troilus and Cressida*, is his equal. And so he has been described as Shakespeare's ideal man of action; nay, it has even been declared that here for once Shakespeare plainly disclosed his own ethical creed, and showed us his ideal, not simply of a man of action, but of a man.

But Henry is neither of these. The poet who drew Hamlet and Othello can never have thought that even the ideal man of action would lack that light upon the brow which at once transfigures them and marks their doom. It is as easy to believe that, because the lunatic, the lover, and the poet are not far apart, Shakespeare would have chosen never to have loved and sung. Even poor Timon, the most inefficient of the tragic heroes, has something in him that Henry never shows. Nor is it merely that his nature is limited: if we follow Shakespeare and look closely at Henry, we shall discover with the many fine traits a few less pleasing. Henry IV. describes him as the noble image of his own youth; and, for all his superiority to his father, he is still his father's son, the son of the man whom Hotspur called a "vile politician." Henry's religion, for example, is genuine, it is rooted in his modesty; but it is also superstitious—an attempt to buy off supernatural vengeance for Richard's blood; and it is also in part political, like his father's projected crusade. Just as he went to war chiefly because, as his father told him, it was the way to keep factious nobles quiet and unite the nation, so when he adjures the Archbishop to satisfy him as to his right to the French throne, he knows very well that the Archbishop *wants* the war, because it will defer and perhaps prevent what he considers the spoliation of the Church. This same strain of policy is what Shakespeare marks in the first soliloquy in *Henry IV.*, where the prince describes his riotous life as a mere scheme to win him glory later. It implies that readiness to use other people as means to his own ends which is a conspicuous feature in his father; and it reminds us of his father's plan of keeping himself out of the people's sight while Richard was making himself cheap by his incessant public appearances. And if I am not mistaken there is a further likeness. Henry is kindly and pleasant to every one as Prince, to every one deserving as King;

and he is so not merely out of policy: but there is no sign in him of a strong affection for any one, such an affection as we recognise at a glance in Hamlet and Horatio, Brutus and Cassius, and many more. We do not find this in *Henry V.*, not even in the noble address to Lord Scroop, and in *Henry IV.* we find, I think, a liking for Falstaff and Poins, but no more: there is no more than a liking, for instance, in his soliloquy over the supposed corpse of his fat friend, and he never speaks of Falstaff to Poins with any affection. The truth is, that the members of the family of Henry IV. have love for one another, but they cannot spare love for any one outside their family, which stands firmly united, defending its royal position against attack and instinctively isolating itself from outside influence.

Thus I would suggest that Henry's conduct in his rejection of Falstaff is in perfect keeping with his character on its unpleasant side as well as on its finer; and that, so far as Henry is concerned, we ought not to feel surprise at it. And on this view we may even explain the strange incident of the Chief Justice being sent back to order Falstaff to prison (for there is no sign of any such uncertainty in the text as might suggest an interpolation by the players). Remembering his father's words about Henry, "Being incensed, he's flint," and remembering in *Henry V.* his ruthlessness about killing the prisoners when he is incensed, we may imagine that, after he had left Falstaff and was no longer influenced by the face of his old companion, he gave way to anger at the indecent familiarity which had provoked a compromising scene on the most ceremonial of occasions and in the presence alike of court and crowd, and that he sent the Chief Justice back to take vengeance. And this is consistent with the fact that in the next play we find Falstaff shortly afterwards not only freed from prison, but unmolested in his old haunt in Eastcheap, well within ten miles of Henry's person. His anger had soon passed, and he knew that the requisite effect had been produced both on Falstaff and on the world.

But all this, however true, will not solve our problem. It seems, on the contrary, to increase its difficulty. For the natural conclusion is that Shakespeare *intended* us to feel resentment against Henry. And yet that cannot be, for it implies that he meant the play to end disagreeably; and no one who understands

Shakespeare at all will consider that supposition for a moment credible. No; he must have meant the play to end pleasantly, although he made Henry's action consistent. And hence it follows that he must have intended our sympathy with Falstaff to be so far weakened when the rejection-scene arrives that his discomfiture should be satisfactory to us; that we should enjoy this sudden reverse of enormous hopes (a thing always ludicrous if sympathy is absent); that we should approve the moral judgment that falls on him; and so should pass lightly over that disclosure of unpleasant traits in the King's character which Shakespeare was too true an artist to suppress. Thus our pain and resentment, if we feel them, are wrong, in the sense that they do not answer to the dramatist's intention. But it does not follow that they are wrong in a further sense. They may be right, because the dramatist has missed what he aimed at. And this, though the dramatist was Shakespeare, is what I would suggest. In the Falstaff scenes he overshot his mark. He created so extraordinary a being, and fixed him so firmly on his intellectual throne, that when he sought to dethrone him he could not. The moment comes when we are to look at Falstaff in a serious light, and the comic hero is to figure as a baffled schemer; but we cannot make the required change, either in our attitude or in our sympathies. We wish Henry a glorious reign and much joy of his crew of hypocritical politicians, lay and clerical; but our hearts go with Falstaff to the Fleet, or, if necessary, to Arthur's bosom or wheresomever he is.[4]

In the remainder of the lecture I will try to make this view clear. And to that end we must go back to the Falstaff of the body of the two plays, the immortal Falstaff, a character almost purely humorous, and therefore no subject for moral judgments. I can but draw an outline, and in describing one aspect of this character must be content to hold another in reserve.

2.

Up to a certain point Falstaff is ludicrous in the same way as many other figures, his distinction lying, so far, chiefly in the mere abundance of ludicrous traits. *Why* we should laugh at a man with a huge belly and corresponding appetites; at the inconveniences he suffers on a hot day, or in playing the footpad, or when he falls down and there are no levers at hand to lift him up again; at the incongruity of his unwieldy bulk and the nimbleness of his spirit, the infirmities of his age and his youthful lightness of heart; at the enormity of his lies and wiles, and the suddenness of their exposure and frustration; at the contrast between his reputation and his real character, seen most absurdly when, at the mere mention of his name, a redoubted rebel surrenders to him— *why*, I say, we should laugh at these and many such things, this is no place to inquire; but unquestionably we do. Here we have them poured out in endless profusion and with that air of careless ease which is so fascinating in Shakespeare; and with the enjoyment of them I believe many readers stop. But while they are quite essential to the character, there is in it much more. For these things by themselves do not explain why, beside laughing at Falstaff, we are made happy by him and laugh *with* him. He is not, like Parolles, a mere *object* of mirth.

The main reason why he makes us so happy and puts us so entirely at our ease is that he himself is happy and entirely at his ease. "Happy" is too weak a word; he is in bliss, and we share his glory. Enjoyment—no fitful pleasure crossing a dull life, nor any vacant convulsive mirth—but a rich deep-toned chuckling enjoyment circulates continually through all his being. If you ask *what* he enjoys, no doubt the answer is, in the first place, eating and drinking, taking his ease at his inn, and the company of other merry souls. Compared with these things, what we count the graver interests of life are nothing to him. But then, while we are under his spell, it is impossible to consider these graver interests; gravity is to us, as to him, inferior to gravy; and what he does enjoy he enjoys with such a luscious and good-humoured zest that we sympathise and he makes us happy. And if any one objected, we should answer with Sir Toby Belch, "Dost thou think, because thou art virtuous, there shall be no more cakes and ale?"

But this, again, is far from all. Falstaff's ease and enjoyment are not simply those of the happy man of appetite;[5] they are those of the humorist, and the humorist of genius. Instead of being comic to you and serious to himself, he is more ludicrous to himself than to you; and he makes himself out more ludicrous than he is, in order that he and others may laugh. Prince Hal never made such sport of Falstaff's person as he himself did. It is *he* who says that his skin hangs about him like an old lady's loose gown, and that he walks before his page like a sow that hath o'erwhelmed all her litter but one. And he jests at himself when he is alone just as much as when others are by. It is the same with his appetites. The direct enjoyment they bring him is scarcely so great as the enjoyment of laughing at this enjoyment; and for all his addiction to sack you never see him for an instant with a brain dulled by it, or a temper turned solemn, silly, quarrelsome, or pious. The virtue it instils into him, of filling his brain with nimble, fiery, and delectable shapes—this, and his humorous attitude towards it, free him, in a manner, from slavery to it; and it is this freedom, and no secret longing for better things (those who attribute such a longing to him are far astray), that makes his enjoyment contagious and prevents our sympathy with it from being disturbed.

The bliss of freedom gained in humour is the essence of Falstaff. His humour is not directed only or chiefly against obvious absurdities; he is the enemy of everything that would interfere with his ease, and therefore of anything serious, and especially of everything respectable and moral. For these things impose limits and obligations, and make us the subjects of old father antic the law, and the categorical imperative, and our station and its duties, and conscience, and reputation, and other people's opinions, and all sorts of nuisances. I say he is therefore their enemy; but I do him wrong; to say that he is their enemy implies that he regards them as serious and recognises their power, when in truth he refuses to recognise them at all. They are to him absurd; and to reduce a thing *ad absurdum* is to reduce it to nothing and to walk about free and rejoicing. This is what Falstaff does with all the would-be serious things of life, sometimes only by his words, sometimes by his actions too. He will make truth appear absurd by solemn statements, which he utters with perfect gravity and which he expects nobody to believe; and honour, by demonstrating that it cannot set a leg, and that neither the living nor the dead can possess it; and law, by evading all the attacks of its highest representative and almost forcing him to laugh at his own defeat; and patriotism, by filling his pockets with the bribes offered by competent soldiers who want to escape service, while he takes in their stead the halt and maimed and the gaol-birds; and duty, by showing how he labours in his vocation—of thieving; and courage, alike by mocking at his own capture of Colvile and gravely claiming to have killed Hotspur; and war, by offering the Prince his bottle of sack when he is asked for a sword; and religion, by amusing himself with remorse at odd times when he has nothing else to do; and the fear of death, by maintaining perfectly untouched, in the face of imminent peril and even while he *feels* the fear of death, the very same power of dissolving it in persiflage that he shows when he sits at ease in his inn. These are the wonderful achievements which he performs, not with the sourness of a cynic, but with the gaiety of a boy. And, therefore, we praise him, we laud him, for he offends none but the virtuous, and denies that life is real or life is earnest, and delivers us from the oppression of such nightmares, and lifts us into the atmosphere of perfect freedom.

No one in the play understands Falstaff fully, any more than Hamlet was understood by the persons round him. They are both men of genius. Mrs. Quickly and Bardolph are his slaves, but they know not why. "Well, fare thee well," says the hostess whom he has pillaged and forgiven; "I have known thee these twenty-nine years, come peas-cod time, but an honester and truer-hearted man—well, fare thee well." Poins and the Prince delight in him; they get him into corners for the pleasure of seeing him escape in ways they cannot imagine; but they often take him much too seriously. Poins, for instance, rarely sees, the Prince does not always see, and moralising critics never see, that when Falstaff speaks ill of a companion behind his back, or writes to the Prince that Poins spreads it abroad that the Prince is to marry his sister, he knows quite well that what he says will be repeated, or rather, perhaps, is absolutely indifferent whether it be repeated or not, being certain that it can only give him an opportunity for humour. It is the same with his lying, and almost the same with his cowardice, the two main vices laid to his charge even by sympathisers. Falstaff is neither a liar nor a coward in the usual sense, like the typical cowardly boaster of comedy. He tells his lies either for their own humour, or on purpose to get himself into a difficulty. He rarely expects to be believed, perhaps never. He abandons a statement or contradicts it the moment it is made. There is scarcely more intent in his lying than in the humorous exaggerations which he pours out in soliloquy just as much as when others are by. Poins and the Prince understand this in part. You see them waiting eagerly to convict him, not that they may really put him to shame, but in order to enjoy the greater lie that will swallow up the less. But their sense of humour lags behind his. Even the Prince seems to accept as half-serious that remorse of his which passes so suddenly into glee at the idea of taking a purse, and his request to his friend to bestride him if he should see him down in the battle. Bestride Falstaff! "Hence! Wilt thou lift up Olympus?"

Again, the attack of the Prince and Poins on Falstaff and the other thieves on Gadshill is contrived, we know, with a view to the incomprehensible lies it will induce him to tell. But when, more than rising to the occasion, he turns two men in buckram into four, and then seven, and then nine, and then eleven, almost in a breath, I believe they partly misunderstand his intention, and too many of his critics misunderstand it altogether. Shakespeare was not writing a mere farce. It is preposterous to suppose that a man of Falstaff's intelligence would utter these gross, palpable, open lies with the serious intention to deceive, or forget that, if it was too dark for him to see his own hand, he could hardly see that the three misbegotten knaves were wearing Kendal green. No doubt, if he _had_ been believed, he would have been hugely tickled at it, but he no more expected to be believed than when he claimed to have killed Hotspur. Yet he is supposed to be serious even then. Such interpretations would destroy the poet's whole conception; and of those who adopt them one might ask this out of some twenty similar questions:—When Falstaff, in the men in buckram scene, begins by calling twice at short intervals for sack, and then a little later calls for more and says, "I am a rogue if I drunk to-day," and the Prince answers, "O villain, thy lips are scarce wiped since thou drunk'st last," do they think that _that_ lie was meant to deceive? And if not, why do they take it for granted that the others were? I suppose they consider that Falstaff was in earnest when, wanting to get twenty-two yards of satin on trust from Master Dombledon the silk-mercer, he offered Bardolph as security; or when he said to the Chief Justice about Mrs. Quickly, who accused him of breaking his promise to marry her, "My lord, this is a poor mad soul, and she says up and down the town that her eldest son is like you"; or when he explained his enormous bulk by exclaiming, "A plague of sighing and grief! It blows a man up like a bladder"; or when he accounted for his voice being cracked by declaring that he had "lost it with singing of anthems"; or even when he sold his soul on Good-Friday to the devil for a cup of Madeira and a cold capon's leg. Falstaff's lies about Hotspur and the men in buckram do not essentially differ from these statements. There is nothing serious in any of them except the refusal to take anything seriously.

This is also the explanation of Falstaff's cowardice, a subject on which I should say nothing if Maurice Morgann's essay, now more than a century old, were better known. That Falstaff sometimes behaves in what we should generally call a cowardly way is certain; but that does not show that he was a coward; and if the word means a person who feels painful fear in the presence of danger, and yields to that fear in spite of his better feelings and convictions, then assuredly Falstaff was no coward. The stock bully and boaster of comedy is one, but not Falstaff. It is perfectly clear in the first place that, though he had unfortunately a reputation for stabbing and caring not what mischief he did if his weapon were out, he had not a reputation for cowardice. Shallow remembered him five-and-fifty years ago breaking Scogan's head at the court-gate when he was a crack not thus high; and Shallow knew him later a good back-swordsman. Then we lose sight of him till about twenty years after, when his association with Bardolph began; and that association implies that by the time he was thirty-five or forty he had sunk into the mode of life we witness in the plays. Yet, even as we see him there, he remains a person of consideration in the army. Twelve captains hurry about London searching for him. He is present at the Council of War in the King's tent at Shrewsbury, where the only other persons are the King, the two princes, a nobleman and Sir Walter Blunt. The messenger who brings the false report of the battle to Northumberland mentions, as one of the important incidents, the death of Sir John Falstaff. Colvile, expressly described as a famous rebel, surrenders to him as soon as he hears his name. And if his own wish that his name were not so terrible to the enemy, and his own boast of his European reputation, are not evidence of the first rank, they must not be entirely ignored in presence of these other facts. What do these facts mean? Does Shakespeare put them all in with no purpose at all, or in defiance of his own intentions? It is not credible.

And when, in the second place, we look at Falstaff's actions, what do we find? He boldly confronted Colvile, he was quite ready to fight with him, however pleased that Colvile, like a kind fellow, gave himself away. When he saw Henry and Hotspur fighting, Falstaff, instead of making off in a panic, stayed to take his chance if Hotspur should be the victor. He *led* his hundred and fifty ragamuffins where they were peppered, he did not *send* them. To draw upon Pistol and force him downstairs and wound him in the shoulder was no great feat, perhaps, but the stock coward would have shrunk from it. When the Sheriff came to the inn to arrest him for an offence whose penalty was death, Falstaff, who was hidden behind the arras, did not stand there quaking for fear, he immediately fell asleep and snored. When he stood in the battle reflecting on what would happen if the weight of his paunch should be increased by that of a bullet, he cannot have been in a tremor of craven fear. He *never* shows such fear; and surely the man who, in danger of his life, and with no one by to hear him, meditates thus: "I like not such grinning honour as Sir Walter hath. Give me life: which if I can save, so; if not, honour comes unlooked-for, and there's an end," is not what we commonly call a coward.

"Well," it will be answered, "but he ran away on Gadshill; and when Douglas attacked him he fell down and shammed dead." Yes, I am thankful to say, he did. For of course he did not want to be dead. He wanted to live and be merry. And as he had reduced the idea of honour *ad absurdum*, had scarcely any self-respect, and only a respect for reputation as a means of life, naturally he avoided death when he could do so without a ruinous loss of reputation, and (observe) with the satisfaction of playing a colossal practical joke. For *that* after all was his first object. If his one thought had been to avoid death he would not have faced Douglas at all, but would have run away as fast as his legs could carry him; and unless Douglas had been one of those exceptional Scotchmen who have no sense of humour, he would never have thought of pursuing so ridiculous an object as Falstaff running. So that, as Mr. Swinburne remarks, Poins is right when he thus distinguishes Falstaff from his companions in robbery: "For two of them, I know them to be as true-bred cowards as ever turned back; and for the third, if he fight longer than he sees reason, I'll forswear arms." And the event justifies this distinction. For it is exactly thus that, according to the original stage-direction, Falstaff behaves when Henry and Poins attack him and the others. The rest run away at once; Falstaff, here as afterwards with Douglas, fights for a blow or two, but, finding himself deserted and outmatched, runs away also. Of course. He saw no reason to stay. *Any* man who had risen superior to all serious motives would have run away. But it does not follow that he would run from mere fear, or be, in the ordinary sense, a coward.[6]

3.

The main source, then, of our sympathetic delight in Falstaff is his humorous superiority to everything serious, and the freedom of soul enjoyed in it. But, of course, this is not the whole of his character. Shakespeare knew well enough that perfect freedom is not to be gained in this manner; we are ourselves aware of it even while we are sympathising with Falstaff; and as soon as we regard him seriously it becomes obvious. His freedom is limited in two main ways. For one thing he cannot rid himself entirely of respect for all that he professes to ridicule. He shows a certain pride in his rank: unlike the Prince, he is haughty to the drawers, who call him a proud Jack. He is not really quite indifferent to reputation. When the Chief Justice bids him pay his debt to Mrs. Quickly for his reputation's sake, I think he feels a twinge, though to be sure he proceeds to pay her by borrowing from her. He is also stung by any thoroughly serious imputation on his courage, and winces at the recollection of his running away on Gadshill; he knows that his behaviour there certainly looked cowardly, and perhaps he remembers that he would not have behaved so once. It is, further, very significant that, for all his dissolute talk, he has never yet allowed the Prince and Poins to *see* him as they saw him afterwards with Doll Tearsheet; not, of course, that he has any moral shame in the matter, but he knows that in such a situation he, in his old age, must appear contemptible—not a humorist but a mere object of mirth. And, finally, he has affection in him—affection, I think, for Poins and Bardolph, and certainly for the Prince; and that is a thing which he cannot jest out of existence. Hence, as the effect of his rejection shows, he is not really invulnerable. And then, in the second place, since he is in the flesh, his godlike freedom has consequences and conditions; consequences, for there is something painfully wrong with his great toe; conditions, for he cannot eat and drink for ever without money, and his purse suffers from consumption, a disease for which he can find no remedy.[7] As the Chief Justice tells him, his means are very slender and his waste great; and his answer, "I would it were otherwise; I would my means were greater and my waist slenderer," though worth much money, brings none in. And so he is driven to evil deeds; not only to cheating his tailor like a gentleman, but to fleecing Justice Shallow, and to highway robbery, and to cruel depredations on the poor woman whose affection he has secured. All this is perfectly consistent with the other side of his character, but by itself it makes an ugly picture.

Yes, it makes an ugly picture when you look at it seriously. But then, surely, so long as the humorous atmosphere is preserved and the humorous attitude maintained, you do not look at it so. You no more regard Falstaff's misdeeds morally than you do the much more atrocious misdeeds of Punch or Reynard the Fox. You do not exactly ignore them, but you attend only to their comic aspect. This is the very spirit of comedy, and certainly of Shakespeare's comic world, which is one of make-believe, not merely as his tragic world is, but in a further sense—a world in which gross improbabilities are accepted with a smile, and many things are welcomed as merely laughable which, regarded gravely, would excite anger and disgust. The intervention of a serious spirit breaks up such a world, and would destroy our pleasure in Falstaff's company. Accordingly through the greater part of these dramas Shakespeare carefully confines this spirit to the scenes of war and policy, and dismisses it entirely in the humorous parts. Hence, if *Henry IV.* had been a comedy like

Twelfth Night, I am sure that he would no more have ended it with the painful disgrace of Falstaff than he ended *Twelfth Night* by disgracing Sir Toby Belch.[8]

But *Henry IV*. was to be in the main a historical play, and its chief hero Prince Henry. In the course of it his greater and finer qualities were to be gradually revealed, and it was to end with beautiful scenes of reconciliation and affection between his father and him, and a final emergence of the wild Prince as a just, wise, stern, and glorious King. Hence, no doubt, it seemed to Shakespeare that Falstaff at last must be disgraced, and must therefore appear no longer as the invincible humorist, but as an object of ridicule and even of aversion. And probably also his poet's insight showed him that Henry, as he conceived him, *would* behave harshly to Falstaff in order to impress the world, especially when his mind had been wrought to a high pitch by the scene with his dying father and the impression of his own solemn consecration to great duties.

This conception was a natural and a fine one; and if the execution was not an entire success, it is yet full of interest. Shakespeare's purpose being to work a gradual change in our feelings towards Falstaff, and to tinge the humorous atmosphere more and more deeply with seriousness, we see him carrying out this purpose in the Second Part of *Henry IV*. Here he separates the Prince from Falstaff as much as he can, thus withdrawing him from Falstaff's influence, and weakening in our minds the connection between the two. In the First Part we constantly see them together; in the Second (it is a remarkable fact) only once before the rejection. Further, in the scenes where Henry appears apart from Falstaff, we watch him growing more and more grave, and awakening more and more poetic interest; while Falstaff, though his humour scarcely flags to the end, exhibits more and more of his seamy side. This is nowhere turned to the full light in Part I.; but in Part II. we see him as the heartless destroyer of Mrs. Quickly, as a ruffian seriously defying the Chief Justice because his position as an officer on service gives him power to do wrong, as the pike preparing to snap up the poor old dace Shallow, and (this is the one scene where Henry and he meet) as the worn-out lecher, not laughing at his servitude to the flesh but sunk in it. Finally, immediately before the rejection, the world where he is king is exposed in all its sordid criminality when we find Mrs. Quickly and Doll arrested for being concerned in the death of one man, if not more, beaten to death by their bullies; and the dangerousness of Falstaff is emphasised in his last words as he hurries from Shallow's house to London, words at first touched with humour but at bottom only too seriously meant: "Let us take any man's horses; the laws of England are at my commandment. Happy are they which have been my friends, and woe unto my Lord Chief Justice." His dismissal to the Fleet by the Chief Justice is the dramatic vengeance for that threat.

Yet all these excellent devices fail. They cause us momentary embarrassment at times when repellent traits in Falstaff's character are disclosed; but they fail to change our attitude of humour into one of seriousness, and our sympathy into repulsion. And they were bound to fail, because Shakespeare shrank from adding to them the one device which would have ensured success. If, as the Second Part of *Henry IV.* advanced, he had clouded over Falstaff's humour so heavily that the man of genius turned into the Falstaff of the *Merry Wives*, we should have witnessed his rejection without a pang. This Shakespeare was too much of an artist to do—though even in this way he did something—and without this device he could not succeed. As I said, in the creation of Falstaff he overreached himself. He was caught up on the wind of his own genius, and carried so far that he could not descend to earth at the selected spot. It is not a misfortune that happens to many authors, nor is it one we can regret, for it costs us but a trifling inconvenience in one scene, while we owe to it perhaps the greatest comic character in literature. For it is in this character, and not in the judgment he brings upon Falstaff's head, that Shakespeare asserts his supremacy. To show that Falstaff's freedom of soul was in part illusory, and that the realities of life refused to be conjured away by his humour—this was what we might expect from Shakespeare's unfailing sanity, but it was surely no achievement beyond the power of lesser men. The achievement was Falstaff himself, and the conception of that freedom of soul, a freedom illusory only in part, and attainable only by a mind which had received from Shakespeare's own the inexplicable touch of infinity which he bestowed on Hamlet and Macbeth and Cleopatra, but denied to Henry the Fifth.

NOTES

1. In this lecture I have mentioned the authors my obligations to whom I
    was conscious of in writing or have discovered since; but other debts
    must doubtless remain, which from forgetfulness I am unable to
    acknowledge.
2. See on this and other points Swinburne, *A Study of Shakespeare* p. 106 ff.
3. Rötscher, *Shakespeare in seinen höchsten Charaktergebilden*, 1864.
4. That from the beginning Shakespeare intended Henry's accession to
    be Falstaff's catastrophe is clear from the fact that, when the two
    characters first appear, Falstaff is made to betray at once the hopes
    with which he looks forward to Henry's reign. See the First Part of
    Henry IV., Act I., Scene ii.
5. Cf. Hazlitt, *Characters of Shakespear's Plays*.
6. It is to be regretted, however, that in carrying his guts away so nimbly
    he "roared for mercy"; for I fear we have no ground for rejecting
    Henry's statement to that effect, and I do not see my way to adopt the
    suggestion (I forget whose it is) that Falstaff spoke the truth when he
    swore that he knew Henry and Poins as well as he that made them.
7. Panurge too was "naturally subject to a kind of disease which at that
    time they called lack of money"; it was a "flux in his purse" (Rabelais,
    Book II., chapters xvi., xvii.).
8. I seem to remember that, according to Gervinus, Shakespeare did
    disgrace Sir Toby—by marrying him to Maria!

Mark Van Doren

Henry IV (1939)

No play of Shakespeare's is better than "Henry IV." Certain subsequent ones may show him more settled in the maturity which he here attains almost at a single bound, but nothing that he wrote is more crowded with life or happier in its imitation of human talk. The pen that moves across these pages is perfectly free of itself. The host of persons assembled for our pleasure can say anything for their author he wants to say. The poetry of Hotspur and the prose of Falstaff have never been surpassed in their respective categories; the History as a dramatic form ripens here to a point past which no further growth is possible; and in Falstaff alone there is sufficient evidence of Shakespeare's mastery in the art of understanding style, and through style of creating men.

The vast dimensions of the comic parts should not be permitted to obscure the merit of the rest. History is enlarged here to make room for taverns and trollops and potations of sack, and the heroic drama is modified by gigantic mockery, by the roared voice of truth; but the result is more rather than less reality, just as a cathedral, instead of being demolished by merriment among its aisles, stands more august. The King of the play is more remote from the audience than any of Shakespeare's kings have been; he is more formal, and speaks with a full organ tone which as Bolingbroke he never used; but that is as it should be in a work which has so much distance to fill between laughter and law, between the alehouse and the throne. Henry wears his robes

From *Shakespeare* by Mark Van Doren, originally published by Henry Holt, 1939. Reprinted by permission of Mrs. Mark Van Doren.

regally, and his sighs because they weigh him down are dignified
and sonorous. One of his cares is that domestic rebellion keeps
him from Jerusalem, where he was sworn

> To chase these pagans in those holy fields
> Over whose acres walk'd those blessed feet
> Which fourteen hundred years ago were nail'd
> For our advantage on the bitter cross.
>
> (1-I.i.24-7)

He knows how to send his voice through four such lines as that,
which in their lack of pause are incantation rather than speech;
though in the second play, when age and illness and despaire of
his son have somewhat shattered his tone, he deepens his style
(III.i; IV, V) to something like the complexity and variety of Shakespeare's dramatic verse at its best.

Another and the chief of his cares is the behavior of his son
who will be Henry V, and who as early as the fifth act of "Richard
II" was causing concern by the amount of time he spent with
Falstaff's dissolute crew. The King preaches more than one sermon to the Prince, and if one were free to choose a companion for
Hal one would certainly prefer the fat knight with the great belly
doublet; for the sermons are heavy with state and conscious of
the speaker's exalted virtue. But one is not free to choose. The
King is after all the King, high away from puns and drunkenness.
And Hal himself, though he will play with Falstaff through ten
long acts, has secretly chosen his father all the while.

> I know you all, and will a while uphold
> The unyok'd humour of your idleness;
> Yet herein will I imitate the sun,
> Who doth permit the base contagious clouds
> To smother up his beauty from the world,
> That when he please again to be himself
> Being wanted, he may be more wonder'd at.
>
> (1-I.ii.218-24)

If this is priggish, and it surely is, we must remember how
conscious Shakespeare's princes always are of their careers, and
we must remember that the uppermost drift of "Henry IV" is
steadily in the direction of Hal's regeneration as Henry V. Falstaff
is an interlude in his life: a circumstance from which Falstaff in
fact derives much of his power. Falstaff like any other man must

have his background, and it had best be a background that moves in time; if he is to be an unkempt knight, there must be banks of knights beyond him in fair dress, in full flower.

Shakespeare never permits us to forget Hal's sober side. Before Shrewsbury he confesses to his father that he has been a truant to chivalry (1-V.i.94). And Warwick assures the King that

> The Prince but studies his companions
> Like a strange tongue, wherein, to gain the language,
> 'T is needful that the most immodest word
> Be look'd upon and learn'd; which once attain'd,
> Your Highness knows, comes to no further use
> But to be known and hated. So, like gross terms,
> The Prince will in the perfectness of time
> Cast off his followers.
>
> (2-IV.iv.68–75)

Humorless as Warwick is, and much as he shocks us who have learned Falstaff's language at the Prince's side, we must recognize here the young man who had killed Hotspur in battle and who will come to such swift maturity in the scene with his dying father's crown (2-IV.v); who will commend the Chief Justice because he had imprisoned a Prince of Wales (2-V.ii); who will mock the expectation of the world and live henceforth a life of formal majesty (2-V.ii); and who at the very end will turn from Falstaff as from an old man he has never seen. This is the young man upon whom Vernon has lavished the brightest vocabulary of solemn praise; on one occasion describing to Hotspur the appearance of Hal and his comrades as they set out for Shrewsbury:

> All furnish'd, all in arms;
> All plum'd like estridges that with the wind
> Bated, like eagles having lately bath'd;
> Glittering in golden coats, like images;
> As full of spirit as the month of May,
> And gorgeous as the sun at midsummer;
> Wanton as youthful goats, wild as young bulls.
> I saw young Harry, with his beaver on,
> His cuisses on his thighs, gallantly arm'd,
> Rise from the ground like feathered Mercury,
> And vaulted with such ease into his seat,
> As if an angel dropp'd down from the clouds;
>
> (1-IV.i.97–108)

and on another occasion crediting the Prince with every attribute
of a knightly soul:

> I never in my life
> Did hear a challenge urg'd more modestly,
> Unless a brother should a brother dare
> To gentle exercise and proof of arms.
> He gave you all the duties of a man,
> Trimm'd up your praises with a princely tongue,
> Spoke your deservings like a chronicle,
> Making you ever better than his praise
> By still dispraising praise valued with you;
> And, which became him like a prince indeed,
> He made a blushing cital of himself,
> And chid his truant youth with such a grace
> As if he mast'red there a double spirit
> Of teaching and of learning instantly.
> There did he pause; but let me tell the world,
> If he outlive the envy of this day,
> England did never owe so sweet a hope,
> So much misconstrued in his wantonness.
>
> (1-V.ii.52-69)

We shall not end by liking Hal better than the Hotspur whom he
challenges and kills, or by preferring the new king of England to
the sometime prince of London's stews. The life of "Henry IV,"
indeed, is not in the handsome boy who will be Henry V. But he is
the foil to that life, the brocaded curtain against which we watch
it moving; he is the mold it is trying to break, the form of which it
is the foe. If he could be broken the life would spill itself meaning-
lessly; whereas nothing is meaningless in "Henry IV," and least of
all this pair of passages in which the first gentleman of England is
so splendidly described.

Not that Hotspur is less the gentleman than Harry, but that
he is more the person, the created speaking man. The King,
comparing him with the Prince, pours on him the most courteous
terms of praise; he is the theme of Honour's tongue, sweet
Fortune's minion and her pride, the very straightest plant
amongst the grove (1-I.i.81-3). And Lady Percy, Hotspur's wife,
speaks of him after his death as Ophelia speaks of the Hamlet she
once knew; he was a miracle of men,

```
        and by his light
Did all the chivalry of England move
To do brave acts. He was indeed the glass
Wherein the noble youth did dress themselves. . . .
In diet, in affections of delight,
In military rules, humours of blood,
He was the mark and glass, copy and book,
That fashion'd others.
```
(2-II.iii.19-32)

But in the same speech Lady Percy lets us know something about her husband which we never know of Harry, and which Shakespeare henceforth will take the pains to publish in the case of any man who immensely interests him. Hotspur had a voice, a particular voice; one so specific in its quality as to sound now in his widow's ears a bit abnormal. "Speaking thick"—speaking, that is, too rapidly, without precise articulation—was the one blemish nature had given him; though even as a blemish it was imitated by others, so that speaking "low and tardily" passed out of fashion while he lived. The torrent of his talk went with the tartness of his tongue and with the rashness of his courage, the quick, busy directness of his purpose. It was this in him, along with his astonishing and unconventional vocabulary, that Lady Percy imitated when she called him "mad-headed ape" and "weasel," and threatened to break his little finger if he withheld his plans from her (1-II.iii). She never learned to swear as well as her master (1-III.i), but she could tell him to lie still, ye thief, as he dropped into her lap like Hamlet into the lap of Ophelia; and it can scarcely be doubted that he lived for her in his voice, as indeed he still lives for any reader of the play.

Northumberland, his father, calls him once "a wasp-stung and impatient fool." He is a high horse with dancing steel for muscles, an uncontrollable charger with gadflies ever at both flanks. It is not ambition that goads him, or any ordinary pride; it is rather a sense of his own superb mettle, a feeling of his strength, a toxin that attacks him because his energy is excessive and finds no outlet in life as most men live it. His scorn for most men takes the form of detesting their pretense; they are but apes of greatness, humbugs who profess the power he has without needing to profess it. He on the contrary, and with a certain perversity,

insists furiously that he is but an ordinary fellow; there is nothing
that he hates, or thinks he hates, more than the extraordinary.
He even fancies that he is a silent fellow, a soldier of few words;
"for I profess not talking" (1-V.ii.92). Yet Northumberland can
chide him for his "woman's mood,"

> Tying thine ear to no tongue but thine own.
>
> (1-I.iii.238)

And the truth is that he talks all the time. He is one of Shakespeare's most copious poets, as well as one of his best.

His earliest appearance in Shakespeare was during the rebellion in "Richard II," when, entering to his father without a nod
for Bolingbroke who stood by, he was asked whether he had
forgotten the noble Duke. His answer was in some indefinable
way impertinent, as if the contempt he was to feel for Bolingbroke as Henry IV already simmered in his blood.

> No, my good lord, for that is not forgot
> Which ne'er I did remember. To my knowledge,
> I never in my life did look on him.
>
> (II.iii.37–9)

If there was impertinence in this it was overlooked, and the
courtesy he followed with was impeccable. But now in "Henry
IV" he is asked by the King why he has not delivered certain
prisoners for whom a messenger has asked him, and although in a
great speech of forty-one lines (1-I.iii.29–69) he puts the reason
off on the affectations of the messenger, and upon

> my impatience
> To be so pest'red with a popinjay,

we learn as soon as the King leaves that the King himself had
been the reason. Hotspur's elders labor to stop his tirade; they
interrupt and rebuke him as many as seven times; but he flows
on, spilling his scorn in flawlessly natural lines of blank verse which
he seems not to recognize as verse. And incidentally we discover
the quality of his feeling towards Bolingbroke on that occasion of
their first meeting.

> I'll keep them all!
> By God, he shall not have a Scot of them;

No, if a Scot would save his soul, he shall not!
I'll keep them, by this hand. . . .
        Nay, I will; that's flat.
He said he would not ransom Mortimer;
Forbad my tongue to speak of Mortimer;
But I will find him when he lies asleep,
And in his ear I'll holla "Mortimer!"
Nay,
I'll have a starling shall be taught to speak
Nothing but "Mortimer," and give it him,
To keep his anger still in motion. . . .
All studies here I solemnly defy,
Save how to gall and pinch this Bolingbroke;
And that same sword-and-buckler Prince of Wales,
But that I think his father loves him not
And would be glad he met with some mischance,
I would have him poison'd with a pot of ale. . . .
Why, look you, I am whipp'd and scourg'd with rods,
Nettled and stung with pismires, when I hear
Of this vile politician, Bolingbroke.
In Richard's time,—what do you call the place?—
A plague upon it, it is in Gloucestershire;
'T was where the madcap duke his uncle kept,
His uncle York; where I first bow'd my knee
Unto this king of smiles, this Bolingbroke,—
'Sblood!—
When you and he came back from Ravenspurgh.
                                        (1-I.iii.213–48)

Northumberland relieves his son's agony; it was at Berkley Castle.

You say true.
Why, what a candy deal of courtesy
This fawning greyhound then did proffer me!
Look, "when his infant fortune came to age,"
And "gentle Harry Percy," and "kind cousin;"
O, the devil take such cozeners!—God forgive me!
Good uncle, tell your tale; for I have done.

His uncle Worcester cannot believe the last remark, and with ponderous irony invites him to go on till he is really done.

I have done, i' faith.

And for the time being he is done. But in the play it is not long until he has started again. The occasion is the rebels' conference at Bangor (1-III.i), and just as he had forgotten the name of Berkley Castle he now has forgotten, or thinks he has forgotten, a map that is necessary to the conference. When they find it for him he settles down to the business of the day; soon, however, to be nettled and stung by what he considers the pompous self-deception of Glendower, the tall Welshman with the deep voice who believes that he is not in the roll of common men, for at his birth the frame and huge foundation of the earth shak'd like a coward, and the heavens were all on fire because this son of Merlin had come to tread the tedious ways of art, of deep experiments. Hotspur hops about like a wasp on a hot griddle. He cannot bear such talk, and of course cannot be still. If the earth shook at Glendower's birth it must have had a kind of colic; the reason, his perverseness insists, was common and prosaic. For there is no such thing as poetry, this magnificent poet declares. His uncle Worcester had once, somewhat in the language of Theseus in "A Midsummer Night's Dream," accused him of apprehending "a world of figures" instead of the plain form of truth (1-I.iii.209–10), but he had let that pass. Now when Glendower, roused to wrath, denies him the virtue of framing ditties lovely well as he himself has done, Hotspur explodes and cries:

> Marry,
> And I am glad of it with all my heart.
> I had rather be a kitten and cry mew
> Than one of these same metre ballad-mongers.
> I had rather hear a brazen canstick turn'd,
> Or a dry wheel grate on the anxle-tree;
> And that would set my teeth nothing on edge,
> Nothing so much as mincing poetry.
> 'T is like the forc'd gait of a shuffling nag.
>
> (1-III.i.127–35)

And after Glendower has left, a speech which commences as an apology mounts quickly to the peak of wrath again:

> I cannot choose. Sometime he angers me
> With telling me of the moldwarp and the ant,
> Of the dreamer Merlin and his prophecies,

> And of a dragon and a finless fish,
> A clip-wing'd griffin and a moulten raven,
> A couching lion and a ramping cat,
> And such a deal of skimble-skamble stuff
> As puts me from my faith. I tell you what:
> He held me last night at least nine hours
> In reckoning up the several devils' names
> That were his lackeys. I cried "hum," and "well, go to,"
> But mark'd him not a word. O, he is as tedious
> As a tired horse, a railing wife;
> Worse than a smoky house. I had rather live
> With cheese and garlic in a windmill, far,
> Than feed on cates and have him talk to me
> In any summer-house in Christendom.
>
> (1-III.i.148–64)

"I tell you what: he held me last night at least nine hours." That is blank verse, but it is also speech, and it is as difficult to scan as a casual remark. In Hotspur Shakespeare has learned at last to make poetry as natural as the human voice—as natural, further-more, as Falstaff's prose, or as the whole conduct of the incompa-rable action which is "Henry IV."

He must have been fond of his creation: of this high-strung youth who was so far above liking the art he mastered, who could be a fine poet without knowing that he was, who indeed made his poetry out of a hot love for nothing except reality and hard sense. For the paradox of Hotspur is the paradox of Shakespeare; the best poet least pampers and preens his talent, and in public at any rate would rather abuse it than take off its edge by boasting of its power to cut. Shakespeare lets Hotspur be proud of his plain-ness—"By God, I cannot flatter" (1-IV.i.6)—but never of his poetry. He lets Worcester criticize his nephew for

> Defect of manners, want of government,
> Pride, haughtiness, opinion, and disdain,
>
> (1-III.i.184–5)

but he will lavish two scenes of the second play upon the memory of a man whose death in the first play he must have regretted as much as the audience did. One of these scenes (II.iii) is that in which Lady Percy tells us how Hotspur had been the glass of

England's fashion and charges Northumberland with his death. The charge is merited, for Northumberland's pretense of illness had been the cause of Hotspur's going unsupported into battle with Prince Hal. The other scene is the opening scene, with its elaborate business of Rumour's false news to Northumberland that his son has won the battle. Dr. Johnson dismissed this business as "wholly useless," but he was wholly wrong. The new play pauses at the start to fix the memory of Hotspur in our minds, to render his death still more unthinkable than it had been, to honor him after his sorry mischance. Shakespeare cannot let him go without such obsequies, and without the suitable spectacle of Northumberland's frenzy once the truth has been made clear to him:

> Now let not Nature's hand
> Keep the wild flood confin'd! Let order die!
> And let this world no longer be a stage
> To feed contention in a ling'ring act;
> But let one spirit of the first-born Cain
> Reign in all bosoms, that, each heart being set
> On bloody courses, the rude scene may end,
> And darkness be the burier of the dead!
>
> (2-I.i.153–60)

The father's turmoil of mind is more than an expression of his conscience; it is an adequate tribute to the finest figure Shakespeare has been able to carve for the serious portion of his History. For Hotspur was very serious. He was almost, indeed, insanely serious. He did not know that he was amusing. He did not understand himself—could not have named his virtues, would never have admitted his limitations. As handsome as Hamlet, and apparently as intelligent, he was not in fact intelligent at all. He was pure illusion, pure act, pure tragedy, just as Falstaff at the opposite pole of "Henry IV" is pure light, pure contemplation, pure comedy.

Falstaff understands everything and so is never serious. If he is even more amusing to himself than he is to others, that is because the truth about himself is something very obvious which he has never taken the trouble to define. His intelligence can define anything, but his wisdom tells him that the effort is not worth while. We do not know him in our words. We know him in his—which are never to the point, for they glance off his center and lead us away along tangents of laughter. His enormous bulk spreads through "Henry IV" until it threatens to leave no room for other men and other deeds. But his mind is still larger. It is at home everywhere, and it is never darkened with self-thought. Falstaff thinks only of others, and of the pleasure he can take in imitating them. He is a universal mimic; his genius is of that sort which understands through parody, and which cannot be understood except at one or more removes. He is so much himself because he is never himself; he has so much power because he has more than that maximum which for ordinary men is the condition of their identity's becoming stated. His is not stated because there is no need of proving that he has force; we feel this force constantly, in parody after parody of men he pretends to be. The parodist, the artist, is more real than most men whom we know. But we cannot fix him in a phrase, or claim more for ourselves than that we have been undeniably in his living presence.

There is a fine thread of personal idiom worked through the text of Falstaff's talk. His private voice rings out in such sentences as these:

> Indeed, you come near me now, Hal.
>
> (1-I.ii.14)

> No; I'll give thee thy due, thou hast paid all there.
>
> (1-I.ii.59–60)

> Indeed, I am not John of Gaunt, your grandfather; but yet no coward, Hal.
>
> (1-II.ii.70-1)

> I'll never wear hair on my face more.
>
> (1-II.iv.153)

> Ah, no more of that, Hal, an thou lovest me!
>
> (1-II.iv.312–3)

> Peace, good Doll! do not speak like a death's head. Do not bid me remember mine end.
>
> (2-II.iv.254-5)

His native speech is casual yet pure, natural yet distinguished, easy and yet expertly wrenched out of line with the conventions of syntax; impossible to define, yet audibly his very own. We hear

it, however, but seldom. Most of the time it is buried under heaps
of talk delivered from a hundred assumed personalities, a hundred fictitious identities.

He is limited as a mimic only by the facts of his physique;
being old and fat, he is short of breath and so must be brief of
phrase.

> Tut, tut; good enough to toss; food for powder, food for
> powder; they'll fill a pit as well as better. Tush, man, mortal
> men, mortal men.
>
>   (1-IV.ii.71-3)

> How now, lad! is the wind in that door, i' faith? Must we
> all march?
>
>   (1-III.iii.102-3)

> How now! whose mare's dead? What's the matter?
>
>   (2-II.i.46-7)

But it will be seen at once—or heard—that he has made the most
of this limitation. Artist that he is, he has accepted its challenge
and employed it in effects that express his genius with a notable
and economical directness. If he must gasp he will make each
further gasp an echo of its fellow—an echo, but with ineffable
additions. His speech then is not merely brief; it is repetitive, it
rolls back on itself, it picks up its theme and tosses it to us again,
with rich improvements.

> Why, Hal, 't is my vocation, Hal. T is no sin for a man to
> labour in his vocation.
>
>   (1-I.ii.116-7)

> If the rascal have not given me medicines to make me
> love him, I'll be hang'd. It could not be else; I have drunk
> medicines.
>
>   (1-II.ii.18-20)

> A plague of all cowards, I say, and a vengeance too!
> marry, and amen! Give me a cup of sack, boy. . . . A plague
> of all cowards! Give me a cup of sack, rogue. Is there no
> virtue extant?
>
>   (1-II.iv.127-32)

If I fought not with fifty of them, I am a bunch of radish.
If there were not two or three and fifty upon poor old Jack,
then am I no two-legg'd creature.

(1-II.iv.205-8)

What, shall we be merry? Shall we have a play extempore?

(1-II.iv.308-9)

Bardolph, am I not fallen away vilely since this last action? Do I not bate? Do I not dwindle? Why, my skin hangs
about me like an old lady's loose gown; I am withered like an
old apple-john.

(1-III.iii.1-4)

I am not only witty in myself, but the cause that wit is in
other men. I do here walk before thee like a sow that hath
overwhelm'd all her litter but one. If the Prince put thee into
my service for any other reason than to set me off, why then
I have no judgement. Thou whoreson mandrake, thou art
fitter to be worn in my cap than to wait at my heels. I was
never mann'd with an agate till now.

(2-I.ii.10-9)

What, a young knave, and begging! Is there not wars? Is
there not employment? Doth not the King lack subjects? Do
not the rebels need soldiers?

(2-I.ii.84-7)

If the cook help to make the gluttony, you help to make
the diseases, Doll. We catch of you, Doll, we catch of you.
Grant that, my poor virtue, grant that.

(2-II.iv.48-51)

Do you think me a swallow, an arrow, or a bullet? Have I,
in my poor and old motion, the expedition of thought?

(2-IV.iii.35-7)

And, once more, its burden, its high business is parody: imitation
not always of another man who is standing by, if it is ever that,
but of some man Falstaff suddenly, without warning, decides to
be. Upon occasion it is the man—the bluff, successful soldier—he
had been trained in his youth to be and has never become, though
he knows the manner perfectly. "Tush, man, mortal men, mortal

men"—there speaks the busy ghost of Sir John Falstaff, who rises
again in "Whose mare's dead? What's the matter?" But there are
many manners, many men. "Do not bid me remember mine
end"—that is dolorously delivered, with a long face that remembers psalms. "I have drunk medicines," "Is there no virtue
extant?", "I am withered like an old apple-john"—in such sighs we
hear a feigned self-pity, a fooling with the music of elegy, which
becomes classic in "A plague of sighing and grief! it blows a man
up like a bladder" (1-II.iv.364–5). In "We catch of you, Doll, we
catch of you" there is a tickling levity, a chuckle and a poke in the
ribs.

The essence of Falstaff is that he is a comic actor, most of
whose roles are assumed without announcement. In at least two
cases he forewarns us: when he proposes to the Prince that they
take turns playing the King (1-II.iv), and when he orders his-page
to help him play deaf before the Lord Chief Justice (2-I.ii).

> My good lord! God give your lordship good time of day. I
> am glad to see your lordship abroad. I heard say your lord-
> ship was sick; I hope your lordship goes abroad by advice.

That is deliberate acting, as is the mournful gesture later on:

> Well, I cannot last ever; but it was alway yet the trick of
> our English nation, if they have a good thing, to make it too
> common.

And the mummery of Falstaff and the Prince as Henry IV provides some of the best stuff in all the play; the Prince, incidentally,
showing both there and elsewhere that he has been Falstaff's
aptest pupil in the school of style, for he can take off both his old
master—"How now, wool-sack! what mutter you?" (1-II.iv.149)—
and his young rival in honor Hotspur (1-II.iv.110–25). But Falstaff's stage acting, first-rate as it is, falls short of the natural
acting he is incessantly busy with, whether the fiction of the
moment be that he is a soldier with secret responsibilities or
whether it be that he is a gay old blade of the town come to chuck
the hostess under the chin and set Doll Tearsheet on his knee.
Under pressure of the necessity to imitate his environment he can
even break into verse, as when the Hostess's theatrical excitement over the little play of Henry IV and his son suggests to him
that he treads a tragic stage:

> For God's sake, lords, convey my tristful queen;
> For tears do stop the flood-gates of her eyes;
>
> (1-II.iv.434-5)

and as when, having so great a desire to hear what news the magnificent Pistol brings of Hal and the kingship, he knows he must fall in with the rascal's style if he is ever to get anything out of him:

> O base Assyrian knight, what is thy news?
> Let King Cophetua know the truth thereof.
>
> (2-V.iii.105-6)

Of course he gets what he wanted; the style works like magic:

> Sir John, thy tender lambkin now is king;
> Harry the Fifth's the man. I speak the truth.
> When Pistol lies, do this, and fig me like
> The bragging Spaniard.
>
> (2-V.iii.122-5)

And it would have been a pity if somewhere in "Henry IV" Falstaff had not added Pistol to his list of roles. For there is nothing more absurd and glorious in Shakespeare than the old-tragedy verse of Ancient Pistol:

> Fear we broadsides? No, let the fiend give fire.
>
> (2-II.iv.196)

> There roar'd the sea, and trumpet-clangor sounds.
>
> (2-V.v.42)

The ripest piece of Falstaff's miming is reserved, however, for a series of scenes toward the close of the second play, when Sir John, recruiting soldiers in Gloucestershire, happens upon an old friend of his London youth, the now doddering Justice Shallow. Shallow has lost all the juices that Falstaff has kept. He is thin and dry, and drones reminiscences in an old man's witless tenor.

> Come on, come on, come on, sir; give me your hand, sir,
> give me your hand, sir. An early stirrer, by the rood! And
> how doth my good cousin Silence?
>
> (2-III.ii.1-4)

Certain, 't is certain; very sure, very sure. Death, as the
Psalmist saith, is certain to all; all shall die.

(2-III.ii.40-2)

I will not excuse you; you shall not be excus'd; excuses
shall not be admitted; there is no excuse shall serve; you
shall not be excus'd. Why, Davy! . . . Davy, Davy, Davy,
Davy, let me see, Davy; let me see, Davy; let me see. Yea,
marry, William cook, bid him come hither. Sir John, you
shall not be excus'd.

(2-V.i.5-13)

His unit of utterance is as brief as Falstaff's, and the Lord knows
he repeats himself; but if any evidence were needed of the muscle
in his big friend's style it could be found at once in the contrast
Shallow provides. For his repetitions are relaxed, nerveless, foolish—the work of weakness, not of a still joyful strength; just as
those of the Hostess are the signs of a fluttering rather than a
doing mind:

I have borne, and borne, and borne, and have been fubb'd
off, and fubb'd off, and fubb'd off, from this day to that day,
that it is a shame to be thought on.

(2-II.i.35-9)

If he swagger, let him not come here; no, by my faith. I
must live among my neighbours; I'll no swaggerers. I am in
good name and fame with the very best. Shut the door;
there comes no swaggerers here. I have not liv'd all this
while, to have swaggering now. Shut the door, I pray you.

(2-II.iv.79-85)

Falstaff, whose memory of Shallow is doubtless less perfect than
he says it is, takes in the truth at a glance; sees that this old forked
radish, this pitiful cheese-paring of a man, lives only in the re-
membrance of his youth; and nobly decides—for even though he
may think to have fun with Shallow later, and cash in on him as a
butt for whom the Prince will pay, there is something noble in the
instantaneous decision—to fall in with his way of speech, to grant
him just what he desires.

Shallow. O, Sir John, do you remember since we lay all night
in the windmill in Saint George's field?

> *Falstaff.* No more of that, good Master Shallow, no more of
> that.
> *Shallow.* Ha! 't was a merry night. And is Jane Nightwork
> alive?
> *Falstaff.* She lives, Master Shallow.
> *Shallow.* She never could away with me.
> *Falstaff.* Never, never; she would always say she could not
> abide Master Shallow.
> *Shallow.* By the mass, I could anger her to the heart. She was
> then a bona-roba. Doth she hold her own well?
> *Falstaff.* Old, old, Master Shallow.
> *Shallow.* Nay, she must be old; she cannot choose but be old;
> certain she's old; and had Robin Nightwork by old Night-
> work before I came to Clement's Inn.
> *Silence.* That's fifty-five year ago.
> *Shallow.* Ha, cousin Silence, that thou hadst seen that that
> this knight and I have seen! Ha, Sir John, said I well?
> *Falstaff.* We have heard the chimes at midnight, Master Shal-
> low.
>
> > (2-III.ii.206–29)

The last and best of these sentences sums up all that Shallow
could hope to say in twenty quavering years, and does it so briefly
that the breath of any hearer must be taken; and expresses its
speaker so completely that he can never be absent from our
consciousness henceforth. We may not know the man who says
this, but we know that a man says it, and we know him better
than we do most members of his race. And we have not failed to
note the magnanimity which after all has been from the beginning the groundwork of his humor: a magnanimity which will
sound once more when, listening to the simple, bemused merriment of Silence as he sings his little songs, he generously puts in
the remark:

> I did not think Master Silence had been a man of this
> mettle.
>
> > (2-V.iii.40)

And Silence responds:

> Who? I? I have been merry twice and once ere now.

The wit of Falstaff's answers when charges of cowardice, treachery, and lying are truly urged against him is the wit of a man who knows that other men are waiting to hear what he will pretend, who he will become, how he will get out of it. "Answer, thou dead elm, answer," "Come," said Poins, "your reason, Jack, your reason." Poins is thirsty for another of Jack's good reasons. He must be patient a while, for Falstaff to make time insists that though reasons were as plenty as blackberries he will give none on compulsion; but in good season it comes: "Why, hear you, my masters. Was it for me to kill the heir-apparent? Should I turn upon the true prince?" (1-II.iv.295-7). Something like that was what Poins and the true Prince wanted, though they could not have predicted it, being no Falstaffs. Like any remark by a great man, it is at the same time surprising and in character; the form of such a man grows clearer with everything he utters, and his dimensions increase. We could not have known that he would say it; and afterwards we cannot imagine him saying anything else or better, though the next thing will be better. "Thy love is worth a million; thou ow'st me thy love" (1-III.iii.155-6). That is better; and so is "I disprais'd him before the wicked, that the wicked might not fall in love with him; in which doing, I have done the part of a careful friend and a true subject, and thy father is to give me thanks for it" (2-II.iv.346-50). That the King does not thank him is not surprising. Falstaff has not expected it.

What now of his vices, and why is it that they have not the sound of vices? None of them is an end in itself—that is their secret, just as Falstaff's character is his mystery. He does not live to drink or steal or foin o' nights. He even does not live in order that he may be the cause of wit in other men. We do not in fact know why he lives. This great boulder is balanced lightly on the earth, and can be tipped with the lightest touch. He cannot be overturned. He knows too much, and he understands too well the art of delivering with every lie he tells an honest weight of profound and personal revelation.

John Dover Wilson

The Falstaff Myth (1943)

Riot and the Prodigal Prince

Falstaff may be the most conspicuous, he is certainly the most fascinating, character in *Henry IV*, but all critics are agreed, I believe, that the technical centre of the play is not the fat knight but the lean prince. Hal links the low life with the high life, the scenes at Eastcheap with those at Westminster, the tavern with the battlefield; his doings provide most of the material for both Parts, and with him too lies the future, since he is to become Henry V, the ideal king, in the play that bears his name; finally, the mainspring of the dramatic action is the choice I have already spoken of, the choice he is called upon to make between Vanity and Government, taking the latter in its accepted Tudor meaning, which includes Chivalry or prowess in the field, the theme of Part I, and Justice, which is the theme of Part II. Shakespeare, moreover, breathes life into these abstractions by embodying them, or aspects of them, in prominent characters, who stand, as it were, about the Prince, like attendant spirits: Falstaff typifying Vanity in every sense of the word, Hotspur Chivalry, of the old anarchic kind, and the Lord Chief Justice the Rule of Law or the new ideal of service to the state.[1]

Thus considered, Shakespeare's *Henry IV* is a Tudor version of a time-honoured theme, already familiar for decades, if not centuries, upon the English stage. Before its final secularization in the

From *The Fortunes of Falstaff*, Chapter II, "The Falstaff Myth," by John Dover Wilson. Reprinted by permission of Cambridge University Press. Copyright © 1943 by Cambridge University Press.

first half of the sixteenth century, our drama was concerned with one topic, and one only: human salvation. It was a topic that could be represented in either of two ways: (i) historically, by means of miracle plays, which in the Corpus Christi cycles unrolled before spectators' eyes the whole scheme of salvation from the Creation to the Last Judgement; or (ii) allegorically, by means of morality plays, which exhibited the process of salvation in the individual soul on its road between birth and death, beset with the snares of the World or the wiles of the Evil One. In both kinds the forces of iniquity were allowed full play upon the stage, including a good deal of horse-play, provided they were brought to nought, or safely locked up in Hell, at the end. Salvation remains the supreme interest, however many capers the Devil and his Vice may cut on Everyman's way thither, and always the powers of darkness are withstood, and finally overcome, by the agents of light. But as time went on the religious drama tended to grow longer and more elaborate, after the encyclopaedic fashion of the middle ages, and such development invited its inevitable reaction. With the advent of humanism and the early Tudor court, morality plays became tedious and gave place to lighter and much shorter moral interludes dealing, not with human life as a whole, but with youth and its besetting sins.

An early specimen, entitled *Youth*[2] and composed about 1520, may be taken as typical of the rest. The plot, if plot it can be called, is simplicity itself. The little play opens with a dialogue between Youth and Charity. The young man, heir to his father's land, gives insolent expression to his self-confidence, lustihood, and contempt for spiritual things. Whereupon Charity leaves him, and he is joined by Riot,[3] that is to say wantonness, who presently introduces him to Pride and Lechery. The dialogue then becomes boisterous, and continues in that vein for some time, much no doubt to the enjoyment of the audience. Yet, in the end, Charity reappears with Humility; Youth repents; and the interlude terminates in the most seemly fashion imaginable.

No one, I think, reading this lively playlet, no one certainly who has seen it performed, as I have seen it at the Malvern Festival, can have missed the resemblance between Riot and Falstaff. The words he utters, as he bounces on to the stage at his first entry, give us the very note of Falstaff's gaiety:

Huffa! huffa! who calleth after me?
I am Riot full of jollity.
My heart is as light as the wind,
And all on riot is my mind,
Wheresoever I go.

And the parallel is even more striking in other respects. Riot, like Falstaff, escapes from tight corners with a quick dexterity; like Falstaff, commits robbery on the highway; like Falstaff, jests immediately afterwards with his young friend on the subject of hanging; and like Falstaff, invites him to spend the stolen money at a tavern, where, he promises, "We will drink diuers wine" and "Thou shalt haue a wench to kysse Whansoeuer thou wilte"; allurements which prefigure the Boar's Head and Mistress Doll Tearsheet.

But Youth at the door of opportunity, with Age or Experience, Charity or Good Counsel, offering him the yoke of responsibility, while the World, the Flesh, and the Devil beckon him to follow them on the primrose way to the everlasting bonfire, is older than even the medieval religious play. It is a theme to which every generation gives fresh form, while retaining its eternal substance. Young men are the heroes of the Plautine and Terentian comedy which delighted the Roman world; and these young men, generally under the direction of a clever slave or parasite, disport themselves, and often hoodwink their old fathers, for most of the play, until they too settle down in the end. The same theme appears in a very different story, the parable of the Prodigal Son. And the similarity of the two struck humanist teachers of the early sixteenth century with such force that, finding Terence insufficiently edifying for their pupils to act, they developed a "Christian Terence" by turning the parable into Latin plays, of which many examples by different authors have come down to us.[4] In these plot and structure are much the same. The opening scene shows us Acolastus, the prodigal, demanding his portion, receiving good counsel from his father, and going off into a far country. Then follow three or four acts of entertainment almost purely Terentian in atmosphere, in which he wastes his substance in riotous living and falls at length to feeding with the pigs. Finally, in the last act he returns home, penniless and repentant, to receive his pardon. This ingenious blend of classical comedy and humanistic morality preserves, it will be noted, the traditional ratio between edification and amusement, and distributes them in the traditional manner. So long as the serious note is duly emphasized at the beginning and end of the play, almost any quantity of fun, often of the most unseemly nature, was allowed and expected during the intervening scenes.

All this, and much more of a like character, gave the pattern for Shakespeare's *Henry IV*. Hal associates Falstaff in turn with the Devil of the miracle play, the Vice of the morality, and the Riot of the interlude, when he calls him "that villainous abominable misleader of Youth, that old white-bearded Satan,"[5] "that reverend Vice, that grey Iniquity, that father Ruffian, that Vanity in years,"[6] and "the tutor and the feeder of my riots."[7] "Riot," again, is the word that comes most readily to King Henry's lips when speaking of his prodigal son's misconduct.[8] And, as heir to the Vice, Falstaff inherits by reversion the functions and attributes of the Lord of Misrule, the Fool, the Buffoon, and the Jester, antic figures the origins of which are lost in the dark backward and abysm of folk-custom.[9] We shall find that Falstaff possesses a strain, and more than a strain, of the classical *miles gloriosus* as well. In short, the Falstaff-Hal plot embodies a composite myth which had been centuries amaking, and was for the Elizabethans full of meaning that has largely disappeared since then: which is one reason why we have come so seriously to misunderstand the play.

Nor was Shakespeare the first to see Hal as the prodigal. The legend of Harry of Monmouth began to grow soon after his death in 1422; and practically all the chroniclers, even those writing in the fifteenth century, agree on his wildness in youth and on the sudden change that came upon him at his accession to the throne. The essence of Shakespeare's plot is, indeed, already to be found in the following passage about King Henry V taken from Fabyan's *Chronicle* of 1516:

> This man, before the death of his fader, applyed him
> unto all vyce and insolency, and drewe unto hym all ryot-
> tours and wylde disposed persones; but after he was admyt-
> ted to the rule of the lande, anone and suddenly he became a
> newe man, and tourned al that rage into sobernesse and
> wyse sadnesse, and the vyce into constant vertue. And for
> he wolde contynewe the vertue, and not to be reduced

> thereunto by the familiarytie of his olde nyse company, he
> therefore, after rewardes to them gyuen, charged theym
> upon payne of theyr lyues, that none of theym were so
> hardy to come within x. myle of such place as he were
> lodgyd, after a day by him assigned.[10]

There appears to be no historical basis for any of this, and Kingsford has plausibly suggested that its origin may be "contemporary
scandal which attached to Henry through his youthful association
with the unpopular Lollard leader" Sir John Oldcastle. "It is noteworthy," he points out, "that Henry's political opponents were
Oldcastle's religious persecutors; and also that those writers who
charge Henry with wildness as Prince find his peculiar merit as
King in the maintaining of Holy Church and destroying of here-
tics. A supposed change in his attitude on questions of religion
may possibly furnish a partial solution for his alleged 'change
suddenly into a new man.'"[11] The theory is the more attractive
that it would account not only for Hal's conversion but also for
Oldcastle's degradation from a protestant martyr and distinguished soldier to what Ainger calls "a broken-down Lollard, a fat
old sensualist, retaining just sufficient recollection of the studies
of his more serious days to be able to point his jokes with them."

Yet when all is said, the main truth seems to be that the
fifteenth and early sixteenth centuries, the age of allegory in
poetry and morality in drama, needed a Prodigal Prince, whose
miraculous conversion might be held up as an example by those
concerned (as what contemporary political writer was not?) with
the education of young noblemen and princes. And could any
more alluring fruits of repentance be offered such pupils than the
prowess and statesmanship of Henry V, the hero of Agincourt,
the mirror of English kingship for a hundred years? In his miracle
play, *Richard II*, Shakespeare had celebrated the traditional royal
martyr;[12] in his morality play, *Henry IV*, he does the like with the
traditional royal prodigal.

He made the myth his own, much as musicians adopt and
absorb a folk-tune as the theme for a symphony. He glorified it,
elaborated it, translated it into what were for the Elizabethans
modern terms, and exalted it into a heaven of delirious fun and
frolic; yet never, for a moment, did he twist it from its original
purpose, which was serious, moral, didactic. Shakespeare plays no

tricks with his public. He did not, like Euripides, dramatize the stories of his race and religion in order to subvert the traditional ideals those stories were first framed to set forth. Prince Hal is the prodigal, and his repentance is not only to be taken seriously, it is to be admired and commended. Moreover, the story of the prodigal, secularized and modernized as it might be, ran the same course as ever and contained the same three principal characters: the tempter, the younker, and the father with property to bequeath and counsel to give. It followed also the fashion set by miracle, morality and the Christian Terence by devoting much attention to the doings of the first-named. Shakespeare's audience enjoyed the fascination of Prince Hal's "white-bearded Satan" for two whole plays, as perhaps no character on the world's stage had ever been enjoyed before. But they knew, from the beginning, that the reign of this marvellous Lord of Misrule must have an end, that Falstaff must be rejected by the Prodigal Prince, when the time for reformation came. And they no more thought of questioning or disapproving of that finale, than their ancestors would have thought of protesting against the Vice being carried off to Hell at the end of the interlude.

The main theme, therefore, of Shakespeare's morality play is the growing-up of a madcap prince into the ideal king, who was Henry V; and the play was made primarily—already made by some dramatist before Shakespeare took it over—in order to exhibit his conversion and to reveal his character unfolding towards that end, as he finds himself faced more and more directly by his responsibilities. It is that which determines its very shape. Even the "fearful symmetry" of Falstaff's own person was welded upon the anvil of that purpose. It is probably because the historical Harry of Monmouth "exceded the meane stature of men," as his earliest chronicler tells us; "his necke . . . longe, his body slender and leane, his boanes smale,"[13]—because in Falstaff's words he actually was a starveling, an eel-skin, a tailor's yard, and all the rest of it—that the idea of Falstaff himself as "a huge hill of flesh" first came to Shakespeare.[14] It was certainly, at any rate in part, in order to explain and palliate the Prince's love of rioting and wantonness that he set out to make Falstaff as enchanting as he could.[15] And he succeeded so well that the young man now lies under the stigma, not of having yielded to the tempter, but of

disentangling himself, in the end, from his toils. After all, Falstaff
is "a devil . . . in the likeness of an old fat man," and the Devil has
generally been supposed to exercise limitless attraction in his
dealings with the sons of men. A very different kind of poet, who
imagined a very different kind of Satan, has been equally and
similarly misunderstood by modern critics, who no longer believing in the Prince of Darkness have ceased to understand him. For,
as Professor R. W. Chambers reminded us in his last public utterance,[16] when Blake declared that Milton was "of the Devil's party
without knowing it," he overlooked the fact, and his many successors have likewise overlooked the fact, that, if the fight in Heaven,
the struggle in Eden, the defeat of Adam and Eve, and the victory
of the Second Adam in *Paradise Regained*, are to appear in their true
proportions, we must be made to realize how immeasurable, how
indomitable, is the spirit of the Great Enemy. It may also be noted
that Milton's Son of God has in modern times been charged with
priggishness no less freely than Shakespeare's son of Bolingbroke.

Shakespeare, I say, translated his myth into a language and
endued it with an atmosphere that his contemporaries would best
appreciate. First, Hal is not only youth or the prodigal, he is the
young prodigal *prince*, the youthful heir to the throne. The translation, then, already made by the chroniclers, if Kingsford be
right, from sectarian terms into those more broadly religious or
moral, now takes us out of the theological into the political
sphere. This is seen most clearly in the discussion of the young
king's remarkable conversion by the two bishops at the beginning
of *Henry V*. King Henry, as Bradley notes, "is much more obviously religious than most of Shakespeare's heroes,"[17] so that
one would expect the bishops to interpret his change of life as a
religious conversion. Yet they say nothing about religion except
that he is "a true lover of the holy church" and can "reason in
divinity"; the rest of their talk, some seventy lines, is concerned
with learning and statecraft. In fact, the conversation of these
worldly prelates demonstrates that the conversion is not the old
repentance for sin and amendment of life, which is the burden,
as we have seen, of Fabyan and other chroniclers, but a repentance of the renaissance type, which transforms an idle and wayward prince into an excellent soldier and governor. Even King

Henry IV, at the bitterest moments of the scenes with his son, never taxes him with sin, and his only use of the word refers to sins that would multiply in the country, when

> the fifth Harry from curbed licence plucks
> The muzzle of restraint.[18]

If Hal had sinned, it was not against God, but against Chivalry, against Justice, against his father, against the interests of the crown, which was the keystone of England's political and social stability. Instead of educating himself for the burden of kingship, he had been frittering away his time, and making himself cheap, with low companions

> that daff the world aside
> And bid it pass.

In a word, a word that Shakespeare applies no less than six times to his conduct, he is guilty of Vanity. And Vanity, though not in the theological category of the Seven Deadly Sins, was a cardinal iniquity in a young prince or nobleman of the sixteenth and seventeenth centuries; almost as heinous, in fact, as Idleness in an apprentice.

I am not suggesting that this represents Shakespeare's own view. Of Shakespeare's views upon the problems of conduct, whether in prince or commoner, we are in general ignorant, though he seems to hint in both *Henry IV* and *Henry V* that the Prince of Wales learnt some lessons at least from Falstaff and his crew, Francis and his fellow-drawers, which stood him in good stead when he came to rule the country and command troops in the field. But it is the view that his father and his own conscience take of his misreadings; and, as the spectators would take it as well, we must regard it as the thesis to which Shakespeare addressed himself.

When, however, he took audiences by storm in 1597 and 1598 with his double *Henry IV* he gave them something much more than a couple of semi-mythical figures from the early fifteenth century, brought up to date politically. He presented persons and situations at once fresh and actual. Both Hal and Falstaff are denizens of Elizabethan London. Hal thinks, acts, comports himself as an heir to the Queen might have done, had she delighted

her people by taking a consort and giving them a Prince of Wales;
while Falstaff symbolizes, on the one hand, all the feasting and
good cheer for which Eastcheap stood, and reflects, on the other,
the shifts, subterfuges, and shady tricks that decayed gentlemen
and soldiers were put to if they wished to keep afloat and gratify
their appetites in the London underworld of the late sixteenth
century. It is the former aspects of the old scoundrel that probably gave most pleasure to those who first saw him on the stage;
and, as they are also those that we moderns are most likely to
miss, I make no apology for devoting most of the rest of this
chapter to an exposition of them.

Sweet Beef

Riot invites Youth, it will be remembered, to drink wine at a
tavern, and tavern scenes are common in other interludes, especially those of the Prodigal Son variety. But Shakespeare's tavern
is more than a drink-shop, while his Riot is not only a "huge
bombard of sack" but also a "roasted Manningtree ox with the
pudding in his belly."

The site of the Boar's Head tavern in Eastcheap is now as
deep-sunk in the ooze of human forgetfulness as that of the
palace of Haroun. But it was once a real hostelry, and must have
meant much to Londoners of the reigns of Elizabeth and James.
Records are scanty, but the very fact that Shakespeare makes it
Falstaff's headquarters suggests that it was the best tavern in the
city. And the further fact that he avoids mentioning it directly,
though quibbling upon the name more than once,[19] suggests, on
the one hand, that he kept the name off the stage in order to
escape complications with the proprietors of the day, and on the
other that he could trust his audience to jump to so obvious an
identification without prompting. In any event, no other tavern in
Eastcheap is at all likely to have been intended, and as Eastcheap is
referred to six times in various scenes, there can be little real
doubt that what Falstaff once calls "the king's tavern"[20] is the
famous Boar's Head, the earliest known reference to which occurs in a will dating from the reign of Richard II.[21] Whether there
is anything or not in Skeat's conjecture that the Glutton in *Piers*

Plowman made it the scene of his exploits like Falstaff,[22] it was a well-known house of entertainment more than two hundred years before Shakespeare introduced it into his play, and had come therefore by his day to be regarded as a historic hostelry, for which reason it was probably already associated in popular imagination with the floating legends of the wild young prince. What, however, seems to have escaped the attention of modern writers is that the house, with a name that symbolized good living and good fellowship above that of any other London tavern, was almost certainly even better known for good food than for good drink.

Eastcheap, there is plenty of evidence to show, was then, and had long been, the London centre at once of butchers and cook-shops. Lydgate, writing in the reign of Henry V, puts the following words in the mouth of his *London Lyckpenny*:

> Then I hyed me into Estchepe;
> One cryes "rybbes of befe and many a pye";
> Pewter pots they clattered on a heap;
> There was a harp, pype, and minstrelsy.

The street was famed, in short, not only for meat and drink, but also for the "noise" of musicians, which belonged to "the old Tauerne in Eastcheap" in *The Famous Victories*, and which "Mistress Tearsheet would fain hear" in Part II of *Henry IV*.[23] As for "rybbes of befe," though we never see or hear of Falstaff eating, or desiring to eat, anything except Goodwife Keech's dish of prawns[24] and the capon, anchovies and halfpenny worth of bread recorded with "an intolerable deal of sack" in the bill found upon him while asleep,[25] Shakespeare none the less contrives to associate him perpetually with appetizing food by means of the imagery that plays about his person. For the epithets and comparisons which Hal and Poins apply to him, or he himself makes use of, though at times connected with his consumption of sack, are far more often intended to recall the chief stock-in-trade of the victuallers and butchers of Eastcheap, namely meat of all kinds, and meat both raw and roast.

Falstaff is once likened to a "huge bombard,"[26] once to a "hogshead,"[27] once to a "tun,"[28] and twice to a "hulk," that is, to a cargo-boat; the nature of the cargo being specified by Doll, who protests to Mistress Quickly, "There's a whole merchant's venture of Bourdeaux stuff in him, you have not seen a hulk better stuffed in the hold."[29] But beyond these there is little or nothing about him in the vintner's line. When, on the other hand, Shakespeare promises the audience, through the mouth of his Epilogue in Part II, to continue the story, with Sir John in it, "if you be not too much cloyed with fat meat," the phrase sums up the prevailing image, constant in reference though ever-varying in form, which the physical characteristics of Falstaff presented to his mind's eye, and which he in turn was at pains to keep before the mind's eye of his public. Changes in London, and even more, changes in the language, have obliterated all this for the modern reader, so that what was intended, from the first, as little more than a kind of shimmering half-apprehended jest playing upon the surface of the dialogue, must now be recovered as a piece of archaeology, that is, as something long dead. The laughter has gone out of it; yet I shall be disappointed if the reader does not catch himself smiling now and again at what follows.

"Call in Ribs, call in Tallow" is Hal's cue for Falstaff's entry in the first great Boar's Head scene; and what summons to the choicest feast in comedy could be more apt? For there is the noblest of English dishes straightaway: Sir John as roast Sir Loin-of-Beef, gravy and all. "Tallow," a word often applied to him, generally in opprobrium, is not rightly understood, unless two facts be recalled: first, that it meant to the Elizabethans liquid fat, as well as dripping or suet or animal fat rendered down; second, that human sweat, partly owing perhaps to the similarity of the word to "suet," was likewise thought of as fat, melted by the heat of the body. The most vivid presentation of Falstaff served up hot, so to say, is the picture we get of him sweating with fright in Mistress Page's dirty linen basket, as it was emptied by her servants into the Thames; and though *The Merry Wives* does not strictly belong to the Falstaff canon, the passage may be quoted here, as giving the clue to passages in *Henry IV* itself. For however different in character the Windsor Falstaff may be from his namesake of Eastcheap, he possesses the same body, the body that on Gad's Hill "sweats to death, and *lards* the lean earth, as he walks along."[30]

"And then," he relates to the disguised Ford,

> to be stopped in, like a strong distillation, with stinking
> clothes that fretted in their own grease! Think of that, a man
> of my kidney! think of that—that am as subject to heat, as
> butter; a man of continual dissolution and thaw; it was a
> miracle to 'scape suffocation. And in the height of this bath,
> when I was more than half stewed in grease, like a Dutch
> dish, to be thrown into the Thames, and cooled, glowing-
> hot, in that surge, like a horse-shoe. Think of that—hissing
> hot: think of that, Master Brook.[31]

The "greasy tallow-catch,"[32] again, to which the Prince compares
him, much to the bewilderment of commentators, betokens, I
believe, nothing more mysterious than a dripping-pan to catch
the fat as the roasting joint turned upon the spit before the fire.
Or take the following scrap of dialogue:

> L. *Chief Justice.* What, you are as a candle, the better part
> burnt out.
> *Falstaff.* A wassail candle, my lord, all tallow—if I did say of
> wax, my growth would approve the truth.
> L. *Chief Justice.* There is not a white hair on your face, but
> should have his effect of gravity.
> *Falstaff.* His effect of gravy, gravy, gravy.[33]

Falstaff's repeated "gravy" is a quibble, of course. But it is not just
a feeble jest upon his table manners, as seems to be usually
assumed: it follows upon the mention of "tallow" and refers to
the drops of sweat that never cease to stand upon his face. In fact,
to use a seventeenth-century expression, applicable to one bathed
in perspiration, he may be said perpetually to "stew in his own
gravy."[34]

Indeed, he glories in the fact. Was it not, according to the
physiological notions of the time, the very warrant of his enormous vitality? Never is he more angered to the heart than when
the Prince likens him one day to a dry withered old apple-john.
His complexion is merely sanguine; heat and moisture mingle to
form the element he moves in; except in moods of mock-repentance he leaves to baser earth the cold and dry of melancholy.[35]

Once we have the trick of it, all sorts of other allusions and
playful terms of abuse are seen to belong to the same category,

while the analogy between that vast carcase, as a whole or in its parts, and roasts of various kinds is capable of almost infinite elaboration. "Chops," for instance, as he is twice called,[36] carries the double significance of "fat cheeks" and "cutlets"; "guts," the Elizabethan word for "tripe," is an epithet that occurs no less than five times;[37] and "sweet beef" as a term of endearment[38] requires no explaining. Nor is he only served up as beef; pork, still more appropriate to the Boar's Head, though brought in less often, provides some magnificent examples. The term "brawn," which means a large pig fattened for the slaughter, is applied to him on two occasions;[39] on his return from Wales the Prince, enquiring of Bardolph, "Is your master here in London? . . . Where sups he? doth the old boar feed in the old frank?"[40] refers to the familiar inn-sign; Falstaff himself declares that he walks the streets followed by the diminutive page "like a sow that hath overwhelmed all her litter but one";[41] last, and best of all, when Doll salutes him between her "flattering busses" as her "whoreson little tidy Bartholomew boar-pig,"[42] she is alluding to the tender sweet-fleshed little sucking-pigs which formed the chief delicacy at Bartholomew Fair.

The mention of Bartholomew Fair, the most popular annual festivity of Elizabethan and Jacobean London, may be linked with two other comparisons, which take us beyond the confines of Eastcheap and help to bestow on Falstaff that "touch of infinity" which Bradley discovers in him, associating him, as they do, with feasting on a vast and communal scale. The first, already quoted above, is the Prince's description of him as a "Manningtree ox with the pudding in his belly,"[43] in other words, as an ox roasted whole and stuffed with sausages, after the fashion of the annual fairs at Manningtree, an Essex town famed for the exceeding fatness of its beasts. But the extremest inch of possibility is reached by Poins when he asks Bardolph "How doth the Martlemas, your master?"[44] Martlemas, or the feast of St. Martin, on 11 November, was in those days of scarce fodder the season at which most of the beasts had to be killed off and salted for the winter, and therefore the season for great banquets of fresh meat. Thus it had been for centuries, long before the coming of Christianity,[45] and thus it remained down to the introduction of the cropping of turnips in the eighteenth century. In calling him a

"Martlemas" Poins is at once likening Falstaff's enormous proportions to the prodigality of fresh-killed meat which the feast
brought, and acclaiming his identity with Riot and Festivity in
general.[46] But perhaps the best comment upon Falstaff as Martlemas comes from Spenser's procession of the seasons in the Book
of Mutabilitie. His November might almost be Falstaff himself,
though the dates prove that the two figures must be independent:

> Next was Nouember, he full grosse and fat,
> As fed with lard, and that right well might seeme;
> For, he had been a fatting hogs of late,
> That yet his browes with sweat did reek and steem,
> And yet the season was full sharp and breem.[47]

One might go to the other end of the scale and point out that
the objects Falstaff chooses as a contrast to his person, objects
excessively thin, wizened or meagre, are likewise often taken
from the food-shops. There is, for instance, the shotten herring,
the soused gurnet, the bunch of radish, the rabbit-sucker or
poulter's hare, and wittiest of all perhaps, the carbonado—the
rasher of bacon, we should say—which he will only allow Hotspur
to make of him, if he is foolish enough to come in his way.[48] But
enough to have shown that by plying his audience with suggestions of the choicest food that London and Eastcheap had to offer,
whenever the person of Falstaff is mentioned, Shakespeare lays
as it were the physical foundations of his Falstaff myth.

The prodigiously incarnate Riot, who fills the Boar's Head
with his jollity, typifies much more, of course, than the pleasures
of the table. He stands for a whole globe of happy continents, and
his laughter is "broad as ten thousand beeves at pasture."[49] But he
is Feasting first, and his creator never allows us to forget it. For in
this way he not only perpetually associates him in our minds with
appetizing images, but contrives that as we laugh at his wit our
souls shall be satisfied as with marrow and fatness. No one has
given finer expression to this satisfaction than Hazlitt, and I may
fitly round off the topic with words of his:

> Falstaff's wit is an emanation of a fine constitution; an
> exuberance of good-humour and good-nature; an overflow-
> ing of his love of laughter and good-fellowship; a giving vent
> to his heart's ease, and over-contentment with himself and
> others. He would not be in character, if he were not so fat as

he is; for there is the greatest keeping in the boundless luxury of his imagination and the pampered self-indulgence of his physical appetites. He manures and nourishes his mind with jests, as he does his body with sack and sugar. He carves out his jokes, as he would a capon or a haunch of venison, where there is *cut and come again;* and pours out upon them the oil of gladness. His tongue drops fatness, and in the chambers of his brain "it snows of meat and drink." He keeps perpetually holiday and open house, and we live with him in a round of invitations to a rump and dozen. . . . He never fails to enrich his discourse with allusions to eating and drinking, but we never see him at table. He carries his own larder about with him, and is himself "a tun of man."[50]

Monsieur Remorse

Like all great Shakespearian characters Falstaff is a bundle of contradictions. He is not only Riot but also Repentance. He can turn an eye of melancholy upon us, assume the role of puritan sanctimony, and when it pleases him, even threaten amendment of life. It is, of course, *mock*-repentance, carried through as part of the untiring "play extempore" with which he keeps the Prince, and us, and himself, entertained from beginning to end of the drama. And yet it is not mere game; Shakespeare makes it more interesting by persuading us that there is a strain of sincerity in it; and it almost completely disappears in Part II, when the rogue finds himself swimming on the tide of success. There is a good deal of it in Part I, especially in the earliest Falstaff scenes.

> But, Hal, I prithee, trouble me no more with vanity. I would to God thou and I knew where a commodity of good names were to be bought.
> Thou hast done much harm upon me, Hal—God forgive thee for it: before I knew thee, Hal, I knew nothing, and now am I, if a man should speak truly, little better than one of the wicked: I must give over this life, and I will give it over: by the Lord, an I do not, I am a villain. I'll be damned for never a king's son in Christendom.[51]

One of his favourite poses is that of the innocent, beguiled by a wicked young heir apparent; he even makes it the burden of his apologia to the Lord Chief Justice at their first encounter. It serves too when things go wrong, when resolute men who have taken £1000 on Gad's Hill are left in the lurch by cowardly friends, or when there's lime in a cup of sack:

> There is nothing but roguery to be found in villainous man, yet a coward is worse than a cup of sack with lime in it. A villainous coward! Go thy ways, old Jack, die when thou wilt, if manhood, good manhood, be not forgot upon the face of the earth, then am I a shotten herring. . . . There lives not three good men unhanged in England, and one of them is fat, and grows old. God help the while! a bad world, I say. I would I were a weaver—I could sing psalms or anything.[52]

But beside this talk of escaping from a wicked world and the toils of a naughty young prince, there is also the pose of personal repentance. At his first entry Poins hails him as Monsieur Remorse, an indication that this is one of his recognized roles among Corinthians and lads of mettle. And we may see him playing it at the opening of act 3, scene 3, when there is no Hal present to require entertaining.

> Well, I'll repent, and that suddenly, while I am in some liking. I shall be out of heart shortly, and then I shall have no strength to repent. An I have not forgotten what the inside of a church is made of, I am a peppercorn, a brewer's horse. The inside of a church! Company, villainous company, hath been the spoil of me.

Such passages, together with the habit of citing Scripture, may have their origin, I have said, in the puritan, psalm-singing, temper of Falstaff's prototype—that comic Lollard, Sir John Oldcastle in the old *Henry IV*.[53] But, if so, the motif, adapted and developed in Shakespeare's hands, has come to serve a different end. In this play of the Prodigal Prince it is Hal who should rightly exhibit moods of repentance; and on the face of it, it seems quite illogical to transfer them to Falstaff, the tempter. Yet there are reasons why Hal could not be thus represented. In the first place, as already noted, repentance in the theological sense, repentance for sin, is not relevant to his case at all, which is rather one of a falling away from political virtues, from the duties laid upon him by his royal vocation. And in the second place, since Henry V is the ideal king of English history, Shakespeare must take great care, even in the days of his "wildness," to guard him from the breath of scandal. As has been well observed by a recent editor: "His riots are mere frolics. He does not get drunk and is never involved in any scandal with a woman."[54] And there is a third reason, this time one of dramatic technique not of morals, why the repentance of the Prince must be kept in the background as much as possible, viz. that as the only satisfactory means of rounding off the two parts, it belongs especially to the last act of the play.

Yet Monsieur Remorse is a good puppet in the property-box of the old morality, and may be given excellent motions in the fingers of a skilful showman, who is laying himself out, in this play especially, to make fun of the old types. Why not shape a comic part out of it, and hand it over to Falstaff, who as the heir of traditional medieval "antics" like the Devil, the Vice, the Fool, Riot and Lord of Misrule, may very well manage one more? Whether or not Shakespeare argued it out thus, he certainly added the ingredient of melancholy, and by so doing gave a piquancy to the sauce which immensely enhances the relish of the whole dish. If only modern actors who attempt to impersonate Falstaff would realize it!

Falstaff, then, came to stand for the repentance, as well as the riotous living, of the Prodigal Son. And striking references to the parable, four of them, seem to show that his creator was fully aware of what he was doing. "What, will you make a younker of me? shall I not take mine ease in mine inn but I shall have my pocket picked?"[55] Sir John indignantly demands of Mistress Quickly, on discovering, or pretending to discover, the loss of his grandfather's seal-ring. The word "younker" calls up a scene from some well-known representation of the parable, in picture or on the stage, a scene to which Shakespeare had already alluded in the following lines from *The Merchant of Venice*:

> How like a younker or a prodigal
> The scarféd bark puts from her native bay,
> Hugged and embracéd by the strumpet wind!
> How like a prodigal doth she return,
> With over-weathered ribs and ragged sails,
> Lean, rent, and beggared by the strumpet wind![56]

Equally vivid is Falstaff's description of the charge of foot he led into battle at Shrewsbury as so "dishonourable ragged" that

"you would think that I had a hundred and fifty tattered prodi-
gals, lately come from swine-keeping, from eating draff and
husks."[57] And seeing that he calls them in the same speech "slaves
as ragged as Lazarus in the painted cloth, where the Glutton's
dogs licked his sores," we may suppose that, here too, he is
speaking right painted cloth, from whence he had studied his
Bible[58]; an inference which seems borne out by his third reference, this time from Part II. Having, you will remember, already
honoured Mistress Quickly by becoming indebted to her for a
hundred marks, that is for over £65, he graciously condescends to
borrow £10 more from her. And when she protests that to raise
the sum she must be fain to pawn both her plate and the tapestry
of her dining-chambers, he replies: "Glasses, glasses, is the only
drinking—and for thy walls, a pretty drollery or the story of the
Prodigal or the German hunting in waterwork is worth a thousand of these bed-hangers and these fly-bitten tapestries."[59] This
is not just the patter of the confidence-trickster; Falstaff, we must
believe, had a real liking for the Prodigal Son story, or why should
that tactful person, mine Host of the Garter Inn, have gone to the
trouble of having it painted, "fresh and new," about the walls of
the chamber that he let to the greasy philanderer who assumed
the part of Sir John, in Windsor.[60] Not being a modern critic, the
good man could not know that his guest was an impostor.

But jollification and mock-repentance do not exhaust Falstaff's
roles. For most of *Henry IV* he plays the soldier, taking a hand in a
couple of campaigns, the first culminating in the death of Hotspur
at Shrewsbury, and the other in the encounter between Prince
John and the Archbishop of York at Gaultree Forest, where the
rebels are finally overthrown. In both of these he performs the
useful dramatic function of supplying the light relief, and in so
doing he exhibits himself as at once the supreme comic soldier of
English literature and a variation of a time-worn theme, the *miles
gloriosus* of Plautus. Before, however, we go to war with him, we
must witness his exploits at Gad's Hill; before we consider his
relation to the braggart of Roman comedy, we must address
ourselves to that vexed problem: was he really a coward? And
since his fate depends entirely upon the countenance of Prince
Hal, there is an even earlier question to be settled: upon what
terms do these two characters associate together? In a word, we

must now survey the fortunes of our jolly knight as Shakespeare represents them to us, within the dramatic frame of the two parts of *Henry IV*.

NOTES

1. In what follows I develop a hint in Sir Arthur Quiller-Couch's *Shakespeare's Workmanship*, 1918, p. 148: "The whole of the business [in *Henry IV*] is built on the old Morality structure, imported through the Interlude. Why, it might almost be labelled, after the style of a Morality title, *Contentio inter Virtutem et Vitium de anima Principis.*"
2. *The enterlude of youth*, ed. by W. Bang and R. B. McKerrow, Louvain, 1905.
3. riot = "wanton, loose, or wasteful living; debauchery, dissipation, extravagance" (*O.E.D.*). Cf. the Prodigal Son, who "wasted his substance with riotous living" (Luke XV. 13).
4. V. C. H. Herford, *The Literary Relations between England and Germany in the Sixteenth Century*, 1886, ch. III, pp. 84–95.
5. Pt. I, 2.4.450 (508); cf. l. 435 (491): "Thou art violently carried away from grace, there is a devil haunts thee in the likeness of an old fat man."
6. *Ibid.* 2.4.442 (500).
7. Pt. II, 5.5.63 (66).
8. Cf. Pt. I, 1.1.85: "Riot and dishonour stain the brow / Of my young Harry"; Pt. II, 4.4.62: "His headstrong riot hath no curb," 4.5.135: "When that my care could not withhold thy riots, / What wilt thou do when riot is thy care?"
9. In particular, the exact significance of the Vice is exasperatingly obscure. Cf. the discussion by Sir E. K. Chambers (*Medieval Stage*, ii, pp. 203-5), who concludes "that whatever the name may mean . . . the character of the vice is derived from that of the domestic fool or jester." I hazard the suggestion that it was originally the title or name of the Fool who attended upon the Lord of Misrule; v. Feuillerat, *Revels of the time of Edward VI*, p. 73: "One vyces dagger & a ladle with a bable pendante . . . deliuerid to the Lorde of Mysrules foole."
10. Fabyan's *Chronicle*, 1516, p. 577.
11. C. L. Kingsford, *The First English Life of King Henry the Fifth*, 1911, pp. xlii, xliii.
12. V. pp. xvi-xix, lviii-lix of my Introd. to *Richard II*, 1939 ("The New Shakespeare").
13. Kingsford, *op. cit.* p. 16.

14. Ainger tries to persuade himself that there was a tradition associating the Lollard, Oldcastle, with extreme fatness; but his editor, Beeching, is obliged to admit in a footnote that he is not aware of any references to this fatness before Shakespeare; *v.* Ainger, *Lectures and Essays*, 1905, i pp. 126–30.

15. Cf. H. N. Hudson, *Shakespeare: his Life, Art and Characters* (ed. 1888), ii, p. 83: "It must be no ordinary companionship that yields entertainment to such a spirit [as Prince Hal's] even in his loosest moments. Whatever bad or questionable elements may mingle with his mirth, it must have some fresh and rich ingredients, some sparkling and generous flavour, to make him relish it. Anything like vulgar rowdyism cannot fail of disgusting him. His ears were never organised to that sort of music. Here then we have a sort of dramatic necessity for the character of Falstaff. To answer the purpose it was imperative that he should be just such a marvellous congregation of charms and vices as he is." See also A. H. Tolman, *Falstaff and other Shakespearian Topics*, 1925, and W. W. Lawrence, *Shakespeare's Problem Comedies*, 1931, p. 64 (an interesting contrast between Hal and Falstaff, Bertram and Parolles).

16. *Poets and their Critics: Langland and Milton* (British Academy Warton Lecture), 1941, pp. 29–30.

17. *Oxford Lectures*, p. 256.

18. Pt. II, 4.5.131.

19. *V.* Pt. I, 2.4.107 (122): "That damned brawn"; Pt. II, 1.1.19: "Harry Monmouth's brawn"; 2.2.143 (159): "Doth the old boar feed in the old frank? / At the old place, my lord, in Eastcheap"; and 2.4.224 (250): "Thou whoreson little tidy Bartholomew boar-pig."

20. Pt. I, 2.2.54 (59). This designation perhaps implies a claim to royal patronage on the proprietor's part, possibly connected with the quasi-historical incident known as the Hurling in Eastcheap, an affray which arose among their retinue while Hal's brothers, the princes John and Thomas, were taking supper at a tavern (unnamed) in Eastcheap, on St. John's Eve, 1410, as is related by Stow (*v.* Kingsford, *op. cit.* p. xxxix).

21. *V.* "East Cheap" in Sugden's *Topographical Dictionary to the Works of Shakespeare.*

22. *V.* note on *Piers Plowman*, Passus v, l. 313, ed. Skeat (Clarendon Press).

23. Pt. II, 2.4.11–12.

24. *Ibid.* 2.1.94 (102) ff.

25. Pt. I, 2.4.523–7 (584–90).

26. *Ibid.* 2.4.440 (497).

27. Pt. II, 2.4.59 (69).
28. Pt. I, 2.4.436 (494).
29. Pt. II, 2.4.59–61 (69–71).
30. Pt. I, 2.2.106 (115).
31. *Merry Wives of Windsor*, 3.5.103–12 (114–24).
32. Pt. I, 2.4.223 (252).
33. Pt. II, 1.2.155–61 (182–4).
34. *V. O.E.D.* "gravy."
35. *V.* p. 224, *Edinburgh University Journal*, Summer 1942 (art. on "Shakespeare's Universe").
36. Pt. I, 1.2.131 (151); Pt. II, 2.4.211 (234).
37. Pt. I, 2.4.222, 252, 440 (251, 286, 498); *ibid.* 3.3.152, 155 (173, 176).
38. Pt. I, 3.3.176 (198).
39. Pt. I, 2.4.107 (122); Pt. II, 1.1.19.
40. Pt. II, 2.2.143 (169).
41. *Ibid.* 1.2.11–12 (13–14).
42. *Ibid.* 2.4.224–5 (250).
43. Pt. I, 2.4.441 (498).
44. Pt. II, 2.2.100 (110).
45. *V.* Sir E. K. Chambers, *Medieval Stage*, ch. XI, "The Beginning of Winter."
46. I owe this point to the late Lord Ernle: writing in *Shakespeare's England* (i, p. 356), he notes: "To Shakespeare's mind the prodigious plenty of Martlemas suggested Falstaff in its proportions."
47. *The Faerie Queene*, Bk. VII, canto vii, st. 40.
48. Pt. I, 5.3.57 (58).
49. George Meredith, *The Spirit of Shakespeare.*
50. *Characters of Shakespeare's Plays* (Hazlitt's *Works*, ed. A. R. Waller and A. Glover, 1902, i. 278).
51. Pt. I, 1.2.80–2, 90–6 (91–2, 102–10).
52. *Ibid.* 2.4.121–29 (137–47).
53. *V. Fortunes of Falstaff*, p. 16 and ch. IV note 20.
54. *V.* p. xi of I *Henry IV*, ed. by G. L. Kittredge (Ginn & Co.). I fancy Hal is just a little tipsy at the beginning of Pt. I, 2.4; but the point is, in general, sound enough, and the more striking that the chroniclers do not hide the fact that Prince Henry was given to sexual intemperance; *v.* Kingsford, *op. cit.* p. 17: "he exercised meanelie the feates of Venus and of Mars, and other pastimes of youth, for so longe as the Kinge his father liued."
55. Pt. I, 3.3.80–3 (90–3). "The alternative title for the Prodigal Son was the 'younger,' as the alternative for the good brother was the 'elder'" (Richmond Noble, *Shakespeare's Biblical Knowledge*, p. 277).

56. *The Merchant of Venice*, 2.6.14–19; cf. 3 *Henry VI*, 2.1.24: "Trimmed like a younker, prancing to his love."
57. Pt. I, 4.2.32–3 (37–9).
58. Cf. *As You Like It*, 3.2.271 (290): "I answer you right painted cloth, from whence you have studied your questions."
59. Pt. II, 2.1.143–7 (155–9).
60. *The Merry Wives*, 4.5.7.

E. M. W. Tillyard

Henry IV (1944)

In an article on *Structural Unity in the two Parts of "Henry IV"* R. A. Law maintains that Part Two is a new structure, an unpremeditated addition. I think so decidedly the other way that I shall treat the two parts as a single play (as Dover Wilson does in the *Fortunes of Falstaff*). Indeed Shakespeare almost goes out of his way to advertise the continuity by keeping the action patently incomplete at the end of the first part. In IV. 4 the Archbishop of York is shown preparing for the rebellious action which is the main political theme of Part Two but which is almost irrelevant to Part One. In V. 2 there is a probable reference forward to the second part. Here Worcester refuses to inform Hotspur of the king's generous consent to confine the battle to a duel between Hotspur and the Prince and of his generous offer of a pardon to all the rebels. Worcester distrusts Henry and probably without reason. Shakespeare was thinking ironically of John of Lancaster's offer of pardon made to the other rebels in the second part, which, though insincere, was trusted. And the first part ends with Henry's sending Prince John and Westmoreland to deal with Northumberland and the Archbishop; an action which is taken up immediately in the second part. Finally, one of the most striking anticipations, pointing to Shakespeare's having planned ahead with much thought, is the talk between Falstaff and the Prince on justice in the scene that first brings them in. The Prince has slipped into the talk of robberies by moonlight an unpleasant

From *Shakespeare's History Plays* by E. M. W. Tillyard, originally published by Chatto and Windus, and Macmillan, 1944 and 1946. Reprinted by permission of Littlefield, Adams, and Company.

reference to the gallows. Falstaff, not relishing it, seeks to turn the conversation with

> And is not my hostess of the tavern a most sweet wench?

But the Prince turns the conversation back to the unpleasant theme. Falstaff again turns the conversation; but the thought of the gallows is too strong for him and he can't help asking,

> Shall there be gallows standing when thou art king? and resolution thus fobbed as it is with the rusty curb of old father antic the law?

The Prince does not say no to this. But the questions are not answered till the end of the second part—indeed they cannot arise again in the first part because the Prince is not yet king—but there Resolution, or Falstaff and his gang, are indeed fobbed with the rusty curb of the Lord Chief Justice or old father antic the law.

The reason why Law wishes to separate the two parts is that he thinks their motives are different. According to him Part One shows the struggle of the Prince and Hotspur culminating in the Battle of Shrewsbury, while Part Two, in strong contrast, shows the Prince in the background not fighting but fought over, as in the Moralities, by the royal household and the Lord Chief Justice on the one hand and by Falstaff, the epitome of the Seven Deadly Sins, on the other. Law was right in seeing the Morality pattern in Part Two, but wrong in not seeing it in Part One likewise. The struggle between the Prince and Hotspur is subordinate to a larger plan.

The structure of the two parts is indeed very similar. In the first part the Prince (who, one knows, will soon be king) is tested in the military or chivalric virtues. He has to choose, Morality-fashion, between Sloth or Vanity, to which he is drawn by his bad companions, and Chivalry, to which he is drawn by his father and his brothers. And he chooses Chivalry. The action is complicated by Hotspur and Falstaff, who stand for the excess and the defect of the military spirit, for honour exaggerated and dishonour. Thus the Prince, as well as being Magnificence in a Morality Play, is Aristotle's middle quality between two extremes. Such a combination would have been entirely natural to the Elizabethans, especially since it occurred in the second book of the *Fairy Queen*. Guyon is at once the Morality figure fought over by the Palmer and Mammon and the man who is shown the Aristotelian allegory of Excess Balance and Defect in Perissa Medina and Elissa. Near the end of the play the Prince ironically surrenders to Falstaff the credit of having killed Hotspur, thus leaving the world of arms and preparing for the motive of the second part. Here again he is tested, but in the civil virtues. He has to choose, Morality-fashion, between disorder or misrule, to which he is drawn by his bad companions, and Order or Justice (the supreme kingly virtue) to which he is drawn by his father and by his father's deputy the Lord Chief Justice. And he chooses Justice. As in the first part the Aristotelian motive occurs, but it is only touched on. After Falstaff has exchanged words with John of Lancaster about his captive Sir John Colevile, he remains on the stage to soliloquise. He calls John a "sober-blooded boy" and blames him for not drinking sack. John is thus cold-blooded and addicted to thin potations; Falstaff himself is warm-blooded and addicted to strong drink. The Prince is the mean, cold-blooded by inheritance but warmed "with excellent endeavour of drinking good and good store of fertile sherris." Temperamentally he strikes the balance between the parsimony of John and the extravagance of Falstaff. He does the same too in his practice of justice. The justice of John of Lancaster in his cold-blooded treatment of the rebels verges on rigour; Falstaff has no general standard of justice at all; Henry V uses his justice moderately in the way he treats his old companions—at least by Elizabethan standards.

I will develop the structure of *Henry IV* in rather fuller detail. The action of the first part opens with high themes of crusades, chivalry, and civil war. But the Prince is not there, and his father laments that he has not got Hotspur for his son. Soon after his words we see the Prince in Falstaff's company, showing, at least superficially, his inclination to idleness and vanity. When they arrange a robbery, his inclination seems confirmed; yet he will join in with a difference, planning with Poins a joke at the expense of Falstaff. Next there is the quarrel between the Percies and the king; and yet another action is planned, this time rebellion. Hotspur is in the very centre of the plot, unlike the Prince, who is only on the edge of his; he also discloses the exaggeration of his passions. From then on the two actions take their course, with various cross-references; the Prince maintaining his negligent aloofness, Hotspur growing more exclusively absorbed. As the action of the Gadshill robbery closes, the Prince hears of the rebellion and decides to join in it, but with how serious intent we cannot say; his resolve to gain amusement by giving Falstaff a charge of foot shows that at any rate he is not exclusively serious. Vanity having had a long turn, Chivalry must now be allowed to work on the Prince. His father rebukes him, and he promises amendment and his resolution to rob Hotspur of his rebellious honours. But what is his resolution worth when soon after at the tavern in Eastcheap he enters with Peto "marching, and Falstaff meets them playing on his truncheon like a fife"? The business of the rebellion proceeds, the rebels raising their forces and Falstaff his ragged company, till the two armies are encamped against each other at Shrewsbury. The crisis occurs in the first scene of the fifth act, where Worcester comes to the king's camp as emissary of the rebels. It is important that Falstaff should be there and that in his presence the Prince should make his choice for chivalry (to which he actually says he has been a truant) by offering to settle the whole matter personally in single fight with Hotspur. Falstaff's speech on honour, which closes the scene, rounds off the main action of the play, for among other things it is really the epitaph of his own defeat. There is no excitement about the Battle of Shrewsbury, for the result has really been settled by the Prince's decision; but it allows Falstaff to come to life again and to acquire a bogus military reputation, which will be an important motive of the second part. In spite of his choice the Prince still finds Falstaff entertaining and backs up his lying claim to have killed Hotspur. He would have perceived, as the spectator should, how the Battle of Shrewsbury reversed the episode of Gadshill. At Gadshill the Prince deprived Falstaff of the money he had stolen from the travellers; at Shrewsbury Falstaff deprived the Prince of the honour of which he had spoiled Hotspur.

In the second part the military theme of rebellion is continued, but the Prince resigns his share in it to his brother John. He has proved his worth in chivalry; he must now prove it in civil life. As in the first part he begins with appearances against him. He has indulged his inclination to vanity by providing Falstaff with a page, and he has applied military methods to civil life (as well as indulging his passions) by striking the Lord Chief Justice. But we learn this by hearsay only: as he draws nearer to the throne the Prince must be less openly given to mischief. In compensation, the opposing principles between which he has to choose are brought face to face, as they never were in the first part. Thus there are two scenes of sparring between Falstaff and the Lord Chief Justice. During the first of these we learn that the Justice has scored a point by having advised the king to post Falstaff to John of Lancaster's army, thus separating him from the Prince. In the middle portion of the play the Morality theme is kept in suspense, while other important business is transacted. The action broadens to include many phases of English life; Falstaff indulges in adventures that have nothing to do with the Prince; the political theme of Henry IV's many troubles draws to a close. Shakespeare naturally reassures us that the main action is only in suspense: for instance in the tavern scene with Falstaff and Doll Tearsheet the Prince recollects his duties when Peto enters with the news that the king is back at Westminster awaiting news of the Yorkshire rebels. The crisis comes just before the king's death, when the Prince persuades his father that he took the crown from his father's bedside in error, not out of indecent haste to begin a riotous reign. We are persuaded too and know that he will accept the rule of the Lord Chief Justice, who committed him to prison, and reject his old companions. Shakespeare knits the end closely not only to the beginning of Part Two but to the whole play. For instance, Falstaff recalls his opposition to his chief enemy and hence the Morality pattern by his last words as he leaves Gloucestershire to salute the new king: "Woe to my Lord Chief Justice." But it is Henry V's words, as he rejects Falstaff, that have the function of gathering the themes together. Henry does not merely preach at Falstaff: every unkind thing he says and every piece of moral advice he gives echo words spoken to or by Falstaff. "Fall to thy prayers" says Henry; and we should think of his earlier words to Falstaff: "I see a good amendment of life in thee, from praying to purse-taking" spoken in the second scene of Part One, and "Say thy prayers and farewell" spoken in a very different tone before the Battle of Shrewsbury. When Henry says

How ill white hairs become a fool and jester,

we should remember (as Falstaff must have remembered) the Chief Justice's words, "There is not a white hair on your face but should have his effect of gravity." And when Henry speaks of the grave gaping for him, we should remember Doll's remark to Falstaff about "patching up thine old body for heaven" and Falstaff's reply of "Peace, good Doll! do not speak like a death's-head; do not bid me remember mine end." These echoes do not make Henry V's speech any kinder but they give it a great deal of point.

The final ratification, through justice administered and chivalric action, of the Prince's two choices is the theme of the next play.

But though *Henry IV* is built on the Morality pattern it is quite without the mental conflict that often marks that pattern, as in *Doctor Faustus*. The action begins at its very latest phase as in *Samson Agonistes* or the *Tempest*. The Prince, though the constant victim of psychological strain, has made up his mind from the start, and any twinges of conscience he feels at his delay in putting his resolutions into action are minor affairs. And unlike Samson he is fully aware that he has made up his mind and is quite spared Samson's pangs of doubt concerning the final issue. In other words there is not the smallest element of tragedy in the main action. When we recollect how powerfully Shakespeare had pictured mental conflict in the Bastard Falconbridge we must conclude that he kept off the tragic because he wished to do so, not because he was incapable of dealing with it at this stage of his development. The above analogy with so superficially different a play as the *Tempest* is strange. Yet it can be extended. Prospero is like the Prince in having already chosen: between reason and passion, forgiveness and revenge. And both plays gain their effect by an unanalysable unity obtained through the subtlest blending of different strains.

Now the Morality pattern of *Henry IV* will have mainly a formal or historical interest, if its hero is an insignificant figure. Of what use thrusting the Prince into the centre, if all the time we look to left and right at Falstaff and Hotspur? The Prince as a character has failed to please greatly, because he appeals less to softer sentiment than Hotspur or Antony, while his imputed

Machiavellianism is quite without the glamour of the same quality in an out-and-out villain like Richard III. Yet I believe that
current opinion is wrong and that he can hold his own with any
character in *Henry IV*. Dover Wilson in his *Fortunes of Falstaff* deserves gratitude for having helped to redress the balance between
the Prince and Falstaff; but as I do not see the Prince altogether as
he does, I will give my version of him.

The Prince as depicted in *Henry IV* (and what follows has no
reference whatever to Henry V in the play which goes by that
name) is a man of large powers, Olympian loftiness, and high
sophistication, who has acquired a thorough knowledge of
human nature both in himself and in others. He is Shakespeare's
studied picture of the kingly type: a picture to which his many
previous versions of the imperfect kingly type lead up: the fulfilment of years of thought and of experiment. Shakespeare sets
forth his character with great elaboration, using both direct description and self-revelation through act and word. Though all
the subtlety is confined to the second, there is no important
discrepancy between the two versions. And first for the Prince's
character as described from without.

At the end of the first scene in which he appears the Prince
assumes the function of chorus to comment on himself: in the
soliloquy beginning "I know you all." Here he pronounces his
knowledge of his present companions and of what they are worth
and the studied deliberateness of his present conduct. For his
kingly style there is Vernon's description of him to Hotspur,

> As full of spirit as the month of May,
> And gorgeous as the sun at midsummer,

and of the godlike ease "like feather'd Mercury" with which he
vaults fully armed onto his horse. His father recognises the comprehensiveness of his mind and passions, when, late in the second
part of the play (IV. 4), he exhorts his son Thomas of Clarence to
cherish his place in the Prince's affections so that he may "effect
offices of mediation" between the Prince's "greatness" and his
other brothers:

> For he is gracious, if he be observ'd.
> He hath a tear for pity, and a hand
> Open as day for melting charity.

> Yet notwithstanding, being incens'd, he's flint,
> As humorous as winter and as sudden
> As flaws congealed in the spring of day.
> His temper, therefore, must be well observ'd.
> Chide him for faults and do it reverently,
> When you perceive his blood inclin'd to mirth;
> But, being moody, give him line and scope,
> Till that his passions, like a whale on ground,
> Confound themselves with working.

But the king is pessimistic. Through the very abundance of his nature the Prince is as subject to excessive evil as to excessive good—

> Most subject is the fattest soil to weeds—

and he thinks the signs are that evil will prevail. But Warwick disagrees, arguing for the power of the Prince's deliberate and sophisticated nature and his appetite for knowledge:

> The prince but studies his companions
> Like a strange tongue, wherein, to gain the language,
> 'Tis needful that the most immodest word
> Be look'd upon and learn'd; which once attain'd,
> Your highness knows, comes to no further use
> But to be known and hated. So, like gross terms,
> The prince will in the perfectness of time
> Cast off his followers; and their memory
> Shall as a pattern or a measure live,
> By which his grace must mete the lives of others,
> Turning past evils to advantages.

Something indeed has to be allowed for in all these testimonies. The Prince in his choric self-comment is concerned first of all with justifying to an Elizabethan audience this apparent degradation of royalty: hence the powerful emphasis on the rich compensation for such degradation—

> My reformation, glittering o'er my fault,
> Shall show more goodly and attract more eyes
> Than that which hath no foil to set it off.

Henry not only describes his son but gives the general version of the princely nature, as can be seen by comparing his words with Belarius's description of the two princes in *Cymbeline*:

Thou divine Nature, how thyself thou blazon'st
In these two princely boys. They are as gentle
As zephyrs, blowing below the violet
Not wagging his sweet head; and yet as rough,
Their royal blood enchaf'd, as the rud'st wind
That by the top doth take the mountain pine
And make him stoop to the vale.

Warwick is preparing for the rejection of Falstaff as well as describing the Prince's character. But, for all these reservations, the speakers do combine to testify to the comprehensiveness of the Prince's mind and the deliberateness of his actions.

External testimony, however, is of small account compared with what is revealed by action and speech; and we must now consider what sort of person the Prince shows himself. This means speaking of his relations to some of the other characters, principally Falstaff. Those who cannot stomach the rejection of Falstaff assume that in some ways the Prince acted dishonestly, that he made a friend of Falstaff, thus deceiving him, that he got all he could out of him and then repudiated the debt. They are wrong. The Prince is aloof and Olympian from the start and never treats Falstaff any better than his dog, with whom he condescends once in a way to have a game. It is not the Prince who deceives, it is Falstaff who deceives himself by wishful thinking. The most the Prince does is not to take drastic measures to disabuse Falstaff; doing no more than repeat the unkind truths he has never spared telling. His first speech to Falstaff ("Thou art so fat-witted . . .") is, as well as much else, a cool statement of what he thinks of him. And the epithet "fat-witted," so plainly the very opposite of the truth in most of its application, is brutally true of Falstaff's capacity for self-deceit. The Prince has a mind far too capacious not to see Falstaff's limitations. In the same scene he plays with him (and with a coolness in full accord with the rejection), when he refers to the gallows. Falstaff dislikes the subject, but the Prince will not let him off. And when later Falstaff tries to attach the Prince to him with "I would to God thou and I knew where a commodity of good names were to be bought," he gets not the slightest encouragement. The Prince just watches and tells the truth. And not in this place alone: it is his habit. He also relishes the ironic act of telling the truth in the assurance that he will thereby deceive: indeed, to such an extent that he once takes big risks and says things which if believed he would have been far too proud to utter. I refer to the episode in the second part (II. 2, at the beginning). This tells us so much of the Prince that it requires close comment.

To understand this scene, we must remember that the Prince has not appeared since the Battle of Shrewsbury, but that he has since been reported to have struck the Lord Chief Justice: the burden of continued chivalrous behaviour at the court has been too great. Thus when he begins "Before God, I am exceeding weary," we naturally conclude that it is of court affairs that he is tired. Poins, with characteristic simplicity, thinks that the Prince's tiredness is but physical and answers with (for him) considerable brightness,

> Is't come to that? I had thought weariness durst not have attached one of so high blood.

The Prince at once begins telling the truth about himself which he knows Poins will fail to understand or believe:

> Faith, it does me; though it discolours the complexion of my greatness to acknowledge it.

In other words, he does find court affairs exhausting; but he is genuinely ashamed to have to admit it. Then he adds,

> Doth it not show vilely in me to desire small beer?

meaning by "small beer" such unexacting company as Poins. Poins misunderstands again, thinking the Prince is talking of the actual liquor, and answers again with (for him) considerable brightness,

> Why, a prince should not be so loosely studied as to remember so weak a composition.

Misunderstood, the Prince is encouraged to be both more confidential about himself and to tell Poins just what he thinks of him.

> Belike then my appetite was not princely got: for, by my troth, I do now remember the poor creature, small beer. But indeed these humble considerations make me out of love with my greatness. What a disgrace is it to me to remember thy name! or to know thy face to-morrow! or to take note how many pair of silk stockings thou hast, viz. these, and

> those that were thy peach-coloured ones! or to bear the
> inventory of thy shirts, as, one for superfluity and another
> for use!

By which the Prince means that he does indeed lack the taste for
royal duties and that it is much more diverting to study human
nature in the shape of that small beer, Poins. And he goes on to
Poins's habits of life, and his illegitimate children. Poins, simple-
mindedly supposing that the Prince's weariness with his duties
has no more depth than his own easy life, asks how many good
young princes would talk so idly when their fathers were "so sick
as yours at this time is." This is a new turn to the conversation
and it gives the Prince an opportunity for confidences he can
count on Poins not to believe or understand:

> *Prince.* Shall I tell thee one thing, Poins?
> *Poins.* Yes, faith; and let it be an excellent good thing.
> *Prince.* It shall serve among wits of no higher breeding than
>   thine.

By this the Prince means that he is willing to say what he is about
to say to people as thick-witted as Poins. Poins, nettled at the
accusation, protests and claims that he can cope with whatever
the Prince has to tell him. Whereupon the Prince unfolds to him
without reserve what he feels about his father. He *is* grieved for
him, but, having acquired a bad reputation, any show of grief
would be interpreted by the ordinary person as sheer hypocrisy.
And so saying he turns on Poins and asks if he is not right on this
point of public opinion.

> *Prince.* What wouldst thou think of me, if I should weep?
> *Poins.* I would think thee a most princely hypocrite.

Delighted that Poins has not believed his confession of grief, the
Prince continues:

> It would be every man's thought; and thou art a blessed
> fellow to think as every man thinks. Never a man's thought
> in the world keeps the road-way better than thine. Every
> man would think me an hypocrite indeed.

He is at once contemptuous of Poins's perception—Poins who had
enjoyed his company and who had not the excuse of the general

public for knowing nothing of his mind—fascinated at the display
of human nature, and relieved at having opened his mind even to
some one whom in so doing he completely bewildered.

So much for the Prince's ironic detachment: the characteristic
and most attractive side of his deliberate way of acting. His
comprehensive nature comes out most brilliantly in an episode
that is usually taken as trivial if not positively offensive: the
foolery of the Prince and Poins with Francis and the other drawers in the Eastcheap tavern, before Falstaff arrives from the
Gadshill robbery. It is a difficult scene, for the editors have not
been able to find any meaning in it that at all enriches the play,
and the sense of one or two sentences remains obscure. But the
general drift should be clear from the Prince's satirical account of
Hotspur killing "six or seven dozen of Scots at a breakfast" at the
end of the incident and from his own reference to "honour" at the
beginning. After what Hotspur has said already of honour earlier
in the play it is impossible that there should not be a connection
between Hotspur and honour here. The Prince has been drinking
and making friends with the drawers of the tavern. He has won
their hearts and learnt their ways:

> To conclude, I am so good a proficient in one quarter of an
> hour that I can drink with any tinker in his own language
> during my life. I tell thee, Ned, thou hast lost much honour
> that thou wert not with me in this action.

In other words the Prince has won a signal victory and great
honour in having mastered this lesson so quickly. It was Johnson
who perceived that the Prince's satire on Hotspur is logically
connected with what goes before and not a mere unmotivated
outburst. But later critics have not given due weight to that
perception. Poins and the Prince have just had their game with
Francis, Poins being as ignorant of the Prince's true meaning as he
was in the scene from the second part just examined.

> *Poins.* But hark ye; what cunning match have you made with
>   this jest of the drawer? Come, what's the issue?
> *Prince.* I am now of all humours that have showed themselves
>   since the old days of goodman Adam to the pupil age of this
>   present twelve o'clock at midnight.

Re-enter Francis.

> What's o'clock, Francis?
> *Fran.* Anon, anon, sir. *Exit.*
> *Prince.* That ever this fellow should have fewer words than a
> parrot, and yet the son of a woman! His industry is upstairs
> and downstairs; his eloquence the parcel of a reckoning. I
> am not yet of Percy's mind, the Hotspur of the north . . .

Johnson saw that the reference to Hotspur connects with the
Prince's declaration that he is "now of all humours," the entry and
exit of Francis with the Prince's comment being a mere interrup-
tion. The Prince's wealth of humours is contrasted with the single
humour of Hotspur. Once again the Prince says just what he
means but in words that will bear another meaning. On the face
of it his words mean that he is greatly excited, being ruled
simultaneously by every human motive that exists; but he also
means that having learnt to understand the drawers he has mastered all the springs of human conduct, he has even then completed his education in the knowledge of men. We can now
understand his earlier talk of honour: he has won a more difficult
action than any of Hotspur's crudely repetitive slaughters of
Scotsmen. Bearing this in mind, we may perceive things at the
beginning of the episode which can easily be passed over. To
Poins's question where he has been the Prince answers:

> With three or four loggerheads among three or four score
> hogsheads. I have sounded the very base string of humility.
> Sirrah, I am sworn brother to a leash of drawers and can call
> them all by their christen names, as Tom Dick and Francis.
> They take it already upon their salvation that though I be
> but Prince of Wales yet I am the king of courtesy.

When the Prince speaks of sounding the base string of humility
he uses a musical metaphor. He means in one sense that he has
touched the bottom limit of condescension. But he means something more: he is the bow that has got a response from the lowest
string of the instrument, namely the drawers. We are to think
that he has sounded all the other human strings already: he has
now completed the range of the human gamut; he is of all
humours since Adam. Now the idea of the world as a complicated

musical harmony was a cosmic commonplace, which would evoke all the other such commonplaces. The drawers are not only the base or lowest string of the instrument; they are the lowest link in the human portion of the chain of being and as such nearest the beasts. And that is why the Prince directly after compares them to dogs by calling them "a leash of drawers." At the risk of being accused of being over ingenious I will add that "sounding" and "base" suggest plumbing the depths of the sea as well as playing on a stringed instrument and that there is a reference to Hotspur's boast earlier in the play that he will

> dive into the bottom of the deep,
> Where fathom-line could never touch the ground,
> And pluck up drowned honour by the locks.

It is not for nothing too that the Prince says the drawers think him the king of courtesy. As I shall point out later this is precisely what Shakespeare makes him, the *cortegiano*, the fully developed man, contrasted with Hotspur, the provincial, engaging in some ways, but with a one-track mind.

There remains a puzzle. Why should the Prince, after Francis has given him his heart, and, symbol of it, his pennyworth of sugar (which he wished he could make two) join with Poins to put him through a brutal piece of horseplay? Is not Masefield justified in his bitter attack on the Prince for such brutality? The answer is first that the Prince wanted to see just how little brain Francis had and puts him to the test, and secondly that in matters of humanity we must not judge Shakespeare by standards of twentieth century humanitarianism. In an age when men watched the antics of the mad and the sufferings of animals for sport we must not look for too much. Further we must remember the principle of degree. At the siege of La Rochelle costly dishes were carried into the town under a flag of truce to a Catholic hostage of noble birth, through a population dying of starvation; and such discrimination between classes was taken for granted. It may look strange when Shakespeare in one play represents the beautiful tact of Theseus in dealing with Bottom and his fellows, and in another allows his king of courtesy to be ungrateful and brutal to Francis. But Francis was a base string; Bottom a tenor string, a man in his way of intelligence and substance. Francis could not expect the same treatment. The subhuman element in the population must have been considerable in Shakespeare's day; that it should be treated almost like beasts was taken for granted.

From what I have said so far about the Prince it turns out that far from being a mere dissolute lout awaiting a miraculous transformation he is from the very first a commanding character, deliberate in act and in judgement, versed in every phase of human nature. But he is more than that. When the drawers think him the "king of courtesy" they know him better than his enemy Hotspur and even his own father do. And when Shakespeare put the phrase in their mouths he had in mind the abstract Renaissance conception of the perfect ruler. I will discuss how this conception enters and affects the play.

First, it is not for nothing that Elyot's *Governor* provided Shakespeare with the episode of the Prince being committed by the Lord Chief Justice. True, Shakespeare modified the episode to suit his special dramatic ends; but he must have known that Elyot held up Prince Hal, even during his father's lifetime, as one who was able to subordinate his violent passions to the sway of his reason. If Shakespeare got an episode from the *Governor* concerning his hero, it is likely that in shaping him he would have heeded the class of courtly manual to which the *Governor* belongs and of which Castiglione's *Cortegiano* was the most famous example. Then, there are passages in *Euphues* which are apt enough to the Prince's case. I do not mean that Shakespeare used them directly, but that, occurring in a conventional didactic book on the education of a typical gentleman, they exemplify the assumptions Shakespeare would have been forced to go on if he meant to picture his perfect prince in accord with contemporary expectation. Here is Euphues's picture of himself uncorrupted by the vices of Naples, as the Prince was uncorrupted by the vices of London:

> Suppose that Naples is a cankered storehouse of all strife, a common stews for all strumpets, the sink of shame, and the very nurse of all sin: shall it therefore follow of necessity that all that are wooed of love should be wedded to lust; will you conclude as it were *ex consequenti* that whosoever arriveth here shall be enticed to folly and, being enticed, of force shall be entangled? No, no, it is the disposition of the thought that altereth the nature of the thing. The sun shineth upon

the dunghill and is not corrupted; the diamond lieth in the fire and is not consumed; the crystal toucheth the toad and is not poisoned; the bird Trochilus liveth by the mouth of the crocodile and is not spoiled; a perfect wit is never bewitched with lewdness neither enticed by lasciviousness.

And here is Lyly's version, put into the mouth of old Fidus, of the central Renaissance doctrine of the all-round man:

And I am not so precise but that I esteem it expedient in feats of arms and activity to employ the body as in study to waste the mind: yet so should the one be tempered with the other as it might seem as great a shame to be valiant and courtly without learning as to be studious and bookish without valour.

Now the Prince in addition to skill in arms has a brilliant and well-trained intellect, which shows itself in his talk with Falstaff, of whose extraordinary character the recollection of a good education is an important part. But the Prince makes not the slightest parade of his intelligence, being apparently negligent of it. And this leads to another mark of the courtier. This is the quality of *sprezzatura* (which Hoby translates by *disgracing* or *recklessness* and to which *nonchalance* may be a modern approximation) considered by Castiglione to be the crown of courtliness, and the opposite of the vice of *affettazione* (translated by Hoby *curiousness*):

Trovo una regula universalissima la qual mi par valer circa questo in tutte le cose umane che si facciano o dicano più che alcuna altra: e ciò è fuggir quanto più si po, e come un asperissimo e periculoso scoglio, la affettazione; e, per dir forse una nova parola, usar in ogni cosa una certa sprezzatura, che nasconda l'arte e dimonstri, ciò che si fa e dice venir fatto senza fatica e quasi senza pensarvi.[1]

Sprezzatura is a genuine ethical quality of the Aristotelian type: the mean between a heavy and affected carefulness and positive neglect. It is in the gift of this crowning courtly quality that the Prince so greatly excels Hotspur. He takes the Percies' rebellion with apparent lightness yet he is actually the hero in it. He gets news of it through Falstaff in the tavern scene after the Gadshill robbery. "There's villainous news abroad" says Falstaff, and goes on to name the different rebels. The Prince, quite unmoved apparently, makes a few idle remarks about Douglas and then goes on to the game of letting Falstaff act his father. Yet at the very end of the scene he lets out his true sentiments with the casual remark, "I'll to the court in the morning." Alone with his father at the court, he is forced by his father's reproaches out of his nonchalance into declaring the full seriousness of his intentions. But this does not stop him in the next scene from relapsing into his apparent frivolity:

> *Enter the* Prince *and* Peto *marching, and* Falstaff *meets them playing on his truncheon like a fife.*

This may be too frivolous for the Italianate courtliness of Castiglione, but Vernon's description of the Prince vaulting with effortless ease onto his horse (quoted in *Shakespeare's History Plays*, p. 257) is the perfect rendering of it. Finally there is the Prince's nonchalant surrender to Falstaff of his claim to have killed Hotspur and his good-humoured but sarcastic willingness to back up Falstaff's lie:

> For my part, if a lie may do thee grace,
> I'll gild it with the happiest terms I have.

Hotspur both offends against the principle of *sprezzatura* in his blatant acclamation of honour, and is satirised by the Prince for the extreme clumsiness of his would-be nonchalance in the very scene where the Prince takes the news of the rebellion so coolly.

> *Prince.* I am not yet of Percy's mind, the Hotspur of the north; he that kills me some six or seven dozen of Scots at a breakfast, washes his hands, and says to his wife 'Fie upon this quiet life! I want work.' 'O my sweet Harry,' says she, 'how many hast thou killed to-day?' 'Give my roan horse a drench,' says he; and answers 'Some fourteen,' an hour after; 'a trifle, a trifle.'

The Prince here is the complete, sophisticated, internationally educated courtier ridiculing the provincial boorishness of Percy, the Hotspur of the north, much like a character in Restoration Comedy ridiculing the country bumpkin.

This is not to say that Hotspur is not a most engaging barbarian; adorable in the openness and simplicity of his excesses, infectious in his vitality, and well-flavoured by his country humour. The child in him goes straight to the female heart; and when his wife loves him to distraction for all his waywardness, we are completely convinced.

NOTE

1. I find one rule that is most general, which in this part, me think, taketh place in all things belonging to a man in word or deed, above all other. And that is to eschew as much as a man may, and as a sharp and dangerous rock, too much curiousness and (to speak a new word) to use in everything a certain disgracing to cover art withal and seem whatsoever he doth and saith to do it without pain and, as it were, not minding it. (Hoby's translation.)

W. H. Auden

The Prince's Dog (1948)

Whoever takes up the sword shall perish by the sword. And whoever does not take up the sword (or lets it drop) shall perish on the cross.

SIMONE WEIL

It has been observed that critics who write about Shakespeare reveal more about themselves than about Shakespeare, but perhaps that is the great value of drama of the Shakespearian kind, namely, that whatever he may see taking place on stage, its final effect upon each spectator is a self-revelation.

Shakespeare holds the position in our literature of Top Bard, but this deserved priority has one unfortunate consequence; we generally make our first acquaintance with his plays, not in the theatre, but in the classroom or study, so that, when we do attend a performance, we have lost that naïve openness to surprise which is the proper frame of mind in which to witness any drama. The experience of reading a play and the experience of watching it performed are never identical, but in the case of *Henry IV* the difference between the two is particularly great.

At a performance, my immediate reaction is to wonder what Falstaff is doing in this play at all. At the end of *Richard II*, we were told that the Heir Apparent has taken up with a dissolute crew of "unrestrained loose companions." What sort of bad company would one expect to find Prince Hal keeping when the curtain rises on *Henry IV*? Surely, one could expect to see him surrounded by daring, rather sinister juvenile delinquents and beautiful gold-

From *The Dyer's Hand and Other Essays*, by W. H. Auden. Reprinted by permission of Random House, Inc.

157

digging whores. But whom do we meet in the Boar's Head? A fat, cowardly tosspot, old enough to be his father, two down-at-heel hangers-on, a slatternly hostess and only one whore, who is not in her earliest youth either; all of them seedy, and, by any worldly standards, including those of the criminal classes, all of them *failures.* Surely, one thinks, an Heir Apparent, sowing his wild oats, could have picked himself a more exciting crew than that. As the play proceeds, our surprise is replaced by another kind of puzzle, for the better we come to know Falstaff, the clearer it becomes that the world of historical reality which a Chronicle Play claims to imitate is not a world which he can inhabit.

If it really was Queen Elizabeth who demanded to see Falstaff in a comedy, then she showed herself a very perceptive critic. But even in *The Merry Wives of Windsor*, Falstaff has not and could not have found his true home because Shakespeare was only a poet. For that he was to wait nearly two hundred years till Verdi wrote his last opera. Falstaff is not the only case of a character whose true home is the world of music; others are Tristan, Isolde, and Don Giovanni.

Though they each call for a different kind of music, Tristan, Don Giovanni, and Falstaff have certain traits in common. They do not belong to the temporal world of change. One cannot imagine any of them as babies, for a Tristan who is not in love, a Don Giovanni who has no name on his list, a Falstaff who is not old and fat, are inconceivable. When Falstaff says, "When I was about their years, Hal, I was not an eagle's talent in the waist; I could have crept into an alderman's thumb-ring"—we take it as a typical Falstaffian fib, but we believe him when he says, "I was born about three in the afternoon, with a white head and something of a round belly."

Time, for Tristan, is a single moment stretched out tighter and tighter until it snaps. Time, for Don Giovanni, is an infinite arithmetical series of unrelated moments which has no beginning and would have no end if Heaven did not intervene and cut it short. For Falstaff, time does not exist, since he belongs to the *opera buffa* world of play and mock action governed not by will or desire, but by innocent wish, a world where no one can suffer because everything he says and does is only a pretense.

Thus, while we must see Tristan die in Isolde's arms and we must see Don Giovanni sink into the earth, because being doomed to die and to go to hell are essential to their beings, we cannot see Falstaff die on stage because, if we did, we should not believe it; we should know that, as at the battle of Shrewsbury, he was only shamming. I am not even quite sure that we believe it when we are told of his death in *Henry V*; I think we accept it, as we accept the death of Sherlock Holmes, as his creator's way of saying, "I am getting tired of this character"; we feel sure that, if the public pleads with him strongly enough, Shakespeare will find some way to bring him to life again. The only kind of funeral music we can associate with him is the mock-requiem in the last act of Verdi's opera.

Domine fallo casto

                      Ma salvaggi l'addomine

Domine fallo guasto.

                      Ma salvaggi l'addomine.

There are at least two places in the play where the incongruity of the *opera buffa* world with the historical world is too much, even for Shakespeare, and a patently false note is struck. The first occurs when, on the battlefield of Shrewsbury, Falstaff thrusts his sword into Hotspur's corpse. Within his own world, Falstaff could stab a corpse because, there, all battles are mock battles, all corpses straw dummies; but we, the audience, are too conscious that this battle has been a real battle and that this corpse is the real dead body of a brave and noble young man. Pistol could do it, because Pistol is a contemptible character, but Falstaff cannot; that is to say, there is no way in which an actor can play the scene convincingly. So, too, with the surrender of Colevile to Falstaff in the Second Part. In his conversation, first with Colevile and then with Prince John, Falstaff talks exactly as we expect—to him, the whole business is a huge joke. But then he is present during a scene when we are shown that it is no joke at all. How is any actor to behave and speak his lines during the following?

> *Lancaster.* Is thy name Colevile?
> *Colevile.* It is, my lord.
> *Lancaster.* A famous rebel art thou, Colevile.
> *Falstaff.* And a famous true subject took him.
> *Colevile.* I am, my lord, but as my betters are,
>   That led me hither. Had they been ruled by me,
>   You would have won them dearer than you have.

> *Falstaff.* I know not how they sold themselves: but thou, like
> a kind fellow, gavest thyself away gratis; and I thank thee
> for thee.
> *Lancaster.* Now have you left pursuit?
> *Westmoreland.* Retreat is made and execution stay'd.
> *Lancaster.* Send Colevile, with his confederates,
> To York, to present execution.

The Falstaffian frivolity and the headsman's axe cannot so directly confront each other.

Reading *Henry IV*, we can easily give our full attention to the historical-political scenes, but, when watching a performance, attention is distracted by our eagerness to see Falstaff reappear. Short of cutting him out of the play altogether, no producer can prevent him stealing the show. From an actor's point of view, the role of Falstaff has the enormous advantage that he has only to think of one thing—playing to an audience. Since he lives in an eternal present and the historical world does not exist for him, there is no difference for Falstaff between those on stage and those out front, and if the actor were to appear in one scene in Elizabethan costume and in the next in top hat and morning coat, no one would be bewildered. The speech of all the other characters is, like our own, conditioned by two factors, the external situation with its questions, answers, and commands, and the inner need of each character to disclose himself to others. But Falstaff's speech has only one cause, his absolute insistence, at every moment and at all costs, upon disclosing himself. Half his lines could be moved from one speech to another without our noticing, for nearly everything he says is a variant upon one theme—"I am that I am."

Moreover, Shakespeare has so written his part that it cannot be played unsympathetically. A good actor can make us admire Prince Hal, but he cannot hope to make us like him as much as even a second-rate actor will make us like Falstaff. Sober reflection in the study may tell us that Falstaff is not, after all, a very admirable person, but Falstaff on the stage gives us no time for sober reflection. When Hal or the Chief Justice or any others indicate that they are not bewitched by Falstaff, reason might tell us that they are in the right, but we ourselves are already bewitched, so that their disenchantment seems out of place, like the presence of teetotalers at a drunken party.

Suppose, then, that a producer were to cut the Falstaff scenes altogether, what would *Henry IV* become? The middle section of a political trilogy which could be entitled *Looking for the Doctor.* The body politic of England catches an infection from its family physician. An able but unqualified practitioner throws him out of the sickroom and takes over. The patient's temperature continues to rise. But then, to everybody's amazement, the son of the unqualified practitioner whom, though he has taken his degree, everyone hàs hitherto believed to be a hopeless invalid, effects a cure. Not only is the patient restored to health but also, at the doctor's orders, takes another body politic, France, to wife.

The theme of this trilogy is, that is to say, the question: What combination of qualities is needed in the Ruler whose function is the establishment and maintenance of Temporal Justice? According to Shakespeare, the ideal Ruler must satisfy five conditions. 1) He must know what is just and what is unjust. 2) He must himself be just. 3) He must be strong enough to compel those who would like to be unjust to behave justly. 4) He must have the capacity both by nature and by art of making others loyal to his person. 5) He must be the legitimate ruler by whatever standard legitimacy is determined in the society to which he belongs.

Richard II fails to satisfy the first four of these. He does not know what Justice is, for he follows the advice of foolish flatterers. He is himself unjust, for he spends the money he obtains by taxing the Commons and fining the Nobility, not on defending England against her foes, but upon maintaining a lavish and frivolous court, so that, when he really does need money for a patriotic purpose, the war with Ireland, his exchequer is empty and in desperation he commits a gross act of injustice by confiscating Bolingbroke's estates.

It would seem that at one time he had been popular but he has now lost his popularity, partly on account of his actions, but also because he lacks the art of winning hearts. According to his successor, he had made the mistake of being overfamiliar—the ruler should not let himself be seen too often as "human"—and in addition, he is not by nature the athletic, physically brave warrior who is the type most admired by the feudal society he is called upon to rule.

In consequence, Richard II is a weak ruler who cannot keep the great nobles in order or even command the loyalty of his soldiers, and weakness in a ruler is the worst defect of all. A cruel, even an unjust king, who is strong, is preferable to the most saintly weakling because most men will behave unjustly if they discover that they can with impunity; tyranny, the injustice of one, is less unjust than anarchy, the injustice of many.

But there remains the fifth condition: whatever his defects, Richard II is the legitimate King of England. Since all men are mortal, and many men are ambitious, unless there is some impersonal principle by which, when the present ruler dies, the choice of his successor can be decided, there will be a risk of civil war in every generation. It is better to endure the injustice of the legitimate ruler, who will die anyway sooner or later, than allow a usurper to take his place by force.

As a potential ruler, Bolingbroke possesses many of the right qualities. He is a strong man, he knows how to make himself popular, and he would like to be just. We never hear, even from the rebels, of any specific actions of Henry IV which are unjust, only of suspicions which may be just or unjust. But in yielding to the temptation, when the opportunity unexpectedly offers itself, of deposing his lawful sovereign, he commits an act of injustice for which he and his kingdom have to pay a heavy price. Because of it, though he is strong enough to crush rebellion, he is not strong or popular enough to prevent rebellion breaking out.

Once Richard has been murdered, however, the rule of Henry IV is better than any alternative. Though, legally, Mortimer may have a good or better right to the throne, the scene at Bangor between Hotspur, Worcester, Mortimer, and Glendower, convinces us that Henry's victory is a victory for justice since we learn that the rebels have no concern for the interests of the Kingdom, only for their own. Their plan, if they succeed, is to carve up England into three petty states. Henry may wish that Hotspur, not Hal, were his heir, because Hotspur is a brave warrior ready to risk his life in battle against England's foes, while Hal appears to be dissipated and frivolous, but we know better. Hotspur is indeed brave, but that is all. A man who can say

> I'll give thrice so much land
> To any well-deserving friend;
> But in the way of bargain, mark ye me,
> I'll cavil on the ninth part of a hair

is clearly unfitted to be a ruler because his actions are based, not on justice, but on personal whim. Moreover, he is not interested in political power; all he desires is military glory.

Thirdly, there is Prince Hal, Henry V-to-be. To everyone except himself, he seems at first to be another Richard, unjust, lacking in self-control but, unfortunately, the legitimate heir. By the time the curtain falls on *Henry V*, however, he is recognized by all to be the Ideal Ruler. Like his father in his youth, he is brave and personable. In addition, he is a much cleverer politician. While his father was an improviser, he is a master of the art of timing. His first soliloquy reveals him as a person who always sees several steps ahead and has the patience to wait, even though waiting means temporary misunderstanding and unpopularity, until the right moment for action comes; he will never, if he can help it, leave anything to chance. Last but not least, he is blessed by luck. His father had foreseen that internal dissension could only be cured if some common cause could be found which would unite all parties but he was too old and ill, the internal quarrels too violent. But when Hal succeeds as Henry V, most of his enemies are dead or powerless—Cambridge and Scroop have no armies at their back—and his possible right to the throne of France provides the common cause required to unite both the nobles and the commons, and gives him the opportunity, at Agincourt, to show his true mettle.

One of Falstaff's dramatic functions is to be the means by which Hal is revealed to be the Just Ruler, not the dissolute and frivolous young man everybody has thought him; but, so far as the audience is concerned, Falstaff has fulfilled his function by Act III, Scene 2 of the First Part, when the King entrusts Hal with a military command. Up to this point the Falstaff scenes have kept us in suspense. In Act I, Scene 2, we hear Hal promise

> I'll so offend to make offense a skill,
> Redeeming time when men least think I will.

But then we watch the rebellion being prepared while he does nothing but amuse himself with Falstaff, so that we are left wondering whether he meant what he said or was only play acting. But from the moment he engages in the political action of the play, we have no doubts whatsoever as to his ambition, capacity, and ultimate triumph for, however often henceforward we may see him with Falstaff, it is never at a time when his advice and arms are needed by the State; he visits the Boar's Head in leisure hours when there is nothing serious for him to do.

For those in the play, the decisive moment of revelation is, of course, his first public act as Henry V, his rejection of Falstaff and company. For his subjects who have not, as we have, watched him with Falstaff, it is necessary to allay their fears that, though they already know him to be brave and capable, he may still be unjust and put his personal friendships before the impartial justice which it is his duty as king to maintain. But we, who have watched his private life, have no such fears. We have long known that his first soliloquy meant what it said, that he has never been under any false illusions about Falstaff or anyone else and that when the right moment comes to reject Falstaff, that is to say, when such a rejection will make the maximum political effect, he will do so without hesitation. Even the magnanimity he shows in granting his old companion a life competence, which so impresses those about him, cannot impress us because, knowing Falstaff as they do not, we know what the effect on him of such a rejection must be, that his heart will be "fracted and corroborate" and no life competence can mend that. It is Hal's company he wants, not a pension from the Civil List.

The essential Falstaff is the Falstaff of *The Merry Wives* and Verdi's opera, the comic hero of the world of play, the unkillable self-sufficient immortal whose verdict on existence is

> *Tutto nel mondo è burla. . . .*
> *Tutti gabbàti. Irridè*
> *L'un l'altro ogni mortal.*
> *Ma ride ben chi ride*
> *La risata final*

In *Henry IV*, however, something has happened to this immortal which draws him out of his proper world into the historical world of suffering and death. He has become capable of serious emotion. He continues to employ the speech of his comic world:

> I have forsworn his company hourly any time this two-and-twenty years, and yet I am bewitched by the rogue's company. If the rascal have not given me medicines to make

me love him, I'll be hanged. It could not be else. I have drunk
medicines.

But the emotion so flippantly expressed could equally well be
expressed thus:

> If my dear love were but the child of state
> It might for Fortune's bastard be unfathered,
> As subject to Time's love or to Time's hate,
> Weeds among weeds, or flowers with flowers
>   gathered.
> No, it was builded far from accident;
> It suffers not in smiling pomp, nor falls
> Under the blow of thralled discontent,
> Whereto th' inviting time and fashion calls.
> It fears not Policy, that heretic
> Which works on leases of short numbered hours,
> But all alone stands hugely politic.

As the play proceeds, we become aware, behind all the fun, of
something tragic. Falstaff loves Hal with an absolute devotion.
"The lovely bully" is the son he has never had, the youth predes-
tined to the success and worldly glory which he will never enjoy.
He believes that his love is returned, that the Prince is indeed his
other self, so he is happy, despite old age and poverty. We,
however, can see that he is living in a fool's paradise, for the
Prince cares no more for him as a person than he would care for
the King's Jester. He finds Falstaff amusing but no more. If we
could warn Falstaff of what he is too blind to see, we might well
say: Beware, before it is too late, of becoming involved with one of
those mortals

> That do not do the thing they most do show,
> Who, moving others, are themselves as stone. . . .

Falstaff's story, in fact, is not unlike one of those folk tales in
which a mermaid falls in love with a mortal prince: the price she
pays for her infatuation is the loss of her immortality without the
compensation of temporal happiness.

Let us now suppose, not only that Falstaff takes no part in the
play, but is also allowed to sit in the audience as a spectator. How
much will he understand of what he sees going on?

He will see a number of Englishmen divided into two parties who finally come to blows. That they should come to blows will in itself be no proof to him that they are enemies because they might, like boxers, have agreed to fight for fun. In Falstaff's world there are two causes of friendship and enmity. My friend may be someone whose appearance and manner I like at this moment, my enemy someone whose appearance and manner I dislike. Thus, he will understand Hotspur's objection to Bolingbroke perfectly well.

> Why, what a candy deal of courtesy
> This fawning greyhound then did proffer me.
> "Look, when his infant fortune came to age,"
> And "gentle Harry Percy" and "kind cousin."
> O the devil take such cozeners.

To Falstaff, "my friend" can also mean he whose wish at this moment coincides with mine, "my enemy" he whose wish contradicts mine. He will see the civil war, therefore, as a clash between Henry and Mortimer who both wish to wear the crown. What will perplex him is any argument as to who has the better right to wear it.

Anger and fear he can understand, because they are immediate emotions, but not nursing a grievance or planning revenge or apprehension, for these presuppose that the future inherits from the past. He will not, therefore, be able to make head or tail of Warwick's speech, "There is a history in all men's lives . . . ," nor any reasons the rebels give for their actions which are based upon anything Bolingbroke did before he became king, nor the reason given by Worcester for concealing the king's peace offer from Hotspur:

> It is impossible, it cannot be
> The King should keep his word in loving us.
> He will suspect us still and find a time
> To punish this offence in other faults.

To *keep his word* is a phrase outside Falstaff's comprehension, for a promise means that at some future moment I might have to refuse to do what I wish, and, in Falstaff's world to wish and to do are synonymous. For the same reason, when, by promising them redress, Prince John tricks the rebels into disbanding their armies and then arrests them, Falstaff will not understand why they and all the audience except himself are shocked.

The first words Shakespeare puts into Falstaff's mouth are, "Now Hal, what time of day is it, lad?" to which the Prince quite rightly replies, "What the devil hast thou to do with the time of day?" In Falstaff's world, every moment is one of infinite possibility when anything can be wished. As a spectator, he will keep hearing the characters use the words *time* and *occasion* in a sense which will stump him.

> What I know
> Is ruminated, plotted, and set down
> And only stays but to behold the face
> Of that occasion that shall bring it on.

> The purpose you undertake is dangerous, the
> time itself unsorted. . . .

> . . . I will resolve to Scotland. There am I
> Till time and vantage crave my company.

Of all the characters in the play, the one he will think he understands best is the least Falstaff-like of them all, Hotspur, for Hotspur, like himself, appears to obey the impulse of the moment and say exactly what he thinks without prudent calculation. Both conceal nothing from others, Falstaff because he has no mask to put on, Hotspur because he has so become his mask that he has no face beneath it. Falstaff says, as it were, "I am I. Whatever I do, however outrageous, is of infinite importance because I do it." Hotspur says: "I am Hotspur, the fearless, the honest, plain-spoken warrior. If I should ever show fear or tell lies, even white ones, I should cease to exist." If Falstaff belonged to the same world as Hotspur, one could call him a liar, but, in his own eyes, he is perfectly truthful, for, to him, fact is subjective fact, "what I am actually feeling and thinking at this moment." To call him a liar is as ridiculous as if, in a play, a character should say, "I am Napoleon," and a member of the audience should cry, "You're not. You're Sir John Gielgud."

In Ibsen's *Peer Gynt*, there is a remarkable scene in which Peer visits the Troll King. At the entertainment given in his honor, animals dance to hideous noises, but Peer behaves to them with perfect manners as if they were beautiful girls and the music ravishing. After it is over, the Troll King asks him: "Now, frankly, tell me what you saw." Peer replies: "What I saw was impossibly ugly"—and then describes the scene as the audience had seen it. The Troll King, who has taken a fancy to him, suggests that Peer would be happier as a troll. All that is needed is a little eye operation, after which he will really see a cow as a beautiful girl. Peer indignantly refuses. He is perfectly willing, he says, to swear that a cow is a girl, but to surrender his humanity so that he can no longer lie, because he cannot distinguish between fact and fiction, that he will never do. By this criterion, neither Falstaff nor Hotspur is quite human, Falstaff because he is pure troll, Hotspur because he is so lacking in imagination that the troll kingdom is invisible to him.

At first, then, Falstaff will believe that Hotspur is one of his own kind, who like himself enjoys putting on an act, but then he will hear Hotspur say words which he cannot comprehend.

> . . . time serves wherein you may redeem
> Your banished honours and restore yourselves
> Into the good thoughts of the world again.

In Falstaff's world, the only value standard is importance, that is to say, all he demands from others is attention, all he fears is being ignored. Whether others applaud or hiss does not matter; what matters is the volume of the hissing or the applause.

Hence, in his soliloquy about honor, his reasoning runs something like this: if the consequences of demanding moral approval from others is dying, it is better to win their disapproval; a dead man has no audience.

Since the Prince is a personal friend, Falstaff is, of course, a King's man who thinks it a shame to be on any side but one, but his loyalty is like that of those who, out of local pride, support one football team rather than another. As a member of the audience, his final comment upon the political action of the play will be the same as he makes from behind the footlights.

> Well, God be thanked for these rebels: they offend none
> but the virtuous. . . .
> A young knave and begging. Is there not employment?
> Doth not the King lack subjects? Do not the rebels need
> soldiers?

Once upon a time we were all Falstaffs: then we became social beings with super-egos. Most of us learn to accept this, but there are some in whom the nostalgia for the state of innocent self-importance is so strong that they refuse to accept adult life and responsibilities and seek some means to become again the Falstaffs they once were. The commonest technique adopted is the bottle, and, curiously enough, the male drinker reveals his intention by developing a drinker's belly.

If one visits a bathing beach, one can observe that men and women grow fat in different ways. A fat woman exaggerates her femininity; her breasts and buttocks enlarge till she comes to look like the Venus of Willendorf. A fat man, on the other hand, looks like a cross between a very young child and a pregnant mother. There have been cultures in which obesity in women was considered the ideal of sexual attraction, but in no culture, so far as I know, has a fat man been considered more attractive than a thin one. If my own weight and experience give me any authority, I would say that fatness in the male is the physical expression of a psychological wish to withdraw from sexual competition and, by combining mother and child in his own person, to become emotionally self-sufficient. The Greeks thought of Narcissus as a slender youth but I think they were wrong. I see him as a middle-aged man with a corporation, for, however ashamed he may be of displaying it in public, in private a man with a belly loves it dearly; it may be an unprepossessing child to look at, but he has borne it all by himself.

> I do walk here before thee like a sow that hath over-whelmed all her litter but one. . . .
> I have a whole school of tongues in this belly of mine, and not a tongue of them all speaks any other word but my name. My womb, my womb undoes me.

Not all fat men are heavy drinkers, but all males who drink heavily become fat. At the same time, the more they drink, the less they eat. "O monstrous! But one halfpenny worth of bread to this intolerable deal of sack!" exclaims Hal on looking at Falstaff's bill, but he cannot have expected anything else. Drunkards die, not from the liquid alcohol they take so much of, but from their refusal to eat solid food, and anyone who had to look after a drunk knows that the only way to get enough nourishment into him is to give him liquid or mashed-up foods, for he will reject any dish that needs chewing. Solid food is to the drunkard a symbolic reminder of the loss of the mother's breast and his ejection from Eden.

> A plague on sighing and grief. It blows a man up like a bladder. . . .

So Falstaff, and popular idiom identifies the kind of griefs which have this fattening effect—eating humble pie, swallowing insults, etc.

In a recent number of *The Paris Review*, Mr. Nicholas Tucci writes:

> The death song of the drunkard—it may go on for thirty years—goes more or less like this. "I was born a god, with the whole world in reach of my hands, lie now defeated in the gutter. Come and listen: hear what the world has done to me."
>
> *In Vino Veritas* is an old saying that has nothing to do with the drunkard's own truth. He has no secrets—that is true—but it is not true that his truth may be found under the skin of his moral reserve or of his sober lies, so that the moment he begins to cross his eyes and pour out his heart, anyone may come in and get his fill of truth. What happens is exactly the opposite. When the drunkard confesses, he makes a careful choice of his pet sins: and these are nonexistent. He may be unable to distinguish a person from a chair, but never an unprofitable lie from a profitable one. How could he see himself as a very significant entity in a huge world of others, when he sees nothing but himself spread over the whole universe. "I am alone" is indeed a true cry, but it should not be taken literally.

The drunk is unlovely to look at, intolerable to listen to, and his self-pity is contemptible. Nevertheless, as not merely a worldly failure but also a willful failure, he is a disturbing image for the sober citizen. His refusal to accept the realities of this world, babyish as it may be, compels us to take another look at this world and reflect upon our motives for accepting it. The drunkard's suffering may be self-inflicted, but it is real suffering and reminds us of all the suffering in this world which we prefer not to think about because, from the moment we accepted this world, we acquired our share of responsibility for everything that happens in it.

When we see Falstaff's gross paunch and red face, we are reminded that the body politic of England is not so healthy, either.

> The Commonwealth is sick of its own choice.
> Their over-greedy love hath surfeited. . . .
> Thou (beastly feeder) art so full of him
> That thou provokest thyself to cast him up.
> So, so, thou common dog, didst thou disgorge
> Thy glutton bosom of the royal Richard. . . .
> Then you perceive the body of our kingdom
> How foul it is: what rank diseases grow,
> And with what danger near the heart of it.

It might be expected that we would be revolted at the sight and turn our eyes with relief and admiration to the Hero Prince. But in fact we aren't and we don't. Whenever Falstaff is on stage, we have no eyes for Hal. If Shakespeare did originally write a part for Falstaff in *Henry V*, it would not have taken pressure from the Cobhams to make him cut it out; his own dramatic instinct would have told him that, if Henry was to be shown in his full glory, the presence of Falstaff would diminish it.

Seeking for an explanation of why Falstaff affects us as he does, I find myself compelled to see *Henry IV* as possessing, in addition to its overt meaning, a parabolic significance. Overtly, Falstaff is a Lord of Misrule; parabolically, he is a comic symbol for the supernatural order of Charity as contrasted with the temporal order of Justice symbolized by Henry of Monmouth.

Such readings are only possible with drama which, like Shakespeare's, is secular, concerned directly, not with the relation of man and God, but with the relations between men. Greek tragedy, at least before Euripides, is directly religious, concerned with what the gods do to men rather than what men do to each other: it presents a picture of human events, the causes of which are divine actions. In consequence, a Greek tragedy does not demand that we "read" it in the sense that we speak of "reading" a face. The ways of the gods may be mysterious to human beings but they are not ambiguous.

There can be no secular drama of any depth or importance except in a culture which recognizes that man has an internal history as well as an external; that his actions are partly in response to an objective situation created by his past acts and the acts of others, and partly initiated by his subjective need to re-create, redefine, and rechoose himself. Surprise and revelation are the essence of drama. In Greek tragedy these are supplied by the gods; no mortal can foresee how and when they will act. But the conduct of men has no element of surprise, that is to say, the way in which they react to the surprising events which befall them is exactly what one would expect.

A secular drama presupposes that in all which men say and do there is a gratuitous element which makes their conduct ambiguous and unpredictable. Secular drama, therefore, demands a much more active role from its audience than a Greek tragedy. The audience has to be at one and the same time a witness to what is occurring on stage and a subjective participant who interprets what he sees and hears. And a secular dramatist like Shakespeare who attempts to project the inner history of human beings into objective stage action is faced with problems which Aeschylus and Sophocles were spared, for there are aspects of this inner history which resist and sometimes defy manifestation.

> Humility is represented with difficulty—when it is shown in its ideal moment, the beholder senses the lack of something because he feels that its true ideality does not consist in the fact that it is ideal in the moment but that it is constant. Romantic love can very well be represented in the moment, but conjugal love cannot, because an ideal husband is not one who is such once in his life but one who every day is such. Courage can very well be concentrated in the moment, but not patience, precisely for the reason that patience strives with time. A king who conquers kingdoms can be represented in the moment, but a cross bearer who every day takes up his cross cannot be represented in art because the point is that he does it every day. (Kierkegaard.)

Let us suppose, then, that a dramatist wishes to show a character acting out of the spirit of charity or agape. At first this looks easy. Agape requires that we love our enemies, do good to those that hate us and forgive those who injure us, and this command is unconditional. Surely, all a dramatist has to do is to show one human being forgiving an enemy.

In *Measure for Measure*, Angelo has wronged Isabella and Mariana, and the facts of the wrong become public. Angelo repents and demands that the just sentence of death be passed on him by the Duke. Isabella and Mariana implore the Duke to show Mercy. The Duke yields to their prayers and all ends happily. I agree with Professor Coghill's interpretation of *Measure for Measure* as a parable in which Isabella is an image for the redeemed Christian Soul, perfectly chaste and loving, whose reward is to become the bride of God; but, to my mind, the parable does not quite work because it is impossible to distinguish in dramatic action between the spirit of forgiveness and the act of pardon.

The command to forgive is unconditional: whether my enemy harden his heart or repent and beg forgiveness is irrelevant. If he hardens his heart, he does not care whether I forgive him or not and it would be impertinent of me to say, "I forgive you." If he repents and asks, "Will you forgive me?" the answer, "Yes," should not express a decision on my part but describe a state of feeling which has always existed. On the stage, however, it is impossible to show one person forgiving another, unless the wrongdoer asks for forgiveness, because silence and inaction are undramatic. The Isabella we are shown in earlier scenes of *Measure for Measure* is certainly not in a forgiving spirit—she is in a passion of rage and despair at Angelo's injustice—and dramatically she could not be otherwise, for then there would be no play. Again, on the stage, forgiveness requires manifestation in action, that is to say, the one who forgives must be in a position to do something for the other which, if he were not forgiving, he would not do. This means that my enemy must be at my mercy; but, to the spirit of charity, it is irrelevant whether I am at my enemy's mercy or he at mine. So long as he is at my mercy, forgiveness is indistinguishable from judicial pardon.

The law cannot forgive, for the law has not been wronged, only broken; only persons can be wronged. The law can pardon, but it can only pardon what it has the power to punish. If the lawbreaker is stronger than the legal authorities, they are powerless to do either. The decision to grant or refuse pardon must be governed by prudent calculation—if the wrong-doer is pardoned, he will behave better in the future than if he were punished, etc. But charity is forbidden to calculate in this way: I am required to forgive my enemy whatever the effect on him may be.

One may say that Isabella forgives Angelo and the Duke pardons him. But, on the stage, this distinction is invisible because, there, power, justice and love are all on the same side. Justice is able to pardon what love is commanded to forgive. But to love, it is an accident that the power of temporal justice should be on its side; indeed, the Gospels assure us that, sooner or later, they will find themselves in opposition and that love must suffer at the hands of justice.

In *King Lear*, Shakespeare attempts to show absolute love and goodness, in the person of Cordelia, destroyed by the powers of this world, but the price he pays is that Cordelia, as a dramatic character, is a bore.

If she is not to be a fake, what she says cannot be poetically very impressive nor what she does dramatically very exciting.

> What shall Cordelia speak? Love and be silent.

In a play with twenty-six scenes, Shakespeare allows her to appear in only four, and from a total of over three thousand three hundred lines, he allots to her less than ninety.

Temporal Justice demands the use of force to quell the unjust; it demands prudence, a practical reckoning with time and place; and it demands publicity for its laws and its penalties. But Charity forbids all three—we are not to resist evil, if a man demand our coat we are to give him our cloak also, we are to take no thought for the morrow and, while secretly fasting and giving alms, we are to appear in public as persons who do neither.

A direct manifestation of charity in secular terms is, therefore, impossible. One form of indirect manifestation employed by religious teachers has been through parables in which actions which are ethically immoral are made to stand as a sign for that which transcends ethics. The Gospel parable of the Unjust Steward is one example. These words by a Hasidic Rabbi are another:

> I cannot teach you the ten principles of service but a little child and a thief can show you what they are. From the child you can learn three things;
> He is merry for no particular reason.
> Never for a moment is he idle.

When he wants something, he demands it vigorously.
The thief can instruct you in many things.
He does his service by night.
If he does not finish what he has set out to do in one
night, he devotes the next night to it.
He and all those who work for him, love one another.
He risks his life for slight gains.
What he takes has so little value for him that he gives up
for a very small coin.
He endures blows and hardships and it matters nothing
to him.
He likes his trade and would not exchange it for any
other.

If a parable of this kind is dramatized, the action must be comic,
that is to say, the apparently immoral actions of the hero must
not inflict, as in the actual world they would, real suffering upon
others.

Thus, Falstaff speaks of himself as if he were always robbing
travelers. We see him do this once—incidentally, it is not Falstaff
but the Prince who is the instigator—and the sight convinces us
that he never has been and never could be a successful highwayman. The money is restolen from him and returned to its proper
owners; the only sufferer is Falstaff himself who has been made a
fool of. He lives shamelessly on credit, but none of his creditors
seems to be in serious trouble as a result. The Hostess may swear
that if he does not pay his bill, she will have to pawn her plate and
tapestries, but this is shown to be the kind of exaggeration
habitual to landladies, for in the next scene they are still there.
What, overtly, is dishonesty becomes, parabolically, a sign for a
lack of pride, humility which acknowledges its unimportance and
dependence upon others.

Then he rejoices in his reputation as a fornicator with whom
no woman is safe alone, but the Falstaff on stage is too old to
fornicate, and it is impossible to imagine him younger. All we see
him do is defend a whore against a bully, set her on his knee and
make her cry out of affection and pity. What in the real world is
promiscuous lust, the treatment of other persons as objects of
sexual greed, becomes in the comic world of play a symbol for the
charity that loves all neighbors without distinction.

Living off other people's money and indiscriminate fornication
are acts of injustice towards private individuals; Falstaff is also

guilty of injustice to others in their public character as citizens. In any war it is not the justice or injustice of either side that decides who is to be the victor but the force each can command. It is therefore the duty of all who believe in the justice of the King's side to supply him with the best soldiers possible. Falstaff makes no attempt to fulfill this duty. Before the battle of Shrewsbury, he first conscripts those who have most money and least will to fight and then allows them to buy their way out, so that he is finally left with a sorry regiment of "discarded unjust serving men, younger sons to younger brothers, revolted tapsters and ostlers trade fallen. . . ." Before the battle of Gaultree Forest, the two most sturdy young men, Mouldy and Bullcalf, offer him money and are let off, and the weakest, Shadow, Feeble and Wart, taken.

From the point of view of society this is unjust, but if the villagers who are subject to conscription were to be asked, as private individuals, whether they would rather be treated justly or as Falstaff treats them, there is no doubt as to their answer. What their betters call just and unjust means nothing to them; all they know is that conscription will tear them away from their homes and livelihoods with a good chance of getting killed or returning maimed "to beg at the town's end." Those whom Falstaff selects are those with least to lose, derelicts without home or livelihood to whom soldiering at least offers a chance of loot. Bullcalf wants to stay with his friends, Mouldy has an old mother to look after, but Feeble is quite ready to go if his friend Wart can go with him.

Falstaff's neglect of the public interest in favor of private concerns is an image for the justice of charity which treats each person, not as a cipher, but as a unique person. The Prince may justly complain:

> I never did see such pitiful rascals

but Falstaff's retort speaks for all the insulted and injured of this world:

> Tut tut—good enough to toss, food for powder, food for powder. They'll fit a pit as well as better. Tush, man, mortal men, mortal men. . . .

These are Falstaff's only acts: for the rest, he fritters away his time, swigging at the bottle and taking no thought for the mor-

row. As a parable, both the idleness and the drinking, the surrender to immediacy and the refusal to accept reality, become signs
for the Unworldly Man as contrasted with Prince Hal who represents worldliness at its best.

At his best, the worldly man is one who dedicates his life to
some public end, politics, science, industry, art, etc. The end is
outside himself, but the choice of end is determined by the particular talents with which nature has endowed him, and the proof
that he has chosen rightly is worldly success. To dedicate one's life
to an end for which one is not endowed is madness, the madness
of Don Quixote. Strictly speaking, he does not desire fame for
himself, but to achieve something which merits fame. Because his
end is worldly, that is, in the public domain—to marry the girl of
one's choice, or to become a good parent, are private, not worldly,
ends—the personal life and its satisfactions are, for the worldly
man, of secondary importance and, should they ever conflict with
his vocation, must be sacrificed. The worldly man at his best
knows that other persons exist and desires that they should—a
statesman has no wish to establish justice among tables and
chairs—but if it is necessary to the achievement of his end to treat
certain persons as if they were things, then, callously or regret-
fully, he will. What distinguishes him from the ordinary criminal
is that the criminal lacks the imagination to conceive of others as
being persons like himself; when he sacrifices others, he feels no
guilt because, to the criminal, he is the only person in a world of
things. What distinguishes both the worldly man and the criminal
from the wicked man is their lack of malice. The wicked man is
not worldly, but anti-worldly. His conscious end is nothing less
than the destruction of others. He is obsessed by hatred at his
knowledge that other persons exist besides himself and cannot
rest until he has reduced them all to the status of things.

But it is not always easy to distinguish the worldly man from
the criminal or the wicked man by observing their behavior and
its results. It can happen, for instance, that, despite his intention,
a wicked man does good. Don John in *Much Ado About Nothing*
certainly means nothing but harm to Claudio and Hero, yet it is
thanks to him that Claudio obtains insight into his own short-
comings and becomes, what previously he was not, a fit husband
for Hero. To the outward eye, however different their subjective
intentions, both Harry of Monmouth and Iago deceive and de-

stroy. Even in their speech one cannot help noticing a certain resemblance between

> So when this loose behaviour I throw off
> And pay the debt I never promised,
> By how much better than my word I am.
> I'll so offend to make offence a skill
> Redeeming time when men least think I will.

and:

> From when my outward action doth demonstrate
> The native act and figure of my heart
> In compliment extern, 'tis not long after
> But I will wear my heart upon my sleeve
> For daws to peck at. I am not what I am. . . .

and the contrast of both to Sonnet 121:

> No, I am that I am; and they that level
> At my abuses reckon up their own.
> I may be straight though they themselves be bevel.

Falstaff is perfectly willing to tell the world: "I am that I am, a drunken old failure." Hal cannot jeopardize his career by such careless disclosure but must always assume whatever manner is politic at the moment. To the degree that we have worldly ambitions, Falstaff's verdict on the Prince strikes home.

> Thou art essentially mad without seeming so.

Falstaff never really does anything, but he never stops talking, so that the impression he makes on the audience is not of idleness but of infinite energy. He is never tired, never bored, and until he is rejected he radiates happiness as Hal radiates power, and this happiness without apparent cause, this untiring devotion to making others laugh becomes a comic image for a love which is absolutely self-giving.

Laughing and loving have certain properties in common. Laughter is contagious but not, like physical force, irresistible. A man in a passion of any kind cannot be made to laugh; if he laughs, it is a proof that he has already mastered his passion. Laughter is an action only in a special sense. Many kinds of action can cause laughter, but the only kind of action that laughter causes is more laughter; while we laugh, time stops and no other kind of action can be contemplated. In rage or hysteria people sometimes are said to "laugh" but no one can confuse the noises they make with the sound of real laughter. Real laughter is absolutely unaggressive; we cannot wish people or things we find amusing to be other than they are; we do not desire them to change them, far less hurt or destroy them. An angry and dangerous mob is rendered harmless by the orator who can succeed in making it laugh. Real laughter is always, as we say, "disarming."

Falstaff makes the same impression on us that the Sinner of Lublin made upon his rabbi.

> In Lublin lived a great sinner. Whenever he went to talk to the rabbi, the rabbi readily consented and conversed with him as if he were a man of integrity and one who was a close friend. Many of the hassidim were annoyed at this and one said to the other: "Is it possible that our rabbi who has only to look once into a man's face to know his life from first to last, to know the very origin of his soul, does not see that this fellow is a sinner? And if he does see it, that he considers him worthy to speak to and associate with." Finally they summoned up courage to go to the rabbi himself with their question. He answered them: "I know all about him as well as you. But you know how I love gaiety and hate dejection. And this man is so great a sinner. Others repent the moment they have sinned, are sorry for a moment, and then return to their folly. But he knows no regrets and no doldrums, and lives in his happiness as in a tower. And it is the radiance of his happiness that overwhelms my heart."

Falstaff's happiness is almost an impregnable tower, but not quite. "I am that I am" is not a complete self-description; he must also add—"The young prince hath misled me. I am the fellow with the great belly, and he is my dog."

The Christian God is not a self-sufficient being like Aristotle's First Cause, but a God who creates a world which he continues to love although it refuses to love him in return. He appears in this world, not as Apollo or Aphrodite might appear, disguised as man so that no mortal should recognize his divinity, but as a real man who openly claims to be God. And the consequence is inevitable. The highest religious and temporal authorities condemn Him as a blasphemer and a Lord of Misrule, as a Bad Companion for mankind. Inevitable because, as Richelieu said, "The salvation of States is in this world," and history has not as yet provided us with any evidence that the Prince of this world has changed his character.

Northrop Frye

The Argument of Comedy (1949)

It is only in Jonson and the Restoration writers that English comedy can be called a form of New Comedy. The earlier tradition established by Peele and developed by Lyly, Greene, and the masque writers, which uses themes from romance and folklore and avoids the comedy of manners, is the one followed by Shakespeare. These themes are largely medieval in origin, and derive, not from the mysteries or the moralities or the interludes, but from a fourth dramatic tradition. This is the drama of folk ritual, of the St. George play and the mummers' play, of the feast of the ass and the Boy Bishop, and of all the dramatic activity that punctuated the Christian calendar with the rituals of an immemorial paganism. We may call this the drama of the green world, and its theme is once again the triumph of life over the waste land, the death and revival of the year impersonated by figures still human, and once divine as well.

When Shakespeare began to study Plautus and Terence, his dramatic instinct, stimulated by his predecessors, divined that there was a profounder pattern in the argument of comedy than appears in either of them. At once—for the process is beginning in *The Comedy of Errors*—he started groping toward that profounder pattern, the ritual of death and revival that also underlies Aristophanes, of which an exact equivalent lay ready to hand in the drama of the green world. This parallelism largely accounts for the resemblances to Greek ritual which Colin Still has pointed out in *The Tempest*.

From *English Institute Essays 1948*. Reprinted by permission of Columbia University Press. Copyright © 1948 by Columbia University Press.

The Two Gentlemen of Verona is an orthodox New Comedy except for one thing. The hero Valentine becomes captain of a band of outlaws in a forest, and all the other characters are gathered into this forest and become converted. Thus the action of the comedy begins in a world represented as a normal world, moves into the green world, goes into a metamorphosis there in which the comic resolution is achieved, and returns to the normal world. The forest in this play is the embryonic form of the fairy world of *A Midsummer Night's Dream*, the Forest of Arden in *As You Like It*, Windsor Forest in *The Merry Wives of Windsor*, and the pastoral world of the mythical sea-coasted Bohemia in *The Winter's Tale*. In all these comedies there is the same rhythmic movement from normal world to green world and back again. Nor is this second world confined to the forest comedies. In *The Merchant of Venice* the two worlds are a little harder to see, yet Venice is clearly not the same world as that of Portia's mysterious house in Belmont, where there are caskets teaching that gold and silver are corruptible goods, and from whence proceed the wonderful cosmological harmonies of the fifth act. In *The Tempest* the entire action takes place in the second world, and the same may be said of *Twelfth Night*, which, as its title implies, presents a carnival society, not so much a green world as an evergreen one. The second world is absent from the so-called problem comedies, which is one of the things that makes them problem comedies.

The green world charges the comedies with a symbolism in which the comic resolution contains a suggestion of the old ritual pattern of the victory of summer over winter. This is explicit in *Love's Labor's Lost*. In this very masque-like play, the comic contest takes the form of the medieval debate of winter and spring. In *The Merry Wives of Windsor* there is an elaborate ritual of the defeat of winter, known to folklorists as "carrying out Death," of which Falstaff is the victim; and Falstaff must have felt that, after being thrown into the water, dressed up as a witch and beaten out of a house with curses, and finally supplied with a beast's head and singed with candles while he said, "Divide me like a brib'd buck, each a haunch," he had done about all that could reasonably be asked of any fertility spirit.

The association of this symbolism with the death and revival of human beings is more elusive, but still perceptible. The fact that the heroine often brings about the comic resolution by disguising herself as a boy is familiar enough. In the Hero of *Much Ado About Nothing* and the Helena of *All's Well That Ends Well*, this theme of the withdrawal and return of the heroine comes as close to a death and revival as Elizabethan conventions will allow. The Thaisa of *Pericles* and the Fidele of *Cymbeline* are beginning to crack the conventions, and with the disappearance and revival of Hermione in *The Winter's Tale*, who actually returns once as a ghost in a dream, the original nature-myth of Demeter and Proserpine is openly established. The fact that the dying and reviving character is usually female strengthens the feeling that there is something maternal about the green world, in which the new order of the comic resolution is nourished and brought to birth. However, a similar theme which is very like the rejuvenation of the *senex* so frequent in Aristophanes occurs in the folklore motif of the healing of the impotent king on which *All's Well That Ends Well* is based, and this theme is probably involved in the symbolism of Prospero.

The conception of a second world bursts the boundaries of Menandrine comedy, yet it is clear that the world of Puck is no world of eternal forms or divine revelation. Shakespeare's comedy is not Aristotelian and realistic like Menander's, nor Platonic and dialectic like Aristophanes', nor Thomist and sacramental like Dante's, but a fourth kind. It is an Elizabethan kind, and is not confined either to Shakespeare or to the drama. Spenser's epic is a wonderful contrapuntal intermingling of two orders of existence, one the red and white world of English history, the other the green world of the Faerie Queene. The latter is a world of crusading virtues proceeding from the Faerie Queene's court and designed to return to that court when the destiny of the other world is fulfilled. The fact that the Faerie Queene's knights are sent out during the twelve days of the Christmas festival suggests our next point.

Shakespeare too has his green world of comedy and his red and white world of history. The story of the latter is at one point interrupted by an invasion from the comic world, when Falstaff *senex et parasitus* throws his gigantic shadow over Prince Henry, assuming on one occasion the role of his father. Clearly, if the Prince is ever to conquer France he must reassert the moral norm. The moral norm is duly reasserted, but the rejection of Falstaff is not a comic resolution. In comedy the moral norm is not morality but deliverance, and we certainly do not feel delivered from Falstaff as we feel delivered from Shylock with his absurd and vicious bond. The moral norm does not carry with it the vision of a free society: Falstaff will always keep a bit of that in his tavern.

Falstaff is a mock king, a lord of misrule, and his tavern is a Saturnalia. Yet we are reminded of the original meaning of the Saturnalia, as a rite intended to recall the golden age of Saturn. Falstaff's world is not a golden world, but as long as we remember it we cannot forget that the world of *Henry V* is an iron one. We are reminded too of another traditional denizen of the green world, Robin Hood, the outlaw who manages to suggest a better kind of society than those who make him an outlaw can produce. The outlaws in *The Two Gentlemen of Verona* compare themselves, in spite of the Italian setting, to Robin Hood, and in *As You Like It* Charles the wrestler says of Duke Senior's followers: "There they live like the old Robin Hood of England: they say many young gentlemen flock to him every day, and fleet the time carelessly, as they did in the golden world."

In the histories, therefore, the comic Saturnalia is a temporary reversal of normal standards, comic "relief" as it is called, which subsides and allows the history to continue. In the comedies, the green world suggests an original golden age which the normal world has usurped and which makes us wonder if it is not the normal world that is the real Saturnalia. In *Cymbeline* the green world finally triumphs over a historical theme, the reason being perhaps that in that play the incarnation of Christ, which is contemporary with Cymbeline, takes place offstage, and accounts for the halcyon peace with which the play concludes. From then on in Shakespeare's plays, the green world has it all its own way, and both in *Cymbeline* and in *Henry VIII* there may be suggestions that Shakespeare, like Spenser, is moving toward a synthesis of the two worlds, a wedding of Prince Arthur and the Faerie Queene.

This world of fairies, dreams, disembodied souls, and pastoral lovers may not be a "real" world, but, if not, there is something equally illusory in the stumbling and blinded follies of the "normal" world, of Theseus' Athens with its idiotic marriage law, of Duke Frederick and his melancholy tyranny, of Leontes and his mad jealousy, of the Court Party with their plots and intrigues. The famous speech of Prospero about the dream nature of reality applies equally to Milan and the enchanted island. We spend our lives partly in a waking world we call normal and partly in a dream world which we create out of our own desires. Shakespeare endows both worlds with equal imaginative power, brings them opposite one another, and makes each world seem unreal when seen by the light of the other. He uses freely both the heroic triumph of New Comedy and the ritual resurrection of its predecessor, but his distinctive comic resolution is different from either: it is a detachment of the spirit born of this reciprocal reflection of two illusory realities. We need not ask whether this brings us into a higher order of existence or not, for the question of existence is not relevant to poetry.

We have spoken of New Comedy as Aristotelian, Old Comedy as Platonic and Dante's *commedia* as Thomist, but it is difficult to suggest a philosophical spokesman for the form of Shakespeare's comedy. For Shakespeare, the subject matter of poetry is not life, or nature, or reality, or revelation, or anything else that the philosopher builds on, but poetry itself, a verbal universe. That is one reason why he is both the most elusive and the most substantial of poets.

Arthur Colby Sprague

Gadshill Revisited[1] (1953)

For about a hundred and eighty years after Sir John Falstaff
for the first time ran roaring from Gadshill, the fact of his
cowardice was taken for granted. Falstaff was immensely popular
with readers and playgoers alike. In the seventeenth century,
allusions to him are far more numerous, by actual count, than
those to any other Shakespearian character,[2] and the terms in
which he is referred to are quite unambiguous. "A thrasonical
puff, and emblem of mock valour," Tom Fuller calls him;[3] and
Dryden, not, I think, inaccurately, describes him as "old, fat,
merry, cowardly, drunken, amorous, vain, and lying." Yet Falstaff's individuality, as Dryden perceived, lay elsewhere:

> That wherein he is singular is his wit, or those things he
> says . . . unexpected by the audience; his quick evasions,
> when you expect him surprised, which, as they are ex-
> tremely diverting of themselves, so receive a great addition
> from his person.[4]

And Dr. Samuel Johnson, agreeing with Dryden, pronounces
Falstaff a coward and defines his wit as consisting "in easy escapes
and sallies of levity."[5]

It was not until 1777 that heresy began. In that year appeared
a long essay of a good deal of subtlety, and even charm, *On the
Dramatic Character of Sir John Falstaff,* by Maurice Morgann. Morgann, a middle-aged civil servant of "uncommon powers," acknowledges that his book was written on a dare, and he dreads

From *Shakespeare Quarterly,* 4 (1953). Reprinted by permission of *Shakespeare Quarterly.*

that it might be taken, as, indeed, it was by many, as a mere exercise in paradox. He recognizes "how universally the contrary opinion prevails"; and that "the appearances" in this case are all against him. Falstaff is involved, almost immediately, "in circumstances of apparent dishonour"; he is called a coward; is seen "in the very act of running away," and "betrayed into those *lies* and *braggadocioes*, which are the usual concomitants of cowardice in military men, and pretenders to valour." What was more, these things are "thrust forward, pressed upon our notice as the subject of our mirth."[6] The grounds for his own belief that Sir John was no coward were of quite another sort, and he asks patience of the reader while he sets forth what "lies so dispersed, is so latent, and so purposely obscured"[7]—the "secret impressions upon us of courage."[8]

Though Morgann's ideas were to prevail, they were not unopposed in his own day. A carefully reasoned reply by Richard Stack appeared in *The Transactions of the Royal Irish Academy*. Dr. Johnson's opinion was twice asked and given. "Why, Sir," Boswell quotes him as saying, "we shall have the man come forth again; and as he has proved Falstaff to be no coward, he may prove Iago to be a very good character."[9] Thomas Davies, too, the actor and bookseller, spoke out, and the point he made was, I think, a telling one: "If the knight is proved to be a man of courage, half the mirth he raises is quite lost and misplaced."[10] What is more curious, Falstaff on the stage remained unregenerate. As he had once been, in this matter of cowardice, so he has remained right down to the present—though such fine actors as Sir Ralph Richardson and (at Stratford) Mr. Anthony Quayle and the late Roy Byford, have dispensed with most of the traditional buffoonery which once disfigured the role.

We have come, indeed, to a parting of ways, the actors keeping straight on as they had been going, the critics, with few exceptions, straying obscurely to the left. Nor was Morgann, with his notion of appearance and reality, his "secret impressions" of courage, a safe guide. Thus, William Lloyd would have Falstaff's delightfully spontaneous rejoinder to the Prince's "Where shall we take a purse tomorrow, Jack?" "Zounds, where thou wilt, lad! I'll make one," a bit of crafty duplicity, with the speaker fully conscious of the incongruity of what he says.[11] And Hazlitt fancies that Falstaff's bill, with its "out-of-the-way charge for capons and sack with only one haif-penny-worth of bread," may have been planted for the Prince to find.[12] (One might question, with equal propriety, whether at the moment of the reading of the bill Sir John, for all his snoring, was really asleep!)

The starting point for such divagations remains the denial of what in the theater seems obvious, the fact of cowardice. Yet Bradley and even Kittredge are among those who have denied it. Bradley, indeed, is not without misgivings. The manner of Falstaff's flight at Gadshill troubles him, if only in a footnote: "It is to be regretted . . . that in carrying his guts away so nimbly he 'roared for mercy'; for I fear we have no ground for rejecting Henry's statement to that effect."[13] He grants, too, that "Falstaff sometimes behaves in what we should generally call a cowardly way." But conduct is not a certain indication of character. "If the word [coward] means a person who feels painful fear in the presence of danger, and yields to that fear in spite of his better feelings and convictions, then assuredly Falstaff was no coward."[14] As for Kittredge, strangely, as it always seemed to me, he had no doubts whatsoever. Even the roaring at Gadshill he denied, or explained away. For once, dramatic evidence went by the board with him, and his Falstaff was *sans peur*, if not quite *sans reproche.*

Among the minority-critics who have held out for cowardice (and John Bailey was one), the foremost is, of course, Professor Stoll. Time after time he has returned to the question, bringing to it his broad knowledge of popular drama and its enduring conventions.[15] Thus, he shows that Falstaff's behavior on the battlefield—his cracking jokes, for instance, or capturing a prisoner of his own, the redoubtable Colevile of the Dale—cannot be taken as evidence of courage, since the mere type-cowards and comic butts of earlier and cruder plays do the like. Sir John's ancestors are a shabby lot, but their existence may as well be acknowledged. In fact, a late-comer to this controversy, who has convinced himself that Falstaff was no braver than he should be, is likely to discover that many of his best arguments have already been used, somewhere, by Mr. Stoll. That they have been so largely disregarded is a little puzzling.

Finally, Professor J. Dover Wilson, though he repeatedly in-

vokes the authority of Johnson in combatting the Romantic critics, is ambiguous on this matter of timidity; or, rather, as it seems
to me, he would have it both ways. Falstaff, during the overpow-
ering of the travelers at Gadshill, is described as "dancing with
rage, on the fringe of the scuffle," and his subsequent flight
becomes as ignominious as the older actors were accustomed to
make it. Indeed, if the Gadshill Scene stood alone, Mr. Wilson is
satisfied that the audience would accept Sir John as "an absolute
coward"—which he will not admit.[16] The representation of cowardice by the right sort of comedian will (he thinks) have produced an effect upon us very different from what might be
expected—affection, even, rather than a "jeering contempt."[17]
The impression of cowardice is dissolved in the mirth of the
Tavern Scene. Falstaff, sensing the plot against him, deliberately
exaggerates, winking to the audience at the moment he begins to
do so. The groundlings might miss the point; there would be
others to whom the question of cowardice was left open to
debate. And Falstaff's "magnificent display of stoutness of heart"
when the Sheriff comes to arrest him, is "the final answer to the
Prince's slanderous story of the events on Gad's Hill, and to our
own receding impressions."[18]

Yet as we pass to still later episodes, it is curious to find
Mr. Wilson taking issue repeatedly with the contentions of the
Morgann school. Falstaff's presence in the thick of battle is no
longer accepted as evidence of valor. His "military reputation is
not only complete bogus, but one of the best jokes in the whole
drama."[19] Had Colevile of the Dale resisted, "we may surmise that
another sham death would have followed the exchange of a few
blows."[20] Even the turning out of poor swaggering Pistol is left to
Bardolph, "while Falstaff, sword in hand, follows up at a discreet
distance behind."[21]

On this whole question of cowardice, then, the earlier critics,
and the actors, are on one side; the later critics, with few exceptions, on the other. Either, that is to say, Falstaff is an egregious
coward; or he is—here there is some want of agreement—a
veteran soldier, usually, and a realist in war; trusted, and not
wholly undeserving of trust; wily, and of great presence of mind;
no Hotspur, of course, but just as certainly, not a coward. The
chief arguments of Morgann and his followers, the arguments

against cowardice, are familiar—Morgann, himself, thought up most of them—and I shall present them only summarily, though I hope with fairness.

There is, first of all, Morgann's bold challenge to the impartial reader: "We all like *Old Jack*" though we so constantly abuse him! But could we like him, vicious as he is, were he actually a coward? Cowardice seems incompatible with our impression of the character as a whole. Our feeling toward Falstaff is altogether different from our feeling toward, say, the cowardly Parolles in *All's Well that Ends Well.*

From impressions and their analysis we pass to inference. Falstaff's military reputation is pointed to with confidence as evidence of desert. Thus, in the dark days before Shrewsbury, the Prince himself entrusts him with the command of a company of foot. Falstaff is present at the King's Council of War; and in the premature account of the outcome of the battle is prominently mentioned among the casualties—"And Harry Monmouth's brawn, the hulk Sir John, Is prisoner." Later we hear of "a dozen Captains" searching anxiously for him while he sups with Mistress Tearsheet. Then, too, a rebel of some note, a knight, Colevile of the Dale, surrenders at once upon hearing who his antagonist is: "I think you are Sir John Falstaff, and in that thought yield me."

Much is made, also, of a relatively inconspicuous episode at the close of the great Tavern Scene in *1 Henry IV.* Bardolph rushes in, with a good deal of nasal clamor, to interrupt the play which Falstaff and Prince Hal are acting: "O, my lord, my lord! the sheriff with a most monstrous watch is at the door"—looking of course, for certain thieves. Falstaff, it is urged, might well be expected to show alarm at this, or even terror. On the contrary, he merely takes hiding behind the arras, where he is presently discovered, not quaking with fear but asleep, and "snorting like a horse."

Later in the same play we have Sir John on the field of battle—and in time, too! He tells us in soliloquy that he has led his poor soldiers where they were slaughtered. He finds himself in the very thick of the fight. Hotspur contends with Prince Hal in single combat. The terrible Douglas suddenly attacks Falstaff. Whereupon Falstaff, no match of course for such an adversary, but never losing his coolness and presence of mind, has recourse to a brilliant stratagem by which he escapes: lives, as is hopefully said of him, to fight another day. As no coward could have slept, earlier, so no coward could now have outwitted death by seeming to die!

The complicated happenings at Gadshill, Morgann takes up last of all, and he admits the possibility that Falstaff in this single instance yielded to a momentary and quite understandable terror (even Bradley, as we saw, was troubled by Sir John's *roaring* as he ran). For an uncompromising defence of the fat hero at this point, one goes to Kittredge. Falstaff, he urges, is under no sort of obligation to fight it out. On the contrary, as a thief caught in the act, it behooves him to take to his heels. "How the fat rogue roar'd!" says Poins, at the end of the Gadshill Scene. But this refers to Falstaff's "vociferous swaggering"—his "Down with them . . . whoreson caterpillars" and so on—as he set upon the travellers—or encouraged poor Bardolph and the others to set upon them! And when the roaring is again mentioned and its precise character specified ("and, Falstaff, you carried your guts away as nimbly . . . and roar'd for mercy, and still run and roar'd, as ever I heard bullcalf"), it is the "only departure from accuracy in Prince Hal's story."

These, then, are the principal arguments which have been used by those who deny that Falstaff was a coward, despite those circumstances of "apparent dishonour" and appearances "singularly strong and striking" which Morgann recognized as likely to sway the judgment of a simple reader. They are arguments which vary a good deal in force; but each of them can, I think, be fairly met.

There is Morgann's argument, first of all, that we could not like "plump Jack" as we do if to his other failings, and quite tipping the balance, were added cowardice. But this is to leave out of account Sir John's years, and it might be added his corpulence. He is obviously disqualified as a combatant—"blasted with antiquity."[22] To expect valor of him is, indeed, to expect too much! And in the Play Scene when, speaking in the person of Prince Hal, he has occasion to praise himself, he makes a point of this: "But for sweet Jack Falstaff, kind Jack Falstaff, true Jack Falstaff, valiant Jack Falstaff, and therefore more valiant being, as he is, old Jack

Falstaff. . . ." Nor need the argument remain hypothetical. For it is quite obvious that Dr. Johnson liked Falstaff, though recognizing the rogue's numerous vices and insisting upon his cowardice. As for his military reputation, I am tempted merely to repeat Professor Dover Wilson's comprehensive description of it as "complete bogus" and "one of the best jokes in the whole drama." Colevile of the Dale has only to learn who his antagonist is, and yields without striking a blow. (His alacrity in yielding does not, indeed, escape comment: "It was more, his courtesy than your deserving," says Prince John to Falstaff, unpleasantly enough.) But if Pistol, the complete coward, is able to take a prisoner on the field of battle, why not his old master, the better man of the two? And Colevile, though his words are not abject like those of Pistol's Frenchman, seems scarcely formidable. Falstaff speaks of him with suspicious emphasis as "a most furious knight and valorous enemy" and of his own "pure and immaculate valour" in taking such a prisoner. Perhaps, the first tribute is as unsubstantial as the second?

But the Prince entrusted Falstaff with the command of a company shortly before Shrewsbury? And this same company, it might be answered, will afford occasion for one of Sir John's happiest monologues; is fully justified, in terms of dramatic economy, by the use made of it! The Prince, too, seems to take the matter lightly. "I'll procure this fat rogue a charge of foot," he says, adding, not I think without relish, "and I know his death will be a march of twelve score." He wants to see Falstaff larding the lean earth once more! Meanwhile, there will be the pleasure of telling him the news:

> I have procured thee, Jack, a charge of foot.
> *Falstaff.* I would it had been of horse.

Later, by the way, Hal entrusts despatches of obvious importance to—of all messengers—Bardolph!

He slept behind the arras—slept soundly and snored. Now this fact has been taken as incontestable proof of high fortitude on the snorer's part. But is it? I would not so far belittle Sir John's sagacity as to believe that what even a minor member of the gang (Gadshill) recognized would not have been perceived by Falstaff— that on this particular expedition they stole "as in a castle, cock-sure."[23] The Prince of Wales, deeply involved as he is, himself, must needs "(if matters should be look'd into) for [his] own credit sake make all whole." Falstaff might well sleep soundly, and, sleeping, contribute to the forwarding of the plot by allowing his pockets to be picked. What is natural in itself has reason as well in the economy of the play as a whole; most of dramatic technique (as I have come to believe) consisting in a playwright's ability to kill more than one bird with a single stone.

Falstaff's behavior at Shrewsbury and Gadshill remains to be considered. At Shrewsbury, then, he led his ragamuffins where they were peppered; is found, himself, where the fighting is fiercest, and escapes death by means of a quite legitimate stratagem. The passing allusion to the destruction of the ragamuffins is impressive when taken out of context. Nor would I impute a sinister motive to old Jack and believe that the securing of their death pay was his object here.[24] Were this so, one would expect some intimation of it in the text. They fell, in any case, almost to a man—and it is convenient for the playwright certainly, and perhaps for Sir John, to have them out of the way. Meanwhile, the soliloquy in which we hear of their fate is worth examining. "Though I could scape shot-free at London," Falstaff begins, "I fear the shot here." Then, starting at the sight of one who has paid his score—"There's honour for you!" "I am as hot as molten lead," he mutters, "and as heavy too. God keep lead out of me! I need no more weight than mine own bowels." For an Elizabethan audience—for, I think, any popular audience—the character of the speech will already have been determined. It is addressed to them, designed for their amusement—a comic monologue spoken by one who does, indeed, "fear the shot" and who will have recourse to whatever shifts he can devise to save that precious carcass of his.

Such shifts and stratagems, far from being incompatible with cowardice on the stage, were its familiar concomitants. Not to go further for an illustration, one turns to *The Famous Victories of Henry the Fifth*. In the old play of that name, well known, it would seem, to Shakespeare, the "Clown" Dericke is an egregious coward; yet he has his wits about him, and most of all when his need is greatest. He boasts of having tickled his nose with a straw, gained in this way the title of "the bloodie souldier," and so escaped combat duty.[25] Taken prisoner, ignominiously enough, during the raid upon the English camp at Agincourt, he manages by an elaborate and very implausible trick to secure his captor's sword, *"hurles him downe"* and is about to kill him when the Frenchman escapes in turn. "What, is he gone?" says Dericke, "Masse, I am glad of it. For, if he had staid, I was afraid he wold have sturd again, and then I should have beene spilt."[26]

"Enter *Douglas*. He fighteth with *Falstaff*, who falls down as if he were dead." I recall a very good performance of *1 Henry IV* at an American repertory theater before a small audience. In the row behind me were two very young girls who clearly had not read the play but, as clearly, were greatly enjoying it. And the happy comment of one of them, wholly spontaneous as it was, delighted me: "He's playing possum!" It came, as I noted, a moment or two after Sir John's descent. To her, as to a good many in that first audience of long ago, he must have seemed to have died indeed. And when, upon the talk of embowelling, Falstaff rose, there came amusement and relief. Though the expedient he practised was, as an eighteenth-century critic stated, "very natural to a coward,"[27] and one which an unfortunate fat man of the same name repeats in *The Merry Wives of Windsor*, it is not, I should say, conclusive evidence of cowardice any more than it is of valor. Relief and amusement come first, and beyond such feelings I doubt if the ordinary spectator goes. Long ere this, he will have made up his mind on the matter of cowardice and will interpret this episode accordingly. And if we, away from the theater, disputing as we do over niceties, are in need of further enlightenment, it comes in the speech immediately following. "The better part of valour is discretion," Falstaff rationalizes. Then, as he looks about him, come thoughts of another sort. "Zounds, I am afraid of this gunpowder Percy, though he be dead. How if he should counterfeit too, and rise?" And, accordingly, to "make him sure," he will thrust his sword into the dead body. If, he adds as an afterthought, he takes upon himself the glory of having slain Hotspur, he may succeed in brazening it out. "Why may not he rise as well as I?" he repeats. There is a double incentive for what he does—fame, yes, but caution as well. Tom Davies who, knowing as he did a great deal about the practical theater, remained undazzled by the brilliance of Maurice Morgann, gave this pas-

sage the emphasis it deserves: "If any proof of [Falstaff's] timidity
be yet wanting, we have, in this scene, such as bids defiance to all
question; for Falstaff, not satisfied with seeing the dead body of
Percy before him, to make all sure, wounds the corpse in the
thigh."[28]

The circumstances of the Gadshill robbery Morgann, for obvious reasons, examined last of all. In the play, it is of some
consequence, however, that the episode comes very early. Shakespeare's practice in matters of exposition is remarkably consistent. Facts and impressions, once imparted, are rarely contradicted, and then in quite unmistakable terms. Even Iago, who for
a few moments may appear to have something of a case against
his master, a still unknown Moor, is soon shown in his true colors
as a designing villain. What is more, the cowardice of Falstaff is
not lightly referred to, or joked about; it receives in the Gadshill
episode what amounts, in dramatic terms, to demonstration.

As Poins outlines the plan, he and the Prince are to set upon
Falstaff, Bardolph, Peto, and Gadshill, and rob them of their
newly acquired booty. The Prince, not unnaturally, wonders
whether "they will be too hard for us"—four men against two.
But Poins reassures him:

> Well, for two of them, I know them to be as true-bred
> cowards as ever turn'd back; and for the third, if he fight
> longer than he sees reason, I'll forswear arms. The virtue of
> this jest will be the incomprehensible lies that this same fat
> rogue will tell us when we meet at supper: how thirty, at
> least, he fought with; what wards, what blows, what ex-
> tremities he endured; and in the reproof of this lies the jest.

Thus, two things are promised: that Falstaff, to translate understatement by understatement, is not likely to do much fighting;
and that, in keeping with his timidity and making it truly diverting, his tales of prowess afterwards will be infinite ("incomprehensible"). Hal is satisfied—and, indeed, Poins knows his man!

At Gadshill, Falstaff has first to endure the distress of being
deprived of his horse—that unfortunate animal!—but being Falstaff is soon able to play upon the familiar theme of his own bulk
quite as happily as his tormentors. He hears that the travellers are
numerous. "Zounds," he cries, "will they not rob us?" And the

Prince: "What, a coward, Sir John Paunch?" "Indeed," he answers, "I am not John of Gaunt, your grandfather; but yet no coward, Hal." "Well, we leave that to the proof." And the proof is soon forthcoming. The travelers, easing their legs by walking down the hill, are pounced upon and relieved of their money, Falstaff setting up a prodigious clamor while this is going on. Once more, to keep these complicated happenings clear, the prince comments:

> The thieves have bound the true men. Now could thou and I rob the thieves and go merrily to London, it would be argument for a week, laughter for a month, and a good jest for ever.

But Falstaff, returning with the booty, is full of satisfaction:

> Come, my masters, let us share, and then to horse before day. An the Prince and Poins be not two arrant cowards, there's no equity stirring. There's no more valour in that Poins than in a wild duck.

It is the note he will sound insistently at the beginning of che Tavern Scene. They are the cowards, not he! He may even believe it, himself. Then,

> *as they are sharing, the Prince and Poins set upon them. They all run away, and Falstaff, after a blow or two* [he is, of course, less nimble than the rest], *runs away too, leaving the booty behind them.*
>
> *Prince.* Got with much ease. Now merrily to horse.
> The thieves are scattered, and possess'd with fear
> So strongly that they dare not meet each other.
> Each takes his fellow for an officer.
> Away, good Ned. Falstaff sweats to death
> And lards the lean earth as he walks along.
> Were't not for laughing, I should pity him.
> *Poins.* How the fat rogue roar'd!

So in *A Midsummer Night's Dream*, Bully Bottom's companions had fled in panic at sight of the ass's head.

George Bartley, a distinguished Falstaff of the early years of the last century and for a long time stage-manager at Covent Garden Theatre, is described as "a courteous, discreet gentleman." He had, nevertheless, a very low opinion of the intelligence of audiences.

"Sir," he would say . . . , "you must first tell them you are
going to do so and so; you must then tell them you are doing
it, and then that you have done it; and then, by G-d" (with a
slap on his thigh), "*perhaps* they will understand you!"[29]

Shakespeare in the present instance might almost be anticipating
the precautions recommended. We are told what will happen;
told, as well, what has happened. And if the actual encounter can
scarcely be interpreted while it is taking place, it is, in Shakespeare's theater, no encounter of phantom-shapes, of dimly outlined silhouettes, but one clearly visible by honest daylight. Misunderstanding could not well have existed. "But yet no coward,
Hal. . . . Well, we leave that to the proof."

More still was promised: "the virtue of this jest . . . the incomprehensible lies." And Falstaff fairly outdoes expectation. In the
study, one may forget or overlook, the visual impressiveness of
his entrance. He and his followers carry battered weapons, their
clothes are stained with blood ("Tell me now in earnest," the
Prince asks later, "how came Falstaff's sword so hack'd?" and Peto
explains, "Why, he hack'd it with his dagger, and said he would
swear truth out of England but he would make you believe it was
done in fight, and persuaded us to do the like"). It is he, Sir John,
who makes complaint, "A plague of all cowards, I say." Deserted,
as he found himself, by those who should have fought beside him,
he had yet borne himself magnificently and escaped only "by
miracle." Poins had prophesied he would claim to have fought
with "thirty, at least," and he reaches fifty—"two or three and
fifty upon poor old Jack." Then, before the fun of the mounting
figures is yet exhausted, he is led to mention casualties: "two
rogues in buckram . . . pepper'd." The same two, as we recognize,
who are so eagerly listening to him now, who can wait, nonetheless, and give their great fish more line, for he is surely caught!

For the actor to wink at his audience, somewhere here, as
Mr. Dover Wilson would have him do, seems to me purely arbitrary. (The meaning of innumerable passages in Shakespeare
could be perverted by means of extra-textual winkings, and it is to
be hoped that the present vogue for imagining them does not
spread to tragedy!) Arbitrary, and also confusing, dividing the
audience at a moment when they should be at one and sharing

their pleasure as good audiences ever do. Above all, for Sir John to appear conscious of his danger thus early, is to anticipate our pleasure in his escape. Whereas, if we are to judge from the text alone, this comes as a magnificent surprise. He seems doomed.

> *Prince.* Mark now how a plain tale shall put you down. Then did we two set on you four and, with a word, outfac'd you from your prize, and have it; yea, and can show it you here in the house. And, Falstaff, you carried your guts away as nimbly, with as quick dexterity, and roar'd for mercy, and still run and roar'd, as ever I heard bullcalf. . . . What trick, what device, what starting hole canst thou now find out to hide thee from this open and apparent shame?
> *Poins.* Come, let's hear, Jack. What trick hast thou now?

And then, and only then (and the actor will not fail to bring out the sudden and dramatic change of speed which marks the moment), Falstaff replies:

> By the Lord, I knew ye as well as he that made ye. Why, hear you, my masters. Was it for me to kill the heir apparent? Should I turn upon the true prince? Why, thou knowest I am as valiant as Hercules; but beware instinct. The lion will not touch the true prince.

Falstaff, as Davies recognized, "is never in a state of humiliation; he generally rises superior to attack, and gets the laugh on his side in spite of truth and conviction."[30] Nevertheless, it is the Prince who recurs to this episode with enjoyment, still gloating over it in *The Second Part of Henry the Fourth*. And Falstaff, having outdone himself with his glorious lion and a prince whose legitimacy is *now*, he says, established (as if there might have been some slight reason to doubt it before!) significantly changes the subject:

> Gallants, lads, boys, hearts of gold, all the titles of good fellowship come to you! What, shall we be merry? Shall we have a play extempore?
> *Prince.* Content—and the argument shall be thy running away.
> *Falstaff.* Ah, no more of that, Hal, an thou lovest me!

As Professor Waldock asked in *The Review of English Studies* some years ago, "What point would there be in such a reply . . . if Falstaff had had the laugh on them all along?"[31] He has extricated himself—"in spite of truth and conviction"—and we in the audience are glad of it. Yet Poins and Prince Hal were right; and for them Gadshill will be, as prophesied, "argument for a week, laughter for a month, and a good jest for ever."

It will be seen, if we look back, that the arguments of those who have denied that Falstaff was a coward are of many different sorts. For the most part, they are suggestive of the study rather than the playhouse. Some, indeed, are abstract, or even syllogistic, like Morgann's *We do not like cowards; we like Falstaff; therefore, Falstaff is not a coward.* Some, again, are based on inferences, sound enough, perhaps, in real life, but untrustworthy in the case of popular drama, as that a coward is unlikely to be found in the thick of the fighting. Often, it is as if the critics were determined to impose their own sense of naturalness on what, in the theater, is the more effective for being extreme—Falstaff's "incomprehensible" lying, for example. Yet Bradley himself perceived that "Shakespeare's comic world" was one of make-believe, "not merely as his tragic world is, but in a further sense—a world in which gross improbabilities are accepted with a smile. . . ."[32]

It remains possible, of course, that with this great character Shakespeare was not contented to work on a single level; so that at one instant we may be back with the Clowns of primitive drama (with Dericke, say, in *The Famous Victories*) and at another are not far from the amiable philosopher of the romantic critics. Thus, the soliloquy on honor seems to me something more than a very witty apology for the speaker's cowardice—though is it not that, as well? We read of an American actor whose fame is associated with this role:

> the shudder with which Hackett spoke the words about Honor, "Who hath it? he that-*died-o'*Wednesday," with its obvious revulsion from even the thought of death, was wonderfully expressive of *Falstaff's* animal relish of life, and also it was supremely comic.[33]

For the cowardice of Falstaff as a comic assumption gives added point to speech after speech, and to deprive the actors of it is to deprive them of a constant source of merriment. "Where," as John Bailey asked, "would be the humour of 'a plague of all cowards' if the speaker were a brave man? Where would be the fun of the 'plain tale' that put his preposterous boastings down if, as we are told, he never meant to be believed?"[34] I would not defend the farcical enormities which have been committed in Falstaff's name by unworthy comedians. Descriptions of the older stage business, whether at Gadshill or Shrewsbury, are sometimes far from edifying. But suppose, merely for the sake of argument, that Sir John *was* a coward—a fat, old, witty, boastful coward.

Early in the *Second Part of King Henry the Fourth*, he seeks to avoid a meeting with the Lord Chief Justice, attempts to hide, then feigns deafness. "Go pluck him by the elbow," the Justice tells his Servant, who does so. (Kittredge, I remember, used to describe this Servant as the Justice's "personal attendant," a "young lawyer," who "thought a lot of himself.") "Sir John!" And Falstaff, as if shocked: "What? A young knave, and begging? Is there not wars? . . . Doth not the King lack subjects?" and so on, all very humiliating to the young man. "You mistake me, sir," he says, but Falstaff continues—and goes too far.

> Why, sir, did I say you were an honest man? Setting my knighthood and my soldiership aside, I had lied in my throat if I had said so.
> *Servant.* I pray you, sir, then set your knighthood and your soldiership aside, and give me leave to tell you you lie in your throat if you say I am any other than an honest man.
> *Falstaff.* I give thee leave to tell me so? I lay aside that which grows to me? If thou get'st any leave of me, hang me; if thou tak'st leave, thou wert better be hang'd. You hunt counter. Hence! avaunt!

Is it not the fact of timidity, here thinly disguised in bluster, which makes the episode diverting?[35]

When the attempt to arrest Falstaff is resisted, a little later, his own part in the ensuing scuffle is not easy to determine. As Professor Shaaber, the Variorum editor, notes, much is left to the actors here; yet he adds, wisely, I think, "There is perhaps a hint in the fact that almost every word Falstaff says is by way of putting Bardolph up to active measures of defense." On the other hand, I should allow Sir John a major share in the routing of Ancient Pistol, in the Tavern Scene. Though Bardolph is at hand, once more, to give assistance, his master seems to have put on a magnificent show of belligerency, at the least; is reported to have hurt Pistol in the shoulder and has to be quieted at last by Doll, who points out that "the rascal's gone." Afterwards, we have speeches of purring self-gratulation ("A rascal bragging slave! The rogue fled from me like quicksilver"), as, to use Mr. Stoll's words, he "prolongs the precious moment, unique and unparalleled in his experience, by continually recurring to it."[36] And perhaps we remember (as we should) Sir John's own description of his opponent earlier in the scene as "a tame cheater. . . . You may stroke him as gently as a puppy greyhound. He'll not swagger with a Barbary hen if her feathers turn back in any show of resistance."

Finally, I would suggest that even single lines and phrases may take on an unexpected impressiveness for us if we return to the earlier conception of the character: to a Falstaff of dexterous evasions and miraculous escapes, lawless in his exaggerations, redoubtable only in repute, and the funnier for being fat and old and a coward. So, in the theater, I have heard Ned Poins lay a sudden emphasis upon two words, just before the Gadshill robbery: "Sirrah Jack, thy horse stands behind the hedge. When thou need'st him, there thou shalt find him. Farewell and *stand fast*"; and their portentousness was of exactly the sort that Sir Toby Belch, sometimes, imparts to a phrase in Sir Andrew's letter: "Fare thee well, and *God have mercy upon one of our souls!*" I conceive, too, of a glint in Falstaff's eye, a certain morbid insistence in his voice, as, at another time, he dwells on the strength of the rebels.

> But tell me, Hal, art not thou horrible afeard? Thou being heir apparent, could the world pick thee out three such enemies again as that fiend Douglas, that spirit Percy, and that devil Glendower? Art thou not horribly afraid? Doth not thy blood thrill at it?

A veteran talking to a young soldier, you may say of the passage—and perhaps it is merely that. Just before Shrewsbury they are talking in a somewhat similar vein.

> *Falstaff.* Hal, if thou see me down in the battle and bestride
> me, so! 'Tis a point of friendship.

It is delivered with a flourish—almost as if in imagination he saw
the Prince of Wales standing over and defending a gallant old
soldier wounded (at any rate, *fallen*) in battle. Hal's quibbling reply
gives him cold comfort: "Nothing but a Colossus can do thee that
friendship. Say thy prayers, and farewell." And Falstaff: "I would
'twere bedtime, Hal, and all well."

The last instance I shall give is from a soliloquy, in which the
Elizabethan actor, standing in the midst of his hearers, would
have directly and familiarly addressed them. Falstaff speaks of
Prince John, who does not appreciate him and cannot be made to
laugh. No wonder, he says, for "this same young sober-blooded
boy" does not drink as he should:

> There's never none of these demure boys come to any proof;
> for thin drink doth so over-cool their blood, and making
> many fish-meals, that they fall into a kind of male greensick-
> ness; and then, when they marry, they get wenches. They
> are generally fools and cowards—which some of us should
> be too, but for inflammation.

For an instant, the joke has become one between Falstaff and
ourselves. He pauses after "cowards"; then, "which some of us"
(Sir John himself, no less!) would certainly be too, except (triumphantly) for the effects of drinking sack! And who could accuse
him of negligence in that regard? *You thought I was confessing, did you?*

I would not seem to attach an undue importance to these
passages. They can be reconciled, each of them, with the Morgann Falstaff. "Would 'twere bedtime, Hal, and all well" is a
sentiment which can be responded to by plenty of soldiers on a
level quite different from that of comic cowardice. And the loss to
the actor—though there is loss—will not be irreparable. On the
other hand, it may be that the consensus among early readers and
critics deserves more emphasis than I have given it. The burden of
proof, as even Morgann recognized, rests upon those who deny
cowardice. Samuel Johnson, as I said earlier, referred twice to
Morgann's *Essay.* On the second occasion, when it is Malone who
records the Doctor's words, they are splendidly comprehensive:
"all he shd. say, was, that if Falstaff was not a coward, Shakspeare
knew nothing of his art."[37]

NOTES

1. A paper read at the Shakespeare Conference at Stratford-on-Avon in August 1951.
2. G. E. Bentley, *Shakespeare and Jonson* (Chicago [1945]), chap. vii.
3. *The History of the Worthies of England*, ed. P. Austin Nuttall (London, 1840), II, 455.
4. "An Essay of Dramatic Poesy," in *Dramatic Essays*, "Everyman's Library," p. 43.
5. *The Plays of William Shakespeare*, ed. Johnson (London, 1765), IV, 356.
6. *An Essay on the Dramatic Character of Sir John Falstaff* (London, 1820), pp. 2, 3.
7. *Ibid.*, p. 4.
8. *Ibid.*, p. 13.
9. James Boswell, *Life of Samuel Johnson*, ed. G. B. Hill and L. F. Powell (Oxford, 1934), IV, 192 note.
10. *Dramatic Miscellanies* (London, 1784), I, 272.
11. *Essays on Shakespeare* (1858), in *I Henry IV*, Furness Variorum Edition, p. 135.
12. *Characters of Shakespeare's Plays*, Bohn ed. (1892), p. 135.
13. *Oxford Lectures on Poetry* (London, 1909), p. 268 note.
14. *Ibid.*, p. 266.
15. *Shakespeare Studies* (New York, 1927); "Recent Shakespeare Criticism," *Shakespeare Jahrbuch*, LXXIV (1938); *Shakespeare and Other Masters* (Cambridge [Massachusetts], 1940); *From Shakespeare to Joyce* (New York, 1944); "Symbolism in Shakespeare," *Modern Language Review*, XLII (1947).
16. *The Fortunes of Falstaff* (Cambridge and New York, 1944), pp. 44, 45.
17. *Ibid.*, p. 47.
18. *Ibid.*, p. 58.
19. *Ibid.*, p. 89.
20. *Ibid.*, p. 87.
21. *Ibid.*, p. 107.
22. *2 Henry IV* I.2.207.
23. *1 Henry IV* II.1.95.
24. Cf. J. W. Fortescue, in *Shakespeare's England*, I,123.
25. *Chief Pre-Shakespearean Dramas*, ed. J. Q. Adams (Boston, etc. [1924]), p. 688.
26. *Ibid.*, pp. 686, 687.
27. Richard Stack, in *1 Henry IV*, Furness Variorum Edition, p. 417.
28. *Dramatic Miscellanies*, I,273.
29. J. R. Planché,, *Recollections and Reflections* (London, 1872), II,208.
30. *Dramatic Miscellanies*, I,237, 238.

31. A. J. A. Waldock, "The Men in Buckram," *Review of English Studies*, XXIII (1947), 19.
32. *Oxford Lectures on Poetry*, p. 270.
33. William Winter, *Shakespeare on the Stage: Third Series* (New York, 1916), p. 359.
34. *Shakespeare* (London, New York, and Toronto, 1929), p. 128.
35. Stoll brackets Falstaff's sidling off at this moment with his behaviour towards Poins in *1 Henry IV* II.4.157, an episode which seems to me less clear in its implications (*Shakespeare Studies*, p. 421).
36. *Ibid.*, p. 425.
37. Boswell, *Life of Johnson*, iv, 515.

Robert Langbaum

Character versus Action in Shakespeare
(1957)

Sympathy would seem to have been responsible in the first place for the psychological interpretation of Shakespeare, and it is no coincidence that the new interpretation made its first appearance in the latter eighteenth century when we note the decline of the dogmatic and the beginning of the sympathetic or humanitarian attitude. Our reading of a Hamlet soliloquy depends, after all, on whether we give more emphasis to Hamlet's moral problem or to his experience in facing the problem. If the moral imperative is uppermost in our minds, we are likely to agree with Hamlet when he chides his delay; we are likely to be concerned with his delinquency and to hope that his confession of guilt will advance him toward the fulfilment of his duty. But if we do not find the moral imperative compelling, we are likely to be less concerned with Hamlet's guilt than with his suffering from the sense of guilt; and we are likely to hope not so much that he will do his duty as that he will free himself from the sense of guilt. Nor will the uncompelling moral imperative strike us as a sufficient motive for so much suffering; in which case we will seek out an underlying motive, less abstract and external, more psychological and even biological, more consonant in other words with our assumptions about the mainsprings of human action. An abstract morality lurking in the dim periphery of our attention can hardly compete with the vivid human being filling the stage. Or to put it con-

From *The Poetry of Experience* by Robert Langbaum (University of Chicago Press, 1986). Originally published by Random House, 1957. Reprinted by permission of the author and The University of Chicago Press.

versely, where dogmatic sanction recedes, sympathy rushes in to
fill the vacuum.

Modern sympathy is even better illustrated when we see it
turned upon Shakespeare's villains, for there it is clearly at odds
with the plot. All the subtleties of nineteenth-century Iago criticism are attempts to account for the fact that, in spite of Iago's
villainy, we find him attractive. We admire him because he has a
strong and clearly defined point of view, and we sympathize with
him because he is on the stage and claims our attention. To the
extent that he is there to be understood, we try to understand
him; we give him our sympathy as a primary condition anterior to
judgment.

Iago was *understood* in the traditional interpretation as well, but
he was understood as congruent with his moral category. When
the moral imperative is, however, less compelling than the sheer
appeal of the human being on the stage, sympathy overflows the
weakened confines of the moral category; so that the modern
reader finds in Iago a life that exceeds the moral category and is
not to be accounted for by it. The modern interest—what we
mean by *character* in fact—is in just that which is incongruent with
the moral category. The modern reader can sympathize with any
character, regardless of his moral position in the plot, provided
only that he is sufficiently central to claim our attention, and has
a sufficiently definite point of view and sufficient power of intellect and will to hold our interest. Thus, sympathy is likely to be
more important than moral judgment in the modern interpretation not only of Iago but also of Shakespeare's Richard III, Macbeth, Shylock and Falstaff, and Marlowe's Tamburlaine, Faustus
and Jew of Malta. If we have no sympathy for the execrable
Aaron of Shakespeare's *Titus Andronicus*, it is not because he is
wicked but because he is too crude and stupid to command our
interest. Where we do find Elizabethan villains attractive, it is in
the same sense and for the same reason that we admire Brown-
ing's duke in *My Last Duchess*.

We know how the decline of the moral sanctions against Jews
and usurers has, by turning our sympathy toward Shylock,
turned *The Merchant of Venice* from a crude comedy into a pathetic if
not tragic drama;[1] and how the modern audience, unable to keep
uppermost in its mind a distinct idea of the social limitations

Malvolio has violated in daring to aspire to a Lady's hand, soon begins to feel sorry for him. Since the comic effect depends specifically on the exclusion of sympathy, it is even more important in comedy than in tragedy that we keep the offended mores in mind—which is why fewer comedies than tragedies survive, and why the comedies that do survive do so through the pathetic or psychological interest that modern readers think they find there.

Falstaff's comic effect has not been impaired. But that is because his comic role has been made philosophical by the modern elevation of his character, an elevation which Stoll attributes to the decline of the chivalric code of honour. We laugh with Falstaff when he makes the common-sense attack upon honour ("Can honour set to a leg?"), because we see him as the witty philosopher of a rival world-view. But according to Stoll, the Elizabethans laughed at him for his transparent attempt to justify his cowardice. They saw him as a self-describing coward turning the general perspective against himself by poking sarcastic fun at himself. Stoll even suggests that Falstaff might have winked at the audience as he "descanted on the duty of discretion."[2] Such humorous self-betrayal would have been no more unpsychological than the startling self-betrayal of Shakespeare's villains in the tragedies.

But whether or not we are willing to go along with Stoll on this point (there is, after all, reason to believe that the laugh on chivalry had begun by Shakespeare's time), the issue between the psychological and anti-psychological interpretations of Falstaff is whether as coward, lecher and glutton he is the butt of the comedy and deservedly outwitted in the end; or whether he is the maker of the comedy, playing the butt for the sake of the humour which he turns upon himself as well as everyone else—whether he is, in other words, victorious in all the wit combats whatever his circumstantial defeat. It is essentially the issue of Hamlet and Macbeth criticism, whether they confront their difficulties or create them; and of Iago criticism, whether he is the villain or as maker of the plot merely playing the villain. In other words, are the characters agents of the plot with only as much consciousness as the plot requires; or have they a residue of intelligence and will beyond what the plot requires and not accounted for by it, so that they stand somehow above the plot, conscious of themselves inside it? The latter view assumes that we can apprehend more about the characters than the plot tells us, assumes our sympathetic apprehension of them.

The Falstaff question has been only less important than the Hamlet question in establishing the psychological interpretation of Shakespeare. Both Hamlet and Falstaff began to appear in their new complex and enigmatic character in the 1770's, the decade of Werther and of a European Wertherism that owed much to an already well-established sentimental tradition in England. Of such a propitious age for psychological criticism, Maurice Morgann, the projector of the new Falstaff, was one of the advanced spirits—liberal in politics, humanitarian in sentiment, and in literature endowed with the new sensibility.

Morgann's sensibility is abundantly illustrated in the *Essay on the Dramatic Character of Sir John Falstaff* (1777), where the perceptions are far in advance of the dialectic. It is his fundamental sympathy for Falstaff that Morgann is trying to explain when he undertakes to prove that, in spite of cowardly actions, "Cowardice *is not* the *Impression*, which the *whole* character of *Falstaff* is calculated to make on the minds of an unprejudiced [i.e. sympathetic] audience." And it is on the ground of experience that he makes the novel distinction between our "*mental Impressions*" and our "*Understanding*" of character—whereby "we often condemn or applaud characters and actions on the credit of some logical process, while our hearts revolt, and would fain lead us to a very different conclusion." The "Understanding" takes cognizance, he says, of "*actions* only," and from these infers "*motives* and *character*; but the sense we have been speaking of proceeds in a contrary course, and determines of *actions* from certain *first principles of character*, which seem wholly out of the reach of the Understanding."[3]

Unfortunately, Morgann is a bit frightened by the revolutionary nature of his case, and tries to prove it to his eighteenth-century readers on their own rationalistic and moral grounds. His essay is therefore valuable for its scattered insights rather than for the hair-splitting, text-citing argument destructive of the dramatic and comic context which he employs in order to uncover in the *actions* he says do not *matter* evidences of Falstaff's courage. It would have required the dialectical equipment of the next century for Morgann to have granted the moral case against Falstaff and accounted for his sympathetic *impression* of him by quite another order of value. Yet the other order of value is certainly implied by Morgann's distinction between the *first principles* of character which we apprehend sympathetically and its manifestations which we judge. It is also implied by his distinction between "*Constitutional Courage*" and the "Courage founded upon *principle*." The latter is moral courage, which comes of conformity to "the prevailing modes of honour, and the fashions of the age." But the former is an existential courage, which "extends to a man's whole life, makes a part of his nature, and is not to be taken up or deserted like a mere Moral quality."[4]

It follows—though Morgann does not specifically articulate the conclusion—that our judgment of Falstaff's moral courage must be problematical because based on a shifting idea of honour; whereas our apprehension of his *constitutional* courage must be certain because based on what he is in himself. Only the double apprehension of character could have given rise to Morgann's perception that character may be incongruous with action, that "the *real* character of *Falstaff* may be different from his *apparent* one," and that an author may give wit, dignity and courage to a character made to seem ridiculous, ignoble and cowardly by all external appearances.[5] The recognition that our *impressions* of a character and even of certain of the character's sentiments and actions may be contradictory of his moral category yet "we know not why, natural," leads to the essential method of all psychological criticism in that it compels us "to look farther, and examine if there be not something more in the character than is *shewn*."[6]

Now it is just the habit in Shakespeare criticism of looking for more than is shown that makes Stoll see red, since he contends that this is to treat the character as historical and that there can be no more in a fictitious character than *is* shown. It is true enough that psychological criticism treats the character as though he had a life of which the action presents only a portion; yet Stoll defines the issue, I think, inadequately. For if we conceive the play as larger than the plot, the part of character uncovered by psychological criticism falls not outside the play but outside the moral categories of the plot. The plot, which we understand through moral judgment, becomes a clearing in the forest; while the play shades off to include the penumbra of forest fringe out of which the plot has emerged, a penumbra which we apprehend through sympathy. Such a conception makes room for psychological criticism by dissolving the limits of character and of the play, by suggesting that the limits are always in advance of comprehension. That is how we come by the modern idea of a masterpiece as an enigma whose whole meaning can never be formulated. Comprehension becomes an unending process, historical and evolutionary; while the play itself moves inviolate down the ages, eluding final formulation yet growing, too, in beauty and complexity as it absorbs into its meaning everything that has been thought and felt about it.

According to this conception, Morgann remains within the play, though outside the categories of the plot, when he undertakes to justify Falstaff by an order of value contradictory of his moral position as comic butt outwitted in the end. The *first principles* of character from which we gain our favourable *impression* of Falstaff are those "qualities of a strong mind, particularly Courage and ability," which attract us in spite of the character's vices. They are sufficient to "discharge that *disgust* which arises from vicious manners; and even to attach us . . . to the cause and subject of our mirth with some degree of affection."[7] But a character without courage and ability cannot long command our interest. That is why Morgann can grant all the other vices attributed to Falstaff, but not cowardice: if we "reckon cowardice among his other defects, all the intelligence and wit [i.e. *ability*] in the world could not support him through a single play."[8] The issue is not moral, it is not that cowardice is the gravest sin; rather it would seem to be whether Falstaff is to exist at all. He is "saturated," says Morgann, "with every folly and with every vice not destructive of his essential character,"[9] with every vice, in other words, except cowardice and stupidity which would be destructive. "Courage and Ability are first principles of Character, and not to be destroyed whilst the united frame of body and mind continues whole and unimpaired; they are the pillars on which he stands firm in spight of all his vices and disgraces."[10]

But in what sense is cowardice destructive of character, when there are after all cowardly characters (Shakespeare's Parolles, Jonson's Bobadil)? Morgann's meaning can, I think, be understood in the terms we have established in this discussion. Courage and ability are necessary if Falstaff is to exist as a *character* in the modern sense, as something more than agent of the plot or representative of a moral category—as a pole for sympathy, with a consciousness in excess of the plot's requirements and a life outside the plot and proof against its accidents. The plot makes him out a coward, "but that is nothing," says Morgann, "if the character itself does not act from any consciousness of this kind, and if our Feelings take his part, and revolt against our understanding."[11] I take this to mean that Falstaff's intention is not to escape danger but to provide humour; just as in the psychological interpretation Iago's intention is to create the plot, and Hamlet's and Macbeth's to exercise their moral sensibility. To entertain so radical an idea, we must have apprehended in these characters a residue of consciousness which is as much a spectator of the action as we are, this consciousness being precisely the quality we apprehend through sympathy.

The fact that our *feelings* should have occasion to revolt against our *understanding* means that we judge this residue of consciousness by an order of value other than moral. Morgann's *courage* and *ability* are existential virtues, virtues which make for the sheer survival of the personality apart from any moral purpose toward which the personality is directed. He speaks at length of the indestructible nature of Falstaff, who, unlike Parolles and Bobadil, is never defeated and never even loses stature from his several disgraces. That is because the disgraces, like the "ill habits, and the accidents of age and corpulence, are no part of his essential constitution . . . they are second natures, not *first*." Falstaff's *first* nature is the "substance of his character [which] remains unimpaired," for "*Falstaff* himself has a distinct and separate subsistence."[12]

Falstaff's courage, remember, is not moral but *constitutional*. It is not Hotspur's kind of courage. It is too bad that Morgann did not undertake the contrast with Hotspur, for it holds good under his interpretation—not to be sure as between cowardice and heroism, but as between two kinds of heroism. If Hotspur is the chivalric hero, Falstaff is the natural hero, the Hero of Existence. His is the courage to be himself, to realize his individuality. He is a hero because of his hard core of character, his fierce loyalty to himself,

because he is more alive than other people. By this peculiarly
modern reading, Falstaff and Hotspur would represent opposite
kinds of heroism both of which go down to defeat; while the
Prince, who temporizes between the two extremes, appropriating
from each the virtues he can turn to his advantage, becomes
prudence triumphant.[13]

Although the eighteenth century could not supply the concepts and vocabulary by which Falstaff might be called a hero,
Morgann is already dealing in the distinctive virtues of the new
heroism when he attacks as mere prudence the moral virtues
Falstaff lacks, and glorifies Falstaff on the ground of his imprudence.

> It may not possibly be wholly amiss to remark in this
> place, that if Sir *John Falstaff* had possessed any of that Cardi-
> nal quality, Prudence, alike the guardian of virtue and the
> protector of vice; that quality, from the possession or the
> absence of which, the character and fate of men in this life
> take, I think, their colour, and not from real vice or virtue; if
> he had considered his wit, not as *principal* but *accessary* only; as
> the instrument of power, and not as power itself; . . . he
> might, without any other essential change, have been the
> admiration and not the jest of mankind.[14]

Without using the word, the passage effectively describes Falstaff
as a hero in the new sense; it contains in brief the whole ethical
attitude of the next century. The attack on prudence is the
beginning of the romantic ethics. Hypocrisy (the denial of one's
own nature) is its worst sin, sincerity (another name for existential courage) its prime virtue. Morgann's Falstaff has the virtues
Blake was to recommend in *The Marriage of Heaven and Hell*: "Prudence is a rich, ugly old maid courted by Incapacity," "He who
desires but acts not, breeds pestilence," "The road of excess leads
to the palace of wisdom." *Excess* explains Falstaff's nature; his
girth, his appetites, his laughter, even his style of wit and the rich
redundancy of his language—all derive their character from excess; yet they are not for that reason vices, as they would be
according to the Aristotelian ethics of the Golden Mean. According to the new ethics, Falstaff's excesses are at once the cause of
his failure and of his distinction.

For he commits what Shelley was to call the "generous error," the error of those who try to live life by a vision of it, thus transforming the world about them and impressing upon it their character. This is the secret of Falstaff's appeal. His vision of life takes over whenever he is on the stage; and everyone on stage with him, most notably the Prince, is drawn into his characteristic atmosphere. The only characters who resist his influence are those who, like the King and Hotspur, never confront him. Yet Falstaff's genius for creating his own environment is dangerous, since the single vision of life cannot be identical with reality and must eventually collide with it. That is why the "generous error" distinguishes the Hero of Existence from what Shelley calls the "trembling throng," who "languish" and are "morally dead," who live eclectically because they have not the courage to live out the implications of their own natures, who are too prudent to venture all on what must turn out to have been a noble delusion.[15]

Dr. Johnson, who saw where Morgann's kind of criticism was leading, said of him: "Why, Sir, we shall have the man come forth again; and as he has proved Falstaff to be no coward, he may prove Iago to be a very good character."[16] Johnson thought he was indulging in witty hyperbole, but the admiration for Falstaff was in fact to be accompanied in the next century by an admiration for Iago and for all characters alive enough to take over the scene, to assert their point of view as the one through which we understand the action. The new existential rather than moral judgment of character was to dissolve dramatic structure by denying the authority of the plot—making the psychologically read play, like the dramatic monologue, depend for its success upon a central character with a point of view definite enough to give meaning and unity to the events, and the strength of intellect, will and passion, the imaginative strength, to create the whole work before our eyes, to give it a thickness and an atmosphere, an inner momentum, a life.

It is, however, in the isolation of character from plot that we can best see the psychological interpretation of Shakespeare as dissolving dramatic structure and leading us toward the dramatic monologue. For in concentrating on the part of character in excess of plot requirements, and in claiming to apprehend more about character than the plot reveals, the psychological interpretation isolates character from the external motivation of plot (such as money, love, power). It makes of character an autonomous force, motivated solely by the need for self-expression. The psychological interpretation of Falstaff rests, for example, on the assumption that Falstaff does not employ his wit for practical advantage, that he makes no secret of his true nature and therefore does not really expect to deceive the other characters but merely to draw them into his jests. Deny this assumption as Stoll does, and you have a Falstaff who menaces the other characters and vies for advantage in the same way as the rival factions of the play's historical episodes. Such a Falstaff must be judged morally and laughed at as a base clown who is deservedly humiliated and outwitted at every turn.

But Morgann's Falstaff employs his wit not as the "instrument of power" but as "power itself." And Hazlitt's Falstaff is less interested in sensual gratification than in his own "ideal exaggerated description" of the life of sensuality and freedom, of a worldview he has taken it upon himself to dramatize.

> His pulling out the bottle in the field of battle is a joke to shew his contempt for glory accompanied with danger, his systematic adherence to his Epicurean philosophy in the most trying circumstances. Again, such is his deliberate exaggeration of his own vices, that it does not seem quite certain whether the account of his hostess's bill, found in his pocket, with such an out-of-the-way charge for capons and sack with only one halfpennyworth of bread, was not put there by himself as a trick to humour the jest upon his favourite propensities, and as a conscious caricature of himself. He is represented as a liar, a braggart, a coward, a glutton, &c. and yet we are not offended but delighted with him; for he is all these as much to amuse others as to gratify himself. He openly assumes all these characters to shew the humourous part of them. . . . In a word, he is an actor in himself almost as much as upon the stage, and we no more object to the character of Falstaff in a moral point of view than we should think of bringing an excellent comedian, who should represent him to the life, before one of the police offices.[17]

Falstaff has no motive other than to exercise his genius for comedy.

Hamlet is in the same way isolated from the plot, when Coleridge explains the intricacies of his character not by referring us to his function in the plot but by referring us to "Shakspere's deep and accurate science in mental philosophy" and to the "constitution of our own minds." Thus, Hamlet's "wild transition to the ludicrous" is explained not as a madness deliberately assumed to deceive the King but as "the expression of extreme anguish and horror." And Hamlet's delay is explained not as due to external obstacles which prevent him from executing the revenge but as due to an "overbalance of imagination" which indisposes him for action.[18] Hazlitt goes even farther by making the delay entirely a matter of Hamlet's preference: "it is more to his taste to indulge his imagination in reflecting upon the enormity of the crime and refining on his schemes of vengeance, than to put them into immediate practice."[19]

The Iago of the psychological interpretation is the Shakespearean character most isolated from plot; for ever since Coleridge's characterization of him as a "motiveless malignity," it has been generally agreed that Iago has nothing to gain from the intrigue he devises to destroy Othello. "He is quite or nearly as indifferent to his own fate as to that of others," says Hazlitt; "he runs all risks for a trifling advantage; and is himself the dupe and victim of his ruling passion—an insatiable craving after action of the most difficult and dangerous kind." He devises the intrigue "as an exercise for his ingenuity" and "to prevent *ennui*."[20] Mere motivation, says Swinburne, would spoil the character of Iago: "A genuine and thorough capacity for human lust or hate would diminish and degrade the supremacy of his evil. He is almost as far above or beyond vice as he is beneath or beyond virtue. And this it is that makes him impregnable and invulnerable."[21]

This last statement carries the isolation of character from plot as far as it will go. The effectiveness of character is made to depend on its inaccessibility to the rational and moral categories of the plot. Falstaff, Hamlet and Iago are geniuses whose only purpose is to express their genius. They are creators of the play who must be judged not as we judge men of action but as we judge artists, by the virtuosity of their creations. It matters less whether they are right than that they accomplish what they set out to be and do—that Falstaff conquer with his wit, that Hamlet gain spiritual ascendancy through his moving and profound exploration of moral experience, and that Iago's intrigue be bold, ingenious and successful.

Such a theory is in its ultimate implication destructive of drama. It destroys the play as an entity distinct from its parts, having a logic, meaning and unity of its own to which the parts are subordinated; for it destroys the objective principles which relate the events and characters to each other and to the whole. By leaving events subject to the will of character, it destroys the logic inherent in the events themselves. And by giving unconditional sympathy to sheer vividness of character, it destroys the moral principle which apportions sympathy among the characters according to their deserts. It leaves an anarchic free-for-all in which the characters compete for a sympathy that depends on the ability to command attention, with the strongest character able to assert his point of view against the general meaning.

What such a theory does is to break down the barriers that hold sympathy in check, subordinating it to the general meaning. It allows sympathy to become a law unto itself, the law of dramatic structure in fact; so that we no longer have the logical unit Aristotle spoke of, with its beginning, middle and end, but rather a succession of whatever characters and events happen to fall within the purview of the character who has captured our sympathy. Instead of a play which is complete because of the working out of its own logic, we have a play whose limits are defined only by the perspective of a central character. Hence the controversy between the anti-psychological critics, who insist that there is only as much character as appears in the play, and the psychological critics, who insist that dramatic characters can be treated as though they were historical, that it is legitimate to speculate upon their lives before and after the play. The question is whether the character is part of a definitive unit, the play; or whether the play is merely an episode in the character's career, an episode whose beginning and end shades off into the rest of his biography. To the extent that perspective replaces logical completeness as the principle of organization, we are moving away from drama toward the dramatic monologue.

There has always been in drama a certain tension between the point of view of each character and the play's final meaning which assigns values to the points of view. And among the audience there has been a corresponding tension between the inclination to be interested in each character out of sheer curiosity and the necessity to judge the characters morally. But character has always given way in drama to general meaning; whereas the nineteenth century preferred to weight the balance in the other direction, to allow the individual point of view and the inclination to be interested in it to have their way against the general meaning. That is what the nineteenth century did with its reading of Shakespeare, where it may not have had the right to, and what it did where it undoubtedly had the right—with its own literature, as in the dramatic monologue.

The dramatic monologue brings to the surface what is underground in drama; what in drama resists the law of the form becomes the law of the dramatic monologue. The sympathy which pulls against the meaning of drama is the meaning and whole *raison d'être* of the dramatic monologue. External and moral relations are still there, but pushed off-stage; they are now the underground and resisting element, the foil against which meaning defines itself. For the meaning of the dramatic monologue derives not from the absorption of the particular in the general but from the defiance of the general. The meaning is not the law which puts character in its place; the meaning *is* character in its unformulated being, in all its particularity.

NOTES

1. There has been, however, no decline in the sanction against tyrannical fathers, who still make excellent butts for comedy provided they are top-dog not under-dog as, in our eyes, Shylock is through his Jewishness. Stoll objects of course to the pathetic Shylock. But I see no alternative if *The Merchant* is to be played at all. A modern audience would not relish the red-wigged, hook-nosed caricature of the Elizabethan stage, nor would they enjoy participating in the unanimous baiting of the lone Jew. The alternative to the modern misinterpretation would seem to be an historically accurate but dead document.
2. *Shakespeare Studies*, p. 468.
3. Ed. W. A. Gill (London: Henry Frowde, 1912), pp. 4–6.
4. p. 23.

5. pp. 14, 148–50.

6. p. 153.

7. pp. 11–12.

8. p. 165.

9. p. 149.

10. p. 165.

11. p. 166.

12. p. 177. "And hence it is," Morgann continues, "that he is made to undergo not one detection only, but a series of detections; that he is not formed for one Play only, but was intended originally at least for two; and the author, we are told, was doubtful if he should not extend him yet farther, and engage him in the wars with *France*." There follows the best explanation I have seen of Falstaff's "disgrace" at the end of *Henry IV Part II*. Since Falstaff interests us by his wit in extricating himself from detections and disgraces, Shakespeare leaves him in disgrace in order that he may get himself out of it in the next play. There is, indeed, no other way of leaving Falstaff, Morgann shrewdly observes, except to leave him dead. For there can be no conclusion of his story in terms of the plot, since his existence has been mainly outside the plot: "He was not involved in the fortune of the Play; he was engaged in no action which, as to him, was to be compleated; . . . he passes thro' the Play as a lawless meteor" (p. 183). Thus, Shakespeare kills him off in *Henry V*, when he has decided not to use him any more.

13. Although Bradley does not carry his reading of the play this far, he calls the Prince "perhaps, the most *efficient* character drawn by Shakespeare," and considers him an unpleasantly calculating person who planned from the start to reject Falstaff: "He is still his father's son, the son of the man whom Hotspur called a 'vile politician.'" ("The Rejection of Falstaff," *Oxford Lectures on Poetry*, London: Macmillan, 1926, pp. 256–57.)

14. pp. 20–21.

15. See the Preface to *Alastor* and the last stanza of *Adonais*.

16. James Boswell, *The Life of Samuel Johnson, LL.D.* (London: J. M. Dent, 1901), III, 230.

17. *Characters of Shakespear's Plays*, pp. 190–91.

18. *Lectures on Shakspere*, pp. 471–73.

19. *Characters*, p. 109.

20. *Characters*, p. 55.

21. *A Study of Shakespeare*, p. 179.

Bernard Spivack

Moral Metaphor and Dramatic Image (1958)

It is hard for us, if not impossible, to regard Falstaff as a villain
in any sense, Shakespeare having marvelously exploited his affinity with the comic aspects of the Vice. But Falstaff's high comedy
is still sufficiently close to its origins in the double nature of his
allegorical forbear to prevent him from being a comic figure
merely. In him the direct accent of the Vice's wit is not quite free
from the faint echo of the Vice's evil. The comic hyperbole describing him as "That villainous abominable misleader of youth" is
his vestigial appendix: it does not actually function in his dramatic
life, but it creates the illness of which he dies. The shadow of a
serious moral judgment hovers about him, disturbing us as it
disturbed Maurice Morgann, and when it finally closes in on him
Falstaff succumbs to the moral severity which is always present in
the traditional stage image of the Vice, no matter how comic his
performance. His banishment and imprisonment are regular punishments for the Vice, who, we must remember, is at bottom a
personification and incorrigible; and we are in debt to Shakespeare's clemency that the fat knight escapes the even more
common punishment of the gallows. If Falstaff's end distresses
Bradley and us, that is because our modern sentiment, innocent
of the old moral and dramatic convention that survives in him and
controls his fate, craves a unified impression consistent with that
side of him into which Shakespeare's genius mainly poured—his
gorgeous wit and innocuous good fellowship. The Elizabethans,
however, habituated by their transitional stage to hybrids of this

From *Shakespeare and the Allegory of Evil,* © 1958, Columbia University
Press. Reprinted by permission of the author and Columbia University
Press.

sort, were completely at home with the double image and the double sentiment.

At any rate, Shakespeare's recollections of the morality Vice confirm his double nature and point the cleavage his role underwent when the dying stage convention of homiletic allegory bequeathed him to the secular drama and to its instinct for artistic discrimination between comedy and tragedy. So long as he remained in the moralities, which lack that instinct because their effort is mainly didactic rather than dramatic, he is an inextricable mixture of farce and high moral seriousness, the source of both the gaiety and gravity of the play. It is only when he is taken over by the secular drama, with its at least partially specialized genres of comedy and tragedy, that he becomes correspondingly specialized, and his intrigue takes on a coloration that conforms to the tragic or comic spirit. But the process is gradual, and in the early years of the seventeenth century the Vice still trails his double nature into both comedy and tragedy, something of a villainous *farceur* in the former and a deadly villain with a farcical style in the latter. His abstract name necessarily disappears, but the allegorical and homiletic method of his performance linger, and so do his traditional intrigue and his characteristic devices of deceit. In comedy his performance is a demonstration of his wit, in tragedy of his villainy. The Elizabethan poets of the secular drama took him as they found him and reworked him gradually, his traditional status and rooted popularity more authoritative for them than the sort of psychological analysis that troubles us today.

C. L. Barber

Rule and Misrule in *Henry IV* (1959)

> If all the year were playing holidays,
> To sport would be as tedious as to work . . .

The two parts of *Henry IV*, written probably in 1597 and 1598, are an astonishing development of drama in the direction of inclusiveness, a development possible because of the range of the traditional culture and the popular theater, but realized only because Shakespeare's genius for construction matched his receptivity. We have noticed briefly in the introductory chapter how, early in his career, Shakespeare made brilliant use of the long standing tradition of comic accompaniment and counterstatement by the clown.[1] Now suddenly he takes the diverse elements in the potpourri of the popular chronicle play and composes a structure in which they draw each other out. The Falstaff comedy, far from being forced into an alien environment of historical drama, is begotten by that environment, giving and taking meaning as it grows. The implications of the saturnalian attitude are more drastically and inclusively expressed here than anywhere else, because here misrule is presented along with rule and along with the tensions that challenge rule. Shakespeare dramatizes not only holiday but also the need for holiday and the need to limit holiday.

It is in the Henry IV plays that we can consider most fruitfully general questions concerning the relation of comedy to analogous forms of symbolic action in folk rituals: not only the likenesses of

From *Shakespeare's Festive Comedy: A Study of Dramatic Form and Its Relation to Social Custom*, 1959. Reprinted by permission of Princeton University Press.

comedy to ritual, but the differences, the features of comic form which make it comedy and not ritual. Such analogies, I think, prove to be useful critical tools: they lead us to see structure in the drama. And they also raise fascinating historical and theoretical questions about the relation of drama to other products of culture. One way in which our time has been seeing the universal in literature has been to find in complex literary works patterns which are analogous to myths and rituals and which can be regarded as archetypes, in some sense primitive or fundamental. I have found this approach very exciting indeed. But at the same time, such analysis can be misleading if it results in equating the literary form with primitive analogues. When we are dealing with so developed an art as Shakespeare's, in so complex an epoch as the Renaissance, primitive patterns may be seen in literature mainly because literary imagination, exploiting the heritage of literary form, disengages them from the suggestions of a complex culture. And the primitive levels are articulated in the course of reunderstanding their nature—indeed, the primitive can be fully expressed only on condition that the artist can deal with it in a most civilized way. Shakespeare presents patterns analogous to magic and ritual in the process of redefining magic as imagination, ritual as social action.

Shakespeare was the opposite of primitivistic, for in his culture what we search out and call primitive was in the blood and bone as a matter of course; the problem was to deal with it, to master it. The Renaissance, moreover, was a moment when educated men were modifying a ceremonial conception of human life to create a historical conception. The ceremonial view, which assumed that names and meanings are fixed and final, expressed experience as pageant and ritual—pageant where the right names could march in proper order, or ritual where names could be changed in the right, the proper way. The historical view expresses life as drama. People in drama are not identical with their names, for they gain and lose their names, their status and meaning—and not by settled ritual: the gaining and losing of names, of meaning, is beyond the control of any set ritual sequence. Shakespeare's plays are full of pageantry and of action patterned in a ritualistic way. But the pageants are regularly interrupted; the rituals are abortive or perverted; or if they succeed, they succeed against odds or in an unexpected fashion. The people in the plays try to organize their lives by pageant and ritual, but the plays are dramatic precisely because the effort fails. This failure drama presents as history and personality; in the largest perspective, as destiny.

At the heart of the plays there is, I think, a fascination with the individualistic use or abuse of ritual—with magic. There is an intoxication with the possibility of an omnipotence of mind by which words might become things, by which a man might "gain a deity," might achieve, by making his own ritual, an unlimited power to incarnate meaning.[2] This fascination is expressed in the poetry by which Shakespeare's people envisage their ideal selves. But his drama also expresses an equal and complementary awareness that magic is delusory, that words can become things or lead to deeds only within a social group, by virtue of a historical, social situation beyond the mind and discourse of any one man. This awareness of limitations is expressed by the ironies, whether comic or tragic, which Shakespeare embodies in the dramatic situations of his speakers, the ironies which bring down the meanings which fly high in winged words.

In using an analogy with temporary king and scapegoat to bring out patterns of symbolic action in Falstaff's role, it will be important to keep it clear that the analogy is one we make now, that it is not Shakespeare's analogy; otherwise we falsify his relation to tradition.[3] He did not need to discriminate consciously, in our way, underlying configurations which came to him with his themes and materials. His way of extending consciousness of such patterns was the drama. In creating the Falstaff comedy, he fused two main saturnalian traditions, the clowning customary on the stage and the folly customary on holiday, and produced something unprecedented. He was working out attitudes towards chivalry, the state and crown in history, in response to the challenge posed by the fate he had dramatized in *Richard II*. The fact that we find analogies to the ritual interregnum relevant to what Shakespeare produced is not the consequence of a direct influence; his power of dramatic statement, in developing saturnalian comedy, reached to modes of organizing experience which primitive cultures have developed with a clarity of outline comparable to that of his drama. The large and profound relations he ex-

pressed were developed from the relatively simple dramatic
method of composing with statement and counterstatement, elevated action and burlesque. The Henry IV plays are masterpieces
of popular theater whose plays were, in Sidney's words, "neither
right tragedies nor right comedies, mingling kings and clowns."

Mingling Kings and Clowns

The fascination of Falstaff as a dramatic figure has led criticism, from Morgann's essay onward, to center *1 Henry IV* on him,
and to treat the rest of the play merely as a setting for him. But
despite his predominating imaginative significance, the play is
centered on Prince Hal, developing in such a way as to exhibit in
the prince an inclusive, sovereign nature fitted for kingship. The
relation of the Prince to Falstaff can be summarized fairly adequately in terms of the relation of holiday to everyday. As the
non-historical material came to Shakespeare in *The Famous Victories
of Henry the Fifth*, the prince was cast in the traditional role of the
prodigal son, while his disreputable companions functioned as
tempters in the same general fashion as the Vice of the morality
plays. At one level Shakespeare keeps this pattern, but he shifts
the emphasis away from simple moral terms. The issue, in his
hands, is not whether Hal will be good or bad but whether he will
be noble or degenerate, whether his holiday will become his
everyday. The interregnum of a Lord of Misrule, delightful in its
moment, might develop into the anarchic reign of a favorite
dominating a dissolute king. Hal's secret, which he confides early
to the audience, is that for him Falstaff is merely a pastime, to be
dismissed in due course:

> If all the year were playing holidays,
> To sport would be as tedious as to work;
> But when they seldom come, they wish'd-for come . . .
> (I.ii.228–230)

The prince's sports, accordingly, express not dissoluteness but
a fine excess of vitality—"as full of spirit as the month of May"—
together with a capacity for occasionally looking at the world as
though it were upside down. His energy is controlled by an

inclusive awareness of the rhythm in which he is living: despite
appearances, he will not make the mistake which undid
Richard II, who played at saturnalia until it caught up with him in
earnest. During the battle of Shrewsbury (when, in Hotspur's
phrase, "Doomsday is near"), Hal dismisses Falstaff with "What! is
it a time to jest and dally now?" (V.iii.57). This sense of timing, of
the relation of holiday to everyday and doomsday, contributes to
establishing the prince as a sovereign nature.

But the way Hal sees the relations is not the way other people
see them, nor indeed the way the audience sees them until the
end. The holiday-everyday antithesis is his resource for control,
and in the end he makes it stick. But before that, the only clear-
cut definition of relations in these terms is in his single soliloquy,
after his first appearance with Falstaff. Indeed, it is remarkable
how little satisfactory formulation there is of the relationships
which the play explores dramatically. It is essential to the play
that the prince should be misconstrued, that the king should see
"riot and dishonor stain" (I.i.85) his brow, that Percy should
patronize him as a "nimble-footed madcap" (IV.ii.95) who might
easily be poisoned with a pot of ale if it were worth the trouble.
But the absence of adequate summary also reflects the fact that
Shakespeare was doing something which he could not summa-
rize, which only the whole resources of his dramatic art could
convey.

It is an open question, throughout *Part One*, as to just who or
what Falstaff is. At the very end, when Prince John observes
"This is the strangest tale that ever I heard," Hal responds with
"This is the strangest fellow, brother John" (V.iv.158–159). From
the beginning, Falstaff is constantly renaming himself:

> Marry, then, sweet wag, when thou art king, let not us that
> are squires of the night's body be called thieves of the day's
> beauty. Let us be Diana's Foresters, Gentlemen of the
> Shade, Minions of the Moon; and let men say we be men of
> good government . . .
>
> (I.ii.26–31)

Here Misrule is asking to be called Good Government, as it is his
role to do—though he does so with a wink which sets real good
government at naught, concluding with "steal":

> . . . men of good government, being governed as the sea is,
> by our noble and chaste mistress the moon, under whose
> countenance we steal.
>
> (I.ii.31–33)

I have considered in an earlier chapter how the witty equivocation
Falstaff practices, like that of Nashe's Bacchus and other apologists for folly and vice, alludes to the very morality it is flouting.[4]
Such "damnable iteration" is a sport that implies a rolling-eyed
awareness of both sides of the moral medal; the Prince summarizes it in saying that Sir John "was never yet a breaker of proverbs. He will give the devil his due" (I.ii.131–133). It is also a game
to be played with cards close to the chest. A Lord of Misrule
naturally does not call himself Lord of Misrule in setting out to
reign, but takes some title with the life of pretense in it. Falstaff's
pretensions, moreover, are not limited to one occasion, for he is
not properly a holiday lord, but a *de facto* buffoon who makes his
way by continually seizing, catch as catch can, on what names and
meanings the moment offers. He is not a professed buffoon—few
buffoons, in life, are apt to be. In Renaissance courts, the role of
buffoon was recognized but not necessarily formalized, not necessarily altogether distinct from the role of favorite. And he is a
highwayman: Shakespeare draws on the euphemistic, mock-chi-
valric cant by which "the profession" grace themselves. Falstaff in
Part One plays it that he is Hal's friend, a gentleman, a "gentleman
of the shade," and a soldier; he even enjoys turning the tables
with "Thou hast done much harm upon me, Hal . . . I must give
over this life, and I will give it over . . . I'll be damn'd for never a
king's son in Christendom" (I.ii.102–109). It is the essence of his
character, and his role, in *Part One*, that he never comes to rest
where we can see him for what he "is." He is always in motion,
always adopting postures, assuming characters.

That he does indeed care for Hal can be conveyed in performance without imposing sentimental tableaux on the action, provided that actors and producer recognize that he cares for the
prince after his own fashion. It is from the prince that he chiefly
gets his meaning, as it is from real kings that mock kings always
get their meaning. We can believe it when we hear in *Henry V* that
banishment has "killed his heart" (II.i.92). But to make much of a

personal affection for the prince is a misconceived way to find meaning in Falstaff. His extraordinary meaningfulness comes from the way he manages to live "out of all order, out of all compass" by his wit and his wits; and from the way he keeps reflecting on the rest of the action, at first indirectly by the mock roles that he plays, at the end directly by his comments at the battle. Through this burlesque and mockery an intelligence of the highest order is expressed. It is not always clear whether the intelligence is Falstaff's or the dramatist's; often the question need not arise. Romantic criticism went the limit in ascribing a God-like superiority to the character, to the point of insisting that he tells the lies about the multiplying men in buckram merely to amuse, that he knew all the time at Gadshill that it was with Hal and Poins that he fought. To go so far in that direction obviously destroys the drama—spoils the joke in the case of the "incomprehensible lies," a joke which, as E. E. Stoll abundantly demonstrates, must be a joke *on* Falstaff.[5] On the other hand, I see no reason why actor and producer should not do all they can to make us enjoy the intellectual mastery involved in Falstaff's comic resource and power of humorous redefinition. It is crucial that he should not be made so superior that he is never in predicaments, for his genius is expressed in getting out of them. But he does have genius, as Maurice Morgann rightly insisted though in a misconceived way. Through his part Shakespeare expressed attitudes towards experience which, grounded in a saturnalian reversal of values, went beyond that to include a radical challenge to received ideas.

Throughout the first three acts of *Part One*, the Falstaff comedy is continuously responsive to the serious action. There are constant parallels and contrasts with what happens at court or with the rebels. And yet these parallels are not explicitly noticed; the relations are presented, not formulated. So the first scene ends in a mood of urgency, with the tired king urging haste: "come yourself with speed to us again." The second scene opens with Hal asking Falstaff "What a devil hast thou to do with the time of day?" The prose in which he explains why time is nothing to Sir John is wonderfully leisurely and abundant, an elegant sort of talk that has all the time in the world to enjoy the completion of its schematized patterns:

Unless hours were cups of sack, and minutes capons, and
clocks the tongues of bawds, and dials the signs of leaping
houses, and the blessed sun himself a fair hot wench in
flame-colored taffeta, I see no reason why thou shouldst be
so superfluous to demand the time of day.

(I.ii.7-13)

The same difference in the attitude towards time runs throughout and goes with the difference between verse and prose medi-
ums. A similar contrast obtains about lese majesty. Thus at their
first appearance Falstaff insults Hal's majesty with casual, off-
hand wit which the prince tolerates (while getting his own back
by jibing at Falstaff's girth):

And I prithee, sweet wag, when thou art king, as God save
thy Grace—Majesty I should say, for grace thou wilt have
none—
Prince. What, none?
Falstaff. No, by my troth; not so much as will serve to be
prologue to an egg and butter.
Prince. Well, how then? Come, roundly, roundly.

(I.ii.17-25)

In the next scene, we see Worcester calling into question the
grace of Bolingbroke, "that same greatness to which our own
hands / Have holp to make so portly" (I.iii.12-13). The King's
response is immediate and drastic, and his lines point a moral that
Hal seems to be ignoring:

Worcester, get thee gone; for I do see
Danger and disobedience in thine eye.
O, sir, your presence is too bold and peremptory,
And majesty might never yet endure
The moody frontier of a servant brow.

(I.iii.15-19)

Similar parallels run between Hotspur's heroics and Falstaff's
mock-heroics. In the third scene we hear Hotspur talking of "an
easy leap / To pluck bright honor from the pale-fac'd moon"
(I.iii.201-202). Then in the robbery, Falstaff is complaining that
"Eight yards of uneven ground is threescore and ten miles afoot
for me," and asking "Have you any levers to lift me up again,
being down?" (II.ii.25-28, 36). After Hotspur enters exclaiming

against the cowardly lord who has written that he will not join
the rebellion, we have Falstaff's entrance to the tune of "A plague
of all cowards" (II.iv.127). And so on, and so on. Shakespeare's art
has reached the point where he makes everything foil to everything else. Hal's imagery, in his soliloquy, shows the dramatist
thinking about such relations: "like bright metal on a sullen
ground, / My reformation, glitt'ring o'er my fault" (I.ii.236-237).
Now it is not true that Falstaff's impudence about Hal's grace
undercuts Bolingbroke's majesty, nor that Sir John's posturing as
a hero among cowards invalidates the heroic commitment Hotspur expresses when he says "but I tell you, my lord fool, out of
this nettle, danger, we pluck this flower, safety" (II.iii.11-12). The
relationship is not one of a mocking echo. Instead, there is a
certain distance between the comic and serious strains which
leaves room for a complex interaction, organized by the crucial
role of the prince. We are invited, by the King's unfavorable
comparison in the opening scene, to see the Prince in relation to
Hotspur. And Hal himself, in the midst of his Boars Head revel,
compares himself with Hotspur. In telling Poins of his encounter
with the drawers among the hogsheads of the wine-cellar, he says
"I have sounded the very bass-string of humility," goes on to note
what he has gained by it, "I can drink with any tinker in his own
language during my life," and concludes with "I tell thee, Ned,
thou hast lost much honour that thou wert not with me in this
action" (II.iv.5, 20-24). His mock-heroic way of talking about "this
action" shows how well he knows how to value it from a princely
vantage. But the remark cuts two ways. For running the gamut of
society *is* an important action: after their experiment with Francis
and his "Anon, anon, sir," the Prince exclaims

> That ever this fellow should have fewer words than a parrot,
> and yet the son of a woman! . . . I am not yet of Percy's
> mind, the Hotspur of the North; he that kills me some six or
> seven dozen of Scots at a breakfast, washes his hands, and
> says to his wife, "Fie upon this quiet life! I want work." "O
> my sweet Harry," says she, "how many hast thou kill'd to-
> day?" "Give my roan horse a drench," says he, and answers
> "Some fourteen," an hour after, "a trifle, a trifle." I prithee
> call in Falstaff. I'll play Percy, and that damn'd brawn shall
> play Dame Mortimer his wife.
>
> (II.iv.110-124)

It is the narrowness and obliviousness of the martial hero that Hal's mockery brings out; here his awareness explicitly spans the distance between the separate strains of the action; indeed, the distance is made the measure of the kingliness of his nature. His "I am not *yet* of Percy's mind" implies what he later promises his father (the commercial image he employs reflects his ability to use, after his father's fashion, the politician's calculation and indirection):

> Percy is but my factor, good my lord,
> To engross up glorious deeds on my behalf . . .
> (III.ii.147-148)

In the Boars Head Tavern scene, Hal never carries out the plan of playing Percy to Falstaff's Dame Mortimer; in effect he has played both their parts already in his snatch of mimicry. But Falstaff provides him with a continuous exercise in the consciousness that comes from playing at being what one is not, and from seeing through such playing.

Even here, where one world does comment on another explicitly, Hotspur's quality is not invalidated; rather, his achievement is *placed*. It is included within a wider field which contains also the drawers, mine host, Mistress Quickly, and by implication, not only "all the good lads of Eastcheap" but all the estates of England.[6] When we saw Hotspur and his Lady, he was not foolish, but delightful in his headlong, spontaneous way. His Lady has a certain pathos in the complaints which serve to convey how all absorbing his battle passion is. But the joke is with him as he mocks her:

> Love? I love thee not;
> I care not for thee, Kate. This is no world
> To play with mammets and to tilt with lips.
> We must have bloody noses and crack'd crowns,
> And pass them current, too. Gods me, my horse!
> (II.iii.93-97)

One could make some very broad fun of Hotspur's preference for his horse over his wife. But there is nothing of the kind in Shakespeare: here and later, his treatment values the conversion of love into war as one of the important human powers. Hotspur has the fullness of life and the unforced integrity of the great aristocrat who has never known what it is to cramp his own style. His style shows it; he speaks the richest, freshest poetry of the play, in lines that take all the scope they need to fulfill feeling and perception:

> oft the teeming earth
> Is with a kind of colic pinch'd and vex'd
> By the imprisoning of unruly wind
> Within her womb, which, for enlargement striving,
> Shakes the old beldame earth and topples down
> Steeples and mossgrown towers. At your birth
> Our grandam earth, having this distemp'rature,
> In passion shook.
> Glendower.   Cousin, of many men
> I do not bear these crossings. Give me leave
> To tell you once again that at my birth
> The front of heaven was full of fiery shapes,
> The goats ran from the mountains, and the herds
> Were strangely clamorous to the frighted fields.
>
> (III.i.28–40)

The established life of moss-grown towers is in Percy's poetic speech, as the grazed-over Welsh mountains are in Glendower's. They are both strong; everybody in this play is strong in his own way. Hotspur's humor is untrammeled, like his verse, based on the heedless empiricism of an active, secure nobleman:

> Glendower. I can call spirits from the vasty deep.
> Hotspur. Why, so can I, or so can any man;
>   But will they come when you do call for them?
>
> (III.i.53–55)

His unconsciousness makes him, at other moments, a comic if winning figure, as the limitations of his feudal virtues are brought out: his want of tact and judgment, his choleric man's forgetfulness, his sudden boyish habit of leaping to conclusions, the noble but also comical way he can be carried away by "imagination of some great exploit" (I.iii.199), or by indignation at "this vile politician, Bolingbroke" (I.iii.241). Professor Lily B. Campbell has demonstrated that the rebellion of the Northern Earls in 1570 was present for Shakespeare's audience in watching the Percy family

in the play.⁷ The remoteness of this rough north country life
from the London world of his audience, as well as its aristocratic
charm, are conveyed when Hotspur tells his wife that she swears
"like a comfit-maker's wife,"

> As if thou ne'er walk'st further than Finsbury.
> Swear me, Kate, like a lady as thou art,
> A good mouth-filling oath; and leave 'in sooth'
> And such protest of pepper gingerbread
> To velvet guards and Sunday citizens.
>
> (III.i.255–259)

It is the various strengths of a stirring world, not deficiencies,
which make the conflict in *1 Henry IV*. Even the humble carriers,
and the professional thieves, are full of themselves and their
business:

> I am joined with no foot land-rakers, no long-staff sixpenny
> strikers, none of these mad mustachio purple-hued malt-
> worms; but with nobility and tranquillity, burgomasters and
> great oneyers, such as can hold in, such as will strike sooner
> than speak, and speak sooner than drink, and drink sooner
> than pray; and yet, zounds, I lie; for they pray continually to
> their saint, the commonwealth, or rather, not pray to her,
> but prey on her, for they ride up and down on her and make
> her their boots.
>
> (II.i.81–91)

In his early history play, *2 Henry VI*, as we have noticed, Shakespeare used his clowns to present the Jack Cade rebellion as a
saturnalia ignorantly undertaken in earnest, a highly-stylized
piece of dramaturgy, which he brings off triumphantly. In this
more complex play the underworld is presented as endemic disorder alongside the crisis of noble rebellion: the king's lines are
apposite when he says that insurrection can always mobilize

> moody beggars, starving for a time
> Of pell-mell havoc and confusion.
>
> (V.i.81–82)

Falstaff places himself in saying "Well, God be thanked for these
rebels. They offend none but the virtuous. I laud them, I praise
them."

The whole effect, in the opening acts, when there is little commentary on the spectacle as a whole, is of life overflowing its bounds by sheer vitality. Thieves and rebels and honest men— "one that hath abundance of charge too, God knows what" (II.i.64)—ride up and down on the commonwealth, pray to her and prey on her. Hotspur exults that "That roan shall be my throne" (II.iii.73). Falstaff exclaims, "Shall I? Content. This chair shall be my state" (II.iv.415). Hal summarizes the effect, after Hotspur is dead, with

> When that this body did contain a spirit,
> A kingdom for it was too small a bound.
>
> (V.iv.89–90)

The stillness when he says this, at the close of the battle, is the moment when his royalty is made manifest. When he stands poised above the prostrate bodies of Hotspur and Falstaff, his position on the stage and his lines about the two heroes express a nature which includes within a larger order the now subordinated parts of life which are represented in those two: in Hotspur, honor, the social obligation to courage and self-sacrifice, a value which has been isolated in this magnificently anarchical feudal lord to become almost everything; and in Falstaff, the complementary *joie de vivre* which rejects all social obligations with "I like not such grinning honour as Sir Walter hath. Give me life" (V.iii.61).

Getting Rid of Bad Luck by Comedy

But Falstaff does not stay dead. He jumps up in a triumph which, like Bottom coming alive after Pyramus is dead, reminds one of the comic resurrections in the St. George plays. He comes back to life because he is still relevant. His apology for counterfeiting cuts deeply indeed, because it does not apply merely to himself; we can relate it, as William Empson has shown, to the counterfeiting of the king. Bolingbroke too knows when it is time to counterfeit, both in this battle, where he survives because he has many marching in his coats, and throughout a political career where, as he acknowledges to Hal, he manipulates the symbols of majesty with a calculating concern for ulterior results. L. C. Knights, noticing this relation and the burlesque, elsewhere in Falstaff's part, of the attitudes of chivalry, concluded with nineteenth-century critics like Ulrici and Victor Hugo that the comedy should be taken as a devastating satire on war and government.[8] But this is obviously an impossible, anachronistic view, based on the assumption of the age of individualism that politics and war are unnatural activities that can be done without. Mr. Knights would have it that the audience should feel a jeering response when Henry sonorously declares, after Shrewsbury: "Thus ever did rebellion find rebuke." This interpretation makes a shambles of the heroic moments of the play—makes them clearly impossible to act. My own view, as will be clear, is that the dynamic relation of comedy and serious action is saturnalian rather than satiric, that the misrule works, through the whole dramatic rhythm, to consolidate rule. But it is also true, as Mr. Empson remarks, that "the double plot is carrying a fearful strain here."[9] Shakespeare is putting an enormous pressure on the comedy to resolve the challenge posed by the ironic perceptions presented in his historical action.

The process at work, here and earlier in the play, can be made clearer, I hope, by reference now to the carrying off of bad luck by the scapegoat of saturnalian ritual. We do not need to assume that Shakespeare had any such ritual patterns consciously in mind; whatever his conscious intention, it seems to me that these analogues illuminate patterns which his poetic drama presents concretely and dramatically. After such figures as the Mardi Gras or Carnival have presided over a revel, they are frequently turned on by their followers, tried in some sort of court, convicted of sins notorious in the village during the last year, and burned or buried in effigy to signify a new start. In other ceremonies described in *The Golden Bough*, mockery kings appear as recognizable substitutes for real kings, stand trial in their stead, and carry away the evils of their realms into exile or death. One such scapegoat figure, as remote historically as could be from Shakespeare, is the Tibetan King of the Years, who enjoyed ten days' misrule during the annual holiday of Buddhist monks at Lhasa. At the climax of his ceremony, after doing what he liked while collecting bad luck by shaking a black yak's tail over the people, he mounted the temple steps and ridiculed the representative of the Grand Llama, proclaiming heresies like "What we perceive through the five senses is no illusion. All you teach is untrue." A few minutes later, discredited by a cast of loaded dice, he was chased off to exile and possible death in the mountains.[10] One cannot help thinking of Falstaff's catechism on honor, spoken just before another valuation of honor is expressed in the elevated blank verse of a hero confronting death: "Can honour . . . take away the grief of a wound? No. . . . What is honour? a word. What is that word, honour? Air." Hal's final expulsion of Falstaff appears in the light of these analogies to carry out an impersonal pattern, not merely political but ritual in character. After the guilty reign of Bolingbroke, the prince is making a fresh start as the new king. At a level beneath the moral notions of a personal reform, we can see a nonlogical process of purification by sacrifice—the sacrifice of Falstaff. The career of the old king, a successful usurper whose conduct of affairs has been sceptical and opportunistic, has cast doubt on the validity of the whole conception of a divinely-ordained and chivalrous kingship to which Shakespeare and his society were committed. And before Bolingbroke, Richard II had given occasion for doubts about the rituals of kingship in an opposite way, by trying to use them magically. Shakespeare had shown Richard assuming that the symbols of majesty should be absolutes, that the names of legitimate power should be transcendently effective regardless of social forces. Now both these attitudes have been projected also in Falstaff; he carries to comically delightful and degraded extremes both a magical use of moral sanctions and the complementary opportunistic manipulation and scepticism. So the ritual analogy suggests that by turning on Falstaff as a scapegoat, as the villagers turned on their Mardi Gras, the prince can free himself from the sins, the "bad luck," of Richard's reign and of his father's reign, to become a king in whom chivalry and a sense of divine ordination are restored.

But this process of carrying off bad luck, if it is to be made *dramatically* cogent, as a symbolic action accomplished in and by dramatic form, cannot take place magically in Shakespeare's play. When it happens magically in the play, we have, I think, a failure to transform ritual into comedy. In dealing with fully successful comedy, the magical analogy is only a useful way of organizing our awareness of a complex symbolic action. The expulsion of evil works as dramatic form only in so far as it is realized in a movement from participation to rejection which happens, moment by moment, in our response to Falstaff's clowning misrule. We watch Falstaff adopt one posture after another, in the effort to give himself meaning at no cost; and moment by moment we see that the meaning is specious. So our participation is repeatedly diverted to laughter. The laughter, disbursing energy originally mobilized to respond to a valid meaning, signalizes our mastery by understanding of the tendency which has been misapplied or carried to an extreme.

Consider, for example, the use of magical notions of royal power in the most famous of all Falstaff's burlesques:

> By the Lord, I knew ye as well as he that made ye. . . . Was it for me to kill the heir apparent? Should I turn upon the true prince? Why, thou knowest I am as valiant as Hercules; but beware instinct. The lion will not touch the true prince. Instinct is a great matter. I was now a coward on instinct. I shall think the better of myself, and thee, during my life—I for a valiant lion, and thou for a true prince. But, by the Lord, lads, I am glad you have the money. Hostess, clap to the doors: watch to-night, pray to-morrow.
>
> (II.iv.295–306)

Here Falstaff has recourse to the brave conception that legitimate kingship has a magical potency. This is the sort of absolutist appeal to sanctions which Richard II keeps falling back on in his desperate "conjuration" (*R.II* III.ii.23) by hyperbole:

> So when this thief, this traitor, Bolingbroke, . . .
> Shall see us rising in our throne, the East,
> His treasons will sit blushing in his face,
> Not able to endure the sight of day . . .
> The breath of worldly men cannot depose
> The deputy elected by the Lord.
> For every man that Bolingbroke hath press'd
> To lift shrewd steel against our golden crown,
> God for his Richard hath in heavenly pay
> A glorious angel.
>
> (*R.II* III.ii.47–61)

In Richard's case, a tragic irony enforces the fact that heavenly angels are of no avail if one's coffers are empty of golden angels and the Welsh army have dispersed. In Falstaff's case, the irony is comically obvious, the "lies are like the father that begets them; gross as a mountain, open, palpable" (II.iv.249–250). Hal stands for the judgment side of our response, while Falstaff embodies the enthusiastic, irrepressible conviction of fantasy's omnipotence. The Prince keeps returning to Falstaff's bogus "instinct"; "Now, sirs . . . You are lions too, you ran away upon instinct, you will not touch the true prince; no—fie!" (II.iv.29–34). After enjoying the experience of seeing through such notions of magical majesty, he is never apt to make the mistake of assuming that, just because he is king, lions like Northumberland will not touch him. King Richard's bad luck came precisely from such an assumption—unexamined, of course, as fatal assumptions always are. Freud's account of bad luck, in *The Psychopathology of Everyday Life*, sees it as the expression of unconscious motives which resist the conscious goals of the personality. This view helps to explain how the acting out of disruptive motives in saturnalia or in comedy can serve to master potential aberration by revaluing it in relation to the whole of experience. So Falstaff, in acting out this absolutist aberration, is taking away what might have been Hal's bad luck, taking it away not in a magical way, but by extending the sphere of conscious control. The comedy is a civilized equivalent of the primitive rite. A similar mastery of potential aberration is promoted by the experience of seeing through Falstaff's burlesque of the sort of headlong chivalry presented seriously in Hotspur.

In order to put the symbolic action of the comedy in larger perspective, it will be worth while to consider further, for a moment, the relation of language to stage action and dramatic situation in *Richard II*. That play is a pioneering exploration of the semantics of royalty, shot through with talk about the potency and impotence of language. In the first part, we see a Richard who is possessor of an apparently magical omnipotence: for example, when he commutes Bolingbroke's banishment from ten to six years, Bolingbroke exclaims:

> How long a time lies in one little word!
> Four lagging winters and four wanton springs
> End in a word: such is the breath of kings.
>
> (*R.II* I.iii.213–215)

Richard assumes he has such magic breath inevitably, regardless of "the breath of worldly men." When he shouts things like "Is not the king's name twenty thousand names? / Arm, arm, my name!" he carries the absolutist assumption to the giddiest verge of absurdity. When we analyze the magical substitution of words for things in such lines, looking at them from outside the rhythm of feeling in which they occur, it seems scarcely plausible that a drama should be built around the impulse to adopt such an assumption. It seems especially implausible in our own age, when we are so conscious, on an abstract level, of the dependence of verbal efficacy on the social group. The analytical situation involves a misleading perspective, however; for, whatever your assumptions about semantics, when you have to *act*, to *be* somebody or become somebody, there is a moment when you have to have faith that the unknown world beyond will respond to the names you commit yourself to as right names.[11] The Elizabethan mind, moreover, generally assumed that one played one's part in a divinely ordained pageant where each man *was* his name and the role his name implied. The expression of this faith, and of the outrage of it, is particularly drastic in the Elizabethan drama, which can be regarded, from this vantage, as an art form developed to express the shock and exhilaration of the discovery that life is not pageantry. As Professor Tillyard has pointed out, *Richard II* is the most ceremonial of all Shakespeare's plays, and the ceremony all comes to nothing.[12] In Richard's deposition scene, one way in which anguish at his fall is expressed is by a focus on his loss of names: he responds to Northumberland's "My Lord—" by flinging out

> No lord of thine, thou haught insulting man,
> Nor no man's lord. I have no name, no title—
> No, not that name was given me at the font—
> But 'tis usurp'd. Alack the heavy day,
> That I have worn so many winters out
> And know not now what name to call myself!
> O that I were a mockery king of snow,
> Standing before the sun of Bolingbroke
> To melt myself away in water-drops!
>
> (*R.II* IV.i.253–262)

His next move is to call for the looking glass in which he stares at his face to look for the meaning the face has lost. To lose one's meaning, one's social role, is to be reduced to mere body. Here again the tragedy can be used to illuminate the comedy. Since the Elizabethan drama was a double medium of words and of physical gestures, it frequently expressed the pathos of the loss of meaning by emphasizing moments when word and gesture, name and body, no longer go together, just as it presented the excitement of a gain of meaning by showing a body seizing on names when a hero creates his identity. In the deposition scene, Richard says "mark me how I will undo myself" (IV.i.203). Then he gives away by physical gestures the symbolic meanings which have constituted that self. When at last he has no name, the anguish is that the face, the body, remain when the meaning is gone. There is also something in Richard's lines which, beneath the surface of his self-pity, relishes such undoing, a self-love which looks towards fulfillment in that final reduction of all to the body which is death. This narcissistic need for the physical is the other side of the attitude that the magic of the crown should altogether transcend the physical—and the human:

> Cover your heads, and mock not flesh and blood
> With solemn reverence. Throw away respect,
> Tradition, form, and ceremonious duty;
> For you have but mistook me all this while.
> I live with bread like you, feel want, taste grief,
> Need friends. Subjected thus,
> How can you say to me I am a king?
>
> (R.II III.ii.171–177)

In expressing the disappointment of Richard's magical expectations, as well as their sweeping magnificence, the lines make manifest the aberration which is mastered in the play by tragic form.

The same sort of impulse is expressed and mastered by comic form in the Henry IV comedy. When Richard wishes he were a mockery king of snow, to melt before the sun of Bolingbroke, the image expresses on one side the wish to escape from the body with which he is left when his meaning has gone—to weep

himself away in water drops. But the lines also look wistfully
towards games of mock royalty where, since the whole thing is
based on snow, the collapse of meaning need not hurt. Falstaff is
such a mockery king. To be sure, he is flesh and blood, of a kind:
he is tallow, anyway. He "sweats to death / And lards the lean
earth as he walks along." Of course he is not just a mockery, not
just his role, not just bombast. Shakespeare, as always, makes the
symbolic role the product of a life which includes contradictions
of it, such as the morning-after regrets when Falstaff thinks of
the inside of a church and notices that his skin hangs about him
like an old lady's loose gown. Falstaff is human enough so that
"Were't not for laughing, . . . [we] should pity him." But we do
laugh, because when Falstaff's meanings collapse, little but make-
believe has been lost:

> *Prince.* Thy state is taken for a join'd-stool, thy golden scep-
> tre for a leaden dagger, and thy precious rich crown for a
> pitiful bald crown.
>
> (II.iv.418–420)

Falstaff's effort to make his body and furnishings mean sovereignty is doomed from the start; he must work with a leaden
dagger, the equivalent of a Vice's dagger of lath. But Falstaff does
have golden words, and an inexhaustible vitality in using them.
He can name himself nobly, reordering the world by words so as
to do himself credit:

> No, my good lord. Banish Peto, banish Bardolph, banish
> Poins; but for sweet Jack Falstaff, kind Jack Falstaff, true Jack
> Falstaff, valiant Jack Falstaff, and therefore more valiant
> being, as he is, old Jack Falstaff, banish not him thy Harry's
> company, banish not him thy Harry's company. Banish
> plump Jack, and banish all the world!
>
> (II.iv.519–527)

I quote such familiar lines to recall their effect of incantation: they
embody an effort at a kind of magical naming. Each repetition of
"sweet Jack Falstaff, kind Jack Falstaff" aggrandizes an identity
which the serial clauses caress and cherish. At the very end, in
"plump Jack," the disreputable belly is glorified.

In valid heroic and majestic action, the bodies of the personages are constantly being elevated by becoming the vehicles of

social meanings; in the comedy, such elevation becomes burlesque, and in the repeated failures to achieve a fusion of body and
symbol, abstract meanings keep falling back into the physical. "A
plague of sighing and grief! it blows a man up like a bladder"
(II.iv.365–366). The repetition of such joking about Falstaff's belly
makes it meaningful in a very special way, as a symbol of the
process of inflation and collapse of meaning. So it represents the
power of the individual life to continue despite the collapse of
social roles. This continuing on beyond definitions is after all
what we call "the body" in one main meaning of the term: Falstaff's belly is thus the essence of body—an essence which can be
defined only dynamically, by failures of meaning. The effect of
indestructible vitality is reinforced by the association of Falstaff's
figure with the gay eating and drinking of Shrove Tuesday and
Carnival.[13] Whereas, in the tragedy, the reduction is to a body
which can only die, here reduction is to a body which typifies our
power to eat and drink our way through a shambles of intellectual
and moral contradictions.

So we cannot resist sharing Falstaff's genial self-love when he
commends his vision of plump Jack to the Prince, just as we share
the ingenuous self-love of a little child. But the dramatist is ever
on the alert to enforce the ironies that dog the tendency of
fantasy to equate the self with "all the world." So a most monstrous watch comes beating at the doors which have been clapped
to against care; everyday breaks in on holiday.

The Trial of Carnival in *Part Two*

In *Part One*, Falstaff reigns, within his sphere, as Carnival; *Part
Two* is very largely taken up with his trial. To put Carnival on trial,
run him out of town, and burn or bury him is in folk custom a
way of limiting, by ritual, the attitudes and impulses set loose by
ritual. Such a trial, though conducted with gay hoots and jeers,
serves to swing the mind round to a new vantage, where it sees
misrule no longer as a benign release for the individual, but as a
source of destructive consequences for society.[14] This sort of
reckoning is what *Part Two* brings to Falstaff.

But Falstaff proves extremely difficult to bring to book—more difficult than an ordinary mummery king—because his burlesque and mockery are developed to a point where the mood of a moment crystallizes as a settled attitude of scepticism. As we have observed before, in a static, monolithic society, a Lord of Misrule can be put back in his place after the revel with relative ease. The festive burlesque of solemn sanctities does not seriously threaten social values in a monolithic culture, because the license depends utterly upon what it mocks: liberty is unable to envisage any alternative to the accepted order except the standing of it on its head. But Shakespeare's culture was not monolithic: though its moralists assumed a single order, scepticism was beginning to have ground to stand on and look about—especially in and around London. So a Lord of Misrule figure, brought up, so to speak, from the country to the city, or from the traditional past into the changing present, could become on the Bankside the mouthpiece not merely for the dependent holiday scepticism which is endemic in a traditional society, but also for a dangerously self-sufficient everyday scepticism. When such a figure is set in an environment of sober-blooded great men behaving as opportunistically as he, the effect is to raise radical questions about social sanctities. At the end of *Part Two*, the expulsion of Falstaff is presented by the dramatist as getting rid of this threat; Shakespeare has recourse to a primitive procedure to meet a modern challenge. We shall find reason to question whether this use of ritual entirely succeeds.

But the main body of *Part Two*, what I am seeing as the trial, as against the expulsion, is wonderfully effective drama. The first step in trying Carnival, the first step in ceasing to be his subjects, would be to stop calling him "My Lord" and call him instead by his right name, Misrule. Now this is just the step which Falstaff himself takes for us at the outset of *Part Two*; when we first see him, he is setting himself up as an institution, congratulating himself on his powers *as* buffoon and wit. He glories in his role with what Dover Wilson has aptly called "comic hubris."[15] In the saturnalian scenes of *Part One*, we saw that it is impossible to say just who he is; but in *Part Two*, Falstaff sets himself up at the outset as Falstaff:

> I am not only witty in myself, but the cause that wit is in other men. . . .

A pox of this gout! or, a gout of this pox! for one or the other
plays the rogue with my great toe. 'Tis no matter if I do halt.
I have the wars for my colour, and my pension shall seem
the more reasonable. A good wit will make use of anything. I
will turn diseases to commodity.

(I.ii.11–12, 273–278)

In the early portion of *Part One* he never spoke in asides, but now
he constantly confides his schemes and his sense of himself to the
audience. We do not have to see through him, but watch instead
from inside his façades as he imposes them on others. Instead of
warm amplifications centered on himself, his talk now consists
chiefly of bland impudence or dry, denigrating comments on the
way of the world. Much of the comedy is an almost Jonsonian
spectacle where we relish a witty knave gulling fools.

It is this self-conscious Falstaff, confident of setting up his
holiday license on an everyday basis, who at once encounters, of
all awkward people, the Lord Chief Justice. From there on, during
the first two acts, he is constantly put in the position of answer-
ing for his way of life; in effect he is repeatedly called to trial and
keeps eluding it only by a "more than impudent sauciness"
(II.i.123) and the privilege of his official employment in the wars.
Mistress Quickly's attempt to arrest him is wonderfully ineffectual; but he notably fails to thrust the Lord Chief Justice from a
level consideration. Hal and Poins then disguise themselves, not
this time for the sake of the incomprehensible lies that Falstaff
will tell, but in order to try him, to see him "bestow himself . . . in
his true colours" (II.ii.186). So during the first two acts we are
again and again put in the position of judging him, although we
continue to laugh with him. A vantage is thus established from
which we watch him in action in Gloucestershire, where the
Justice he has to deal with is so shallow that Falstaff's progress is a
triumph. The comedy is still delightful; Falstaff is still the greatest
of wits; but we are constantly shown fun that involves fraud.
Falstaff himself tells us about his game, with proud relish. Towards the end of the play, Hal's reconciliation with his father and
then with the Lord Chief Justice reemphasizes the detached vantage of judgment. So no leading remarks are necessary to assure
our noting and marking when we hear Falstaff shouting, "Let us
take any man's horses; the laws of England are at my commandment. Blessed are they that have been my friends, and woe unto

my lord chief justice!" (V.iii.140-144). The next moment we watch Doll and the Hostess being hauled off by Beadles because "the man is dead that you and Pistol beat among you" (V.iv.18). Many of the basic structures in this action no doubt were shaped by morality-play encounters between Virtues and Vices,[16] encounters which from my vantage here can be seen as cognate to the festive and scapegoat pattern. The trial of Falstaff is so effective *as drama* because no one conducts it—it happens. Falstaff, being a dramatic character, not a mummery, does not know when he has had his day. And he does not even recognize the authority who will finally sentence him: he mistakes Hal for a bastard son of the king's (II.iv.307). The result of the trial is to make us see perfectly the necessity for the rejection of Falstaff as a man, as a favorite for a king, as the leader of an interest at court.

But I do not think that the dramatist is equally successful in justifying the rejection of Falstaff as a mode of awareness. The problem is not in justifying rejection morally but in making the process cogent *dramatically*, as in *Part One* we reject magical majesty or intransigent chivalry. The bad luck which in *Part Two* Falstaff goes about collecting, by shaking the black yak's tail of his wit over people's heads, is the impulse to assume that nothing is sacred. In a play concerned with ruthless political maneuver, much of it conducted by impersonal state functionaries, Falstaff turns up as a functionary too, with his own version of maneuver and impersonality: "If the young dace be a bait for the old pike, I see no reason in the law of nature but I may snap at him" (III.ii.356-359). Now this attitude is a most appropriate response to the behavior of the high factions beneath whose struggles Falstaff plies his retail trade. In the Gaultree parleys, Lord John rebukes the Archbishop for his use of the counterfeited zeal of God—and then himself uses a counterfeited zeal of gentlemanly friendship to trick the rebels into disbanding their forces. The difference between his behavior and Falstaff's is of course that Lancaster has reasons of state on his side, a sanction supported, if not by legitimacy, at least by the desperate need for social order. This is a real difference, but a bare and harsh one. After all, Falstaff's little commonwealth of man has its pragmatic needs too: as he explains blandly to the Justice, he needs great infamy, because "he that buckles him in my belt cannot live in less" (I.iii.159-160).

The trouble with trying to get rid of this attitude merely by getting rid of Falstaff is that the attitude is too pervasive in the whole society of the play, whether public or private. It is too obviously *not* just a saturnalian mood, the extravagance of a moment: it is presented instead as in grain, as the way of the world. Shakespeare might have let the play end with this attitude dominant, a harsh recognition that life is a nasty business where the big fishes eat the little fishes, with the single redeeming consideration that political order is better than anarchy, so that there is a pragmatic virtue in loyalty to the power of the state. But instead the dramatist undertakes, in the last part of the play, to expel this view of the world and to dramatize the creation of legitimacy and sanctified social power. Although the final scenes are fascinating, with all sorts of illuminations, it seems to me that at this level they partly fail.

We have seen that Shakespeare typically uses ritual patterns of behavior and thought precisely in the course of making clear, by tragic or comic irony, that rituals have no *magical* efficacy. The reason for his failure at the close of *Part Two* is that at this point he himself uses ritual, not ironically transformed into drama, but magically. To do this involves a restriction instead of an extension of awareness. An extension of control and awareness is consummated in the epiphany of Hal's majesty while he is standing over Hotspur and Falstaff at the end of *Part One*. But *Part Two* ends with drastic restriction of awareness which goes with the embracing of magical modes of thought, not humorously but sentimentally.

It is true that the latter half of *Part Two* very effectively builds up to its finale by recurrent expression of a laboring need to be rid of a growth or humor. King Henry talks of the body of his kingdom as foul with rank diseases (III.i.39), and recalls Richard's prophecy that "foul sin gathering head / Shall break into corruption" (III.i.76–77). There are a number of other images of expulsion, such as the striking case where the rebels speak of the need to "purge th' obstructions which begin to stop / Our very veins of life" (IV.i.65–66). Henry himself is sick in the last half of the play, and there are repeated suggestions that his sickness is the consequence both of his sinful usurpation and of the struggle to defend it. Since his usurpation was almost a public duty, and his defense of order clearly for England's sake as well as his own advantage, he becomes in these last scenes almost a sacrificial figure, a king who sins for the sake of society, suffers for society in suffering for his sin, and carries his sin off into death. Hal speaks of the crown having "fed upon the body of my father" (IV.v.160). Henry, in his last long speech, summarizes this pattern in saying:

> God knows, my son,
> By what bypaths and indirect crook'd ways
> I met this crown; and I myself know well
> How troublesome it sat upon my head.
> To thee it shall descend with better quiet,
> Better opinion, better confirmation;
> For all the soil of the achievement goes
> With me into the earth.
>
> (IV.v.184–191)

The same image of burying sin occurs in some curious lines with which Hal reassures his brothers:

> My father is gone wild into his grave;
> For in his tomb lie my affections . . .
>
> (V.ii.123–124)

This conceit not only suggests an expulsion of evil, but hints at the patricidal motive which is referred to explicitly elsewhere in these final scenes and is the complement of the father-son atonement.

Now this sacrificial imagery, where used by and about the old king, is effectively dramatic, because it does not ask the audience to abandon any part of the awareness of a human, social situation which the play as a whole has expressed. But the case is altered when Hal turns on "that father ruffian" Falstaff. The new king's whip-lash lines stress Falstaff's age and glance at his death:

> I know thee not, old man. Fall to thy prayers.
> How ill white hairs become a fool and jester!
> I have long dreamt of such a kind of man,
> So surfeit-swell'd, so old, and so profane;
> But being awak'd, I do despise my dream.
> Make less thy body, hence, and more thy grace;
> Leave gormandising. Know the grave doth gape
> For thee thrice wider than for other men.
>
> (V.v.51–58)

The priggish tone, to which so many have objected, can be explained at one level as appropriate to the solemn occasion of a coronation. But it goes with a drastic narrowing of awareness. There are of course occasions in life when people close off parts of their minds—a coronation is a case in point: Shakespeare, it can be argued, is simply putting such an occasion into his play. But even his genius could not get around the fact that to block off awareness of irony is contradictory to the very nature of drama, which has as one of its functions the extension of such awareness. Hal's lines, redefining his holiday with Falstaff as a dream, and then despising the dream, seek to invalidate that holiday pole of life, instead of including it, as his lines on his old acquaintance did at the end of *Part One*. (Elsewhere in Shakespeare, to dismiss dreams categorically is foolhardy.) And those lines about the thrice-wide grave: are they a threat or a joke? We cannot tell, because the sort of consciousness that would confirm a joke is being damped out: "Reply not to me with a fool-born jest" (V.v.59). If ironies about Hal were expressed by the context, we could take the scene as the representation of his becoming a prig. But there is simply a blur in the tone, a blur which results, I think, from a retreat into magic by the *dramatist*, as distinct from his characters. Magically, the line about burying the belly is exactly the appropriate threat. It goes with the other images of burying sin and wildness and conveys the idea that the grave can swallow what Falstaff's belly stands for. To assume that one can cope with a pervasive attitude of mind by dealing physically with its most prominent symbol—what is this but magic-mongering? It is the same sort of juggling which we get in Henry IV's sentimental lines taking literally the name of the Jerusalem chamber in the palace:

> Laud be to God! Even there my life must end.
> It hath been prophesied to me many years,
> I should not die but in Jerusalem . . .
>
> (IV.v.236–238)

One can imagine making a mockery of Henry's pious ejaculation by catcalling a version of his final lines at the close of *Richard II* (V.vi.49–50):

> Is this that voyage to the Holy Land
> To wash the blood from off your guilty hand?

An inhibition of irony goes here with Henry's making the symbol do for the thing, just as it does with Hal's expulsion of Falstaff. A return to an official view of the sanctity of state is achieved by sentimental use of magical relations.

We can now suggest a few tentative conclusions of a general sort about the relation of comedy to ritual. It appears that comedy uses ritual in the process of redefining ritual as the expression of particular personalities in particular circumstances. The heritage of ritual gives universality and depth. The persons of the drama make the customary gestures developed in ritual observance, and, in doing so, they project in a wholehearted way attitudes which are not normally articulated at large. At the same time, the dramatization of such gestures involves being aware of their relation to the whole of experience in a way which is not necessary for the celebrants of a ritual proper. In the actual observance of customary misrule, the control of the disruptive motives which the festivity expresses is achieved by the group's recognition of the place of the whole business within the larger rhythm of their continuing social life. No one need decide, therefore, whether the identifications involved in the ceremony are magically valid or merely expressive. But in the drama, perspective and control depend on presenting, along with the ritual gestures, an expression of a social situation out of which they grow. So the drama must control magic by re-understanding it as imagination: dramatic irony must constantly dog the wish that the mock king be real, that the self be all the world or set all the world at naught. When, through a failure of irony, the dramatist presents ritual as magically valid, the result is sentimental, since drama lacks the kind of control which in ritual comes from the auditors' being participants. Sentimental "drama," that which succeeds in being neither comedy nor tragedy, can be regarded from this vantage as theater used as a substitute for ritual, without the commitment to participation and discipline proper to ritual nor the commitment to the fullest understanding proper to comedy or tragedy.

Historically, Shakespeare's drama can be seen as part of the process by which our culture has moved from absolutist modes of thought towards a historical and psychological view of man. But though the Renaissance moment made the tension between a magical and an empirical view of man particularly acute, this pull is of course always present: it is the tension between the heart and the world. By incarnating ritual as plot and character, the dramatist finds an embodiment for the heart's drastic gestures while recognizing how the world keeps comically and tragically giving them the lie.

NOTES

1. See *Shakespeare's Festive Comedy*, pp. 12–13.
2. Fascination with the abuse of ritual is nowhere clearer than in Marlowe's *Tamburlaine* and *Dr. Faustus*.
3. The use of analogies like the scapegoat rituals can be misleading, or merely amusing, if the pattern is not rigorously related to the imaginative process in the play. Janet Spens, a student of Gilbert Murray's, wrote in 1916 a brief study which attempted to establish the presence of ritual patterns in Shakespeare's work (*An Essay on Shakespeare's Relation to Tradition*, Oxford, 1916). She throws out some brilliant suggestions. But her method for the most part consists of leaping intuitively from folklore to the plots of the plays, via the hypothesis of lost intermediary folk plays; and the plots, abstracted from the concrete emphasis of their dramatic realization, can be adjusted to square with an almost unlimited range of analogies. Miss Spens argues, for example, that because Antonio in *The Merchant of Venice* is enigmatically detached from personal concerns, and because in accepting the prospect of death at Shylock's hands he says "I am the tainted wether of the flock," he "is" the Scapegoat. To be sure, at a very general level there is a partial analogy to scapegoat rituals, since Antonio is undertaking to bear the consequence of Bassanio's extravagance; and perhaps the pound of flesh motif goes back ultimately, through the tangle of legend and story tradition, to some such ceremonial. But there is no controlling such analogies if we go after them by catching at fragments of narrative; and one can understand, on that basis, the impulse to give up the whole approach as hopelessly capricious.

    The case is altered, however, if attention is focused, not on this or that group of people in this or that story, but on the roles the persons are given in the play. When we are concerned to describe

dramatic form—the rhythm of feeling and awareness in the audience which is focused through complementary roles in the fable
and implemented by concrete patterns of language and gesture—
then the form of rituals is relevant to the form of the plays as a
parallel expression of the same kind of organization of experience.

4. See *Shakespeare's Festive Comedy*, pp. 67–73.
5. *Shakespeare Studies*, pp. 403–433.
6. See Empson, *Pastoral*, pp. 42ff.
7. Lily B. Campbell, *Shakespeare's Histories, Mirrors of Elizabethan Policy* (San Marino, 1947), pp. 229–238.
8. "A Note on Comedy," *Determinations*, ed. by F. R. Leavis (London, 1934).
9. *Pastoral*, p. 46.
10. See James G. Frazer, *The Scapegoat* (London, 1914), pp. 218–223 and passim.
11. I am indebted to my colleagues Professor Theodore Baird and Professor G. Armour Craig for this way of seeing the relation of names to developing situations.
12. See *Shakespeare's History Plays* (New York, 1946), pp. 245ff.
13. See *Shakespeare's Festive Comedy*, pp. 67–73, for the relation of Falstaff to Nashe's pageant figure of Bacchus, to Shrove Tuesday and other mummery roles where the praise of food, drink, and folly was a traditional holiday exercise.
14. The ritual of Carnival in Italy and its relation to Italian comedy has recently been exhibited in Professor Paolo Toschi's *Le origini del teatro italiano* (Torino, 1955) with a fullness and clarity made possible by the rich popular Italian heritage.
15. *The Fortunes of Falstaff* (New York, 1944), Ch. V, "Falstaff High on Fortune's Wheel," p. 94.
16. *Ibid.*, pp. 17–22.

G. K. Hunter

Shakespeare's Politics and the Rejection of Falstaff (1959)

When Heminge and Condell called the First Folio "Mr. William Shakespeare's Comedies, Histories, & Tragedies" they raised not only the first but also the basic question about the English History Plays—a question which remains unanswered to-day, though it has continued in various guises to provoke critical speculation throughout the whole of the intervening period. For the difficulty raised by an assumption that there is a *genre* "History Play," parallel to "Comedy" or "Tragedy" is one that lies at the centre of any serious critical response to these plays.

It is tempting to dismiss the Heminge and Condell title as a confusion of subject (history) with form (comedy/tragedy), and certainly there was much muddling of the terms at this time; but a close comparison of *Richard II* (say) with *Hamlet* (or *Richard III* with *Macbeth*) soon reveals why the History plays cannot be regarded as simply Tragedies (or Comedies) in an English historical setting. *Richard II* leaves us concerned with the *national* consequences of the hero's death; in no comparable way are we concerned at the end of *Hamlet* with the political future of Denmark. Hamlet is a man first and a prince second; Richard II is judged first as a king; the personal judgment on him as a man can modify but not alter this primary verdict.

There is good ground for judging the History Play on its own, unique, terms; but we should notice that this takes the resonance out of most critical pronouncements. We lose the idea of a form

From *Critical Quarterly* 8 (1959). Reprinted by permission of the author.

which is defined by its aiming at certain long-established, much-discussed ends (as the "end" of tragedy is said to be the effecting of catharsis through the exercise of pity and terror), and we lose those cross-lights from other successful practitioners in the *genre* (as the practice of Sophocles or Racine helps to define the unique quality of Shakespearian tragedy).

The earliest (Neo-classical) critics, like Dryden, seem to have inferred from this lack of background that the History Plays were not real "art," and therefore beneath the kind of critical procedure that involved The Rules. Gildon (1710) went so far as to say that they "mix comic and tragic, and being histories, contain no fable or design"; Dr. Johnson does not deny the general point and Mrs. Montagu pleads for pardon only on the ground of the pleasure given: "But, if the pedantry of learning could ever recede from its dogmatical rules, I think this play [*Henry IV*] instead of being condemned for being of that species, would obtain favour for the species itself."

The "irregularity" which these critics detected in their pleasure did not, of course, upset the Romantic critics; but our original question, "Has the History Play a basic form or only a basic content?" did not cease to affect criticism. Romantic concern with the human attractiveness or otherwise of the characters made the uncertainty about form felt in a rather different way; for where Comedy and Tragedy invite us to identification with or dissociation from central characters in fairly obvious and traditional ways, the History Play provides no such obvious directives to our sympathies and the question naturally takes the form, "with whom, in such plays, are our sympathies supposed to rest, with the humanly attractive (Richard II, Falstaff) or with the historically successful (i.e. the politically able)—Bolingbroke, Hal?" And in this form the problem is still with us.

The commonest Romantic attitude is in fact one which very obviously carries on Neo-classical doubts about the "seriousness" of History Plays. The nineteenth century saw few dissidents from the view that the plays were pageant-like in intention—"six full-length portraits of the Kings of England" as Dowden phrased it, and justified by the patriotism of the Armada period rather than by any truly artistic ends. The prevailing belief that Shakespeare was a poet of natural endowment rather than painstaking accomplishment seemed to find a particular demonstration here, a demonstration buttressed by the supposed "fact" that his earliest History Plays (the *Henry VI* series) were mere revampings of original work by real intellectuals (Marlowe, Greene, Nashe, etc.), while the later ones were seen as carrying on a line of least resistance to the national clamour for "such stimulus as visible reminders of England's past could give" (Charlton). This viewpoint is nicely epitomised by Raleigh who tells us: "Plays founded on English history were already popular when Shakespeare began to write; and while he was still an apprentice their tragic possibilities had been splendidly demonstrated in Marlowe's *Edward II.*" It is probably worth pointing out that the basis of scholarly "fact" for both these ideas has now been removed. The evidence against the first ("revamping") notion was presented by Peter Alexander in 1929; evidence against the second has been slowly accumulating throughout this century (e.g. in Charlton and Waller's edition of *Edward II* and in Rossiter's edition of *Woodstock*); by 1953 F. P. Wilson could say, "for all we know there were no popular plays on English history before the Armada and . . . Shakespeare may have been the first to write one." The possibility that it was Shakespeare who invented the History Play alters startlingly many preconceptions about the author, but this is not the place to follow its implications. The point to be made here is that under these earlier preconceptions analytical criticism lay dormant while critics concentrated on the material, presented, Elton remarks, "in the manner of Scott."

The general Romantic quest for knowledge of the characters beyond what the play provided was easier to pursue in the Histories than in the Comedies or Tragedies, and to some extent more legitimate, given the fact the added material was "true" and so could not compromise the factual truth of the plays. In this context one can see why Scott marks the limit normally allowed to Shakespeare's "art" in the presentation of his sources (or rather *source*, since only one—Holinshed's Chronicle—was acknowledged). The most popular Waverley novels in the period— *Ivanhoe* and *The Talisman*—manipulate individuals in the interest of general historical colouring; human responses are grossly simplified by the need to make them illustrate the temper of the time in which they are set, and modern-thinking individuals do not appear. If this was Shakespeare's "manner," clearly the effort to get the historical material into focus was a basic critical necessity.

The view that Shakespeare presented the past but hardly interpreted it was further strengthened for the nineteenth century by a feeling for that common bond of patriotism which bound sixteenth-century playwright and nineteenth-century audience together. This provided a point of view which was general enough not to present those dangers to [Romantic] poetry that Shelley had detected in more precise moral or political formulations:

> A poet . . . would do ill to embody his own conceptions of right and wrong, which are usually those of his place and time, in his poetical creations which participate in neither.

From this point of view if Shakespeare had had precise notions of good and bad statesmanship he would inevitably have been a lesser Shakespeare—"of an age" rather than "for all time." The English Histories are in fact a great testing-ground for the question whether the poet achieves universality by avoiding particulars or whether (to quote Lily B. Campbell) "the poet must be reckoned . . . a man who can be understood only against the background of his own time."

The "Scott-like," factual and patriotic approaches of the nineteenth century all pointed to the first of these alternatives, and in general the History Plays fitted into the perspectives so arranged. One reign, however (as depicted by Shakespeare), seems particularly difficult to take in this light; *Henry IV* presents very prominently a debate between the private values of Falstaff and the public values of the House of Lancaster, and this culminates in the rejection of Shakespeare's best-loved character. Does not the shock that this gives to popular expectation imply that Shakespeare was deeply and personally involved in the political reasoning that leads to the Rejection? Modern minds tend to suppose it does, but though the Rejection has long been regretted, the conflict of values was not invoked by earlier critics. Maurice Morgann in all his long defence of Falstaff found no need to denigrate the Prince, and even as late as Dowden the Rejection raises no real moral difficulty. Dowden treats Hal and Falstaff, in fact, quite separately—one under "English History" and one

under "Humour"; the real-life, successful Englishness of Henry V
is sufficient to glorify him as "the apostle of fact" without raising
doubts about the moral validity of such factualness as would
trouble more modern minds.

Very shortly after Dowden, however, it becomes apparent
that the quality of patriotism was more strained than the Victori-
ans had allowed and a lot less universal. A Radical critic like Shaw
was soon rating Shakespeare for passing through "a worldly
phase in which he tried to thrust such a Jingo hero as Henry V
down our throats." More recent knowledge of Shakespeare's debt
to the official Homilies and other Elizabethan blandishments has
often reinforced modern disenchantment with patriotism and
politics. Thus J. F. Danby remarks that "the theology of the plays
is the no-theology of Tudor propaganda . . . their no-morality
that claims rebellion is always wicked." Twentieth century critics
have seldom been willing to deny that the plays are involved with
political ideas; yet the political successes these lead to are not of a
kind likely to be popular to-day; the question of what we are to do
about this admiration for the author's intelligence coupled to a
distaste for his ideas is the question round which swings nearly all
twentieth century criticism of the History Plays. Comparatively
few critics have been prepared to condemn Shakespeare because
of his ideas, and the commonest response is that Shakespeare's
attitude was somehow divided: he presents Tudor political ideas,
true, but at the same time he sees behind the facade; the plays do
not say to the heart what they seem to say to the mind; Shakespeare's plot may seem to praise the "vessel of clay" Bolingbroke,
but the poetry truly exalts the "vessel of porcelain" Richard II (the
phrases are Yeats's).

It is at this point in the history of criticism that the crucial
status of the Rejection for the whole interpretation of the History
Plays becomes apparent, and a review of attitudes to this episode
soon makes the dominance of the "divided-mind" approach fairly
obvious. Here, as so often elsewhere in Shakespeare, A. C. Bradley is the dominant modern critic. The defence of Falstaff was
fully briefed by Maurice Morgann in 1777, but it was left for
Bradley in 1902 to redraw the perspectives of the plays from the
"human" point of view of Falstaff. For Bradley, Falstaff grew too
big, too lovable and too human a character for the plot to have

power to reject him; rather it was that the warmly human in
Shakespeare came to reject the fish-cold, plot-controlling Lancastrians. For Charlton, Shakespeare is coming to see that politics is
a dirty business even as he presents it, and though none of the
plays actually turns on "the sense that what is good in the world
of politics is entirely unrelated to and generally the opposite of
what makes for goodness in the moral life," this is the sense with
which the plays leave us. The spontaneous Hotspur is to be
preferred to the calculating Hal, and this preference is echoed
again and again, for example by Palmer (1945) though Palmer
takes the more modern line that Shakespeare was neutral in the
conflict. Most recently of all D. A. Traversi has reiterated his
"sense . . . that success in politics implies moral loss, the sacrifice
of more attractive qualities in the distinctively personal order."
The strongest argument for the rejection of Hal would seem to
derive from a view of these plays in the line of Shakespeare's
development, especially in the phase "from *Henry V* to *Hamlet*"
described by Granville-Barker in 1925. Una Ellis-Fermor's essay
on "Shakespeare's Political Plays" treats the subject fully from this
point of view. Shakespeare was orthodox in accepting the need
for strong personal rule, but increasingly he saw the hollowness
behind the imposing public face, and in the Roman History Plays
(the logical development of the English ones) he revealed the
moral bankruptcy of political success.

Against this grouping of critics who see Shakespeare as protected by a layer of irony from any identification with the ethic of
political success, and in the end rejecting public values, we may set
another grouping of critics who do not rely primarily on evidence
of a divided mind. John Dover Wilson, E. M. W. Tillyard, Theodore Spencer, A. P. Rossiter, Lily B. Campbell and M. C. Bradbrook agree in one thing at least, that they see Shakespeare as
primarily the spokesman of his own age, as the proponent of a
particular point of view; though of course they interpret the
political and practical aspects of his attitude in such a way that
keeps them dissociated from modern anti-democratic politics of a
theoretically similar kind. When Tillyard started to write on the
History Plays he found that he would have to instruct his readers
first of all in the ruling concepts that governed Elizabethan political thinking. He did this in *The Elizabethan World Picture*, and even so,

more than a third of his actual *Shakespeare's History Plays* is taken up with background material. Tillyard and all these writers redefine politics as concerned with *Order*, implying a reflection in the State of cosmic order in the heavens and psychological order in the soul of man, so that a "political play" comes to involve almost of necessity the spiritual and psychological dimensions that modern political discussions are normally condemned for lacking. Yet these dimensions are not added to Shakespeare without some cost in freezing into a rigid scheme the originally plastic materials. Even if we do not go as far as Lily B. Campbell and see the plays as fully meaningful only to Elizabethan historians, there is a general supposition that the common reaction against the nastiness of the Lancasters can be explained away in terms other than human. The subject matter of *Henry IV* can be seen as "the education of the Prince"; Hal becomes a representative of the golden mean between Falstaff and Hotspur (the deficiency and the excess of honour); Falstaff himself acquires a heritage of conventional attributes from the Fool, the Vice, the Parasite, the Braggart Soldier, etc. The structure of the plays (as the subject becomes "moral") comes to seem dependent on that of the Morality plays. Thus the subject (moralised history) finds a form which expresses its tensions fully in dramatic shape—the total design being spread across eight, or even ten, plays, and articulating the parts into a vast but coherent expression of typical Elizabethan political thinking.

The result of this wholesale rethinking of the History Cycle is certainly impressive. No one writing to-day could pretend not to have learned a great deal from this approach—which we may label "formalist" because of its concern to approach the meaning through the formal organisation of the play. Yet a perception of abstract patterns, a defence of Hal out of Aristotle, and a Rejection of Falstaff as the type of Riot cannot be taken to answer completely objections which are framed on different and yet still justified responses. We may legitimately add the relation of Mean and Deficiency to that of friend and companion when we speak of Hal and Falstaff, but we only sidestep the problem of the Rejection—which arises from a sense of human betrayal—if we suppose that the non-human components in the relationship cancel out the human ones, and this is especially fallacious in the theatre.

We may also object that these critics sacrifice the individual play to the total design, denying our natural response to immediate events by pointing to remote consequences or antecedents in the historical cycle. Thus it is said that the beginning of Part two of *Henry IV* is intelligible only if we remember the end of Part one, that Shakespeare intends our response to *Henry V* and *Henry VI* to be conditioned by our memories of *Richard II*, and so on. All the evidence points, however, to the fact that the basic unit of Shakespeare's theatre was the single play; some historical knowledge is certainly assumed in the audience (not unnaturally—it was just over a hundred years since Bosworth Field), but the requirement to keep details of the whole cycle in mind seems to take the plays out of the theatre, or at least to imply a coterie audience-response more proper to Bayreuth than the Globe.

Indeed though the critics who seek for Shakespeare's personal attitudes and those who seek for a formal skeleton of typical ideas are generally opposed, one approach they seem to have in common: a sense of the insufficiency of the separate plays and a desire to import intensity and significance from outside. The formalist critics explain *Henry IV* by viewing it against the pattern of pre-Tudor history which Shakespeare derived from Hall's Chronicle; the subjective critics deduce its significance from the place it occupies in the development of Shakespeare's thought. The two attitudes cannot be combined easily; if we are looking for a third possibility should we not look at just this point they agree in rejecting—the self-sufficiency of the separate play?

In fact, though competing arguments from outside may seem to make Hal good and Falstaff bad (or vice versa), neither *Henry IV* play makes such a discrimination. The conflict between Falstaff and the House of Lancaster is never one which divides along the line between Moral and Immoral. Both sides are equally amoral. Both Hal and Falstaff seek to manipulate or interpret the plot to their own advantage: each is the impresario of his own performance, putting on and taking off masks as the situation allows. Hal sees the action as his own development in time, history leading up to the glorious reign of Henry V, with himself in the present popular role of wild-oat-sowing aristocrat; Falstaff on the other hand sees it as a comedy, takes the action out of time whenever he can, swells out the present moment to a rounded forgetfulness, and casts himself as Master of Revels. Hal's grasp on the future moves is matched only by Falstaff's capacity to sidestep time and logic, to move from one lie or attitude faster than his pursuers can. This aspect has been well expressed by Van Doren: "he is so much himself because he is never himself . . . the essence of Falstaff is that he is a comic actor, most of whose roles are assumed without announcement."

The opposition in the play is clearly enough the cause of the opposition between formalist and subjective critics, which I have discussed above. If we are to allow for the total effect of the play which *dramatises* these oppositions, clearly enough we must find a point of focus which will allow both sides to make their effects. And this involves more than a statement that Shakespeare was neutral: if the play is to hang together it must hold out the possibility of comprehension *somewhere*. If we are not to relapse into the sense that the History Plays are simply pageants we must find a definition of Shakespeare's concern for the private values of the individual which will not deny his concern for good government. L. C. Knights has recently advanced from the subjective side a treatment which goes some way towards this, speaking not only of Shakespeare's "refusal to let the abstract and general obscure the personal and specific" but also saying "he made no arbitrary separation between what is politics and what is not." Yet I do not think that Knights allows sufficiently for Shakespeare's perception that the King or Governor may sometimes have to sacrifice his own private good for the public good of others and here the Rejection is obviously crucial. Knights's basic question, "How does this affect relations between men? What kind of man acts in this way? How does he further make himself by so acting?" do not allow sufficiently for the current of opinion in the plays that a King must be kingly to be admirable and that kingliness is at times quite monstrously inhuman. The status of the scapegoat-king may throw some light on what seems to be required here. The scapegoat reigns in honour, even adoration, but then he is slaughtered mercilessly and his death rejoiced over as taking away the sins of the nation. One can see how irrelevant to such a figure are questions of the kind Knights has proposed. It may seem a long way from the anthropological subtleties of *The Golden Bough* to the straightforward modern history of Shakespeare's day, but enough of the old capacity to hold contrary attitudes to sovereignty together survived into the Tudor period to give meaning to type figures like "the Scourge of God" (see Battenhouse on Marlowe's *Tamburlaine*) and into our own lifetime to give power to a book like Kafka's *Castle*. Some such undogmatic subtlety of approach is certainly needed if we are to hold together in a sympathetic unity the multifarious perceptions of the English History Plays.

BOOKS MENTIONED

Charles Gildon, "Remarks on the Plays of Shakespeare," Rowe's edn. of Shakespeare, vii (1710)

Mrs. Montagu, *An Essay on Shakespeare* (1769)

Maurice Morgann, "An Essay on the Dramatic Character of Sir John Falstaff" (1777), rept. D. N. Smith, *Eighteenth Century Essays on Shakespeare* (1903)

Edward Dowden, *Shakespeare* (1875)

A. C. Bradley, "The Rejection of Falstaff," *Fortnightly Review* (1902), rept. *Oxford Lectures* (1909)

G. B. Shaw, *Dramatic Opinions* (1906)

W. A. Raleigh, *Shakespeare* (1909)

H. B. Charlton, *Shakespeare, Politics and Politicians* (1929)

Mark Van Doren, *Shakespeare* (1939)

Theodore Spencer, *Shakespeare and the Nature of Man* (1942)

John Dover Wilson, *The Fortunes of Falstaff* (1943)

E. M. W. Tillyard, *Elizabethan World Picture* (1943); *Shakespeare's History Plays* (1944)

Una Ellis-Fermor, *The Frontiers of Drama* (1945)

John Palmer, *Political Characters of Shakespeare* (1945)

Lily B. Campbell, *Shakespeare's Histories: Mirrors of Elizabethan Policy* (1947)

D. A. Traversi, "*Henry IV, Part I,*" *Scrutiny* XV (1947), rept. *Shakespeare from Richard II to Henry V* (1958)

J. F. Danby, *Shakespeare's Doctrine of Nature* (1949)

M. C. Bradbrook, *Shakespeare and Elizabethan Poetry* (1951)

F. P. Wilson, *Marlowe and the Early Shakespeare* (1953)

L. C. Knights, *Shakespeare's Politics* (British Academy Lecture 1957)

R. J. Dorius

A Little More than a Little (1960)

By showing us the power and frailty of seven kings, Shake-speare's nine English history plays (excluding *Henry VIII*) imply a standard of good kingship which no one of his kings, except possibly Henry V, fully attains. Both this standard and Henry's relationship to it have puzzled many commentators, and with good reason, since the great tragedies imply somewhat different standards, with far more emphasis upon heroic action. The tragic hero's willingness to take terrible risks, to throw away power and life itself for a cause, is not demanded of the kings of the histories. By and large, except for Richard III, they are more conservative; their mission is less to question and dare than to reconcile and maintain. They are absorbed less with the state of man than with practical politics; their problem is not why but how. It follows that they cannot risk the "tragic waste" precipitated by the inflexible high-minded resolve of the heroes. Indeed, the overweening am-bition of a partly tragic character like Hotspur is seen in the context of the histories as slightly comic.

What seems to set off the values of these plays most markedly from those of the tragedies is the importance given by the histo-ries to the virtues of prudence and economy. For in the chronicle plays these are the essential qualities, together with strength of character—kingliness—for a ruler's governance both of himself and his realm. To what degree the importance of these qualities in Shakespeare, up to the turn of the century, is related to the poet's response to crises of his own day, or to the spectacle of an older

From *Shakespeare Quarterly*, 11 (1960). Reprinted by permission of *Shakespeare Quarterly*.

England wasted for a hundred years through the incompetence or violence of a succession of weaklings, usurpers, and tyrants, it is difficult to say. But it is clear that the fullest exploration of the significance of prudence and economy in state affairs, and thus also of their opposites—carelessness, excess, waste, and disease, is to be found in the sequence running from *Richard II* through *Henry V*. It is with the development of these themes of good husbandry and extravagance through the metaphoric language of this tetralogy, and especially of *Richard II*, that this paper will be chiefly concerned. The thematic imagery of these plays possesses a logic and coherence striking enough to justify numerous comparisons between images of different dramas and the assumption that the group forms, in essential features, if not perhaps in initial conception or over-all effect, a unified design.

From Richard's "I wasted time, and now doth time waste me" at the beginning of the series to Henry V's weighing time "Even to the utmost grain" at the end, a concept of good husbandry presides like a goddess over the turbulent experiences of these plays. The assumption behind this emphasis upon watchful economy seems to be that life and power are precious gifts and that to squander them or to misdirect them is a crime against God and the state. And to be careless is to hand one's life and throne over to the initiative of others, who may turn both to their own ends. A negligent and heedless prince, like Richard II, creates a vacuum of power which must be filled, and invites disaster. Throughout, waste or destruction is associated in these plays with an apparently antithetical theme—fatness or excessive growth. Both are the extremes of which economy is the mean, or the ends to which extravagance in man or government might lead. We frequently find in these plays a kind of logical or psychological relationship between the stages of a process from health to disease, marked by metaphors depicting carelessness, eating or sleeping, deafness or blindness, rioting, fatness or excess, sickness, waste, barrenness, and death. The general movement of *Richard II* and of the cycle through *2 Henry IV* is from youthful or springtime luxuriance to aged or wintry barrenness. Of course these polarities are developed more fully in the later Shakespeare. But the well-known association in the great tragedies between images of excess or disease and faults ranging from mere folly to crime is already fully developed in these histories. The significance of Hamlet's dark reference to the world as "an unweeded garden That grows to seed" and to man as a beast whose chief good is "but to sleep and feed" is greatly heightened if seen through the preoccupation with things gross in nature and men in the English histories.

The collaboration of plot, character, and thematic imagery to create a unity of tone and meaning is so intimate in these plays that a word or metaphor can be said to be deepened into character or extended into plot. Thus in *Henry IV* the pervasive imagery of extremes is in a sense embodied both in a lean king of state literally worn away with anxiety and in a fat king of revels surrounded by slivers of himself, "Pharaoh's lean kine." Shape is at least partly an index to character. Everywhere the ideal king, the "figure of God's majesty," is contrasted with the "ugly form Of base and bloody insurrection. . . ."[1] Frequently fast follows feast, early death follows premature growth, in emphatic contrast. In the theatre, the sickness of the divided commonwealth is visibly present in the range of physical proportions of the characters on the stage. In Part II (III.i), the spectacle of the harassed lonely king watching through the night is preceded by the convivial brawling involving fat Saturn and Tearsheet-Venus "in conjunction" and followed by the pricking of the ragamuffins, as Falstaff misuses the king's press. It is almost as though these wastrels, like the crown itself, were, as the Prince says, feeding "upon the body of my father" (IV.v.160).

The most important antitheses in the histories are often sharpened by what appear to be minor tricks of language. The merry word-games in which the Prince and Falstaff engage, the matchings of "unsavory similes" of fatness and thinness, represent a comic playing with political and moral themes at the core of these plays. One of Falstaff's favorite puns points up the connection between waste and fatness. "Your means are very slender, and your waste is great," says the Chief Justice, posed against Falstaff at the beginning of Part II, and Falstaff replies, "I would my means were greater and my waist slenderer" (I.ii.160–163). Tagged as Sir John Paunch by Hal, Falstaff rejoins, "Indeed, I am not John of Gaunt, your grandfather . . ." (I:II.ii.70–71). What begins in a word or name can come to suggest a way of life. One of the polar oppositions to the careless John who sleeps upon benches afternoons and has the "disease of not list'ning" (II:I.ii.138) is this care-worn John who puns on his own name before Richard II:

> For sleeping England long time have I watch'd;
> Watching breeds leanness, leanness is all gaunt.
>
> (II.i.77–78)

We usually find in the histories that the responsible man and state are thin, the heedless usually fat. Honor-seeking Hotspur, "Amongst a grove the very straightest plant," can be contrasted not only with Falstaff, "out of all order, out of all compass," who reduces honor to a word, but with Richard II, who stoops "with oppression" of the "prodigal weight" of his nobles. Indeed, imagery of over-eating is applied both to the rightful ruler and the usurper, as the sickness of the head of the state develops. From Gaunt's remark about the "eager feeding" which "doth choke the feeder," young Richard (II.i.37), to Worcester's criticism in *Henry IV* of the lean king who once set out to purge the state of its excesses, is in many ways a single movement. Henry IV, made "portly" by the help of the Percies,

> did oppress our nest;
> Grew by our feeding to so great a bulk
> That even our love durst not come near your sight
> For fear of swallowing. . . .
>
> (I:V.i.61–64)

The eaters are eaten and the would-be physicians become centers of contagion. The lean may wax and the fat wane, but all go to extremes. Henry IV speaks what might be the motto of the histories: "a little More than a little is by much too much" (I:III.ii.72–73). Implicit everywhere is the unrealized possibility in both man and state of a kind of Aristotelian norm, an ideal of moderation or of equilibrium among opposing forces.

As these quotations have shown, images from the contemporary psychology of the humors help to shape the larger conceptual framework of these plays. The centrality of these metaphors is suggested by the frequency with which characters who fulfill at times a choral role employ them. It is but a step from fatness to disease. Occasionally rising toward the end of his life above his absorption in self-pity, Richard prophesies a growing sickness he failed to cure when he was himself king: the time will come that "foul sin gathering head Shall break into corruption" (V.i.58–59). Meanwhile, as in *Hamlet* (III.iv.148–149), "rank corruption, mining all within, Infects unseen," and the infection spreads before it is finally lanced. Henry IV, like Richard before him, becomes increasingly a helpless observer of a malady he cannot cure:

> Then you perceive the body of our kingdom,
> How foul it is; what rank diseases grow,
> And with what danger, near the heart of it.
>
> (II:III.i.38–40)

Henry at least faces more frankly than Richard the fact that he himself is the sick heart. In Part II, the Archbishop, though a rebel, maintains a very detached attitude toward the civil war. He speaks of the discontent following the supplanting of Richard by Bolingbroke as a sickness of the "beastly feeder," the people themselves, who are like dogs that alternately sate themselves and "disgorge" successive kings: "The commonwealth is sick of their own choice; Their over-greedy love hath surfeited" (II.iii.87–88). Later he includes two reigns and both royalists and rebels in a general indictment:

> we are all diseas'd
> And with our surfeiting and wanton hours
> Have brought ourselves into a burning fever,
> And we must bleed for it; of which disease
> Our late King, Richard, being infected, died.
>
> (II:IV.i.54–58)

And, though he disclaims it, he also tries to become England's physician,

> To diet rank minds sick of happiness
> And purge the obstructions which begin to stop
> Our very veins of life.

"Surfeiting" and "wanton" are above all the words for Richard II. The disease which begins in the mind of this king spreads to the body of the state and to its noblemen, and the judicious bleeding and purging of England are delayed throughout three plays, until

the "mood" (and "mode") is changed, and the "soil" of Henry IV's
dubious achievement goes with him into the earth (II:IV.v.190–
200). To trace this creeping infection to its source, a closer analysis of related themes in *Richard II* is now in order.

II

Themes of negligence, excess, and waste are developed in
Richard II primarily through several strands of imagery—those of
time, the garden and sickness, and the farm and death. All are
interrelated in a play whose poetic unity has in the last decade
been demonstrated many times. When Richard, the state's time-
keeper, threatens to appropriate the titles and property which
banished Bolingbroke should inherit from John of Gaunt, York
sternly equates the rights of inheritance with cosmic law:

> Take Hereford's rights away, and take from Time
> His charters and his customary rights;
> Let not to-morrow then ensue to-day;
> Be not thyself—for how art thou a king
> But by fair sequence and succession?
>
> (II.i.195–199)

To interrupt the succession of father to son is to endanger the
blood descent from king to king, even to unking a rightful sovereign. It is to question the very foundations of what the Gardener
(in III.iv) calls "law and form and due proportion," to make time
itself have a stop. The suggestion is that "Time" draws up all
charters and alone gives them meaning. Within forty lines of this
warning we learn that the king is indeed not himself, but "basely
led By flatterers . . . ," and within a hundred that the discon-
tented nobles have decided to seize the time to "make high majesty look like itself. . . ." Bolingbroke is later accused of having
returned to England "Before the expiration of thy time" (the
prescribed six years of banishment), and of taking "advantage of
the absent time." But Richard's time is "absent" less because he is
away in Ireland when Bolingbroke returns than because he has
failed to act promptly within it and has abused it. And yet the
usurper compounds Richard's crimes. Confronted by the king's

loyal friends, Bolingbroke claims "I am a subject, And I challenge law" (II.iii.133–134). York's reply, however, suggests that Hereford is plucking or seizing (the play's words for the usurper) for his own ends the law and time ignored by Richard. York has had a "feeling" for the injury done Bolingbroke,

> But in this kind to come, in braving arms,
> Be his own carver and cut out his way
> To find out right with wrong—it may not be. . . .
>
> (II.iii.141–145)

Since Richard is himself, as we soon see, a far more clumsy "carver," he is soon cut out of both kingship and kingdom. In the exacting world of the histories, to lose the initiative—or even to act prematurely, like Hotspur—may be to lose one's life. Bolingbroke is above all a master of timing.

. . . .

III

Richard's failure as watchful gardener and physician bequeaths to his successor a realm fat and very sick. The grieving queen suggests an intimate cause-and-effect relationship between the two reigns when she fancies herself giving birth to Bolingbroke, her "sorrow's dismal heir" (II.ii.62), almost as though he were begotten by Richard's folly. But the play's poetic justice is not so simple. Bolingbroke's watchful shrewdness collaborates with Richard's ineffectuality to turn Fortune's wheel. The two men, like other protagonists in Shakespeare, are functions of each other and of their total situation. They are locked in a grim dance in which Richard's weakness opens the way to power for Bolingbroke, and Bolingbroke's silent strength matches Richard's expectations of annihilation. Metaphors of water and of moving buckets suggest a Bolingbroke on high poised and ready to flood a royal reservoir that empties itself. But judgments in the later histories are kinder to the wastrel Richard than to the politician Bolingbroke, whose usurpation and killing of a king are thought more heinous than all of Richard's folly. Though a trimmer, Bolingbroke cannot weed his own garden, for his foes are "en-

rooted with his friends . . ." (II:IV.i.207). In a long speech to
Prince Hal in *1 Henry IV*, troubled Henry sees Richard's blind
rioting recapitulated in his son, perhaps as a punishment for
Henry's own "mistreadings." This comparison between Richard
and Hal affords us a convenient vantage point for pursuing thematic imagery of waste and excess through succeeding plays of
this group. Analysis will be centered upon three or four critical
passages and the character of Falstaff.

After the excesses of Richard's reign, the Lancastrians reject
fatness and imprudence in both man and commonwealth. This
rejection underlies the famous first interview of Henry with his
son, the Prince's first soliloquy, and the Prince's later banishment
of Falstaff. Henry tells Hal that when he himself courted the
crown, his own state, "Seldom but sumptuous, show'd like a feast
And won by rareness such solemnity" (III.ii.57–59). The politician's view of public appearance as strategy could scarcely be
further refined. In sixty-odd lines, Henry employs "seldom" three
times to refer to his activities and reenforces it with a dozen other
words suggesting economy. In a score of very different terms,
however, Henry says that men were with King Richard's presence "glutted, gorg'd, and full," for he,

> being daily swallowed by men's eyes,
> They surfeited with honey and began
> To loathe the taste of sweetness. . . .
>
> (70–72, 84)

Kingship is here a kind of candy which should be given the people
infrequently, probably when one wishes something from them.
Three of Henry's verbs are especially significant:

> And then I stole all courtesy from heaven,
> And dress'd myself in such humility
> That I did pluck allegiance from men's hearts. . . .
>
> (50–52)

It is unnecessary to apply these words to Hal to observe that his
seldomness (and his careful "dress") has something in common
with that of his father. Indeed, as prince (though not as king), his
seldom-acting in the interests of the state is rather like Henry's
seldom-appearing, but it commits him to greater personal risks.

Though Hal spends his youth as a madcap of "unyok'd humour" desiring small beer and as a friend of the "trunk of humours," he seems to know from the beginning what he is doing. In his first soliloquy (I.ii.219-241) he exhibits the theatrical sense of timing of other Shakespearian heroes, sharpened to a remarkable degree. He says he will "imitate the sun" which "doth permit" the clouds to "smother up his beauty," so that his eventual shining will be "more wonder'd at." One of his figures about holidays employs his father's terms: "when they seldom come, they wish'd-for come, And nothing pleaseth but rare accidents." He wants his reformation to "show more goodly and attract more eyes Than that which hath no foil to set it off." This is surely the returning prodigal calculating every effect: he will "offend to make offence a skill." Part of this attitude derives from the emphasis upon absoluteness in the heroic code, according to which it is no "sin to covet honor," and "Two stars" cannot "share" in glory (I:V.iv.64-65). It derives also from the necessity of the protagonist in Shakespeare to have a "dainty" ear, from his necessity to collaborate in the nick of time with his fate: "the readiness is all." "Percy is but my factor . . . ," the Prince tells his father,

> To engross up glorious deeds on my behalf;
> And I will call him to so strict account
> That he shall render every glory up. . . .
> (I:III.ii.147-150)

Bolingbroke's earlier imagery of "more" and "less" here becomes financial. This young accountant will appear to be eating and sleeping, but when Hotspur's bond of honor has matured, Hal will spring to life and exact both principal and interest, "Or I will tear the reckoning from his heart" (152). Behind this ferocity of course lies the ancient notion of the conqueror's (like the cannibal's) gaining the strength and virtue of the conquered. But the Prince's accounting reminds us of the very different "trim reckoning" by which Falstaff reduces honor to a word, and we must turn to the knight who only reckons his sack to understand more fully why the Prince seems to be eating his cake and having it too.

When Henry V banishes the "tutor and the feeder of my riots" at the end of Part II, he speaks of his companionship with Falstaff as a "dream," which—"being awak'd" and watching for sleeping

England—he now despises (II:V.v.53–55). The younger Henry apparently dreams of Falstaff as Richard II seemed to dream of Bolingbroke in England's garden, but unlike Richard, he does not succumb to his nightmare. Some critics have been offended by an image (among others) from Henry's rejection speech which the metaphors we have been following should help to deepen and justify: "Make less thy body, hence, and more thy grace; Leave gormandizing" (56–57). To throw these words and this controversial scene into larger perspective, we must give appropriate emphasis to the virtues of law and order embodied in the Chief Justice and of prudence and economy running through all of the histories. And we must remember the surprising seriousness with which Falstaff defends himself and the Prince promises to banish him ("I do, I will") during the mock interview—really the trial of a way of life—in Part I (II.iv.462–528). Both seem to know from the beginning that this dream will end. But the complexity of Falstaff and of our attitudes toward him is the best measure of the delicate balance among political and moral attitudes maintained throughout these plays.

The sympathy of the world has always been with the fat knight, and the popularity of these plays would be vastly reduced if, unimaginably, he were not in them. The Prince's turning from "plump Jack," "All the world," can be seen as the rejection of fuller life in favor of power, of being for becoming. That Jack is perhaps an inevitable companion for the Prince, Henry IV makes plain when he associates fatness with nobility in speaking of his son: "Most subject is the fattest soil to weeds; And he, the noble image of my youth, Is overspread with them" (II:IV.iv.54–56). But in a comic but highly significant defense of the medicine he recommends for every illness, Falstaff says that the royal blood or soil in Hal was originally "lean, sterile, and bare" and had to be "manured, husbanded, and till'd" with "fertile sherris" to make Hal "valiant" (II:IV.iii.92–135). Falstaff's phenomenal attractiveness and his mockery of honor and all state affairs give us, among other things, just the insight we need into the "cold blood" of the Lancasters, and also into the dying chivalric code for which his "catechism" (I:V.i.128–140) is a kind of epitaph or *reductio ad absurdum*. But the parallels between the sustained imagery we have been following and Shakespeare's characterization of Falstaff em-

phasize a darker side of this hill of flesh and illuminate his profoundly functional role in this entire cycle of plays.

Far from threatening the structure of the histories, as some
have maintained, Falstaff is one of their central organizing symbols. It is tempting to guess that Shakespeare rapidly found the
imagery drawn from nature and animal life which is so marked a
feature of the style of *Henry VI* and, far more subtly and intri-
cately, of *Richard II*, inadequate for his increasingly complicated
meanings. However we account for it, he developed or chanced
upon another and far more expressive vehicle for the ideas of the
sick state and king associated in *Richard II* with the overgrown
garden. The final evolution of the metaphor of the fat garden and
of the sick body politic is probably the fat man. Metaphors from
the unweeded garden may underline or even symbolize the sickness of the realm, to be sure, but the tun of man can also, if as
alert and witty as Falstaff, make the best possible case for fatness,
for the "sin" of being "old and merry," for "instinct" and life
rather than grinning honor and death. And he can afford us the
point of view from which thinness and economy can be seen as
inadequate or unpleasant characteristics. Thus he can throw into
clearer relief the entire political and personal ethic of the histories. If we compare the relatively simple equivalence between the
physical ugliness of the "elvish-mark'd, abortive, rooting hog,"
Richard III, and the disordered state, on the one hand, with the
ambivalent richness of the relationships between the "shapes" of
Falstaff and rebellious England, on the other, we can have a
helpful index of the deepening of Shakespeare's thought and his
growing mastery of his medium over the five or six years (1592–3
to 1597–8) that separate the first of the major histories from the
greatest.

Falstaff, then, is both the sickness of the state, the prince of
the caterpillars preying on the commonwealth, and the remedy
for some of its ills. And his role dramatizes the gulf between the
essential virtues of the private man and those of the ruler, for
we see in *Antony*, the feast which nourishes the one often sickens
the other. Timeless Falstaff is in a curiously reciprocal relationship with time-serving Henry IV, for they are the principal com-
petitors for the Prince's allegiance, in affording by precept and
example radically contrasting mirrors for the young magistrate.

But the usurper who disdained to follow the example of rioting Richard, as we have seen, finds his eldest son rioting with Falstaff—a kind of embodiment of Henry's inability to weed his own garden. Both the politician and the reveler must disappear from the world of young Henry V before he can find his own voice somewhere between them. He had to befriend Falstaff to know this man's gifts and "language," and in the "perfectness of time" he had to act to arrest the threat of such "gross terms" to the kingdom (II:IV.iv.68–75). The threat is real, for Falstaff is almost the result of a process similar to that referred to by the Archbishop in defending the rebels in Part II: "The time misord'red doth, in common sense, Crowd us and crush us to this monstrous form . . ." (II:IV.ii.33–34). We can hardly sentimentalize a Falstaff who says he will "turn diseases to commodity" (II:I.ii.277), when we remember the Bastard's great attack upon "commodity" (opportunism, time-serving) in the nearly contemporary King John.[2] And we cannot ignore the outrageousness of Falstaff's cry upon hearing of Hal's succession, just before he himself is banished: "Let us take any man's horses; the laws of England are at my commandment" (II:V.iii.141–142). Falstaff threatens to usurp the "customary rights" of time, governed as he says he is only by the moon, and to make the law "bondslave" to lawlessness.

Falstaff is depicted in language very similar to that employed in two of the most vivid pictures of disorder in all of Shakespeare, both of them from 2 Henry IV. Once in a kind of mock despair, the wily Northumberland prays that "order die! And let this world no longer be a stage To feed contention in a ling'ring act . . ." (I.i.154–156). Later, the dying king, apprehensive lest his realm receive the "scum" of "neighbour confines" and become a "wilderness," fears that Hal will

> Pluck down my officers, break my decrees;
> For now a time is come to mock at form.
> Harry the Fifth is crown'd. Up, vanity . . . !
> For the Fifth Harry from curb'd license plucks
> The muzzle of restraint, and the wild dog
> Shall flesh his tooth on every innocent.
>   (IV.v.118–120, 131–133)

The formless man, "vanity in years," who has mocked at all forms of honor has been the prince's closest companion, potentially a powerful voice in state affairs. The real target of the "fool and jester" has been the "rusty curb of old father antic the law" (I:I.ii.69–70), and the violence in the lines above of "wild dog" and "flesh" reminds us of the "butcher" of the histories, Richard III, and of the cormorant-villains of the tragedies. The rejection of Falstaff marks the new king's turning from the negligence and excess that had nearly destroyed England since the reign of Richard II. As the young king dismisses one tutor and embraces another in the Chief Justice, he cultivates his garden in "law and form and due proportion":

> The tide of blood in me
> Hath proudly flow'd in vanity till now.
> Now doth it turn and ebb back to the sea,
> Where it shall mingle with the state of floods
> And flow henceforth in formal majesty.
> (II:V.ii.129–133)

The proud river of the private will has become the sea of life of the commonwealth. The blood which here as in the tragedies is the basis of both mood and mind is purged. The man who said he was of all humors comes to achieve the "finely bolted" balance which Henry once thought characterized the traitor Scroop:

> spare in diet,
> Free from gross passion or of mirth or anger . . .
> Not working with the eye without the ear,
> And but in purged judgment trusting neither.
> (H.V., II.ii.131–136)

Henry V is by no means the kind of hero we would admire fully in the tragedies. But the Choruses which celebrate his virtues make perfectly plain that this trim watcher rises from his father's vain engrossing of "cank'red heaps" of gold to genuine magnanimity—the fearless sun king:

> A largess universal, like the sun,
> His liberal eye doth give to every one,
> Thawing cold fear.
> (Pro.4.43–45)

NOTES

1. References to Part 2 of *Henry IV* are indicated thus: II:IV.i.39–40. All readings are from the *Complete Works*, edited by G. L. Kittredge, Boston, 1936.

2. As has frequently been observed, the Falstaff of Part II is a less complicated and attractive figure than the Falstaff of Part I. Increasingly obsessed with his age, his aches and diseases, and, being rarely in the company of the Prince, at once more arrogant and less witty, he seems to embody less of the high-spiritedness which the Lancastrians lack and more of the corruption which threatens to engulf the kingdom.

Jonas A. Barish

The Turning Away of Prince Hal (1965)

The rejection of Falstaff,[1] like much else in Shakespeare, has tended to turn a searchlight on us, and make ourselves reveal ourselves either as moralists or as sentimentalists. Shakespeare preserves such a delicate balance, throughout the two parts of *Henry IV*, between authority and rebellion, business and pleasure, sobriety and negligence, that the final episode almost invites us to view them in the light of our own deep preferences. If we range ourselves naturally on the side of authority, with its promise of order and justice, we will tend to endorse the casting off of the embodiment of disorder, the enemy-in-chief of the Lord Chief Justice. We will be gratified by the reckoning with misrule that has been so long in coming. We will subscribe to the authorized versions of the incident—to Prince John of Lancaster's opinion, for example, that his brother, the new king, has behaved handsomely to his old associates. If, on the other hand, our instincts prompt us to range ourselves more strongly on the side of freedom and spontaneity, we may tend to remember the vitality in Falstaff more than his lawlessness; we may recall his panegyric to sack more vividly than his fleecing of Shallow, and we will doubtless compare it in its favor with the official treachery practised by Prince John in Gaultree Forest. We will then find the rejection scene an affront, Hal a preaching humbug, and the whole episode a distasteful illustration of the incompatibility of kingship with kindness.[2]

From *Shakespeare Studies* 1 (1965). Reprinted by permission of the author and the Chairman of the Board of Trustees of the Center for Shakespeare Studies.

Either of these formulations certainly oversimplifies, but my own instincts lead me to suspect that the latter view is the truer one, and that Bradley's essay still remains the soundest statement of the case. Bradley, it will be recalled, felt that the planned deterioration of Falstaff in 2 *Henry IV*, carried out by Shakespeare with remarkable thoroughness, still could not prevail over the vitality intrinsic to the character (who embodies "the bliss of freedom gained in humour"); and that, conversely, the fact that the rejection is indeed necessary to the welfare of the kingdom, and that the Prince has, in some sense, been rejecting Falstaff all along, could not dispel our feeling that the terms of the rejection are too peremptory and too scathing.[3]

I should like to ask whether we do not arrive at much the same view if we take a different route, and consider the incident not so much as a detail in a Bradleyan character analysis as in the light of Shakespearean dramaturgy in general, by measuring it against the pattern of other plays, especially the comedies. I think that when we do, we find Bradley's strictures confirmed. We find that the false notes struck by the new king in his speech to his old tavernmate—the sanctimoniousness, the dishonest retrospective revision of the relations between himself and Falstaff, whereby the latter is turned into his "misleader," so that he can be more stingingly dismissed, and the king appear correspondingly more magnanimous—that these notes ring especially false because they impose a constricting rather than a liberating interpretation on all that we have witnessed up to this moment.

They also transfer us forcibly from the domain of comedy to the grimmer realm of history. In so doing, they help us to see what differentiates comic drama from history play. History, it would seem, lends itself better to the shape of tragedy than of comedy. In historical plays like *Richard III* and *Richard II*, tragic structure seems to arise naturally from chronicled event. As the erring kings reach the period of their acts or sufferings, they seem to crystallize almost without pressure into tragic protagonists; the playwright need only follow the grain of history. But as Falstaff, the greatest comic character in Shakespeare, nears the end of *his* reign, the comic mould must be broken by violence, and the comic resolution harshly suppressed. C. L. Barber has shown how Falstaff recreates the figure of the Lord of Misrule who must, for the health of the community, be cast out once his moment of triumph has passed.[4] It only remains to underline the fact that the realization of this pattern, in which the Lord of Misrule becomes a scapegoat, is not a comic but a tragic fulfillment.

In the comic world, it is those whom Barber designates as the kill-joys—the putters-down of mirth, the sour-faced guardians of authority or censorious moralism—who are chased from the stage so that joy may reign unconfined. Given the choice between a drunken sensualist like Sir Toby Belch and a prescriptive authoritarian like Malvolio, comedy opts for the former: the sensualist, however chastened and curbed of his disruptive tendencies, remains to participate in the communal festivities of the finale, while the foiled authoritarian stalks furiously from the scene. Similarly, at the end of *The Merchant of Venice, Much Ado about Nothing,* and *As You Like It,* it is the masquers and revellers who command the stage, while the enemies of pleasure—Shylock, Don John, the melancholy Jaques—hold themselves aloof, or take flight, or retreat into sterile solitude. The enemies of pleasure, we notice, are two of them villains: inability to enter into the festive mood is closely bound up with an inability to respond warmly to others, to form close attachments, to give freely and lovingly of oneself. But history imposes a bleaker design: at the end of *2 Henry IV* it is the kill-joys who win out, and the spirit of Carnival who is gorgonized by a stony British stare, and placed under lock and key in the Fleet.[5]

I have labelled these remarks "The Turning Away of Prince Hal" to underscore the element of *self*-rejection involved in the new king's action. The just-crowned Henry V declares with no slight emphasis that he is not the thing he was, that he has turned away his former self, and expects to do as much with those who kept him company. For a Shakespearean hero, this is an oddly self-mutilating declaration. Shakespearean drama normally works toward a synthesis, in which characters find themselves enhanced in their sympathies and more varied in their responses than before. The range of their appreciation has widened; they have learned to value things they once slighted; in tragedy this enlarged appreciativeness often constitutes a partial compensation for the protagonist's loss of worldly greatness.

Shakespearean comedy customarily finds its characters in a moment of idleness, in a recreative suspension of what has been or will be their "normal" life. After the games and improvisations of *Love's Labor's Lost*, the death of the Princess' father comes to recall us, along with the characters, to a sterner world of adversity and business. In *A Midsummer Night's Dream* the young lovers live through a spell of bewitchment, of abandonment to the irrational and quirky depths in themselves, before waking to daylight and normalcy. Waking, they recall in wonder the strange shapes traced on their memories by the events they have dreamed over-night.

In both these cases the interval of play or dream is conceived as a positive experience. The pleasant proclivities in themselves to which the young heroes and heroines of *Love's Labor's Lost* give rein—for wit and impromptu ceremony, for love and poetry and disguise, for feasts of language and masques of folly—are presented in the most attractive terms. These activities are conceived not only as suitable to the youth of the participants, but as enriching. The first sign of wisdom in the young men is not the little academe they aspire to found, but their renunciation of it, their surrender to the presence of the ladies and the delights of the season. If, in their wooing and revelling, they proceed a new way into folly, it is a folly that involves a happy attentiveness, however incomplete, to others beside themselves, a potential lessening, at least, of the egoistic self-absorption with which they took up their roles as philosophers in the academe. When at the height of the festivity, the shadow of death falls on the mirth, it does not repudiate the mirth, but places it within a larger perspective, renders it doubly precious by underscoring its fragility, even as it hints at its inadequacy. The twelve-month penance proposed by the Princess is not intended to wipe out the memory of the "courtship, pleasant jest, and courtesy" (V.ii.789)[6] offered to the ladies, but to chasten its extravagances, to put it to the test under severer conditions. There is no doubt that the young lords require a lesson in humanity—this much is proved by their callousness toward the rustics during the pageant of the Worthies, and reiterated by Rosaline's last words to Berowne—but no one suggests that the holiday interlude has in itself been reprehensible or immoral.

In *A Midsummer Night's Dream*, even more explicitly, the dream sequence proves potent enough to cast a prospective richness over the future lives of the lovers. Hermia will be the more loved by Lysander for his having momentarily strayed to Helena, and Helena will be the more cherished by Demetrius for his having yielded to a freak of folly, and courted Hermia. Demetrius' folly, we should notice, begins before the play does, and supplies the basis for its action. The enchantments of the night in the palace wood return him not to the condition he was in when he entered the wood, but to where he was before the play began, in love with his first love, his true love, Helena. The confusions provoked by the magic flower-juice have simply allowed the capricious and vagrant impulses in the lovers to play themselves out at farce tempo, as in a movie speed-up. At dawn the lovers do not merely come to their senses, or to themselves; they come to selves renewed and refreshed by the night's adventures. The sound of horns and hunting that fills the wood as Theseus takes to the chase conveys us into the bracing air of daytime reality, but the nocturnal spell proves able to sustain itself. When Oberon and his train return at nightfall to scatter blessings on the newly wedded couples, we see the witchery of the preceding night continuing, visibly, to shed its benefits on the spirits of the lovers.

Prince Hal, like the king and courtiers in *Love's Labor's Lost*, has been on holiday, as he told us in his first soliloquy. Like the young lovers of *A Midsummer Night's Dream* he has been dreaming: he has "long dreamt of such a kind of man" (V.v.53). And it has been a dream of love: if the prince has not loved Falstaff, Falstaff has certainly loved the prince. As a symbol of "the supremacy of the imagination over fact,"[7] Falstaff has glittered as enticingly as the moonlight in the Athens wood; as the incarnation of play, he has outstripped the young lords of Navarre even in their most inspired moments of sonneteering and masquerading. Following the lead of the comedies, then, we would expect the dream, the holiday, the moment of love, to have left some precious residue in the prince's spirit. We might suppose that certain human propensities were better cultivated at Eastcheap than at court: the free pleasuring of the senses, the capacity to live in the present, undistracted by vain regrets over the past or empty wishes about the future, the love of wit and mirth, the invigorating skepticism toward received opinion and official rhetoric.

But unlike the heroes of the comedies, Hal is ashamed of his holiday, and he despises his dream. He recoils from his former lover with more of a shudder than Titania from the memory of

Bottom. Nowhere does his final speech allow for the possibility that the sportive interlude was valuable. Where his counterparts in the comedies incorporate the holiday or the dream into their fuller waking lives, the new king dismisses it as a spell of "riot," a moment of worthless disorder. Instead of a synthesis, in which an enlarged sense of human possibility emerges from the dialectic between duty and holiday, or dream and waking, we have a forcible sundering of the two kinds of experience, and a walling of them off into the noncommunicating realms of Good and Bad.

The sundering is accompanied, inevitably, by a shrinking. Prince Hal is rightly said by Tillyard to be, in his tavern days, of a "comprehensive nature,"[8] responsive to the whole range of human potentiality. When he sounds the base string of humility in the company of the drawers, Hal is putting himself in vital touch with the whole spectrum of English life. He claims such a microcosmic comprehensiveness for himself when he announces that he is "of all humours that have showed themselves humours since the old days of goodman Adam" (1H4, II.iv.104–6). In Tillyard's gloss, he is claiming to be "ruled simultaneously by every human motive that exists." Now, his coronation accomplished, we find that he has cultivated this wide responsiveness only to disavow it and deliver homilies on it, that he is bent on rooting out of himself the variousness of feeling he once prided himself on— that, in short, his comprehensive nature is comprehensive no more, but partial and exclusive.

He now takes the attitude toward his tavern truancy that has always been taken in court circles. The main extenuation of his scapegrace ways, by sympathetic counsellors, has been the hope that he would at length reject them. The Earl of Warwick, comforting the sick Henry IV, tries to reassure him concerning Hal's wildness:

> The Prince but studies his companions
> Like a strange tongue, wherein, to gain the language,
> 'Tis needful that the most immodest word
> Be look'd upon and learnt; which once attain'd,
> Your Highness knows, comes to no further use
> But to be known and hated. So, like gross terms,
> The Prince will, in the perfectness of time,
> Cast off his followers; and their memory

Shall as a pattern or a measure live
By which his Grace must mete the lives of others,
Turning past evils to advantages.

(2H4 IV.iv.68-78)

The prince, thus, is defended on the ground that he is getting to
know the seamy side of life, acquainting himself with vices so as
to hate and shun them, as men learn foul words in foreign
tongues in order to purify their vocabularies. The only available
justification for Hal's misbehavior is one that frankly regards it as
a deviation into *evils*, immersion in an alien element from which, it
is piously hoped, *advantages* may one day ensue. Hal is not thought
to have anything in common with his tavernmates, nor have they
anything to teach him except the unattractiveness of vice.

This remains essentially the approved view after the accession. The Archbishop of Canterbury, at the beginning of *Henry V*,
describes the young king's reformation as a descent of grace. In
the Archbishop's eyes the king has been a prodigal, who on
reaching the throne renounced the sins for which wise men
censured him when he was prince: "his addiction was to courses
vain, / His companies unletter'd, rude, and shallow, / His hours
fill'd up with riots, banquets, sports" (I.i.54-6). Banquets and
sports, we note, the pastimes of the holiday world, are here made
nearly synonymous with "riots," the key term of disapproval, for
which no favorable senses occur in Shakespeare. Henry IV, wistfully comparing his son to Harry Percy, saw "riot and dishonour"
staining his son's brow. In the eyes of the guardians of order,
Falstaff himself symbolizes Riot.[9] The prince's tavern life was
"vain"—frivolous and empty. His companions were "rude" and
"shallow," capable only of being a coarsening influence. When the
new king, at his coronation, adopts the same vocabulary, when he
bids the Lord Chief Justice "speak to that vain man," when he
charges Falstaff with having been "the tutor and the feeder of
[his] riots," he serves notice that he has absorbed the viewpoint of
the establishment; he now sees his acquaintance with Falstaff as a
wholly negative experience, an initiation into evil that has taught
him what to shun.

"How ill white hairs become a fool and jester!" Folly, in Shakespeare, usually proves to be an inescapable condition of life, to

which no one is immune, and jesters, to quote a perhaps not altogether trustworthy witness, "do oft prove prophets." Those who most fiercely claim exemption from folly are usually those suffering from hubris, for whom comic chastisement or tragic humbling is in store: the young men in *Love's Labor's Lost*, the fiery Lear. Acceptance of one's folly amounts to an acceptance of one's own earthy composition, and that of others: in both comic and tragic actions it forms an indispensable stage on the road to self-fulfillment. The newly crowned Henry V, by his categorical dismissal of folly, pursues the reverse course: he seeks to disclaim what he formerly acknowledged, his proneness to error, his membership in the race of goodman Adam. The rejection of Falstaff is part of a process in which, in the words of the Archbishop of Canterbury, "Consideration like an angel came / And whipp'd th'offending Adam out of him" (*H5*, I.i.28–9)—whereby the king disclaims the component of common clay in himself and sets himself apart from the stock of Adam. We are hardly surprised when later on, at the battlefield in France, he approves the execution of Bardolph without a flicker of recognition of the former association between them.

Now it is true that Hal is not the hero of a comedy, or of a tragedy, and that the experiences of romantic love, usually central to the comic formula, or of worldly ruin, central to tragedy, are here beside the point. It is true also that comic and tragic heroes ordinarily suffer from some defect of vision or error of feeling—Berowne's excessive penchant for mockery, Demetrius' whimsical fancy for Hermia—that must be corrected by whatever humbling experiences the plot affords. Hal, it may be argued, as the hero of a history play, suffers from no such defect. His task, according to the chief moralistic view, is not so much to understand himself, or to reform himself in any substantial way, as to fit himself to be the kind of king who will rule England wisely, and he is from the start in possession of his own best course. Eastcheap is not for him a regenerative wood, but a school of squalor where he learns plain truths about his future subjects and his realm. Even his most expansive moments, it may be urged, such as that with the drawers, are tinged with calculation; Hal is practising sounding the base string so as to be able later to play the whole gamut of the viol of state. But the more we insist on the element of planning in the Eastcheap truancy, the more we turn Hal into a cardboard prince, incapable from the outset of responding to the vitality of Falstaff. Under these conditions, the sojourn in the tavern becomes little better than an empty masquerade, and the gratuitous emphasis of the rejection speech seems more bizarre and inappropriate than ever. If, on the other hand, we grant the reality of the lure of Falstaff, as we surely experience it, and if we acknowledge what we plainly observe to be the case, that Falstaff delights the prince, then we find the exigencies of the history play leading to a "reformation" that we can only feel as a dehumanization.

Doubtless by progressively transforming revelry into misrule, during the latter scenes of 2 *Henry IV*, Shakespeare has done what he could to justify dramatically the moralistic position. Having chosen to make Hal into the hero-king, a combination of both human and political virtues, he prepares the way for the crisis by making us reject Falstaff first. But those critics who have espoused the fierce tone as well as the dogma of the rejection scene have tended to give the episode a purely institutional reading. They have subscribed to the official doctrine according to which the prince makes himself the mirror of all Christian kings by disowning his past self. But Shakespearean characters do not achieve greatness by self-truncation, nor by adopting a priggish tone toward their own past misdeeds (if misdeeds they have committed). To banish plump Jack is to banish what is free and vital and pleasurable in life, as well as much that is selfish and unruly—not all the world perhaps, but more of it than either we or Hal can do without.

History thus defeats those who would defy it by trying to live in a changeless present or an undiminished youth, or in a realm of pure play. It awards its favors to those who can make themselves its servants by curbing their own human fullness. The history play as a genre—the Lancastrian tetralogy at least—takes an optimistic view of the process. It strives to present it as benign, so that the irresponsibles, who would flourish in comedy, are felt to deserve their defeat, while the exponents of order, however repressive, are felt to warrant our allegiance. In a later Shakespearean play a similar dilemma turns to tragedy. Antony and Cleopatra attempt to integrate into their public selves precisely the folly that Hal excludes from his: feasting, sensuality, music, sport and idleness. In their case the spirit of the tavern is installed at the heart of their beings as monarchs; instead of being curbed and disciplined, it expands till it disables them as rulers. Their progress reverses Hal's: they start with business, empire, authority, the tyranny of time and the consciousness of limits, and end with play, sensuality, time transposed into eternity, and all limits obliterated and transcended. In their case holiday gradually invades the conduct of imperial business till it engrosses them utterly; the life of kingship gradually becomes the dream, the life of pleasure the engulfing, transcending reality. Where Hal fits himself as a ruler by scrapping part of his humanity, Antony and Cleopatra unfit themselves by fostering the totality of theirs. Only the Egyptian transvaluation by which things melt into and become each other's opposites permits them to translate their political failure into a spiritual victory.

This play too has tended to expose its readers as moralists and sentimentalists. Those who see in Falstaff chiefly a portent of disorder, to be rightly spurned by a repentant Hal come to his senses after a prodigal sowing of wild oats, also tend to see a cautionary tale in the story of Antony and Cleopatra, a homily against adultery and a warning against the neglect of serious business. Those who see in the sacrifice of Falstaff a near-tragic reproof of life by the tyrannical demands of state tend also to see in the deaths of Antony and Cleopatra a triumphant escape from the clutches of the same tyranny. In neither case, one suspects, can the conflicting forces be made to merge lastingly, or reach a stable equilibrium. Too many contradictory conditions exist to be satisfied. Life contains more than any given configuration in it can ever adequately embody, especially if that configuration straddles the public and private worlds as hugely as do the destinies of the English throne or the dynastic concerns of Egypt and ancient Rome. One must accept the fact that in one case political success is achieved at the cost of a constricted sensibility, in the other that a magnified sensibility is achieved at the price of imperial defeat.

NOTES

1. The present essay, in slightly different form, was delivered as a paper before the Shakespeare section of the Modern Language Association, at its annual convention, in New York, December, 1964.

2. The New Variorum Edition of the play, ed. Matthias Shaaber (Philadelphia, 1940), pp. 584-99, provides plentiful examples of both views,
but particularly of the second, or sentimentalist view, the moralistic
position, in its fullest development, being a more recent phenomenon.
The Summer, 1956 (VII, #3) issue of *Shakespeare Quarterly*, a Supple-
ment to the New Variorum Edition of *1 Henry IV*, ed. G. Blakemore
Evans, contains a survey of later comment, in the Appendix, pp. 78-
94. To the work of the two chief moralist critics, J. Dover Wilson and
E. M. W. Tillyard, one may add such footnotes as Hugh Dickinson,
"The Reformation of Prince Hal," *SQ*, XII (1951), 33-46, and Peter J.
Seng, "Songs, Time, and the Rejection of Falstaff," *ShS*, XV (1962),
31-40.

3. A. C. Bradley, "The Rejection of Falstaff," *Oxford Lectures on Poetry*,
2nd ed. (London, 1909), pp. 247-73. I should add that in addition to
Bradley and Barber (cited below), the critics who seem to me to have
written most illuminatingly on Prince Hal and Falstaff are Harold C.
Goddard, *The Meaning of Shakespeare* (Chicago, 1951), I, 167-213; Derek
Traversi, *Shakespeare from Richard II to Henry V* (Stanford, 1957),
pp. 162-165; and J. A. Bryant, Jr., "Prince Hal and the Ephesians,"
Sewanee Review, LXVII (1959), 204-19. The last-named essay, though it
does not engage in debate with the moralist critics, constitutes one of
the best rejoinders to them from a point of view explicitly Christian
and theological. Goddard, II, 184-209, and Traversi, *An Approach to
Shakespeare*, 2nd ed. (New York, 1956), pp. 235 ff., have also written
penetratingly on the relations between love and power in *Antony and
Cleopatra*, proposing a thesis essentially the same as that adopted in the
final two paragraphs of the present essay.

4. *Shakespeare's Festive Comedy* (Princeton, 1959), pp. 192-221. Barber's comments on the rejection scene (pp. 218-20) tend to corroborate Bradley. Barber's anthropological Falstaff had of course been anticipated
by J. Dover Wilson, *The Fortunes of Falstaff* (New York, 1943), pp. 25-31,
and J. I. M. Stewart, *Character and Motive in Shakespeare* (New York,
1947), pp. 135-9; and was reinforced by Philip Williams, "The Birth
and Death of Falstaff Reconsidered," *SQ*, VIII (1957), 356-65.

5. Nothing said of Falstaff in the present essay need invalidate the
propositions about him as a dramatic character made by such psychoanalytic critics as Franz Alexander and Ernst Kris, or such students of
Elizabethan theatrical convention as E. E. Stoll and Bernard Spivack.
Falstaff doubtless does represent, as Alexander suggests in "A Note
on Falstaff," *Psychoanalytic Quarterly*, II (1933), 592-606, "the wholly
self-centered pleasure-seeking principle," "the deep infantile layers of
the personality," which the prince must master in himself before
becoming a fully balanced adult. And he doubtless represents as well a

"depreciated father-figure," the psychological need to repudiate whom explains (without necessarily dramatically justifying) the "pointed cruelty" of the rejection scene (Ernst Kris, "Prince Hal's Conflict," *Psychoanalytic Quarterly,* XVII [1948], 487–506). He is, further, the braggart soldier described by Stoll in *Shakespeare Studies* (New York, 1927), pp. 403–490, and the Vice of the sixteenth century stage psychomachia described by Spivack in *Shakespeare and the Allegory of Evil* (New York, 1958), pp. 87–91. But in all these guises he continues to incarnate "freedom gained in humour," as Bradley phrases it (p. 262), to whom we respond even in his deterioration; in whom vitality persistently triumphs over old age, vice, and disease; and who "cannot be crushed with a plot," even if the plot is devised by Shakespeare. I would subscribe to William Empson's feeling, in "Falstaff and Mr. Dover Wilson," *Kenyon Review,* XV (1953), 221, 256, that "the main fact about Falstaff . . . is that it is hard to get one's mind all round him," and that "it is hard to defend this strange figure without doing it too much."

6. Citations from Shakespeare are to the edition of George Lyman Kittredge (Boston, 1936).
7. Goddard, I, 179, 183.
8. *Shakespeare's History Plays* (London, 1944), p. 274.
9. See *The Fortunes of Falstaff,* pp. 17–25.

Sigurd Burckhardt

"Swoll'n with Some Other Grief": Shakespeare's Prince Hal Trilogy (1968)

I speak of peace, while covert enmity
Under the smile of safety wounds the world;
And who but Rumour, who but only I,
Make fearful musters and prepared defence,
Whiles the big year, swoll'n with some other grief,
Is thought with child by the stern tyrant war,
And no such matter?

(2 Henry IV, Induction)

In *Der bestrafte Brudermord*—a seventeenth-century German version of the Hamlet story, which appears to be derived from the lost "Ur-Hamlet"—Hamlet rids himself of Rosencrantz and Guildenstern (as Shakespeare was to call them) by a neat and simple stratagem. As he marches between them, their pistols aimed at him from either side, he suddenly ducks; by sheer reflex, the two courtiers pull their triggers and shoot each other dead. The stratagem illustrates nicely how to win by the dialectical, *divide et impera* or *tertius ridens* method. The dialectician is not such a fool as himself to take arms against a sea of troubles; he divides his troubles into antitheses and makes them take arms against each other. If he can make no sense of "being," he pairs it off against "non-being," and presto! he emerges in possession of "becoming," historical process and metaphysical certitude. For a mere trick, dialectics has earned handsome (but unhappily only paper) profits.

From *Shakespearean Meanings* by Sigurd Burckhardt, 1968. Reprinted by permission of Princeton University Press.

Shakespeare does not allow his Hamlet to play it; perhaps that is one measure of his difficulties. The Prince likewise rids himself of Rosencrantz and Guildenstern, but not quite by the *tertius ridens* method. He has to do more than duck; he has to act and make himself co-responsible (with Claudius) for the courtiers' death. Now it is they who are in the middle, "between the fell, incensèd points / Of mighty opposites." Hamlet claims that they "sit not near [his] conscience"; but what about Ophelia, who perishes between the same fell points? And in any case he finds *himself* one of the mighty opposites; for him, "to be" and "not to be" do not cancel each other into a higher synthesis.

Dialectics is an ordering device; it orders by arranging disorder symmetrically. We do not resort to it as long as we know, or think we know, where and wherein order resides; we resort to it when we do not know, or pretend not to know, where our quest for order is taking us. The dialectician acts as though he had fully accepted the challenge of disorder and were seriously engaged in meeting it. What he forgets, or chooses to ignore, is that dialectical conflict is a question-begging device. Whatever victories are won in this way are won by prearrangement.

There are various possible images of order; traditionally, that of the Christian West has been the triad. Unlike the circle (the image of divine order), the triad allows for discord, as any image of human order must; the base points are seen as potentially or actually in conflict. But at the same time it provides the apex where conflict can be arbitrated and resolved. For any level where conflict can arise there is a next higher level of appeal—the whole forming a pyramid, with God or some other absolute as the supreme arbiter.

If this is our image of order, it is natural that we should think of disorder as a triad minus the apex—as conflict where there is no higher court of appeal. Dialectics undertakes to reconstruct the apex from the base points, once the former can no longer be assumed as known. But the fact is that the apex *is* known; it is given by the symmetry of the image. Dialectical conflict is an instance not so much of disorder as of order *manqué*. It is a duel, trial by combat. A duel differs from normal, "orderly" trials only in that the court speaks through the outcome rather than *in propria persona*. This may not be very consoling to the losing combatant, who may be so unreasonable and dialectically unenlightened as to feel that *he* was in the right and should have won. But it is most reassuring to the observing dialectician, who can persuade himself that once again disorder has brought forth order. If it had, the birth would be miraculous; in fact it is simply a *petitio principii.*

All this may seem an odd preamble to an interpretation of Shakespeare's Prince Hal plays. But I hope to show that in these plays Shakespeare took a much more searching look at the problem of disorder than he had in the earlier histories. He had long since discovered that the apex had disappeared or become inaccessible; he now finds that even the remnant is more than he can safely take for granted.

I

Symmetry is so satisfying an arrangement because it gives scope to our secret lust for combat and disorder even while reassuring us that we are ultimately safe. We may think as we wish of Hal's famous soliloquy in *1 Henry IV*—"I know you all, and will a while uphold"—we *are* reassured by it. Between rebellion and misrule, between hot pride and slippery wit, sword-edged honor and fat-bellied self-indulgence, we know there is an axis of symmetry and a *tertius ridens*. Order will emerge in the end, not necessarily because it has proved its superior title but because the two kinds of disorder will kill and cancel each other.

1 Henry IV seems to reach this point of satisfying resolution when Hal stands between what he assumes to be the corpses of Hotspur and Falstaff and speaks over each the appropriate obsequies. If the stage were simply a mirror of reality, its order and disorders, here the ordering would seem achieved. But of course it is not; no sooner has Hal walked off than disorder arises in massive palpability:

> 'Sblood, 'twas time to counterfeit. . . . Counterfeit? I lie, I am no counterfeit. To die is to be a counterfeit, for he is but the counterfeit of a man who hath not the life of a man; but to counterfeit dying when a man thereby liveth, is to be no counterfeit, but the true and perfect image of life in-

deed. . . . I am afraid of this gunpowder Percy though he be
dead. How, if he should counterfeit too and rise? By my
faith, I am afraid he would prove the better counterfeit.
Therefore I'll make him sure; yea, and I'll swear I killed him.
Why may not he rise as well as I?

(V.iv.113–28)

Not only *may* Hotspur rise but he *will*—as soon as the scene is
ended and his "body" has been lugged off the stage. Like other
leading actors in tragedies and histories, he makes a living by
counterfeit dying, and to do so "is to be no counterfeit, but the
true and perfect image of life indeed." Falstaff's rising destroys all
kinds of reassuring symmetries, the first being that of stage and
world. *Sub specie realitatis*, his claim to being Hotspur's killer is
exactly as good, or bad, as Hal's, just as his pretense of having died
on the field of honor is exactly as good, or bad, as Hotspur's.
Simply by refusing to submit to the agreeable fiction that there is
an axis of symmetry between on-stage and off-stage and that
reality and its representation correspond to each other in perfect
balance, Falstaff throws us and the play back into dizzying confusion.

The confusion is covered up—at a price. In order to reestablish
the stage-world balance, Hal lures—not to say bribes—Falstaff
back into fictionality:

Come, bring your luggage nobly on your back.
For my part, if a lie may do thee grace,
I'll gild it with the happiest terms I have.

(V.iv.160–62)

He manages to sound magnanimous about it, but is he doing
more than making a virtue of necessity? For the "truth," in this
confusion of counterfeits, is with Falstaff; he is the only one at
this point who is not a "double man":

Falstaff. No, that's certain; I am not a double man. . . . There
is Percy. If your father will do me any honor, so; if not, let
him kill the next Percy himself. . . .
Hal. Why, Percy I killed myself, and saw thee dead.
Falstaff. Didst thou? Lord, Lord, how this world is given to
lying! I grant you I was down and out of breath, and so
was he. . . .

(V.iv.141–50)

Falstaff is ready to split the credit for Hotspur's killing: if Hal supports him in his "lie," he will sustain Hal in Hal's "lie." And this bargain does represent some sort of truth, or at least of justice. For no matter who has run his sword through Hotspur in the make-belief of the stage, dramatically and morally it is Falstaff's role to kill him and to be killed by him; in the dialectic of the play's structure, he is a hero, while Hal is the *tertius ridens*. Strangely, it is he, the creature of Shakespeare's imagination rather than of history, who in the end asserts himself as the reality principle incarnate, reminding us that disorder is not slain as neatly and inexpensively as the calculated symmetrics of dialectics would have us believe. Very likely his creator planned him as Hal means to use him: as a foil, with Hotspur as a counterfoil. But he would not stay so corseted; he outgrew his preassigned measure and function. In the end, while he does not seriously disquiet us— Shakespeare, when he has need, is a master at letting us have our cake and eat it—Falstaff *remains*, the bulky remainder of a division which was calculated at $2 \div 2 = 1$, but which would not come out even.

II

1 *Henry IV* is designed toward the release of combat. We watch the opponents quarrel; lay their plans, and gather their forces; march toward Shrewsbury, and fail in last-minute negotiations, until by Act v, scene iii, we are ready for that discharge of tension which of itself seems to create a sense of order.

2 *Henry IV* promises to repeat the design. Once again the rebels plot and march; once again the king takes countermeasures. But this time the encounter takes place in the first part of Act IV—and in Gaultree Forest of infamous memory. We are denied the release of battle; the confrontation ends in the treachery of John of Lancaster. The rebels, promised redress of their grievances, are tricked into dismissing their army; as soon as they have done so, they are seized and executed, while their dispersing soldiers are pursued and slain.

In the innocent days of moral and psychological criticism, John's bloody equivocation used to be roundly condemned; critics made no secret of their distaste for a play which seemed, for its satisfactory outcome, to depend on so mean a stratagem. Of late we have become more sophisticated; we talk about the larger political design, the education of Hal, and the utter wickedness of rebellion in Tudor doctrine. We are warned not to take Gaultree Forest too seriously: for an Elizabethan audience, rebels deserved no better. What Prince John dispenses is, after all, a kind of "justice," though somewhat "rigorous": "Temperamentally [Hal] strikes the balance between . . . John and . . . Falstaff. . . . The justice of John in his cold-blooded treatment of the rebels verges on rigour; Falstaff has no general standard of justice at all."[1]

I suggest that if an interpreter finds himself driven, by the tenor of his argument, into such euphemizing, there is something badly wrong with the argument. We always misread Shakespeare if our reading compels us to make light of cruelty and treachery— especially where these are not condemned and in some manner disowned in the play itself. More shocking even than Gaultree itself is the fact that it is accepted almost without comment. Prince John hardly troubles to justify himself; the transaction is between the rebels and "God":

> Strike up the drums, pursue the scattered stray.
> God, and not we, hath safely fought today.
>
> (IV.ii.120–21)

The king, when he is informed by letter of "the manner how this action hath been borne," says nothing explicit about it. But his reaction is telling: it is upon receiving the news of victory that he falls into his final illness:

> And wherefore should these good news make me
>   sick?
> Will Fortune never come with both hands full,
> But write her fair words still in foulest letters?
>
> (IV.iv.102–04)

The only extended commentary is Falstaff's praise of sherris-sack, which invites comparison with the Bastard's "commodity" speech in *King John*. There a peaceful "composition," healing in itself though achieved at some cost in loyalty, was flayed in explicitly moral terms; now an act of slaughter, made possible by a signal abuse of trust, is described as a matter of metabolism. Gaultree Forest becomes more troublesome by being treated with cold matter-of-factness.

But our trouble is by no means simply moral; Shakespeare frustrates an almost physical need for a discharge of tension. Gaultree Forest is, to be sure, a "fact of history," but if Shakespeare felt that he could not, in honesty, leave it out of his account, he had the option of giving it little or no dramatic weight. He might have relegated it to a report—with the appropriate sad commentary on the questionable shifts kings sometimes find themselves driven to. Instead, he designs his play so that Gaultree looms as a second Shrewsbury, only to deceive our expectations both dramatically and morally. What is more, he gives us clear warning of what he is about:

> I speak of peace, while covert enmity
> Under the smile of safety wounds the world . . .
> Make fearful musters and prepared defence,
> Whiles the big year, swoll'n with some other grief,
> Is thought with child by the stern tyrant war,
> And no such matter.
>
> (2 Henry IV, Induction)

These lines have usually been glossed—no doubt correctly—as alluding to contemporary political events, particularly to the false rumors of a Spanish invasion which alarmed England in 1596. But their much more immediate and revealing reference is to the play they introduce—to its false expectations and false promises of safety, indeed to its general sense of false pregnancy.

The question we must ask of 2 *Henry IV* is, I think, quite different from those which have commonly been asked. Many critics have marked the play off as unworthy of Shakespeare, a chore he assumed unwillingly and discharged carelessly. More recently, under the leadership of Tillyard and J. Dover Wilson, it has been interpreted as the second step in Hal's *gradus ad regnum*, his preparation for the royal office. The newer criticism has the virtue of assuming a serious intention on Shakespeare's part; but I do not see, any more than Derek Traversi and Clifford Leech, how 2 *Henry IV* can be interpreted as part of a continuous ascent. How does Hal say?

From a God to a bull? A heavy descension! It was Jove's case.
From a prince to a prentice? A low transformation! That
shall be mine; for in everything the purpose must weigh
with the folly.

(II.ii.192–96)

Here the immediate reference is to his disguise as a tapster; but
we need only remember the Gadshill robbery and its sequel in
1 *Henry IV* to see what broader meanings attach to this "heavy
descension." There is, throughout Part II, a musty atmosphere as
of stale air in closed rooms, of moral and physical debility. The
tapster scene is to Gadshill very much as Gaultree is to Shrewsbury. The question to ask is: What is the purpose that weighs
with such dramaturgical folly? What is that other, unexpressed,
stifled grief with which 2 *Henry IV* goes pregnant?

III

I quoted John's summing up of the "battle" of Gaultree Forest:
"God, and not we, hath safely fought today." The piety is more
offensive than the treachery, even though John seems to be
saying no more than Harry will say after the Battle of Agincourt.
Why? Because John perverts the very principle of trial by combat
to which he appeals. Combat as a means of discovering truth and
doing justice can have only one justification: that it be open, with
the outcome in genuine doubt, so that God *can* render His verdict.
At Agincourt there is some meaning to the claim that God has
spoken; there is none at Gaultree. I believe that Shakespeare
intends to underscore the difference when he has Harry say, after
Agincourt:

O God, Thy arm was here;
And not to us, but to Thy arm alone
Ascribe we all! When, *without stratagem,*
But in plain shock and even play of battle,
Was ever known so great and little loss
On one part and on th' other. Take it, God,
for it is none but Thine!

(*Henry V*, IV.viii.111–17—my italics)

I shall have to return to Harry's oddly strenuous insistence on the
non nobis, Te Deum theme. (After Shrewsbury, God is not even
mentioned.) At the moment my point is that John has not submit-
ted his case and cause to God's judgment but has preempted that
judgment and foisted his own treacherous equivocation off on us
as God's voice. In terms of triadic order, he has construed the
apex by identifying it with one of the base (very base!) points. And
in doing so he has transformed the figure from a triangle into a
line. We shall presently explore the implications of this "low
transformation."

One thing is immediately clear: the order he represents—that
of Lancastrian and post-Lancastrian England—has become *secular.*
The sanctions it rests on are not divine or cosmic but at best
pragmatic. The shift to secularity finds its most palpable expression in the unexpected fulfillment of the prophecy that Henry IV
will die in "Jerusalem." Throughout the two parts of *Henry IV* the
king speaks of his purpose to wash away the stain of Richard's
sacred blood by leading a crusade to the Holy Land, but the very
forces he has set free by his usurpation prevent his doing so. He
cannot "get away"—get away, that is, from the consequences of
the act to which he and all his successors owe the crown. Blindly
he hopes that he can regain the lost religious sanction, only to
discover on his deathbed that the prophecy on which his hope was
based had a secular rather than a sacred meaning—that his final
destination is not the Holy City of Christendom but a chamber in
Westminster Palace.[2]

The age of holy wars is past. When, in the night before
Agincourt, Harry disputes with Williams and Bates about the
king's accountability for the afterlife of those who die in his wars,
we need to be as much aware of what he *cannot* answer as of what
he can and does answer:

> *King.* Me thinks I could not die anywhere so contented as in
> the King's company, his cause being just and his quarrel
> honourable.
> *Will.* That's more than we know.
> *Bates.* Aye, or more than we should seek after; for we know
> enough if we know that we are the King's subjects. If his
> cause be wrong, our obedience to the King wipes the
> crime of it out of us.

> Will. But if the cause be not good, the King himself hath a
> heavy reckoning to make. . . . I am afeard there are few
> die well that die in a battle. . . . Now, if these men do not
> die well, it will be a black matter for the King that led
> them to it.
>
> (IV.i.132–52)

To which Harry has but one reply:

> Every subject's duty is the King's, but every subject's soul is
> his own.
>
> (IV.i.185–86)

This is cold, secular comfort. What he ought to be able to answer
Williams is what Richmond told his men before Bosworth Field:

> God and our good cause fight upon our side. . . .
> Then, if you fight against God's enemy,
> God will in justice ward you as His soldiers.
>
> (Richard III, V.iii.240–54)

Since the king claims to be God's representative, his cause ought
to be God's cause, his wars holy wars, and those who die for him
[Him] ought to be martyrs. To die for the king should *ipso facto* be a
"good end," washing away prior sins and earning the reward of
eternal salvation.

But of course Harry can answer nothing of the sort. His
father's yearning to lead a crusade was already an anachronism
and even as such tainted with policy:

> To lead out many to the Holy Land,
> Lest rest and lying still might make them look
> Too near unto my state.
>
> (2 Henry IV, IV.v.211–13)

Bolingbroke's political testament undergoes exactly the same
shift as the meaning of "Jerusalem." The holy war having been
prevented by the very forces it was meant to check, the dying
king urges his son to engage in "foreign quarrels" (in sharp
contrast to his sentiments as recorded by Holinshed):

> Therefore, my Harry,
> Be it thy course to busy giddy minds
> With foreign quarrels, that action, hence borne out,
> May waste the memory of former days.
>
> (IV.v.213–16)

This is realism rather than cynicism: a clear-eyed recognition and acceptance of the fact that kingship, if it ever was divine, is no longer so. What is cynical is the pretense of John of Lancaster (and many statesmen since) that, though every subject's soul is his own when he is asked to fight *for* the king, it is *ipso facto* the Devil's if he chooses to fight against him.

IV

To return to the structural argument. Two things about 2 *Henry IV* are clear: it is designed to culminate in Hal's accession; and it disappoints our expectation (aroused by the play itself) of reaching that point through the "plain shock and even play of battle." To gauge our disappointment, we need only imagine the following: that Shakespeare had written *Henry IV* in one part, climaxing in the battle of Shrewsbury; that the king had died right after the battle, so that Hal's accession would have followed immediately upon his battlefield triumph; and that Hal had at that point exposed Falstaff's cowardice and lies, making them the occasion of rejecting him and signifying his own resolution to be a just and sober as well as valiant king. The distortion and telescoping of historical facts would have been no worse than what Shakespeare permits himself elsewhere; and I am by no means the first to suggest that such a way of managing the story would have been dramatically much more satisfying than the two-part arrangement Shakespeare chose.

What would have been lost? Very little of Falstaff; whatever Shakespeare does with him in Part II, except for the rather pathetic lechery, he has done already and better in Part I. To compare the capture of Sir John Coleville with the "killing" of Hotspur, for example, is to notice not just a repetition but a "heavy descension," analogous to that from Gadshill to the taproom and from Shrewsbury to Gaultree. We would miss Justice Shallow, but only as one more figure in Shakespeare's vast gallery of comic portraits. The only matters of dramatic weight that probably would have had to be sacrificed are the action involving the Chief Justice and the episode of the premature seizure of the crown.

No one, as far as I know, has tried to make much of the latter; so what is left is the Chief Justice, and it is hardly surprising that the play's defenders have made him the pivotal figure. The argument runs thus: of the two royal virtues, valor and justice, the Prince proves his title to the first in Part I and to the second in Part II. Moreover, the rejection of Falstaff must be adequately prepared; Shakespeare does so by showing how Falstaff takes himself and his claims on Hal more and more seriously, until in the coronation scene he clearly overreaches himself and precipitates his own disgrace. The specifically political conflict, with its conclusion in Gaultree Forest, plays a very minor role in this account. (Some critics of this persuasion manage not to mention it at all.) The major antagonists, corresponding to Falstaff and Hotspur in Part I, are Falstaff and the Chief Justice; when Hal sides with Justice and rebukes Misrule, his *gradus ad regnum* is completed.

The interpretation has much to recommend it, especially neatness; but it will hardly bear scrutiny. I noted that it fails to account for the play's sense of debility and decline. But if that seems too subjective and intangible a factor, there is still the political action. Why would Shakespeare burden his play with this dramatic and moral abortion, if it did not even serve his end? Why, on the other hand, would he reduce to a mere mention the most famous and dramatic episode in the Hal legend: the striking of the Chief Justice? The episode had become virtually canonical; and it is difficult to imagine a scene better suited to Shakespeare's purpose, *if* that purpose were to show Hal learning to respect the law's majesty. Instead, what do we see of the Prince? Nothing in Act I; the Poins and tapster scenes in Act II; nothing in Act III and for most of Act IV; the seizing of the crown at the end of Act IV; and, finally, the elevation of the Chief Justice and the rejection of Falstaff in Act V. The rebels are given greater scope than that.

In fact, up to the point of his seizing the crown, it appears that Hal is quite deliberately being kept *out of* the play. Of the only two scenes he is given prior to that point, the second (II.iv) is almost wholly dominated by Falstaff and his gentlewomen; the Prince's puny jest is just sufficient—and is *meant*—to remind us of the lost glories of the corresponding scene in Part I (II.iv). And the first, with Poins, has no action; except for a good deal of aimless banter and the quick planning of the tapster scene, we hear only of Hal's weary resignation to the role of wild prince which common opin-

ion compels him to keep up. Not only are his appearances grudging; they are intended for little else than to let us *know* that they
are grudging.

If Hal's participation in the "low" action is designedly minimal,
in the "action of state" it is, except for the very end, reduced to
nothing. Again Shakespeare takes pains to make us conscious of
the lack. At the conclusion of the tapster scene Peto enters breath-
lessly with news of the king's being at Westminster and receiving
alarming reports from the North. Hal responds:

> By heaven, Poins, I feel me much to blame
> So idly to profane the precious time,
> When tempest of commotion, like the south
> Borne with black vapour, doth begin to melt
> And drop upon our bare unarmed heads.
> Give me my sword and cloak. Falstaff, good night.
>
> (II.iv.390–95)

Spoken like a Prince—and in orotund blank verse. But what
happens? The next scene shows the king in Westminster, deeply
troubled by the rebellion and resolving to meet it; Hal is not
present. Nor is he with the king's forces in Yorkshire. In IV.iv,
again in Westminster, the king inquires after him and is told that
he is hunting at Windsor—or, it may be, dining in London, "with
Poins and other his continual followers." In any case he is not at
court; he arrives only after the king has been stricken and seems
to be dead.

Again the inevitable comparison with *1 Henry IV* makes this
absence even more pointed. In the great post-Gadshill scene, Hal
treated a summons from the king with wonderfully inventive
levity; there was nothing in the style of "I feel me much to blame"
and "Give me my sword and cloak. Falstaff, good night!" All the
same, he did appear before his father, did pledge himself to fight
Hotspur, and was given "sovereign charge" of the king's forces.
And, of course, he went on to become the hero of Shrewsbury—
rather more so, be it noted, than Shakespeare's sources gave
warrant for. From *The Famous Victories* Shakespeare refused to take
what seems to have been another noted scene in the legend: Hal's
coming before the king in a cloak full of eyelet-holes and needles
(to signify his being on needles until he has seized the crown) and

with dagger drawn. Hal's "Give me my sword and cloak" is the only remnant of this scene—just enough to warn the audience that here again their expectation will be disappointed.

Thus 2 *Henry IV* is littered with rejections of dramatic opportunities, or rather of dramatic obligations, incurred partly by the structure of the play itself, partly by what we will (and are carefully reminded to) expect from 1 *Henry IV*, and partly by what we expect from the established legend. Shakespeare rejects not whole incidents but rather the scenes to which they would naturally give rise: the actual dramatic confrontation and "showdown." We *hear* of Hal's striking the Chief Justice but we do not see it; we *hope* for a major encounter between Hal and Falstaff but are disappointed; we *expect* a confrontation between Hal and the king but are denied it; we *are sure* that there will be a battle between the king's forces and the rebels but are cheated of it. The play seems a series of "fearful musters and prepared defense— and no such matter." The children of the "stern tyrant war"— confrontation, encounter, conflict, battle—are one by one killed in the womb; and since drama is conflict, it seems as though Shakespeare set about deliberately strangling his play.

Clearly the theory that in Part II Hal proves himself just (as in Part I he proved himself valorous), while it has a certain *a priori* plausibility, is sadly lacking in dramatic substance. But just as clearly the play is *about* Hal and culminates in his accession. What, then, is Hal's role; what does he *do*, except remind us that he is doing nothing? The answer is simple: prior to his accession, Hal has one role only—that of heir, of *successor*.

He nowhere shows the slightest concern with justice until after he is king. The serious part of his conversation with Poins turns on the succession: Poins cannot believe that Hal is sincerely grieved by his father's illness, which promises to speed him to the throne; and Hal wearily acknowledges that common opinion can hardly think otherwise. The scene with Falstaff has nothing to do with justice. In his soliloquy by the king's bed, Hal is full of resolution; but what he thinks about is the crown and how he means to keep it:

> Lo, where it sits,
> Which God shall guard; and put the world's whole
>   strength

Into one giant arm, it shall not force
This lineal honour from me. This from thee
Will I to mine leave, as 'tis left to me.

                                    (IV.v.43–47)

In the following dialogue with his father, the latter does raise the
problem of justice:

Pluck down my officers, break my decrees;
For now a time is come to mock at form.

                                    (IV.v.118–19)

But Hal hardly responds to it; he is entirely taken up with convincing the king that when he took the crown he was not
prompted by an unfilial wish to succeed before his time. With Hal
on the scene, the dramatic focus is always on the succession.

I am not arguing that justice is irrelevant to 2 *Henry IV*; on the
contrary, it is manifestly the controlling theme of the subplot
between Falstaff and the Chief Justice, with Justice Shallow in a
subsidiary role. This subplot is concluded and determined by the
young king at play's end; and in that sense and to that degree it
does involve him. But I *am* arguing that this involvement is designedly minimal and late. To describe Hal as playing the same
role with respect to justice that he played in Part I with respect to
valor is to distort and ignore the play's dramatic logic for the sake
of a far too neat and symmetrical scheme—for the sake of a
symmetry, I might add, to which the play bids a troubled, anxious
farewell.

Our seeing Hal as stripped of all roles except that of successor
helps us account for several oddities. It accounts for the omission
of the scene in which Hal strikes the Chief Justice; it accounts for
his non-appearance at court and his non-participation in the affairs of the realm. It also brings into focus another oddity, which
has attracted some critical attention. In his soliloquy, Hal apostrophizes the crown; when he justifies himself to the dying king, he
claims to quote this apostrophe:

I spake unto this crown as having sense,
And thus upbraided it: . . .

                                    (IV.v.158–59)

But, strangely, what he quotes himself as having said differs from
what we have just heard him say. If the difference were great and

intended to deceive the king about Hal's true feelings, we would simply conclude that Hal is being hypocritical. But that is clearly neither the case nor the intention; there is no reason why he should not quote himself as exactly as he claims to be doing. Why the misquote?

I believe this is one of the many instances where Shakespeare does something odd because he wants to startle us into paying close attention. If we do so, we find that the difference between the two apostrophes is one of metaphor rather than of feeling or motive. In his soliloquy, Hal calls the crown a *"lineal* honor" (rather strangely, since the one standard attribute of a crown, other than its being gold, is that it is a circle, a round or "rigol"). He is determined to keep the *line* of succession unbroken. But in his subsequent self-quoting, he uses a different metaphor:

> Thus, my most royal liege,
> *Accusing* it, I put it on my head,
> To *try* with it, as with an *enemy*
> That had before my face murdered my father,
> The *quarrel* of a true inheritor.
>
> (IV.v.165–69—my italics)

Now it is combat—more precisely trial by combat—that is insisted on. The crown comes to Hal not as a lineal honor but, paradoxically, as both the object of combat ("true inheritor") and the antagonist ("enemy"). The Prince, in his capacity as successor, sees himself as the challenger in a just "quarrel" which he is eager to "try."

What are we meant to make of this mass of oddities? It would seem that we need to think carefully about the problem of *succession*. What is it? What does it rest on? What does it entail? It is time to think before we can go back to quoting.

V

Not that the question of succession has been ignored by Shakespeare scholarship. It has been shown that the governing theme of the history plays, derived by Shakespeare from Hall's *Union of the Noble and Illustre Famelies of Lancastre and Yorke*, is that of the disturbed succession. But I shall argue that for Shakespeare the disturbance was vastly more radical and encompassing than we have realized; that it involved not merely England but the entire moral universe; and, most importantly, that its consequences were *irreversible*. To put it somewhat provocatively: in the deposition of Richard II Shakespeare discovered the decomposition of a world picture; we are wrong in assuming that his world picture was still that of Hall and Tudor doctrine.

Succession in the usual sense—the transfer of sovereign power—is actually only a special case of succession. The transfer of sovereign power is an event very much like other events involving the transfer of energy; if we assume that the universe in its physical-moral totality is governed by uniform laws, it makes no difference, in principle, whether the force being transferred is kinetic energy passing from one billiard ball to another or sovereign power passing from one magistrate to another. The reason it does seem to make a difference is that we have come to think of the physico-moral universe as two distinct universes and of the laws governing them as two distinct kinds of law. For us a law of succession (in the narrow sense) is man-made, changing with time, place, and social circumstances; whereas for most of us even today, and for all of us until quite recently, a law of physical succession is, or was, universal and eternal in its operation. In terms of legal philosophy: we regard social laws as *positive* (man-made) and scientific laws as *natural* (inherent in the structure of the universe or given by its creator).

On the whole, when it came to succession, the sixteenth century did not make this distinction. The law governing the transfer of sovereign power—primogeniture—had all the prestige and sanctions of divine prescription; it was a "natural" law like other natural laws, instituted by God for the ordering of events. The physical and moral universe was still one and indivisible, a basically juridical order in which "law" had the sense of rule or decree. The immense success of the natural sciences since then—especially when coupled with the ill success of our efforts to find just, stable, and universal social arrangements—destroyed that faith and that unity. Still it was by no means as naïve as we thought. We are now beginning to realize that scientific laws are no more "natural," universal, and immutable than social laws.

The universe is coming to be *one* again, the only difference being that its laws—i.e., the order we find in it—are positive rather than natural or divine.

We know now that scientific laws imply "models"; the models are man-made and stand or fall by their ability to order events. The model of the world underlying the concept of mechanical causality is no "truer" than the model underlying primogeniture, is in fact very much of the same kind. If, and as long as, it is successful in ordering the transfer of force, it will serve; if it proves inadequate for that purpose, we start looking for a better model. In other words, the real change that has taken place over the last three hundred years is that the world, which used to be seen (and more importantly, felt) as divinely ordered, now appears to us as ordered by our needs and for our ends. Still, the belief in natural law dies hard, because it answers to our profoundest need: to find, in the purposeless flux of time and energy, that ultimate permanence without which, it seems, we cannot make sense of our experience. We have made a religion of science not because we revered science but because we needed a religion; now that this religion is also failing us, we must see how we will orient ourselves in a universe that is wholly secular. Will we learn to manage a world that is entirely ours to manage?

Laws of succession, then, order the transfer of sovereign power, that power being conceived not as the property of the particular "body" or magistrate who at a given moment holds and exercises it, but as inhering in and emanating from some being or entity which is considered eternal or almost so. God, the nation, the sovereign people, even the "blood royal" all share this quality of permanence. Nevertheless it is not a matter of indifference where a given society believes that power to reside, and hence how it orders its transfer from one bearer to another. For the mode of transfer implies a model of the universe, a picture of how events must succeed each other to be orderly, intelligible, *legitimate*. A man who has a concept of legitimacy different from mine lives not just in a different society but in a different world.

At first glance it seems obvious that Shakespeare's histories recognize only one mode of succession as truly legitimate: primogeniture. Other modes—particularly succession by combat, as described in Frazer's *Golden Bough*—seem clearly illegitimate; indeed they are not alternate modes so much as lapses into chaos. (Succession by popular election can readily be interpreted as a variant of succession by combat.) All the same it would be very easy for an anthropological critic to read the history plays as recording a series of successions by combat, in which kings who are lacking in potency are supplanted (and usually killed) by others who prove their right to the title by their ability to seize it. Indeed, if this critic were rigorously descriptive and inferred the law of succession in the histories strictly from the actual events, he could not possibly arrive at the law of primogeniture. Richard II to Henry IV, Henry VI to Edward IV, Edward V to Richard III, Richard III to Henry VII—by the combat mode this succession is close to "unbroken," certainly much less broken than under the mode of primogeniture. Depending on the model we choose, the same sequence will appear as either reasonably orderly or disastrously chaotic.

Of course, if we chose the combat model we would completely pervert the meaning of Hall and other Tudor historians and do at least some violence to Shakespeare's. Still I cannot help asking: how much violence? Tudor political theorists and propagandists were always ready to quote St. Paul to the effect that all power is from God, whence it followed that the subject owed obedience, as a matter of religious duty, to the *de facto* ruler. It does not take much thought to discover that this argument implies a combat model of succession; a little more thought may even lead to the suspicion that there is a remarkably close, perhaps necessary, connection between this model and a divinely ruled universe. However that may be, the Tudors were not foolhardy enough to rest their title on the Pauline principle alone; a great deal of effort and ingenuity was expended in proving that the title was (primo-genitively) legitimate. Tudor propaganda left little to chance; it worked both sides of the royal road. The title was legitimate beyond question; and even if it was not, it still was. Heads the king won, tails the doubting subject lost—his head most likely if he was rash enough to ask for the toss.

I do not mean that the deception was conscious; the apologists of the Tudor establishment were, I expect, all honorable men, and in any case there is hardly a limit to the inconsistencies men manage sincerely to believe where their needs and vital interests are at stake. Without question the Elizabethans believed that legitimacy and orderly succession went by primogeniture. But the idea that combat was an acceptable way of discovering God's will and verdict was still very much alive—vestigially even in the ritual of succession. (The English coronation ceremony provides for a "King's Champion," who offers to prove his sovereign's title by combat against any and all challengers.) The sense was still strong that there are important occasions where the truth of a claim and the justice of a cause can be determined only by an "appeal to arms," the presiding judge in this court of last appeal being God. Under these circumstances it was natural that even thoughtful men should, as occasions demanded, feel quite untroubled about applying one or the other of these concepts of legitimacy, or even both simultaneously, without realizing that they entailed mutually inconsistent world pictures. But I believe that Shakespeare—who was a more than ordinarily thoughtful man—did see the inconsistency.

. . . .

   The burden of my argument—the point of this interpretation of the Hal trilogy—is this: Shakespeare, having discovered that the "most fine, most honoured, most renowned" golden unity of the Elizabethan world picture was in truth a lethal mixture of two mutually inconsistent and severally inadequate models of succession, but that to reject both meant imprisonment and sterility, first tried a dialectical solution (1 Henry IV) and next a dis-solution (2 Henry IV and Henry V). The solution, he found, rested on a petitio principii; the several dissolutions entailed severe sacrifices—most importantly, the sacrifice of true legitimacy. Each in its own way was "swoll'n with some other grief"; but it was a grief that had to be borne and born, if bearing, generation, succession was to continue.
   I realize that I have credited Shakespeare with what appears to be a very modern and still largely scientific concept: that of the model. I must now credit him with another, closely related one: complementarity. I am in fact saying that, some three centuries before Niels Bohr, Shakespeare discovered the need of complementarity—i.e., of operating with two mutually inconsistent and severally inadequate models because, and as long as, a single,

consistent, and adequate model has not been found. Complementarity differs from and is superior to mixing because it remains aware of its "illegitimacy" and *pays the price* of choosing one model or the other. It does not pretend to be a solution, hence does not close the road of discovery but on the contrary compels us to take the risk of following it. Its passionate demand for order forces us to leave the safe prison of a static, once-for-all world picture, to suffer the grief of imperfection and disorder and the joy of genuine action and creativity. Complementarity, in short, asserts the value of *human action in time*—which is to say, of history, of drama.

I credit Shakespeare with discovering these concepts not because I want to "modernize" him but because I see no other way of accounting for the observable facts of the second tetralogy. How else are we to explain the sequence Shrewsbury-Gaultree Forest-Agincourt? How else are we to explain the strange frustration of our combativeness, which appears to be the "law" of *2 Henry IV*, and on the other hand the almost total indulgence of this same combativeness which governs most of *Henry V*? How— to descend to the level of textual cruxes—are we to explain the oddity of Hal's two apostrophes of the crown? How—to mention one more item from what could easily be extended into a very long list—are we to explain the fact that the crown comes to Hal both by seizure and by lineal descent—that he takes, before the appointed time, what becomes his at the appointed time? Why this filial, lineal piety so oddly yoked with creative impatience? Wherever we look, we find complementarity.

Hal's seizure of the crown is the figure of Shakespeare's "seizure" of history. Of course, he found the episode in his sources, but that is precisely the point. He likewise found other episodes in his sources—most signally that of Hal's striking the Chief Justice. Many of these he reduced to dramatic insignificance, but this one he makes his own. Not wilfully, not for theatrical effect, but because in it he discovers the very metaphor of his effort and enterprise: to write "creative history," to find meaning and order both in the succession of historical events and in the succession of his dramatic explorations. Truly and reverently looked at, recorded history answers *to* his quest and question; but it does not *answer* it. Instead of providing him with the definitive model of succession and success, to be retraced by him in simple piety—or instead of meeting him with blank silence and leaving him free to impose on it whatever pattern happens to suit him—it supplies him with a metaphor. And the metaphor is one of *complementarity*, of either-or. It is neither a mixture nor a synthesis, but a metaphor: that strange entity which demands to be analytically dissolved because it *means* and creatively "made good" because it *is*. It is pregnant, hence promises birth; but the birth is never certain, while labor and pain *are* certain. Is even the father certain? Can we be sure of legitimacy? Will the offspring be the child of passion or of duty, of self-assertive lust or submissive routine? There are no guarantees, only the risk and the will—the need—to order.

IX

To state my argument in terms of the "price paid," the following schema emerges. Richard II, refusing to pay any price whatever, in the end pays most heavily; he finds himself compelled to retreat into the sterile though poignant pathos of non-success and non-succession. Prince Hal of *1 Henry IV* tries to avoid paying the price by dialectical design: he exploits the combat model by pitting disorder against rebellion, but hopes to escape the consequences of this model by superior management. He is literally the "know-you-all," the omniscient and almost omnipotent dramatist, seemingly involved but actually secure. And he almost brings it off; *1 Henry IV* is not by accident the "best play" of the trilogy. If the problem of succession were solvable by dramaturgic skill, here it would be solved; if dialectical "wit" were the ultimate wisdom, Hal's obsequies over Hotspur and Falstaff might be the last word. But, as we saw, Hal's solution is half a lie; to sustain it, he must also sustain Falstaff's half-lie. Disorder is not vanquished; Falstaff survives by playing dead, and the rebellion survives, at least in part, by Northumberland's playing sick. If disorder has lost a good deal of its vitality, so has order (witness *2 Henry IV*), for the simple reason that order, under the dialectical scheme, depends on disorder as symmetry depends on contrast. Without two such splendid foils as Hotspur and Falstaff to flash in mock-heroic combat, Hal finds himself sadly reduced.

In 2 *Henry IV* he (and Shakespeare—the two are the same)
accepts the necessity of paying the price; and the price is self-
denial, withdrawal. Now there is no theatrical cashing in on the
combat model: on exciting clashes and encounters, on tense confrontations; the "due process" of lineality prevails. A fetid domes-
ticity, a weary rather than vigorous air of expectancy, blankets
the whole. What vigor there is comes from Falstaff and even so is
generated by contrast:

> If you do not all show like gilt twopences to me, and I in the
> clear sky of fame o'ershine you as much as the full moon
> doth the cinders of the element, which show like pins' heads
> to her, believe not the word of the noble.
>
> (IV.iii.54–60)

As usual, he is in the right; for if the capture of Coleville was not
exactly an act of heroism, it shines brightly in comparison to the
victory won by John of Lancaster. But there is no longer room in
England for the combat kind of disorder—which is not exactly to
say that order has prevailed. Disorder has taken the meaner and
more indirect forms of corruption and equivocation: partial justice, bribery, false promises, and bad debts—disorders rather than
disorder. The body politic no longer suffers from a raging fever
but from ill humors—that's the humor of it. The "high terms" of
a proud and combative nobility have deteriorated into the ludicrous fustian of Pistol, the gentle poetry of ladies into the grubby
prose of Doll Tearsheet:

> She bids you on the wanton rushes lay you down
> And rest your gentle head upon her lap,
> And she will sing a song that pleaseth you
> And on your eyelids crown the god of sleep.
>
> (*1 Henry IV*, III.i.214–17)

but:

> Ah, you sweet little rogue, you! Alas, poor ape, how thou
> sweat'st! Come, let me wipe thy face, come on, you whore-
> son chops. Ah, rogue! i' faith, I love thee.
>
> (*2 Henry IV*, II.iv.233–36)

A world seems to have come to an end.

True, there is the Lord Chief Justice. But there are likewise
the little justices, the Shallows, in whom the current of the law,

however pure at the fountainhead, will ultimately stagnate. The new England seems to have little room for high drama; it breeds the comedy of humors and of satire. John of Gaunt's "sceptred isle" has become Nashe's *Isle of Dogs*. At the top, the lineal succession is by way of being secured, justice is being maintained, order upheld; why do we miss the bright spark of metal on metal? Why do we feel oppressed by the insistent organicity of this order, the sequence of growth and decay?

> *Shallow.* Death, as the Psalmist saith, is certain to all; all shall die.
>   How a good yoke of bullocks at Stamford fair?
> *Silence.* By my troth, I was not there.
> *Shallow.* Death is certain. Is old Double of your town living yet?
> *Silence.* Dead, sir.
> *Shallow.* Jesu, Jesu, dead! A' drew a good bow; and dead! John a' Gaunt loved him well, and betted much money on his head. Dead! . . . How a score of ewes now?
> *Silence.* Thereafter as they be. A score of good ewes may be worth ten pounds.
> *Shallow.* And is old Double dead?
>
>   (III.ii.41–58)

Yes, old "double" is dead. Succession is no longer won by competition and at hazard; it breeds. Let time and nature have their course, and it will come to you: death is certain. Order is no longer something wrought, the reward of struggle and design, but something self-perpetuating, the endless sequence of cause and effect. The blood royal, too precious to be shed on the battlefield, flows sluggishly through sober veins. It is sadly in need of artificial stimulation:

> The second property of your excellent sherris is, the warming of the blood; which, before cold and settled, left the liver white and pale, which is the badge of pusillanimity and cowardice; but the sherris warms it and makes it course from the inwards to the parts extreme. It illumineth the face, which as a beacon gives warning to all the rest of this little kingdom, man, to arm. And then the vital commoners and inland petty spirits muster me all to their captain, the heart, who, great and puffed up with this retinue, doth any deed of courage; and this valor comes of sherris.
>
>   (IV.iii.110–22)

Even valor is a matter of what "comes of" what.

This is the quality of by far the largest part of *2 Henry IV*. We are constantly aware of Hal, to be sure, but only as the "next in line." He no longer directs the action or designs the confrontations; he lets himself be carried where, by lineality and with the aid of his brother's indirection, he is destined to be carried: to the throne.

NOTES

1. E. M. W. Tillyard, *Shakespeare's History Plays* (New York, 1962), p. 302.
2. The story of the prophecy, as of the intended crusade, Shakespeare found in Holinshed. What he did not find there was the stress on secularization. The effect of the story in Holinshed is that Henry IV died piously. The crusade is not a long-nourished, repeatedly frustrated plan, nor is it linked to Henry's guilt and doubtful title. Henry announces it for the first and only time shortly before his death and justifies it in thoroughly medieval fashion: "For it grieved him to consider the great malice of Christian princes, that were bent upon a mischievous purpose to destroy one another, to the peril of their own souls, rather than to make war against the enemies of the Christian faith, as in conscience (it seemed to him) they were bound." He is stricken, not upon receiving the news of Gaultree Forest, but while praying at the shrine of St. Edward; and the "Jerusalem" where he dies, though not the Holy City, seems at least to be in the Cathedral (it is "next at hand" and belongs to the abbot of Westminster) rather than in the palace.

D. J. Palmer

Casting off the Old Man: History and St. Paul in *Henry IV* (1970)

I

Biblical quotations abound in Shakespeare's two *Henry IV* plays, and most of them are made by Falstaff, whose allusions, as Richmond Noble says, "are the aptest in the whole of the plays."[1] They are also, of course, singularly profane in Falstaff's mouth, and his "damnable iteration" of Scripture, we may suspect, is a relic of his former identity as Sir John Oldcastle, the name of Prince Hal's riotous companion in that execrable play, *The Famous Victories of Henry the Fifth*. It seems that after borrowing the name of his fat knight from the older play, Shakespeare subsequently rechristened him as Falstaff out of deference to the family feelings of Oldcastle's Elizabethan descendant, Lord Cobham.[2] For the historical Oldcastle, as the Epilogue in Part Two tells us, "died a martyr, and this is not the man." He was in fact a Lollard burned at the stake for his faith during the reign of Henry V, and honoured by the more zealous Protestants of Shakespeare's day as one of the early heroes of their cause. A familiarity with the Bible was therefore particularly, if scurrilously, appropriate to the first Sir John, and no doubt this irreverent representation of his ancestor as a pseudo-puritan offended Lord Cobham as much as the imputation of cowardice.

Prince Hal, however, knows his Bible at least as well as Falstaff, and in the concluding couplet of his soliloquy at the end of the first tavern scene,

From *Critical Quarterly*, 12 (1970). Reprinted by permission of the author.

I'll so offend to make offence a skill,
Redeeming time when men think least I will,

(1.2.209–10)[3]

editors have noted the echo of St. Paul's *Epistle to the Ephesians*:

Take hede therefore that ye walke circumspectly, not as
fooles but as wise,

Redeeming the time: for the days are evil.

(5:15–16)[4]

The aptness and full significance of this allusion, however, remain
to be explored. Preserving an essential distinction between the
fool and the wise man, Hal's resolve "to make offence a skill"
parallels Falstaff's virtuosity in avoiding reproof by turning offence into an ingenious and apparently harmless display of wit,
while Hal's promise to redeem the time follows Falstaff's mock-
determination, "I must give over this life, and I will give it over"
(1.2.92). The soliloquy clearly has an important dramatic function: it distinguishes the Prince at the beginning of the play from
the wild youth that others, including Falstaff and the King, suppose him to be, and in so doing it puts an entirely new complexion
upon the traditional legends of the riotous Prince, such as those
represented on the stage in *The Famous Victories*.

As Falstaff says, but in two senses that he is not aware of, "the
true prince may, for recreation sake, prove a false thief" (1.2.149).
Behind Falstaff's back, Poins and Hal plot the Gadshill robbery as
a "jest," "for recreation sake," to prove Falstaff himself "a false
thief," that is, a liar and no thief at all. But at a deeper level in the
play, the "recreation" signifies that "reformation" which Hal
promises in his soliloquy at the end of this scene. The soliloquy
therefore states the central business of both plays, to show us the
process by which Hal is to redeem the time; it also insists that
Hal's "reformation" will be not so much an amendment of life, as
a "recreation" of his true identity in men's eyes. "Never call a true
piece of gold a counterfeit," Falstaff tells him at the abrupt end of
the "play extempore," "thou art essentially made without seeming
so" (2.4.476). Moreover, this "recreation" of the true Prince also

reflects Shakespeare's artistic and historical purpose in the two plays, which are themselves presented to us "for recreation sake."

Hal's allusion to the words of St. Paul is thus at the heart of the dramatic structure. It is no accident that the Eastcheap community is described to Hal in Part Two as "Ephesians, my lord, of the old church" (2.2.143), for when Hal's promise to redeem the time is eventually fulfilled at the end of Part Two, his rejection of Falstaff ("I know thee not, old man")[5] again recalls the Apostle's injunctions to the Ephesians:

> That is, that ye cast of, concerning the conversation in the time past, the olde man, which is corrupt through the deceivable lustes,
>
> And be renewed in the spirit of your minde,
>
> And put on the new man, which after God is created in righteousnes, and true holines.
>
> Wherefore cast of lying, & speake everie man trueth unto his neighbour: for we are members one of another.
>
> (4:22-5)

Paul speaks of a metaphorical "olde man," the unregenerate Adam in the self, and Hal addresses an all too substantial counterpart, but one surely well qualified to recognise the appropriateness of the text. If we can suppose so, Shakespeare's old man must have found the Biblical context as a whole particularly galling:

> Let no man deceive you with vaine wordes: for suche things commeth the wrath of God upon the children of disobedience.
>
> Be not therefore companions with them.
>
> (5:6-7)
>
> And be not drunke with wine, wherein is excess.
>
> (5:18)

The page in the Geneva Bible which Hal seems to have had particularly in mind bears the heading over its double columns, "Put on the new man . . . Awake from slepe," words which must have struck a responsive chord in the imagination of the author of *A Midsummer Night's Dream* (where Bottom himself, in his garbled fashion, has occasion to recall the Apostle on the subject of dreams and visions):[6]

> Wherefore he saith, Awake thou that slepest, and stand up from the dead, & Christ shal give thee light.
>
> (5:14)

So Hal says in his rejection speech:

> I long have dreamt of such a kind of man,
> So surfeit swell'd, so old, and so profane;
> But, being awak'd, I do despise my dream.
>
> (5.4.50–2)

If there is an ironic echo of this image of awakening and standing up from the dead at the end of Part One when Falstaff arises from the dead on the battlefield ("Counterfeit? I lie, I am no counterfeit: to die is to be a counterfeit," 5.4.114), then it is also remembered in Hal's last interview with his dying father in Part Two, when he mistakes sleep for death and prematurely removes the crown to the distress of his waking father. "Ye were once of darkenes," says Paul (5:8), and it is true that Hal was formerly one of the "squires of the night's body" (Part One, 1.2.23), but when he assumes the crown, he will "have no fellowship with the unfruteful workes of darkenes, but even reprove them rather" (5:11). Finally, Hal stands up from the dead, not only as his father's rightful successor, but in his renewed existence on Shakespeare's stage.[7] The history play itself is redeeming time.

Henry IV therefore owes considerably more to St. Paul's *Epistle to the Ephesians* than the passing reference noted by the commentators. The use of these allusions to relate the beginning of Part One to the end of Part Two reinforces the arguments of those who regard the two plays as structurally unified although individually self-contained. The theme of time's redemption and the renewal of life also links the two plays with the comedies. In addition, it does not seem likely, as some have suggested, that Hal's soliloquy in the second scene of Part One is an interpolation inserted when Shakespeare was revising the play, since the very phrase which carries such a burden of dramatic significance, "redeeming time," is integrated with the language of Part One as a whole, as well as being carried through to Part Two.

II

The influence of the earlier Tudor morality drama upon the structure of the *Henry IV* plays has often been observed. In treating the theme of Hal's "reformation," Shakespeare naturally turned to the "prodigal son" motif of the interludes, and Falstaff is actually referred to in terms of the leading comic character of the morality plays, as "that reverend vice." More specifically, Paul A. Jorgensen[8] has pointed out that one such interlude, *Lusty Juventus* (c. 1550), anticipates Shakespeare in making the same allusion to St. Paul:

> Saint Paul unto the Ephesians giveth good exhortation,
> Saying, walk circumspectly, redeeming the time,
> That is, to spend it well, and not to wickedness incline.

Jorgensen also notes that this text was introduced into the Homily for Rogation Week, where many in Shakespeare's audience must have become familiar with it. But his explanation of the text "as meaning to take full advantage of the time that man is given here on earth for salvation," however theologically correct, falls a long way short of its significance in relation to Hal's situation and purpose, because it overlooks the primary importance of the etymological association with buying and selling. Even the lines from *Lusty Juventus* paraphrase "redeeming the time" as "to spend it well." Strictly the word means "buying back," as in redeeming a debt: in the language of the pawnshop, even today, it has no theological overtones.

The marginal glosses to the text in the Geneva Bible explain the word in these terms:

> Selling all worldlie pleasures to bye time . . . In these perilous dayes & crafte of the adversaries, take hede how to bye again the occasions of godlines, which the worlde hathe taken from you.

So in his soliloquy Hal says he will "pay the debt I never promised" (1.2.202), and the language of settling debts is heard throughout Part One.

The days of Henry IV are indeed evil and perilous, as the King's speech opening the play makes clear. The disastrous consequences of the deposition of Richard are felt throughout the land, in "the intestine shock And furious close of civil butchery." In an attempt to redeem his guilt, the King has vowed a crusade to the Holy Land,

> Over whose acres walk'd those blessed feet
> Which fourteen hundred years ago were nail'd
> For our advantage on the bitter cross.
>
> (1.1.25–7)

To walk circumspectly (or rather to march "in mutual well-be-seeming ranks") in the path of his Redeemer is the vow that Bolingbroke will never redeem; the very act of usurpation was that of an oath-breaker, and the rebels know him as a man who will not pay the debt he promised.

After the succeeding tavern scene and Hal's soliloquy, the rebels are introduced, and Hotspur exhorts his companions to purge the dishonour of their complicity in the usurpation:

> Yet time serves wherein you may redeem
> Your banish'd honours, and restore yourselves
> Into the good thoughts of the world again.
>
> (1.3.180–2)

In their very different context, Hotspur's words echo those of Hal's resolve in the soliloquy of the previous scene. Worcester finds another motive for rebellion, in self-defence rather than high principle, but he also uses the language of redemption:

> To save our heads by raising of a head:
> For bear ourselves as even as we can,
> The King will always think him in our debt,
> And think we think ourselves unsatisfied,
> Till he hath found a time to pay us home.
>
> (1.3.284–8)

The first three scenes of Part One therefore establish the theme of "redeeming time" in relation to each of the play's three worlds: the court, the tavern, and the rebel camp. The talk of dues and payment heard in the tavern scenes must also be related to the major preoccupations of the play. Falstaff, for instance, "will give the devil his due," but his other accounts must be settled by Hal on his behalf:

> Prince. Why, what a pox have I to do with my hostess of the
> tavern?
> Falstaff. Well, thou hast call'd her to a reckoning many a time
> and oft.
> Prince. Did I ever call thee to pay thy part?
> Falstaff. No; I'll give thee thy due, thou hast paid all there.
>
> (1.2.46–51)

At the end of the second tavern scene, when Hal discovers in the
pocket of the sleeping Falstaff the outstanding account for that
"intolerable deal of sack," he also speaks of the money taken at
Gadshill, which "shall be paid back again with advantage"
(2.4.528).

Thus, when Hal promises his father in the interview scene of
Part One to "redeem all this on Percy's head," the appropriateness
of his analogy has by this point been well established in the play:

> Percy is but my factor, good my lord,
> To engross up glorious deeds on my behalf;
> And I will call him to so strict account
> That he shall render every glory up,
> Yea, even the slightest worship of his time,
> Or I will tear the reckoning from his heart.
>
> (3.2.147–52)

The interview scene closes with the King's line, "Advantage feeds
him fat while men delay," which is Falstaff's cue to begin the
following scene with a reference to his fancied loss of weight ("Do
I not dwindle?") suggesting also the dwindling of his role in the
increasing imminence of more urgent affairs. He makes another
vow of amendment, echoing that we have just heard from Hal:
"Well, I'll repent, and that suddenly, while I am in some liking"
(3.3.5). He was, he says, virtuous once, and "paid money that I
borrowed—three or four times." So too before the battle of
Shrewsbury, Falstaff confides his fear to the Prince before launching upon his "catechism" of honour:

> Falstaff. I would 'twere bed-time, Hal, and all well.
> Prince. Why, thou owest God a death. (Exit)
> Falstaff. 'Tis not due yet; I would be loath to pay him before
> his day. What need I be so forward with him that calls not
> on me? . . . What is honour? A word. What is that word?
> Honour. What is that honour? Air? A trim reckoning!
>
> (5.1.125–40)

These illustrations demonstrate how central is that Pauline phrase, "redeeming time," to the play's concern with the proper time for settling debts of one kind or another. The very language of the play is coloured by this Biblical allusion, which in its sense of redeeming a promise relates to the many oaths that are sworn and foresworn in the course of the action, and so to the idea of honour, (honour is "a word," but a word that should be kept), while the phrase also expresses that sense of time as a commodity spent well or ill in the play. When the days are evil, and the time is out of joint ("Find we a time for frighted peace to pant," sighs the King in the play's opening lines), the idleness of the tavern life with its "play extempore" ("What a devil hast thou to do with the time of the day?" as Hal demands of Falstaff), is contrasted with the hasty impatience of Hotspur:

> O gentlemen, the time of life is short!
> To spend that shortness basely were too long
> If life did ride upon a dial's point,
> Still ending at the arrival of an hour.
>
> (5.2.82–5)

"The time will come," Hal promises his father, and with a sense of mounting urgency in the play, the hour arrives at Shrewsbury: "What, is it a time to jest and dally now?" For the dying Hotspur, "life, time's fool, And time, that takes survey of all the world, Must have a stop," but for Hal in his triumph, "the day is ours" at the end of Part One and his father acknowledges, "Thou hast redeem'd thy lost opinion."

III

"Redeeming time when men think least I will," Hal speaks not of being renewed in the spirit of his mind, but rather of renewing his reputation in the minds of others. He intends to "falsify men's hopes," to "show more goodly and attract more eyes." Hotspur has a similar understanding of honour, as being restored "into the good thoughts of the world again," though of course he has a misplaced conception of how this is to be achieved. What men think, both collectively as the world at large, and as particular individuals, is of crucial concern throughout both plays. Facing his father's suspicion that he is even in collusion with the rebels, Hal replies,

> Do not think so; you shall not find it so:
> And God forgive them that so much have sway'd
> Your Majesty's good thoughts away from me!
> I will redeem all this on Percy's head.
>
> (3.2.129–32)

Such a sustained association with men's thoughts suggests that for Shakespeare the word "redeem" not only bore its etymological sense of settling a debt, but also, through a species of pun, attached itself to the meaning of "deem." To be restored from disgrace into men's good thoughts is thus to be "re-deemed."

"I would to God thou and I knew where a commodity of good names were to be bought," says Falstaff to Hal (1.2.80), and honour and reputation in Part One have had as much to do with what men call one as with what they think of one. A man is known by his name, and Falstaff is a master of giving good names to bad things:

> Marry, then, sweet wag, when thou art King, let not us that are squires of the night's body be called thieves of the day's beauty; let us be Diana's foresters, gentlemen of the shade, minions of the moon; and let men say we be men of good government, being governed, as the sea is, by our noble and chaste mistress the moon, under whose countenance we steal.
>
> (1.2.22–8)

The Ephesians were worshippers of Diana, and so Falstaff can argue, " 'tis no sin for a man to labour in his vocation" (1.2.102). Does not St. Paul exhort the Ephesians to "walke worthie of the vocation whereunto ye are called" (4:1)?

Talk of being "called" to a reckoning, to a "strict account" (e.g., 1.2.48, 3.2.49, 5.1.128, all quoted above) is thus related to the importance of names and titles in the play. What a man is called by, and what he is called to, are, in the strict meaning of the word, his "vocation," and to be worthy of his vocation as Prince is Hal's chief concern in Part One. When he reappears in the tavern after the Gadshill robbery, he shows a wry sensitivity to the names he is called by the potboys:

> I have sounded the very base-string of humility. Sirrah, I am
> sworn brother to a leash of drawers and can call them all by
> their christen names, as Tom, Dick, and Francis. They take it
> already upon their salvation that though I be but Prince of
> Wales yet I am the king of courtesy; and tell me flatly I am no
> proud Jack, like Falstaff, but a Corinthian, a lad of mettle, a
> good boy—by the Lord, so they call me—and when I am
> King of England I shall command all the good lads of East-
> cheap. They call drinking deep, dyeing scarlet; and when you
> breathe in your watering, they cry "hem!" and bid you play it
> off. To conclude, I am so good a proficient in one quarter of
> an hour that I can drink with any tinker in his own language
> during my life.
>
> (2.4.3–16)

There follows the jest with Poins at Francis' expense, an episode
that seems to have baffled satisfactory interpretation. But to
understand the point of Hal's joke, we should note his reference
to being called "a Corinthian," for the Corinthians, like the Ephesians, were exhorted by Paul to mend their ways, and offered
advice on vocation:

> Let every man abide in the same vocation wherein he was
> called.
>
> Art thou called being a servant? Care not for it; but if yet
> thou maist be free use it rather.
>
> (I Corinthians, 7:20-21)

So in stage-managing his play extempore with Francis, Hal plays
upon the multiple meanings of "vocation," calling his name, and
talking of his calling, while Poins calls him to a reckoning:

> *Prince.* Come hither, Francis.
> *Francis.* My lord?
> *Prince.* How long hast thou to serve, Francis?
> *Francis.* Forsooth, five years, and as much as to—
> *Poins* (within). Francis!
> *Francis.* Anon, anon, sir.
> *Prince.* Five year! by'r lady, a long lease for the clinking of
>   pewter. But Francis, darest thou be so valiant as to play
>   the coward with thy indenture and show it a fair pair of
>   heels and run from it?
>
> (2.4.37–47)

In Francis, Hal is parodying himself as a fellow-Corinthian and a fellow-apprentice, and the repetition of "Anon, anon, sir," like the stage-direction at the end of the joke, "*Here they both call him: Francis stands amazed, not knowing which way to go,*" dramatises Hal's critical reflection upon his own neglect of his vocation: "Away, you rogue! Dost thou not hear them call?" It is certainly Hal's private joke as far as both Francis and Poins are concerned, and one that expresses a very different mood from the confident, even complacent, tone of the soliloquy at the end of the first tavern scene. He is close here to the mood of Hamlet's "O what a rogue and peasant slave am I!"

Hal's problem is to seem what he is, to be given his due, and to be called by his proper name ("Prince Hal" itself reflects an indecorous mixture of formality and familiarity). He is, in Falstaff's words, "essentially made without seeming so," a peculiar irony for one whose title is "heir apparent." It is small comfort to hear from Falstaff in jest what he would claim from all men in earnest:

> By the Lord, I knew ye as well as he that made ye. Why hear you, my masters: was it for me to kill the heir apparent?
> (2.4.258-9)

Unfortunately, it is only too true that Falstaff knows the Prince no better than "he that made ye," his own father. But the "open and apparent shame" which the Gadshill adventure was intended to fix upon Falstaff is thus turned instead upon the Prince himself.

In the self-assured vein of his soliloquy, Hal compared himself to the sun,

> That when he please again to be himself,
> Being wanted, he may be more wondered at.
> (1.2.193-4)

Ironically, this "policy" of withholding oneself from the public eye to be the more admired is the very same argument which his father uses to reproach Hal for keeping low company (and the irony is doubled when we recall that in *Richard II* it was this Bolingbroke who courted popular favour in an undignified fashion: "Off went his bonnet to an oyster wench"). The premises of Hal's self-justification are thus invalidated in the interview scene,

and it is a much chastened Prince who now promises in the
plainest terms,

> I shall hereafter, my thrice-gracious lord,
> Be more myself.
>
> (3.2.92–3)

On Shrewsbury field, the King shamefully lends his name and
identity to others to protect himself in battle, and when Douglas
encounters him and supposes he is addressing yet another decoy,

> What art thou
> That counterfeit'st the person of a king?
>
> (5.3.27–8)

the question cuts deeply into Bolingbroke's dubious claim to the
title. By contrast, Hal's decisive encounter with his namesake
begins with a declaration of his true identity:

> *Hotspur.* If I mistake not, thou art Harry Monmouth.
> *Prince.* Thou speak'st as if I would deny my name.
> *Hotspur.* My name is Harry Percy.
> *Prince.*   Why then I see
>   A very valiant rebel of the name.
>   I am the Prince of Wales.
>
> (5.3.59–63)

Seen on the stage, Hal is quite literally now in his true colours,
bearing over his armour the heraldic insignia of the heir apparent.
This transformation was earlier described in what are surely the
play's most magnificent lines, spoken by Vernon in answer to
Hotspur's scornful enquiry about "the nimble-footed madcap
Prince of Wales, And his comrades that daff'd the world aside And
bid it pass":

> All furnish'd, all in arms;
> All plum'd like estridges, that with the wind
> Bated like eagles having lately bath'd;
> Glittering in golden coats, like images;
> As full of spirit as the month of May,
> As gorgeous as the sun at midsummer;
> Wanton as youthful goats, wild as young bulls.
> I saw young Harry with his beaver on,
> His cushes on his thighs, gallantly arm'd,
> Rise from the ground like feathered Mercury,

And vaulted with such ease into his seat
As if an angel dropp'd down from the clouds
To turn and wind a fiery Pegasus,
And witch the world with noble horsemanship.

(4.1.97–110)

All the "wild" and "wanton" energies of youth, associated in legend with the "madcap Prince," are here beautifully assimilated to the imagery of natural vitality, and transcended by the picture of the rider on his horse, the traditional emblem of disciplined energy and good government. Hal has "put on the new man."

IV

Hal's tribute to Hotspur, also reported by Vernon,

He gave you all the duties of a man,
Trimm'd up your praises with a princely tongue;
Spoke your deservings like a chronicle,

(5.2.56–8)

reminds us that the chronicle, the record of history, is the final arbiter of reputation. The chronicler himself, "redeeming time," gives honourable men their due, restoring them into the good thoughts of the world again. Shakespeare's treatment of Hal's "reformation" in terms of men's judgements of him rather than any sudden moral conversion on his part reflects his attitude to the stories of the Prince's reprobate youth as unauthoritative material, distinct from the authentic matter of historical record. The very existence of these stories must have demonstrated to Shakespeare how prone are men's minds to invent and credit fiction and to entertain conjecture—a phenomenon which as poet and dramatist he naturally exploited, and which throughout his work was obviously one of his deepest and most abiding interests.

As Vernon says, the Prince is "So much misconstrued in his wantonness" (5.2.69). The lines in which Hal protests to his father,

in reproof of many tales devis'd,
Which oft the ear of greatness needs must hear,
By smiling pick-thanks and base newsmongers,

(3.2.23–5)

follows Holinshed's account of the supposedly riotous youth as a
fabrication, so many "tales" and "slanderous reports":

> Whilest these things were a dooing in France, the lord Hen-
> rie prince of Wales, eldest sonne to king Henrie, got knowl-
> edge that certeine of his fathers servants were busie to give
> informations against him, whereby discord might arise be-
> twixt him and his father: for they put into the kings head,
> not onelie what evil rule (according to the course of youth)
> the prince kept to the offense of manie: but also what great
> resort of people came to his house, so that the court was
> nothing furnished with such a traine as dailie followed the
> prince. These tales brought no small suspicion into the kings
> head, least his sonne would presume to usurpe the crowne,
> he being yet alive, through which suspicious gelousie, it was
> perceived that he favoured not his sonne, as in times past he
> had doone.
>   The Prince sore offended with such persons, as by slan-
> derous reports, sought not onelie to spot his good name
> abrode in the realme, but to sowe discord also betwixt him
> and his father, wrote his letters into everie part of the
> realme, to reproove all such slanderous devises of those that
> sought his discredit.[9]

Even the word "pick-thanks" is taken from Holinshed: "Thus
were the father and sonne reconciled, betwixt whome the said
pick-thanks had sowne division."[10]
    "Let no man deceive you with vain words": it is certainly
appropriate that in the tavern world, which has attached itself to
history by "slanderous report," Falstaff should be the embodiment of lies, "gross as a mountain, open, palpable." In his account
of the men in buckram, we see the very process by which history
is translated into fiction, and his "play extempore" bears the same
relationship to Shakespeare's history play as the unlicensed tales
of the wild Prince do to the authentic versions of the chronicle.
Falstaff habitually takes the Lord's name in vain; he also takes in
vain all titles of honour: they are "a word," no more.
    It is supremely ironical, but presumably a sheer coincidence,
that a play so deeply concerned with the "commodity of good
names" and "vocation" should have run into difficulties over the
name and reputation of its chief slanderer. When Shakespeare

redeemed Oldcastle from the posthumous ignominy of his stage identity, he baptised the fat knight after the cowardly figure of Sir John Fastolfe, who had made a brief début in the poet's first history play, and was there condemned as one who

> Doth but usurp the sacred name of knight,
> Profaning this most honourable order.
>
> (*The First Part of King Henry VI*, 4.1.42-3)

Even this reincarnation was to provoke some complaint that Shakespeare had taken another good name in vain, and later in the seventeenth century Thomas Fuller tried to do for Sir John Fastolfe what Shakespeare had done for the Prince, to rescue him from ill-fame:

> Now as I am glad that *Sir John Oldcastle* is *put out*, so I am sorry that *Sir John Fastolfe* is *put in*, to relieve his memory in this base service, to be the *anvil* for every *dull wit* to strike upon. Nor is our Comedian excusable, by some alteration of his name, writing him *Sir John Falstafe* (and making him the *property* of *pleasure* for King *Henry* the fifth, to abuse) seeing the *vicinity* of sounds intrench on the memory of *that worthy Knight*, and few do heed the *inconsiderable difference* in spelling of their name.
>
> (*The Worthies of England*, 1662)[11]

The difference in spelling, however, is sufficient to achieve a certain propriety in the first syllable of Falstaff's name.

Hal keeps his promise to call Hotspur to "so strict account That he shall render every glory up," and in his defeat Hotspur surrenders his "proud titles" to the Prince. But what is the nature of the honour so won by Hal at the end of Part One? There is little glorification of Hal's victory; it is rather the hollowness of Hotspur's conception of honour that is stressed. Hal's generosity to his dead enemy is certainly noble:

> Thy ignominy sleep with thee in the grave
> But not remembered in thy epitaph.
>
> (5.3.100-1)

But far from coveting the admiration of men's thoughts at the end of the play, Hal is contemptuously acquiescent in Falstaff's demand to be given the official credit for Hotspur's fall:

> For my part, if a lie may do thee grace,
> I'll gild it with the happiest terms I have.
>
> (5.3.156–7)

The Prince, one feels, is more genuinely concerned about his personal relationship with his father, and more deeply affected by the pointless death of the young Hotspur; he is content to let the rest go, just as he orders Douglas to be set free without claiming ransom. Hal has come a long way since the desire of the soliloquy to "show more goodly and attract more eyes."

In the eyes of true judgement (and in the theatre Shakespeare flatters us with this vantage point), such a refusal to court public esteem will commend itself all the more favourably. "Nothing confutes me but eyes, and nobody sees me," says Falstaff, even as we watch him desecrate the body of Hotspur. If honour lives only in men's eyes and opinions, it is a very ambiguous and unstable commodity, as Hal has now learned:

> An habitation giddy and unsure
> Hath he that buildeth on the vulgar heart
>
> (Part Two, 1.3.89–90)

When the days are evil, where does true judgement of honour reside? This, however, is where Part Two takes up the story.

V

Lord Cobham, and Thomas Fuller too, might well have turned against the poet himself Rumour's words in the Prologue to Part Two:

> Upon my tongues continual slanders ride,
> The which in every language I pronounce,
> Stuffing the ears of men with false reports.
>
> (6–8)

Indeed, with an aggressive swipe worthy of Ben Jonson, and striking the discomfiting note which is characteristic of this play, Rumour identifies "the still-discordant wavering multitude" with his present theatre-audience:

> But what need I thus
> My well-known body to anatomize
> Among my household?
>
> (20-2)

Here in the theatre Rumour recognizes his home, the place where men's judgements and imaginations are exercised upon the illusions they see and hear. Rumour is the presiding spirit of Part Two, and Falstaff is his Apostle: "Lord, Lord, how subject we old men are to this vice of lying" (3.2.294). But the course of the play is to fulfil the words of that other Apostle, "that ye cast of, concerning the conversation in time past, the olde man, which is corrupt through the deceivable lusts . . . and put on the new man":

> Wherefore cast of lying, & speake everie man trueth unto his neighbour: for we are members one of another.
>
> (*Ephesians*, 4:22-5)

With Hotspur gone, the prevailing mood of Part Two is set by its old men: Northumberland, Falstaff, the Lord Chief Justice, that other Justice, Shallow, and of course the King himself. There is much talk of sickness and death, and the time is burdened with memories of the past and anticipations of things to come. As the Archbishop of York says, "The commonwealth is sick of their own choice . . . What trust is in these times? . . . Past and to come seems best; things present worst" (1.3.86-108). Even more than was the case in Part One, the days are evil, and "we are time's subjects" (1.3.110).

Hal's reappearance in the tavern, after his personal triumph at the end of Part One, is a reversion that defeats our expectations, in a play full of false anticipation. The "weary" Prince who makes his entrance in 2.2. is a very different figure from the buoyant confident youth who promised to redeem the time in Part One, and who there seemed about to "witch the world with noble horsemanship." He now appears oppressed, in accord with the disenchantment of this old men's world, and bitter in his self-reproach. "What a disgrace is it to me to remember thy name," he says unflatteringly to Poins, whose equally bald rejoinder raises the very question in our minds concerning Hal's apparent relapse after his achievement on Shrewsbury field:

How ill it follows, after you have laboured so hard, you
should talk so idly! Tell me, how many good young princes
would do so, their fathers being so sick as yours at this time
is?

(2.2.27–30)

Stung by the reproof coming from such a quarter, Hal's reply
goes to the heart of the play's concern with slanderous rumour,
opinion, and men's judgements:

> *Prince.* Marry, I tell thee it is not meet that I should be sad,
> now my father is sick; albeit I could tell to thee—as to one
> it pleases me, for fault of a better to call my friend—I
> could be sad and sad indeed too.
> *Poins.* Very hardly upon such a subject.
> *Prince.* By this hand, thou thinkest me as far in the devil's
> book as thou and Falstaff for obduracy and persistency: let
> the end try the man. But I tell thee my heart bleeds
> inwardly that my father is so sick; and keeping such vile
> company as thou art hath in reason taken from me all
> ostentation of sorrow.
> *Poins.* The reason?
> *Prince.* What wouldst thou think of me if I should weep?
> *Poins.* I would think thee a most princely hypocrite.
> *Prince.* It would be every man's thought; and thou art a
> blessed fellow to think as every man thinks.

(2.2.37–54)

With the death of the King imminent, a sudden display of
grief from his successor would be construed as hollow indeed,
particularly in one whose former estrangement from the court
was on every tongue of Rumour. The very depth of Hal's genuine
feelings for his father, far more than a mere politic concern of the
Prince for his reputation, cannot tolerate the prospect of such an
imputation being put upon the most intimate relationship of his
life. But this is indeed what happens later in the play, when Hal's
misprision of his father's sleep leads to the King's misprision of
Hal's motives for removing the crown:

> *Prince.* I never thought to hear you speak again.
> *King.* Thy wish was father, Harry, to that thought.
> I stay too long by thee, I weary thee.

Dost thou so hunger for mine empty chair
That thou wilt needs invest thee with my honours
Before thy hour be ripe?

(4.5.92-7)

In Part One, Hal's vow to redeem the time signified the need to recover an essentially personal esteem, to be recognised for what he is, "heir apparent." In this sequel, the course of time is to lead him, not to his true name and vocation, but to a new name and vocation as King. Now "redeeming time" signifies a duty to the nation as a whole, for the time is out of joint, and the sick commonwealth must be rejuvenated, the divided realm reunited as "members one of another":

King. Then you perceive the body of our kingdom
     How foul it is; what rank diseases grow,
     And with what danger, near the heart of it.
Warwick. It is but as a body yet distempered
     Which to his former strength may be restored
     With good advice and little medicine.

(3.1.38-43)

The Hal of Part One fulfilled his vow by defeating young Hotspur; in Part Two, it is the old man who must be cast off, though not in the sense that the King suspects.

"You that are old consider not the capacities of us that are young," as Falstaff says (1.2.165). The old indeed totally misjudge the young, and in harbouring very similar expectations of Hal, one in fear and the other in hope, both the King and Falstaff misconstrue the times to come:

The blood weeps from my heart when I do shape
In forms imaginary, th' ungirded days
And rotten times that you shall look upon
When I am sleeping with my ancestors.
For when his headstrong riot hath no curb,
When rage and hot blood are his counsellors,
When means and lavish manners meet together,
O, with what wings shall his affections fly
Towards fronting peril and oppos'd decay!

(4.4.58-66)

But Hal's youth has no more "headstrong riot" in it than the youth of Justice Shallow: "Jesu, Jesu, the mad days that I have spent! and to see how many of my old acquaintance are dead!" (3.2.32–3). Time past and future lives in "forms imaginary," and Shallow's wonderful reminiscences ("every third word a lie," says Falstaff) exemplify how natural it is to turn history into mythology and legend.

The consciousness of time in Part Two is developed into the idea of history itself, as the play looks both before and after, through the long memories of old men and through their anticipations of the future. In this respect the dialogue between the King and his wise counseller Warwick in 3.1. is of central significance. Reflecting ruefully upon the former allegiances of Richard's time between men now bitter enemies, the King sees "the revolution of the times" as merely the flux and mutability of Nature, in which man is helplessly and unpredictably tossed and turned by "necessity":

> how chances mock,
> And changes fill the cup of alteration
> With divers liquors! O, if this were seen,
> The happiest youth, viewing his progress through,
> What perils past, what crosses to ensue,
> Would shut the book and sit him down and die.
>   (3.1.51–6)

In his reply Warwick advances a different conception of history, not as some impersonal, inscrutable decree in "the book of fate," but as an essentially human process, analogous to Nature's laws of organic growth rather than to lawless mutability:

> There is a history in all men's lives,
> Figuring the natures of the times deceas'd;
> The which observ'd a man may prophesy,
> With a near aim, of the main chance of things
> As yet not come to life, who in their seeds
> And weak beginning lie intreasured.
> Such things become the hatch and brood of time;
> And by the necessary form of this . . .
>   (3.1.80–7)

Warwick's point of view lends quite a different significance to the idea of historical "necessity"; instead of being mere victims of blind circumstance, as the King supposes, men can and must

direct their lives by reaping advantage from experience. It is
Warwick who later correctly prophesies that

> The Prince will, in the perfectness of time,
> Cast off his followers; and their memory
> Shall as a pattern or a measure live,
> By which his Grace must mete the lives of other,
> Turning past evils to advantages.
>
> (4.4.74–8)

Hal's progress through both plays demonstrates that life is
not "time's fool," as Hotspur believed, but a meaningful and
purposeful relationship between past and future. What will appear to Hal's contemporaries (and to legend) as a sudden and
unpredictable "revolution of the times" has been presented to us a
wise use of time on Hal's part, and also a process of developing
wisdom and insight from the moment of that over-simplified,
over-confident view of things expressed in the soliloquy at the
beginning of Part One. Hal is to inherit a usurped crown and its
attendant evils, that have driven his father into his grave, and he
is to succeed, not by "indirect crook'd ways" but by the "plain and
right" inheritance of the "hatch and brood of time" from "the
times deceas'd." Youth does not usurp age, although age may
often suppose so, and feel itself cast off. In the larger design of the
play, and of Nature, time is redeemed as youth matures, and
assumes the burdens which age can carry no more. Shakespeare's
reading of history in Part Two, like that of Warwick, is related to
the wider perspectives of natural processes.

When at his father's death Hal puts on the new man with "this
new and gorgeous garment, majesty," he is royally proclaimed by
a stage-direction which indicates his change of name, habit, and
company: "*Enter* KING HENRY THE FIFTH, *attended.*" In losing his
father he has also cast off the old man:

> And, Princes all, believe me, I beseech you,
> My father is gone wild into his grave,
> For in his tomb lie my affections;
> And with his spirits sadly I survive,
> To mock the expectation of the world,
> To frustrate prophecies, and to raze out
> Rotten opinion, who hath writ me down
> After my seeming.
>
> (5.2.122–9)

Such sad mockery of expectation is seen in the rejection of Falstaff, which we have been led to anticipate from the very start, but which we actually witness with a feeling of regret, for in banishing the old man, as in burying his father, Hal has also cast off his youth.

NOTES

1. Richmond Noble, *Shakespeare's Biblical Knowledge* (1935), p. 169. An indispensable but far from complete treatment of the subject.
2. See Introduction to *The First Part of King Henry IV* (new Arden Shakespeare), edited by A. R. Humphreys (1960), pp. xxxix–xlii.
3. Quotations of Shakespeare's text are from *The Complete Works*, edited by Peter Alexander (1951).
4. Quotations from the Bible are from *The Geneva Bible: A Facsimile of the 1560 Edition* (Madison, Milwaukee, and London, 1969).
5. "I know you not" is also the Bridegroom's reply to the foolish virgins (*Matthew*, 25:12).
6. "The eye of man hath not heard, the ear of man hath not seen, man's hand is not able to taste, his tongue to conceive, nor his heart to report, what my dream was" (4.1.20–2). Cf. *1 Corinthians*, 2:9.
7. A well-known Elizabethan tribute to the power of the history play to restore the dead to life and so to redeem the time is Thomas Nashe's allusion to Shakespeare's *Henry VI Part One* in *Pierce Penilesse His Supplication to the Divell* (1592):

   > How would it have ioyed braue *Talbot* (the terror of the French) to thinke that after he had lyne two hundred yeares in his Tombe, hee should triumphe againe on the Stage, and haue his bones new embalmed with the teares of ten thousand spectators at least, (at seuerall times) who, in the Tragedian that represents his person, imagine they behold him fresh bleeding?

   Quoted in E. K. Chambers, *William Shakespeare: A Study of Facts and Problems* (2 vols., 1930), II.188.
8. Paul A. Jorgensen, *Redeeming Shakespeare's Words* (Berkeley and Los Angeles, 1962), pp. 52–69.
9. Humphreys, *ed. cit.*, p. 177.
10. *ibid*, p. 179.
11. Quoted in Chambers, II.244.

Paul A. Gottschalk

Hal and the "Play Extempore" in *I Henry IV* (1974)

The great tavern scene of *I Henry IV* (II.iv) is the longest of the play and the most elaborate, ranging over five hundred lines from the gulling of Francis and the attempted showing-up of Falstaff to the Sheriff's sudden entry and Hal's imminent departure for court. Understandably, the scene has attracted a number of critical studies relating its parts to one another or to the play as a whole,[1] and certainly its richness and complexity warrant any attempt to clarify the aesthetic unity that lies beneath. Yet for all this complexity, the scene progresses smoothly enough, looking back toward Gadshill in its first half and forward to the royal palace in the second, back toward Hal's disgrace and forward to his redemption. This shift coincides with what, in view of the impending confrontation of Hal with his father, is clearly the crisis of the scene: the staging of the "play extempore," in which first Falstaff and then Hal assumes the role of King Henry lecturing his truant son. The importance of this episode has already been underlined in Richard L. McGuire's "The Play-within-the-Play in *I Henry IV*" (*Shakespeare Quarterly*, 18 [1967], 47–52), where it is treated, indeed, as the crisis in Hal's development as hero. Dealing with the play extempore as an example of the Elizabethan play within a play, McGuire states that Hal attains "discovery of self through pretense" (p. 52), that, in acting out his role of King, he comes to realize it is time for the change he had predicted in his soliloquy of I.ii and thus time at last to reject Falstaff. In response to Falstaff's mock plea against banishment, Hal's final words in

From *Texas Studies in Literature and Language*, 15.4 (1974). Reprinted by permission of The University of Texas Press.

the episode—"I do, I will"—are spoken "as Prince *and* King" (p. 50). "This short reply after much rhetoric and repetition," says McGuire, "underlines the change in character and the finality of the renunciation" (p. 50).

Despite its humor, then, the play episode is highly serious drama, and McGuire's study is important in showing how this may be so. Yet this study is itself somewhat distortive. The play episode is not technically a play within a play at all; for that reason, we shall see, it cannot lead to "discovery of self through pretense" and thus is not crucial in the way that McGuire suggests.[2] Both the nature of the play episode as play and its function as Hal's crisis need to be reexamined.

Indeed, the very notion of Hal's crisis in this play is problematic. McGuire's interpretation becomes puzzling the moment we apply the principle that change of character onstage can be indicated only by change in the personage's avowed attitude, by change in his actions, or by comments from other characters. The last we do not find until the King's praise of Hal in Act III and Vernon's in Act IV. As to change in attitude, Hal's "I will" is no more than a summary of his soliloquy at the end of I.ii, in which he first reveals his intention to renounce Falstaff and his companions. Finally, if Hal's words "I do" promise a present change in his actions, as at first they seem to do, the promise remains unfulfilled. When, moments later, the Sheriff enters seeking Falstaff, Hal lies to protect his friend.[3] As soon as his interview with his father is over, Hal returns to the tavern, and his exploits there merely perpetuate the humor of earlier scenes. And when at the end of the play Falstaff claims credit for killing Hotspur, Hal acquiesces in the deceit:

> For my part, if a lie may do thee grace,
> I'll gild it with the happiest terms I have.
>
> (V.iv.161–162)[4]

Hal has not renounced Falstaff in the play episode. Falstaff continues to woo Hal, Hal to contemn Falstaff (as he did in his first lines of the play) but also to sport with him and, when the chips are down, to help him. In short, nothing has happened—and nothing does happen subsequently in the play that would not have occurred had the play scene never taken place. The play episode is not a "discovery of self through pretense," because Hal has discovered nothing that he did not already know in I.ii. It is not a crisis in character because his character shows no change. In the play scene, nothing really happens. Indeed, we might ask ourselves, what *could* happen? Hal has already made his crucial commitment to regality in Act I; he carries it out in Act V and again in Act V of Part 2. Between the moment of decision and the moment of action, what is there to dramatize? Shakespeare was to work again at that problem in *Hamlet*, but Hal is not like Hamlet. If we analyze dramatic character into *potential* to perform a given action and *probability* of performing it, we see that in *Hamlet* the discrepancy between these two is enormous. The horizons of Hamlet's character are so vast, his potential for a wide variety of actions so broad, that the probability of his committing any one action is proportionately nebulous. In Hal, however, potential and probability are virtually identical. While Hamlet's character doesn't organize around his task, Hal's does. His time, too, is out of joint, but on the whole he seems quite pleased that he was born to set it right.

Therefore, *1 Henry IV* is a play without a normal climax.[5] Shrewsbury is at once its moment of crisis and its moment of resolution. Hal's royal identity and his merely provisional relationship with Falstaff are announced in the soliloquy of I.ii, not as a grasping towards identity, as in Hamlet's soliloquies, but as a moral *fait accompli*. But this identity is latent. Throughout almost all of both parts of *Henry IV* it remains in solution, invisible to Hal's companions, but not manifest until, first at Shrewsbury and then in the final rejection of Falstaff, it crystallizes openly and irrevocably.

Shakespeare's strategy in the play is to hide the inevitable fulfillment of Hal's character from Hal's contemporaries while revealing it to us. It is the same technique he had used shortly before in *Richard III*. Richard, however, must overcome a long series of obstacles on his way to success, while Hal faces only one crucial act in each part of *Henry IV*: the battle with Hotspur and the rejection of Falstaff. So although the basic problem of plot is much the same in *Richard III*, *Henry IV*, and *Hamlet*, the solutions differ, for Hal's character is simpler than Hamlet's and his goal closer than Richard's. Shakespeare's solution in *1 Henry IV* is to provide Hal with three analogous episodes of promise, episodes that seem to build toward the ultimate fulfillment of Shrewsbury while in fact doing little or nothing to bring it about. Each episode is followed by an apparent moral relapse to further maintain the suspense. First comes Hal's promise to himself in the soliloquy of I.ii, followed by the robbery at Gadshill; then the play episode, a promise to Falstaff, followed by Hal's protecting Falstaff from the Sheriff; and finally the throne room scene, in which Hal promises allegiance to his father—and then procures Falstaff his commission in the royal army.

To further the illusion of progress, these episodes are climactically arranged. The soliloquy is mere statement, completely hidden from all other characters in the play, and represents Hal's potential at its most latent. In the play episode Hal's regality becomes more overt, but only in the apparent context of play and only in the world of the tavern. In the throne room scene, however, the early promise of the soliloquy becomes a solemn oath to the King: it is both overt and totally serious. Finally, at Shrewsbury, the promise is fulfilled in action. When, therefore, McGuire says, "we never again see Falstaff and Hal together as they were before the play-within-the-play" (p. 50), he is right, but the stress must be laid on the "we never see": although the relationship of Hal and Falstaff is consistent throughout, the point of view from which it is shown us systematically shifts.[6] Thus, these promissory episodes do not simply mark time until Shrewsbury. If they are not crises, they are moments of heightened definition in the developing portrait of the young man who will be King.

The play episode begins its contribution to this portrait by bringing the immediately antecedent action into new focus, just as the soliloquy of I.ii refocuses the action of that scene. There, however, the effect is quite clear: Hal simply detaches himself morally from his companions ("I know you all . . ."). But here Hal must ultimately detach himself not only from Falstaff, the embodiment of amoral irresponsibility, but also from Francis and Hotspur, each in his own way an embodiment of loyalty so blind that it becomes irresponsibility too, of a different sort from Falstaff's but no less dangerous.[7] Yet, as in the earlier scene, Hal at first seems to be moving further and further away from commitment as the scene progresses, as he transposes the many-faceted world of *I Henry IV* into play. First, he plays at being a tapster, a Francis. Then, as Francis's single-minded simplicity reminds him of Hotspur's, he prepares to play that worthy: "I prithee call in Falstaff. I'll play Percy, and that damn'd brawn shall play Dame Mortimer his wife" (II.iv.122–124). There follows the attempted trapping of Falstaff, in which the reality of thievery becomes play (Falstaff's disguise of valor, complete with costume: the bloodied garments and hacked swords) within play (Poins and Hal having robbed the robbers—and with their own costumes of buckram) within play ("By the Lord, I knew ye as well as he that made ye"), the momentary butt of which is Hal himself, ironically most out of touch with the hopes of the theater audience just when Falstaff claims to have recognized the true Prince by instinct. The playfulness of the scene culminates in Falstaff's proposal, "What, shall we be merry? Shall we have a play extempore?" There is a momentary jockeying for position as Hal answers, "Content— and the argument shall be thy running away," and Falstaff retorts, "Ah, no more of that, Hal, an thou lovest me!" (ll. 308–313). We scarcely have time to ponder Falstaff's conditional before the Hostess bursts in to announce that a nobleman has just arrived from the court. Falstaff is sent out to speak with him, returns with word that Hal is to go to court in the morning, and begs Hal to "practise an answer" for the King (l. 412). Hal's reply seems to revive the momentarily interrupted atmosphere of play and, finally, to bring into it the two chief remaining figures from the world of *Henry IV*: Hal as Prince, and the King himself. "Do thou stand for my father," Hal tells Falstaff, "and examine me upon the particulars of my life" (ll. 413–414). A skit of some sort has been in the offing throughout the entire scene—first one on Hotspur and Lady Percy, then on Falstaff's running away, now on an event that has yet to occur: the confrontation of Henry IV and Prince Hal.

What makes this skit unusual among Elizabethan and Jacobean plays within plays is precisely that it is a "play extempore": both characters create their own roles as they go along. What is more, we see with increasing clarity that what the roles—and role-playing itself—mean to each is quite different.

For the chief temptation that Falstaff poses as a vice-figure is to reduce all things to play. The humor of the "men in buckram" episode stems from the very havoc that Falstaff's narration plays with reality as he creates a world where honor, valor, and mathematical identity itself are mere shadows, a world that denies the earnestness, practicality, and logic that are the forte of the two Henrys. Now in the play extempore Falstaff, sensing impending danger, begins to move the King himself into this unreal world; he makes Henry speak "in King Cambyses' vein," and in Euphues's as well.[8] McGuire suggests that the style is Falstaff's conception of kingly speech, that he is trying to be realistic,[9] but Falstaff has a very precise, self-conscious awareness of the rhetorical figure he is cutting: he is not imitating kingly speech, he is parodying it, reducing kingship to literary convention, making reality a fiction. Thus, King Henry's agony over Hal's truancy becomes, in Falstaff's hands, a ludicrous exercise in euphuism. And that is precisely Falstaff's point. Falstaff's rhetoric picks up some dignity only when he turns to his own praises, and then changes again as he breaks off and addresses Hal more directly: "And tell me now, thou naughty varlet, tell me where hast thou been this month?" (ll. 473–475). The shift is deliberate and effective. Its friendly, teasing informality places Hal's offense precisely in the light in which Falstaff wants it to be considered.

Finally, Falstaff's reaction when Hal "deposes" him takes his dangerous lack of earnestness a step further. If, as McGuire suggests (p. 50), his chief concern is to maintain his position by having Hal "practise an answer," he might reasonably be concerned that Hal has not done so. But his reaction to the "deposition" indicates that that is not what is on his mind at all: "Depose me? If thou dost it half so gravely, so majestically, both in word and matter, hang me up by the heels for a rabbit-sucker or a poulter's hare" (ll. 478–481). His concern is for the pure virtuosity with which he has played his role. He does not even embrace the opportunity to show Hal how the Prince should speak to the King but here again, as with the men in buckram, abdicates prudence and gives himself to the jest of the moment: Hal as king speaks of grievous complaints against the Prince, and " 'Sblood, my lord," replies Falstaff indecorously, "they are false! Nay, I'll tickle ye for a young prince, i' faith" (ll. 488–489). Role-play becomes his world, its practical implications forgotten. The game, to borrow from Dr. Johnson, is the Cleopatra for which he loses the world and is content to lose it. If Falstaff's hope lies in maintaining the verisimilitude of the play, he has undermined his hope. But if his hope—and the chief temptation he presents to the Prince—is to reduce the serious to play, the real to unreal, we see him here in a moment of triumph, and the Prince, if he does not counteract this temptation, in a moment of extreme moral danger.

When Hal "deposes" Falstaff, the crisis of the scene has arrived: "Dost thou speak like a king? Do thou stand for me, and I'll play my father" (ll. 476–477). First Falstaff acts the king, and now Hal will. But whose king will he act? If Falstaff's—that is, if he turns kingship into play—then the play world dominates political reality for Hal, and Falstaff wins.

But Shakespeare has already indicated that Hal will mean something radically different when *he* acts the king. We begin to see the difference at the very moment that the world of the skit first begins to separate itself from the reality of Eastcheap, the moment that real objects become props. "This chair shall be my state, this dagger my sceptre, and this cushion my crown," proclaims Falstaff. "Thy state," replies Hal, "is taken for a join'd-stool, thy golden sceptre for a leaden dagger, and thy precious rich crown for a pitiful bald crown" (ll. 415–420). Dr. Johnson wished that Hal's reply had been omitted, in that "it contains only a repetition of Falstaff's mock-royalty."[10] But Hal is repeating the lines with a difference. Falstaff is more interested in the props than in what they symbolize ("This chair . . . this dagger . . . this cushion") while to Hal the props as such are remote and what they represent foremost in his mind: not only does he reverse Falstaff's syntactic order, citing the royal object before its stage symbol, but he refers to the object specifically ("*thy* state") and to the symbol indefinitely ("*a* join'd stool"), while his adjectives build up into an eloquent climax ("Thy state . . . thy golden sceptre . . . thy precious rich crown"). Falstaff transforms the crown into a cushion; Hal sees the cushion but thinks of the actual state, scepter, and crown of England.[11] In these two apparently similar speeches of Falstaff and Hal, the throne and the Falstaff world are implicitly debating the issue shortly to be raised in greater earnest: the relative reality of each to the other.

The second intimation that Hal will play the king with a difference comes when Falstaff concludes his king speech: "And tell me now, thou naughty varlet, tell me where hast thou been this month?" and Hal makes no answer. Indeed, what sort of an answer might he make? Falstaff presumably hopes for the sort he himself would give, one that would reduce the whole problem to felicitous jest. But Hal does not reply in the role Falstaff has assigned him; he will not mock himself. Instead, deposing Falstaff, he himself becomes king,[12] and his first words indicate in their terseness and sobriety the seriousness of the confrontation that is to occur in III.ii:

> Now, Harry, whence come you?
> . . . .
> The complaints I hear of thee are grievous.
>
> (ll. 484, 486–487)

And when Falstaff breaks his role to heighten the jest—"Nay, I'll tickle ye for a young prince, i' faith"—Hal turns the jest back to seriousness: "Swearest thou, ungracious boy? Henceforth ne'er look on me" (ll. 488–491).

In the lines that follow, one could debate whether Hal is speaking as the king or as himself. McGuire observes that Hal's tirade against Falstaff, though it is rant, is what Hal conceives to be kingly rant (p. 49); yet it is also reminiscent of the contempt that Hal has shown for Falstaff earlier in the scene:

> Call in ribs, call in tallow.
>
> (l. 125)

> These lies are like their father that begets them—gross as a mountain, open, palpable. Why, thou clay-brain'd guts, thou knotty-pated fool, thou whoreson obscene greasy tallow-catch—
>
> (ll. 249–253)

The tone is darker, but the style remains much the same. The ambiguity is resolved, of course, in the epiphanic moment when Falstaff pleads "banish not him thy Harry's company" and Hal replies, "I do, I will" (ll. 526, 528). McGuire says that here Hal is speaking "as Prince *and* King," but, we have seen, Hal as prince never rejects Falstaff. Rather, he is speaking first as player-king and then in his actual role of future king, and we see that the two roles are continuous, that, in fact, Hal hasn't been acting at all.

And that is his response to Falstaff's transformation of the serious into play: he has transformed play back into reality. This reality comes bursting in on them in the form of the Sheriff, and Falstaff, falling asleep behind the curtain, hides from it both in deed and in spirit. Meanwhile, the Prince has the last word on the thievery game—which he cancels by returning the money—and moves on to his encounter with his father, an encounter that will take place as predicted.

There is not, then, a single play extempore in *I Henry IV*: there are two, Falstaff's and Hal's, each moving away from the actual present, but one toward the unreal, the other toward the future. This ambivalence is possible precisely because the play is extemporaneous, without script or predetermined action. In genuine plays within plays, as in any regular play, the action is presented as autonomous, the events portrayed as beyond the control of either actor or spectator. A play creates its own world; whatever its relevance to the real world, there can be no question of identity. The actor, as Antonin Artaud puts it, is "entirely penetrated by feelings that do not benefit or even relate to his real condition,"[13] and so is the actor-analogue of a play within a play. But neither actor in the play within *I Henry IV* possesses such autonomy. There is no script, no mimetic *a priori*, and both must shape their roles from whole cloth out of their own characters, their own penchant for involvement in the action that they portray. By its very nature, the play cannot be seen as separate from them.

Falstaff becomes absorbed in the play; as we watch him, the dimension of the actor behind the role sometimes fades away. "Play out the play," he cries, with the sheriff at the door. "I have much to say in the behalf of that Falstaff" (ll. 531–532). And indeed we cannot define Falstaff solely as the shrewd, ambitious parasite that he would appear without the roles that he continually plays. It is the wholeheartedness with which he plays them, the enthusiasm with which he invests his whole personality in the unreal and the impossible, that sets him aside from the other vice characters and eirons that inhabit the world of drama. But in the world of *Henry IV* he is dangerous precisely because he testifies to the primacy of the play world and thus to the unreality of the political.

Hal, on the other hand, is ultimately not playing at all. The fictional world he creates is, in fact, not fictional. It is separated from actuality not as an object of the imagination but as an object of prediction. The poet, as Sidney observes, does not affirm, but Hal's half of the skit ends on a mimetic affirmation which he immediately extends into the reality of the future: "I do, I will." It has often been suggested that the play scene parodies the encounter of King and Prince in III.ii,[14] but that, in effect, is merely what Falstaff wants it to do, since the end of parody is to undermine the serious; Falstaff wants the tavern to define the throne room. Hal brings about the precise opposite. The destiny that defines his character transmutes play into sudden prophecy: the duties of the throne define this moment in the tavern. For the second time, and through the very medium that threatens it the most, Hal's latent regality becomes manifest.

If the play episode does not mark a major shift in Hal's character, it does mark a major shift in the point of view of the play itself. The skit begins by showing us Hal's duties under the aspect of Falstaff; it concludes by showing Falstaff under the aspect of royalty. And it is thus that we shall see Falstaff henceforth, for England is not playing his game, and his actions as he carries a bottle of sack into battle, leads his men to slaughter, and stabs the dead Hotspur, justify the Prince's disgust. From now on, and throughout Part 2 as well, Falstaff stands in the shadow of royalty until at last, fulfilling his prophecy of the play extempore, King Henry V banishes him and commits himself, as he knew all along that he must, to an action in which Falstaff can play no part.

NOTES

1. See Fredson Bowers, "Hal and Francis in *King Henry IV, Part 1*," *Renaissance Papers, 1965*, publication of Southeastern Renaissance Conference (Durham, N.C., 1966), pp. 15–20; Waldo F. McNeir, "Structure and Theme in the First Tavern Scene of *Henry IV, Part One*," *Essays on Shakespeare*, ed. Gordon Ross Smith (University Park, Pa., 1965), pp. 67–83; and S. P. Zitner, "Anon, Anon: or, a Mirror for a Magistrate," *SQ*, 19 (1968), 63–70. An ambiguously entitled essay is F. M. Salter's "The Play within the Play of *First Henry IV*," *Transactions*

of the *Royal Society of Canada*, 3rd ser., vol. 40, sec. 2 (May, 1946), 209–223, which deals with the relation of the comic to the historical plot.

2. McGuire is disputing Dieter Mehl's point that plays staged by protagonists and involving "startling shifts of identities" are "a distinctly Jacobean feature" ("Forms and Functions of the Play within a Play," *RenD*, 7 [1965], 41–61, at p. 50). But Mehl seems to mean shifts from role-playing to actuality in such a way that one "may sometimes wonder whether the characters are still acting their parts or speaking in person" (Mehl, p. 50), rather than shifts in the character itself. As we shall see, neither situation applies to *I Henry IV*, though the latter comes close.

3. McGuire takes issue with McNeir (p. 79), who says that "the whole world of Falstaff hangs in the balance" pending Hal's words to the Sheriff, McGuire maintaining that Hal has already in effect made up his mind in the play episode (p. 50 and n.). But that this moment is in fact tense on the stage and that Hal does not resolve the tension by renouncing Falstaff here and now calls precisely into question what he means by "I do, I will."

4. The word "grace" marks the shift between these lines and Falstaff's final rejection: "Make less thy body, hence, and more thy grace . . ." (Part 2, V.v.56). Here, as throughout, I follow the argument of G. K. Hunter, "*Henry IV* and the Elizabethan Two-Part Play," *RES*, n.s. 5 (1954), 236–248, that Shakespeare took responsibility for the thematic coherence of the two parts of *Henry IV* even if he did not originally plan for the second; certainly, Hal's rejection of Falstaff is predicated in Part 1: see Harold Jenkins, *The Structural Problem in Shakespeare's Henry the Fourth* (London, 1956), reprinted in R. J. Dorius, ed., *Discussions of Shakespeare's Histories* (Boston, 1964), pp. 41–55.

5. See Fredson Bowers, "Shakespeare's Art: The Point of View," in *Literary Views*, ed. Carroll Camden (Chicago, 1964), pp. 45–58.

6. Note that whereas Hal's encounter with his father (III.ii) seems *to us* to mark a major estrangement of Hal from Falstaff, in fact Falstaff's position is consolidated once the interview is gotten over: "I am good friends with my father, and may do anything. . . . I have procured thee, Jack, a charge of foot" (III.iii.203–204, 208–209).

7. For a development of this point, see Bowers, "Hal and Francis in *King Henry IV*, Part 1," pp. 18–20.

8. See notes in the New Variorum edition of *I Henry IV*, ed. Samuel Burdett Hemingway (Philadelphia, 1936), pp. 161–164. Arnold Davenport sees an additional parallel in both substance and style to the dialogue on love vs. kingship in II.ii of Lyly's *Campaspe*, where Hephestion upbraids Alexander for wishing to relinquish his royal

station and duties over the love of an unworthy captive girl ("Notes on Lyly's 'Campaspe' and Shakespeare," *Notes and Queries*, 199 [n.s. 1, 1954], 19–20), while G. B. Harrison sees a parody of the style and repertory of the Admiral's Men ("Shakespeare's Actors," in *A Series of Papers on Shakespeare and the Theater*, Shakespeare Association [London, 1927], pp. 62–87, esp. pp. 76–79). All three arguments suggest a reduction—for those in Shakespeare's audience who detect the allusions—of the serious to play.

9. Thus, when the Hostess interrupts, "he must silence her, the symbol of his bawdy-house, tavern-frequenting aspect of character, before he may imitate Henry Bolingbroke and speak to Hal" (p. 49).

10. Cited in Hemingway, ed., New Variorum edition, p. 159.

11. See Richard Farmer's observation (cited in New Variorum, p. 160): "This is an apostrophe of the prince to his absent father, not an answer to Falstaff," which is a necessary complement to McNeir's comment that "the signs of Falstaff's assumed royalty in throne, sceptre, and crown are reduced by Hal's literal directness to what they are—a joined-stool, a leaden dagger, and a bald crown" (McNeir, p. 77).

12. For the dramatic effectiveness of this visual stage metaphor, see McGuire, p. 49.

13. "The Theater and the Plague," in *The Theater and Its Double*, tr. Mary Caroline Richards (New York, 1958), p. 24. Even in such an extreme case as *The Spanish Tragedy*, this general principle holds true for the play within the play insofar as we see Hieronimo *as playing* Soliman: the role is analogous to reality and will erupt into reality, but it is not identical to it. If it were, there would be no suspense in the play within *The Spanish Tragedy*.

14. For an able counterargument to this view, see McGuire, pp. 49–52.

Robert G. Hunter

Shakespeare's Comic Sense As It Strikes Us Today: Falstaff and the Protestant Ethic (1978)

If there are such things as antibodies (and I am told that there are), then let there be such things as antiembodiments and let Falstaff be one. Let him also be an embodiment (there is plenty of room), for Falstaff embodies a large part of my subject, Shakespeare's comic sense. Simultaneously he antiembodies the Protestant ethic. What he is, it is not. What it is, he is not. Did Shakespeare's comic sense serve the body politic by generating Falstaff in an attempt to immunize comparatively Merrie England against those foreign organisms, the Puritan Saints? If so, the attempt failed, and Shakespeare knew it would. The Henriad, I will maintain but not demonstrate, dramatizes, in the rejection of Falstaff, the victory of the Protestant ethic, presenting that social triumph as a psychological event, the decision of Henry the Fifth to labor in his vocation, to do his duty in that royal station to which it pleased God to call him.

Thus Falstaff came into being, almost four centuries ago, during the first insurgency of the Protestant ethic and, perhaps, in response to it. Today we are celebrating the bicentennial of one of that ethic's more elaborate offspring. And do we not sense today that we are living through the decadence and disappearance of the ethic, that we watch going down the great drain of history what Shakespeare saw coming up it? What will take the ethic's place? That seems to me one of today's more nagging questions,

From *Shakespeare, Pattern of Excelling Nature*, ed. David Bevington and Jay L. Halio. Reprinted by permission of the author and Associated University Presses.

and I haven't the vaguest notion of its answer. But we might explore the question by consulting the comic sense of our particular oracle. Let us have a look first at the ethic and then at Falstaff as antiembodiment of it.

The phenomenon that I claim Falstaff antiembodies is authoritatively described and accounted for by Max Weber in *The Protestant Ethic and the Spirit of Capitalism.* Weber identifies the main characteristic of that ethic as "worldly asceticism . . . a fundamental antagonism to sensuous culture of all kinds." He sees the ethic as the result of two theological causes, one Lutheran and one Calvinist. The Lutheran cause is the "conception of the calling." In reacting against the monastic ideal Luther did not entirely repudiate the worthiness of ascetic self-denial. What he did was to replace the insistence upon withdrawal from the world with a "valuation of fulfilment of duty in worldly affairs as the highest form which the moral activity of the individual could assume." To this exaltation of the importance of laboring in one's vocation was added the Calvinist notion of absolute predestination. If you believe that humanity has been irretrievably divided into the elect and the reprobate, then it becomes a matter of some importance to convince yourself that you are a member of the right group. "In order to attain that confidence intense worldly activity is recommended as the most suitable means. It and it alone disperses religious doubts and gives certainty of grace." As a paradoxical result, Protestantism, which proclaims that works are useless as a means of gaining salvation, ends by finding them "indispensable as a means . . . of getting rid of the fear of damnation." "Getting rid of fear" is a key phrase for an understanding of the psychological power of the Protestant ethic and of Falstaff as a compendious alternative to that ethic. Hope of eternal life gets rid of the fear of death. Faith in our election gets rid of the fear of eternal damnation, and contemplating the success of our worldly activity ratifies our faith in election. Success is evidence of salvation. The Protestant ethic is a superb strategy for getting rid of those fears which are inherent in the human condition, fears of time, of death, and of damnation. It is one of the greatest in what Freud calls "the great series of methods devised by the mind of man for evading the compulsion to suffer."

Falstaff is an anthology of such methods. I count and will try to define five, taking them in the order Shakespeare presents them to us. The first I label "living within appetite," the second "play," the third "success," the fourth "carnival," and the last, "hope." Of these the first, second, and fourth are in direct opposition to the ideals and practices of the Protestant ethic. The third and the last are distorted imitations of Protestant ethic methods and I will call them serious parodies, though it makes me uneasy to claim that anything about Falstaff is serious.

The first of Falstaff's methods is the most effective and also the most difficult to sustain. It is common to all of us, originates in infancy, and antedates the fear of time itself. Our first clock is appetite, and time first presents itself to us as that which intervenes between appetite and its satisfaction, and its rebirth. The time we thus perceive through appetite is circular in nature, a time of eternal return. A day is that which separates breakfast from breakfast. There is nothing to fear in time thus perceived as circular, as the element in which pleasure, the satisfaction of appetite, takes place. And much in the reality we begin to perceive outside our bodies appears to confirm the truth of time's circularity. The sun also ariseth, and the sun goeth down and hasteth to the place where he arose. Spring, summer, autumn, winter— spring. Not much of this appetitive, circular time has passed, however, before its passing forces upon us the knowledge that our understanding of time is incomplete. The bodies whose appetites we have satisfied change permanently. Today is not yesterday despite the similarity in breakfasts. Summer returns but last summer will never return. Time, we find, is rectilinear, the shortest possible distance between birth and death. With that discovery our fear of time is born, and our minds must devise methods for evading the suffering in that fear. The method of the Protestant ethic is to glorify time's rectilinearity, to proclaim time the element not of pleasure, but of duty, of the worldly achievement that ratifies faith in our election. This, however, is not Falstaff's way.

Henry IV, Part One opens with the King doing desperate battle against the implacability of rectilinear time. "Find we a time" is his plea. A time for peace, for the establishment of order, for the crusade, the achievement that will expiate Richard's murder and convince the King that his soul is saved after all. The second scene begins when Falstaff first waddles into our consciousness on the line, "Now, Hal, what time of day is it, lad?" a question whose total banality inspires Hal to a rather wonderful tirade on the question: "What a devil hast thou to do with the time of the day?", a question that Hal himself proceeds to answer: "Unless hours were cups of sack, and minutes capons, and clocks the tongues of bawds, and dials the signs of leaping-houses. . . ." Hal's conditional answers his interrogative. Falstaff's clock is Falstaff's paunch and the time it tells is circular, revolving from thirst to sack to thirst to sack. From hunger to capon to hunger to capon. From lust to wench to lust to fair, hot wench. Falstaff copes with the fact of time's linearity by stoutly denying it, by doing his best to live his life within the circular time of appetite. Such a life would be a life without fear of time, but of course no moderately conscious life can be so lived. It's not just that capons, sack, and wenches refuse to arrive on schedule—though that is annoying enough. The rectilinearity of time is constantly being forced upon our unwilling minds. Even our best friends are in the habit of saying things like "gallows," and when we try tactfully to change the subject to something pleasant like "a most sweet wench," they refuse to cooperate and we end up depressed, "as melancholy as a gib cat, or a lugged bear."

When this happens to Falstaff, he moves to his second strategy. He answers the reproaches of his superego with the exhilarating language of play—purely verbal play at first. Falstaff copes with melancholy by playing with Hal at finding similes for it: a gib cat, a lugged bear, an old lion, a lover's lute, the drone of a Lincolnshire bagpipe, a hare, the melancholy of Moor-ditch. Having thus put the forces of his conscience on the defensive, he proceeds to polish them off by employing his favorite play method, role-playing. Falstaff has the ability to make anything appear ridiculous by pretending to be it. Here he represses his own tendencies to contrition by pretending to be contrite: "But Hal, I prithee trouble me no more with vanity . . . thou hast done much harm upon me, Hal, God forgive thee for it: before I knew thee, Hal, I knew nothing, and now am I, if a man should speak truly, little better than one of the wicked." What Poins calls "Monsieur Remorse" is Falstaff's first and in some ways best role. Nowhere does Shakespeare make it clearer how the humorous man copes with the certainty of death and the possibility of damnation. By parodying his own fears, Falstaff answers the challenge Hamlet gives the skull of Yorick: he makes us laugh at that. But of course it is not just himself that Falstaff is mocking here. Monsieur Remorse is pretty clearly a Puritan gentleman. He is one of the Protestant Saints whom the Prince of Wales has so far misled as to make him doubt his own election and fear that his conduct indicts him as little better than one of the reprobate. Not only does Falstaff's role-playing purge him of his own melancholy, it accuses the Protestant ethic of being a role that the Puritan thinks (or pretends to think) he is playing in earnest. But it is not only the specific mockery, the parochial satire that the Protestant ethic would find offensive. Falstaff's roles release him from the depressing confines of reality and that, unless done religiously, will not do. Play in all its forms, from morris-dancing to the great Globe itself, is an inadmissible alternative to laboring soberly in one's vocation. But Falstaff, *homo ludens*, goes on playing. On Gadshill and in the tavern his roles increase and multiply: the young desperado ripping off the fat chuffs who batten on the commonwealth ("They hate us youth"); the battered survivor of a better time who sees a virile world of courage and honor among thieves degenerating, disintegrating around him: "Go thy ways, old Jack, die when thou wilt—if manhood, good manhood, be not forgot upon the face of the earth, then am I a shotten herring . . ."; and Sir John Fairbanks, Sr., driving before him two, four, seven, nine, eleven men in buckram; and finally, of course, the King, the Prince, himself. So Falstaff's Protean mind copes with itself, represses and escapes its fears by becoming not dying Jack Falstaff but anything and everything, turning all things to laughter.

But again this is not enough. On the morning after the night before the body whose appetites have been so assiduously satisfied informs the Protean mind that time is rectilinear and he is but Falstaff and a man: "Do I not bate? Do I not dwindle? Why, my skin hangs about me like an old lady's loose gown. I am withered like an old apple-john." And we get a reprise of Monsieur Remorse, rather more Romanist in his second version, I think. Clearly, sterner measures than play are called for. Living in appetite is the strategy of the infant. Play is the strategy of the child. Falstaff is never such a fool as to put away childish things. He knows he needs all the strategies he can get. While retaining the two I have already identified, he moves to those of the mature man and specifically to an antiversion of the Protestant ethic itself. Having parodied the remorse of the Puritan, he now more seriously parodies its results: the determination to labor in one's vocation.

When, in their first scene, Hal interrupts the finer flights of Monsieur Remorse to ask Jack Falstaff where they should take a purse tomorrow, he gets the reply, " 'Zounds, where thou wilt, lad, I'll make one." Upon which the prince observes, "I see a good amendment of life in thee, from praying to purse-taking." Monsieur Remorse's rejoinder is a model of Christian forbearance: "Why, Hal, 'tis my vocation, Hal, 'tis no sin for a man to labor in his vocation." If one wished to be unfair to the Protestant ethic (and I do), one could say that Weber's description of the shift in Christian morality from the medieval exaltation of the monastic ideal to the seventeenth-century Puritan enshrinement of capitalist worldly asceticism is encapsulated in Hal's phrase "from praying to purse-taking." Falstaff's methods in purse-taking are not commercial and therefore his calling is not lawful. But he is not really a highwayman either. The night's exploits on Gadshill are closer to play than to vocation, an especially exciting game of cops-and-robbers. Ordinarily and whenever possible, Falstaff combines the crafts of the professional soldier and the confidence-man. He combines them very successfully. The £300 that he extorts from reluctant draftees compares favorably with the £250 Shakespeare is estimated to have made in a good year and very favorably indeed with the £20 annual salary of the Stratford schoolmaster. And Falstaff is a success on the battlefield as well. He does his duty by leading or somehow chivvying his soldiers into a position where they can be thoroughly peppered, and then he distinguishes himself by stabbing the corpse of Hotspur in the thigh. Does he expect anyone to believe that he and not Hal has killed Harry Percy? It doesn't matter, for there are distinct orders of success in lying. A liar may succeed because he is believed or because he cannot be contradicted. Falstaff is content with the more modest degree, and thus he achieves one of those reputations, common enough in fields other than the military, for having done something or other at some time or other.

The result of these successful labors is the Sir John Falstaff of *Henry the Fourth, Part Two*: Jack Falstaff with his familiars, John with his brothers and sisters, and Sir John with all Europe. Such are the secular rewards of laboring in one's vocation—self-fulfillment and a sense of one's identity confirmed by the respect of the community. And there is no strategy more successful than success for concealing from us our participation in the common human condition. For the Puritan, of course, the rewards of such laboring also include the conviction of one's election and a consequent faith in one's eternal salvation. Falstaff does not go that far, not by some distance. Indeed, his profession is an extension of his play. He has added a new dimension to his role-playing and has begun to pretend really to be what he is pretending to be. To what extent that makes him different from the rest of us, including the ethical Protestants, I must leave it to the subtler masters of the dramaturgical school of social psychology to decide. My point is that as a technique for dealing with our fears of time and death, becoming Sir John with all Europe works very well. Monsieur Remorse is no longer needed to repress the natterings of the superego. Being Sir John is enough.

Or almost enough, for again the body reminds us of our inevitable predicament. The owner of Sir John's urine may have more diseases than he knows for, but Sir John is aware of a good number of them: "A pox of this gout! or a gout of this pox! for the one or the other plays the rogue with my great toe." That great toe, long invisible to its owner's eye, is transmitting the body's tedious message: you cannot conquer time. Falstaff's fourth method for jamming that communication is related to all of the previous three. Carnival is an attempt to regain occasionally and temporarily the bliss of living within appetitive time. It is that period which society sets aside for sanctioned play, for humor, wit, and role-playing. It is the necessary holiday in which we may rest from doing our duties in that station to which it has pleased God to call us. Except, of course, that the Puritans recognized no such necessity. They were opposed to Carnival, but they were equally opposed to Lent—not because they found its lugubrious self-denials distasteful (though they knew there was no merit in them) but because they thought it should be Lent all the year round. Once more, Sir John embodies a different point of view. After a hard day's labor devoted to evading the Lord Chief Justice, placating Mistress Quickly, devising methods for bilking Master Dommelton the slops-maker, and avoiding the importunities of a dozen sweating captains—after such a day, the warrior deserves his repose. Wine, women, and song, sack and canary, Doll Tearsheet and Sneak's noise—all the components of an ideal saturnalia are present in the great festive scene of *Henry IV, Part Two*. But Shakespeare is here aiming to present us with the real as well as the ideal, and real saturnalia has indecorous results: vomit, urine, syphilis, and violence. Our women enter talking of wine and its effects and when asked how she is doing now, Doll replies, "Better than I was—hem!" That "hem," I suspect, is Shakespeare's suggestion to his boy-actor that he should indicate audibly but nonverbally why Doll is doing better than she was. Sir John enters with song: "When Arthur first in court," and urine: "Empty the jordan." A bout of wit follows between Doll and Falstaff on the subject of who is responsible for whose venereal disease. The episode with Pistol brings us to violence and Sir John's valor inspires Doll to ask her little, tidy, Bartholomew boar-pig when he will leave fighting a-days and foining a-nights and begin to patch up his old body for heaven. *Carpe diem* is a motto of carnival, but one of the things we ask of saturnalia is that it make us forget why it is that we want to seize the day. Doll's comment is malapropos and her most flattering busses cannot make Falstaff forget the consequences of linear time: "I am old. I am old." And finally, in spite of the fun and games with Hal and Poins, it looks as if Shakespeare were going to let Falstaff be frustrated by age and time and by the demands of his vocation, for "The man of action is called on" and must leave the sweetest morsel of the night unplucked. Farewells must be said: "Well, fare thee well. I have known thee these twenty-nine years, come peascod-time, but an honester and truer-hearted man. . . ." I thoroughly agree with the Arden editor's note on peascod-time: "The precision with which Mistress Quickly dates a 29-year-old meeting is entirely touching." Just how entirely that is, however, can be understood only if one apprehends the bawdy of "peascod," and to do that one must reverse the syllables. Doing so emphasizes that the time that finally triumphs here is appetitive and circular. Bardolph reenters with a command: "Bid Mistress Tearsheet come to my master." Poins was wrong: desire has not outlived performance. Codpiece time comes round again and Plump Jack lives!

This is a heartening conclusion to a brilliant scene and yet we suspect Shakespeare of suggesting that Falstaff is coming to the end of his strategies. This suspicion is strengthened by the King's magnificent speeches in the next scene on the book of fate, the revolution of the times, and the necessity of meeting one's necessities. The scene that follows informs us that old Double is dead and John of Gaunt, who loved him well, is dead and death is certain, very sure, all shall die, and that the one way left of coping with that perception seems to be to let one's shallow mind wander quickly to the price of a good yoke of bullocks at Stamford Fair. Yet Falstaff continues to labor cheerfully in his fraudulent vocation, and it is not until act 5, scene 3 that we discover that he has been doing battle with time and the prospect of death by employing one strategy more than the four we have already examined. Pistol interrupts senility's saturnalia in Gloucestershire with news of yet another death: the old king is dead as nail in door. Falstaff, whom Shallow and Silence have kept quietly amused to this point, now explodes with excitement: "I am Fortune's steward . . . I know the young King is sick for me . . . the laws of England are at my commandment . . . woe to my Lord Chief Justice!" This is the revelation of a life illusion. Since the first time we saw him in the second scene of the Henriad, Falstaff has never repeated to Hal or us his speculations on what will happen when the Prince becomes the King. We realize that he much overestimates Hal's devotion to sack and laughter, but we have small reason to know, until we find out, that Falstaff thinks Hal's accession will put the laws of England at Sir John's commandment. What here stands revealed is Falstaff's last strategy, his secular, temporal version of a religious faith in one's election to eternal salvation. Falstaff copes with his condition by living in hope, as which of us does not. We must cling to our faith in that intervening event (the doctorate, tenure, the professorship, retirement) which will with millennial effect transform the quality of our existence. Delusive hope was included in Pandora's box lest we should despair and destroy ourselves. What kills Sir John is the destruction of his delusive hope and the consequent knowledge that his future does not exist.

He would have died anyway. Falstaff, like everybody else, is killed by death. But that death is designed by Shakespeare to show us something. The King kills Falstaff's heart, but what impels the King to do so is the desire to do his royal duty by laboring in his vocation. I lack the time to demonstrate why I think Henry of Monmouth stands for the Protestant ethic but I believe that, consciously or not, Shakespeare has transposed into his early-fifteenth-century action the uncompleted spiritual and political struggles of the 1590s. Hal's psychomachia is a battle between Carnival and Lent, and Falstaff is on the losing side. Hal and the Protestant Ethic reject Falstaff, but Shakespeare does not reject Falstaff nor does he reject Hal for rejecting Falstaff.

Falstaff defines the Protestant Ethic by being what it isn't, but also by being a different variety of what it is: a means of coping with the fears engendered by the realities of the human condition. The ethic defeats Falstaff because of the superior strength that derives from the religious faith on which it is based—a faith that enables it to cope with our fears by denying that the realities that inspire them are ultimately real, by asserting that linear time will give way to eternity and that death is a transition to eternal life. Falstaff's being what he is, however, poses a great question to the ethic's answer: may not the ethic's faith be as illusory a strategy as any of Falstaff's, finally a form of delusive hope itself? Hal, in accepting his necessary form, must reject Falstaff because the Protestant ethical form cannot encompass the question Falstaff poses. But Shakespeare's art can and does. It encompasses, as always, question and answer and the questioning of the answer. And the questioning of the questioning, for what is the Falstaff action but a demonstration of the inevitable inadequacy of the strategies of which his character is composed? Shakespeare's sense, whether comical or tragical or tragical-comical-historical-pastoral, seems to me to be always interrogative. For me the great thing about Shakespeare's art is its ability simultaneously to reveal and accept our inadequacies, above all the inadequacy of our answers. The motto carved on the temple of our particular oracle is, "Your answers questioned here."

Ronald R. Macdonald

Uneasy Lies: Language and History in Shakespeare's Lancastrian Tetralogy (1984)

There has always been uncertainty about what we call Shake-speare's "histories." The genre (if it is a genre) seems inherently unstable under critical scrutiny, always threatening to become something else, to slide over into other generic modes about which there is firmer agreement, to become simply tragedy (*Richard II*) or comedy (*1 Henry IV*), or dramatic satire (*2 Henry IV*). Yet, with the possible exception of early work like *The Comedy of Errors*, Shakespeare seems never to have been willing to accept the traditional genres quite as he found them, and the evidence of impurity, even in the lighthearted romantic comedies, is well known. We will never find in the Shakespearean canon the kind of generic purity that a more strictly classical temperament would consider indispensable.

Yet something does distinguish Shakespeare's histories, particularly the mature work of the second tetralogy here to be considered. I hope I will not be accused of tautology in saying that the "something" is a scrupulous concern for history, for by "history" I do not mean a narrative of events, the "story" of the past, but a concern with processes and the inner necessities of historical change, the mechanisms of transition, the deep and nearly invisible shifts in thinking and assumptions that form the basis of what we call in retrospect, and partly for interpretive convenience, "epochs." History in this sense was, for Shakespeare, not a compilation of events (set down in the chronicles in apple-pie

From *Shakespeare Quarterly*, 35 (1984). Reprinted by permission of *Shakespeare Quarterly*.

order), on which he could hang a series of brilliantly conceived (if fundamentally ahistorical) dramatic characters. It was, rather, an extra-personal—if not quite impersonal—phenomenon, playing itself out in different registers in the huge cast of characters that peoples the tetralogy. I am aware that it is not usual to credit Shakespeare with this kind of sophisticated historical understanding; indeed, it is only in our century that it has become usual to credit him with sophistication at all.[1] Yet I do so, for once we have abandoned the "native wood-notes wild" hypothesis, rich and complex vistas are open to us. Protests about over-reading often mask a nostalgia for a simple and "natural" Shakespeare, whose small Latin and less Greek are part of his charm. I believe that no reading which makes sense can fairly be called an over-reading.

Because I have said roughly what I mean by history, and because I will refer to "myths" in what follows, I had better say roughly what I mean by myths. I mean neither those colorful tales of gods and goddesses in ancient times, nor "archetypal" patterns in the plays themselves, but, quite simply, the stories men tell one another to achieve political order and consensus. Let me begin by proposing a theory, itself perhaps a myth of origins, which suggests why it is that men speak of kings as "anointed," as deputies elected by the Lord, and what they hope to accomplish by speaking in this by no means inevitable fashion.

Say that the language of sacred kingship arises in response to a fundamental contradiction in the feudal system as Shakespeare understood it. That contradiction may be brought to the surface by wondering why a feudal system should have a king at all, for feudal society is marked by the formation of *many* centers of power, independent families with bands of retainers, each internally bound together by blood ties and *comitatus* loyalty. To speak of a centralized monarchy in a situation which yields, in effect, a number of private armies verges on paradox. I make no attempt to explain (for I really do not know) why it is that monarchies arise in the first place. Perhaps the explanation implicit in 1 Samuel.viii, that the presence of a common enemy leads a pluralistic tribal society to seek centralized leadership, is as good as any. My subject is not, in any case, the origin of monarchy, but the linguistic conventions that sustain it, the conventions that attempt to manage certain fundamental contradictions which threaten disruption.

It seems clear that in a feudal system the language of sacred kingship does not begin by naming those powers and perquisites that are naturally present in the person of the king and in the monarchic institution, but by naming precisely those that are not naturally present. The king is not called "God's anointed," one does not speak of the divinity that hedges a king because the king really *is* supreme and untouchable, but because he is patently vulnerable, because in many ways his position is the shakiest one in the pluralistic feudal world. If there is something shrilly hysterical about Richard's manic swing from the extreme position that sees the king as inviolate and inviolable, to the equally extreme position that sees him as the quintessential victim (kings may be deposed, slain in war, poisoned by their wives, killed as they sleep—"all murthered," says Richard), there is yet the force of insight in his extremity. And we remember that the phrase about the divinity that hedges a king comes from the fratricidal Claudius of Denmark, the most unanointed, so to speak, of Shakespearean monarchs. We may admire (some may even envy) the cool arrogance it must take for one in his position to use the phrase, but we will scarcely accept it from him without protest.

The vocabulary is thus deployed in an attempt to patch up a contradiction, to redress an imbalance, to achieve political consensus. As long as the achieved consensus remains virtually unanimous, as long as it is taught early on to the young, like the very language on which it depends for transmission, it can continue to masquerade, however uneasily, as a description of the nature of things. Thanks to an apparently incorrigible tendency of the human mind to confound culture and nature,[2] it will be understood not as a collective fabrication of the social order with discernible historical origins, but as a part of the metaphysical order handed down from on high at the creation.

But such consensuses are notoriously fragile. Any essentially secular and social construct, which has managed to get itself promoted to the status of the nature of things, so that it is viewed as the original creation of God and an expression of His will, is liable to be asked for its credentials, to prove that its origin lies in the mind of God, and not, as it seems to do as a matter of fact, in the minds of men. The initiative may well come from a child, who has as yet to master the language of the social order to the point where it is part of his unconscious stock-in-trade. In fact, as we shall see, it is more accurate to say that such a child has not yet allowed that language to master him. "The emperor has no clothes," the candid child observes in Andersen's tale. He has not yet come under the sway of the bizarre notion that the emperor's word is as good as the fact; and, not being subject to this mastering assumption, he will not be surprised to learn that the insane project of appearing in public stark naked originated with an unscrupulous tailor in possession of a bright idea. In what follows, we will encounter the emperor in the slender person of King Richard II, the child in the more robust person of Henry Bullingbrook, and the tailor in the huge bulk of Jack Falstaff.

What follows also falls into three parts, corresponding roughly to the dialectical moments of thesis, antithesis, and synthesis. The first part ends with Richard, whose thesis has collided with the antithetical Bullingbrook and his fellow conspirators, including Hotspur. The second ends with Hotspur, who has now become the antithesis of an antithesis in that he is engaged in conspiracy against the very Lancastrian throne he has previously helped to establish. His veering about expresses what will happen to Bullingbrook as Henry IV, and it is on the complex figure of the new king, traversed by contradiction, yet attempting a reluctant and uneasy synthesis, that the third part comes to rest. The triadic structure of my argument thus seeks to reveal some unsuspected similarities among three heterogeneous and apparently ill-sorted figures, and to plot those figures as three points converging.

I

Briefly, what the emperor learns from the child and what Richard learns from Bullingbrook is that you don't need any water at all (let alone all the water in the rough, rude sea) to wash the balm off an anointed king. The usurpation brings to awareness the essentially secular, *fabricated* character of the political order. The awareness arrives with the force of Platonic anamnesis, the unforgetting of what we knew all along; in contemporary terms it effects what Freud called the return of the repressed. Amidst the wreckage of the institution of sacred kingship,

Richard must learn, somewhat in the manner of Molière's bourgeois gentleman, that he has actually been speaking prose all his
life. His words have no privileged efficacy, certainly not the magical force that the old consensus seemed to confer upon them.
Perhaps even more important, his power to silence others depends solely on their acquiescing in being silenced. Here is Thomas Mowbray responding to Richard's sentence of banishment:

> A heavy sentence, my most sovereign liege,
> And all unlook'd for from your Highness' mouth.
> A dearer merit, not so deep a maim
> As to be cast forth in the common air,
> Have I deserved at your Highness' hands.
> The language I have learnt these forty years,
> My native English, now I must forgo,
> And now my tongue's use is to me no more
> Than an unstringed viol or a harp,
> . . . . .
> Within my mouth you have enjail'd my tongue,
> Doubly portcullis'd with my teeth and lips, . . .
> (I.iii.154-62, 166-67)[3]

These are the words of an old loyalist, assenting to the underlying assumption that the king's speech (his sentence in a number
of senses) has force. But even in this apparently unproblematic,
ritualistic tribute to the king's verbal efficacy, there lurk certain
troubling hints of what has been repressed, and now fairly clam-
ors for expression. For in saying that he deserves a better fate at
Richard's hands, Mowbray must allude, whether he intends to or
not, to his loyal silence concerning Richard's conniving in the
murder of Thomas of Woodstock, a very real silence that precedes
any ritualistic sentence of banishment and the merely metaphorical silence attendant upon it. Richard has "enjail'd" Mowbray's
tongue in the perfectly ordinary sense that he has gotten him to
promise to keep quiet about the murder of Woodstock. That
Mowbray now abides by this promise is not the result of some
mysterious power inhering in the words of the king, but the
result of his loyalty and sense of personal honor. And it is precisely on this prior silence, the product of the give and take of
political conspiracy, that such power as Richard has very materially rests.

It is remarkable that Shakespeare nowhere passes moral judgment on the murder of Woodstock. It may, indeed, and for all we are told, have been the smartest thing to do in the circumstances. Perhaps it has been Richard's only means of consolidating his power, hard won from the Lords Appellant in the previous decade. But what really interested Shakespeare was that the move, whatever its merits, was *truly* political, a matter of agreements, trade-offs, the give and take of bargains. Whatever the circumstances of Woodstock's death, and whoever is implicated, Richard has not brought it about by a magical decree. But in banishing Mowbray, Richard attempts to take refuge in the notion of the king's magical and ritual power. In so doing he becomes embroiled in enormous difficulty, for he attempts to solve a real problem by imaginary means.

This is not to deny, of course, that there will be plenty of occasions when it will be expedient and shrewd for the king to speak as if he had not only magical powers, but a virtual monopoly of divine vengeance. Henry IV will do this repeatedly, usually with an eye for contingencies, and very much alive to the possibility that no one will believe him. But this is still to speak politically, to use the vocabulary of sacred kingship as a special language aimed at bringing about secular solutions. It is not to embrace as truths those things the special language enables you to say.

But Richard does not use the language of sacred kingship: he allows it to use him. In surrendering himself entirely to the assumptions inherent in the system, he represses the altogether pertinent fact that the divinity that hedges a king is an ambiguous concept. If there really is such a divinity, it hedges a king in two senses: it hedges him in, and it hedges him off; it at once protects him, and sets real limits to his power. It is surely the second meaning that Richard has forgotten in his attempt to cover political action with ritualistic and magical means, to deny the palpable contradiction of a divinely anointed king engaging in political maneuvering.

This is perhaps Richard's real abdication, that in insisting on his role as *rex*, he forgets he must also be *dux*,[4] and the scene later on (IV.i), where he actually gives Bullingbrook the crown,' is but the seal and capstone to it. Richard's attempt to deny the historical and political character of his world is no more successful than most attempts at repression, though it is only in the heightened vision of drama that the repressed returns with the signal clarity with which Henry Bullingbrook returns to England. But there is much that is deeply and humanly moving about Richard's failure, and it is certainly a mistake to read his tragedy simply as a tragedy of character, the collapse of a shrill and rather precious neurotic in a situation that could have been successfully managed by a different personality. Shakespeare certainly differentiated Richard's personality profoundly, he certainly succeeded in creating a compelling and complex dramatic person, but this should not obscure the fact that it is Richard's distinct and unenviable role to enact and clarify certain paradoxes that do not stem from his idiosyncrasies, but are latent in the political order.[5] He must live those paradoxes for all to see, and not the least of these is the fact that the more he insists on his power as the anointed king, the less real power he wields.

Richard is abetted in contradiction by his friends quite as much as by his enemies. There is much talk of flatterers and flattery in *Richard II*, and the Lancastrian faction is fond of conjuring the bogey of hypocritical and ill-intentioned friends, who are leading the king astray for self-serving reasons. But a careful search of the play will fail to turn up any clear-cut examples of such friends. It is as if the Lancastrians, in speaking of evil flatterers, were trying to evoke the world of the first tetralogy with its stage villains and quasi-devils, as well as its saviors. Such talk has ultimately the effect of reminding us of the altogether different world we have entered with the second tetralogy. That world is too stubbornly concrete to yield to the simple moral patterns that men try to impose on it.

Evidence of this concreteness is partly furnished by the inadequacy of the existing idiom to manage the complexities of the actual, historical situation. Those critical of Richard are, willynilly, his flatterers quite as much as those who remain loyally silent. Here is Gaunt, for instance, advising Richard from his deathbed:

> Now He that made me knows I see thee ill,
> Ill in myself to see, and in thee, seeing ill.
> Thy death-bed is no lesser than thy land,

> Wherein thou liest in reputation sick,
> And thou, too careless patient as thou art,
> Commit'st thy anointed body to the cure
> Of those physicians that first wounded thee.
> A thousand flatterers sit within thy crown,
> Whose compass is no bigger than thy head,
> And yet, [incaged] in so small a verge,
> The waste is no whit lesser than thy land.
>
> (II.i.93–103)

In the very act of denouncing flatterers, Gaunt is constrained to use the language of sacred kingship, to speak of the king's anointed body, and to suggest the analogy between the health of that body and the health of the land as a whole. It is not that Gaunt wishes to flatter Richard (quite the opposite), but that the only language available to him contains and supports the contradictions and confusions in the system of sacred kingship that are emerging with the return of Bullingbrook. Gaunt's deathbed speech is in reality a tissue of proverbs and homilies, all a good deal too neat to manage the concrete complexities of the historical moment:

> Methinks I am a prophet new inspir'd,
> And thus expiring do foretell of him:
> His rash fierce blaze of riot cannot last,
> For violent fires soon burn out themselves;
> Small show'rs last long, but sudden storms are short;
> He tires betimes that spurs too fast betimes;
> With eager feeding food doth choke the feeder;
> Light vanity, insatiate cormorant,
> Consuming means, soon preys upon itself.
>
> (II.i.31–39)

It is not that Gaunt's string of proverbs does not contain some truth, but that it is not prophetic in any useful sense. His speech becomes, with its iterations and heavy emphases, an attempt to conjure an England which, if it ever existed at all, is now certainly dying along with Gaunt himself:

> This blessed plot, this earth, this realm, this England,
> This nurse, this teeming womb of royal kings.
> . . . . .

> This land of such dear souls, this dear dear land,
> Dear for her reputation through the world,
> Is now leas'd out—I die pronouncing it—
> Like to a tenement or pelting farm.
> England, bound in with the triumphant sea,
> Whose rocky shore beats back the envious siege
> Of wat'ry Neptune, is now bound in with shame,
> With inky blots and rotten parchment bonds;
> That England, that was wont to conquer others,
> Hath made a shameful conquest of itself.
> Ah, would the scandal vanish with my life,
> How happy then were my ensuing death!
>
> (II.i.50–51, 57–68)

We will meet this relatively flat-footed repetitiveness in the discourse of others: it is always an indication that the speaker is in the presence of a concrete circumstance he has no real power to control. Gaunt's concluding wish that his death might be a sacrifice to relieve England of scandal contains the residue of magical thinking. If there is a way out of difficulty, it lies not in magical expiation, but in facing language and the ambiguities it generates, perhaps in working through those "inky blots and rotten parchment bonds" that Gaunt simply wishes away in contempt.

The homiletic idiom is bankrupt in the world of *Richard II*, for it has no power to govern the ways in which men really behave. Bullingbrook significantly ignores it. Not for him the consolations of philosophy:

> Teach thy necessity to reason thus:
> There is no virtue like necessity.
> Think not the King did banish thee,
> But thou the King. Woe doth the heavier sit
> Where it perceives it is but faintly borne.
> Go, say I sent thee forth to purchase honor,
> And not the King exil'd thee.
>
> (I.iii.277–83)

This begins to anticipate Polonius, and it has about the same success in restraining Bullingbrook as Polonius' wise saws have in restraining Laertes. Bullingbrook will not pretend that he has banished the king: he will, indeed, banish him. My point is simply that Richard is not the only one in the play who unreflectingly

allows the established idiom to speak in him, rather than using
that idiom in all self-consciousness as a means to a political end.
Richard's volatile personality drives him to extreme positions, to
be sure, but those positions do have the merit of exposing the
contradictions inherent in the established idiom that everyone
else is willing to leave unexamined. Thus to Aumerle's and Car-
lisle's gentle promptings to action, Richard characteristically responds with a metaphor that he does not quite recognize as a
metaphor:

> So when this thief, this traitor Bullingbrook,
> Who all this while hath revell'd in the night,
> Whilst we were wand'ring with the antipodes,
> Shall see us rising in our throne, the east,
> His treasons will sit blushing in his face,
> Not able to endure the sight of day,
> But self-affrighted tremble at his sin.
>
> (III.ii.47–53)

Richard takes the extreme position that, if what the language of
sacred kingship seems to be saying is really true, if he really is
God's anointed, then he should not have to lift a finger to retain
his kingdom. Battles are, of course, not won with glorious angels
in heavenly pay, but Richard's uncompromising stand, by taking
the established idiom at its word, at least tests that idiom, ultimately finding it inadequate to the real and historical facts of the
matter. Having wrung from the idiom a confession of its real
inadequacy, Richard will go on to remake a poetic language
which, if impotent, is still in touch with a tangible world:

> In winter's tedious nights sit by the fire
> With good old folks and let them tell [thee] tales
> Of woeful ages long ago betid;
> And ere thou bid good night, to quite their griefs,
> Tell thou the lamentable tale of me,
> And send the hearers weeping to their beds.
> For why, the senseless brands will sympathize
> The heavy accent of thy moving tongue,
> And in compassion weep the fire out,
> And some will mourn in ashes, some coal-black,
> For the deposing of a rightful king.
>
> (V.i.40–50)

This is in many ways the discourse we have known all along, and Richard's characteristic extravagance, his narcissism, his tendency to see himself as a character in a story ("For God's sake, let us sit upon the ground / And tell sad stories of the death of kings," III.ii.155–56) are fully in evidence. But what is in some respects the most extravagant image of his farewell to his queen, the image of the firelogs weeping at his fate, is grounded in observation of the concrete. Anyone who has ever watched a green log burn will know what he is talking about, and anyone who has built a fire with green wood will know that it can "weep" a fire out. This is a fundamentally sounder metaphor (and Richard treats it *as* a metaphor, and nothing more) than talk of angels in heavenly pay. Green logs are real. Angels must remain a supposition.

It is not, of course, that Richard achieves an idiom adequate to political realities, though he does achieve an authentic idiom. He rises to a self-conscious mastery of language that no one else in this play approaches. Richard perhaps glimpses the fact that language, like magic, must be discounted before it can become effective. The man who invokes divine vengeance and expects a prompt bolt of lightning may have a long wait in store for him. He hasn't, after all, completed the trick, for though he may well and truly have sawed the lady in half, he hasn't put her back together again. To insist on what is ultimately fictional power ends up in exposing real weakness. But real weakness, properly managed, may result in real power. It is certainly possible, for instance, to invoke divine vengeance, and all the while be perfectly clear in your mind that divine vengeance has a reputation for unreliability, that it frequently fails to materialize, and, that when it does, it has a notorious tendency to miss its mark. The question here will be the expediency of invoking divine vengeance in the first place. If the truculent and fractious persons with whom you have to deal happen also to be superstitious, you might well murmur something about heavenly retribution. And if something fairly momentous has *already* happened, a decisive battle, say, the victor may choose to call his victory divine vengeance with relative impunity. He invokes it, in effect, after the fact.

But these are matters for the precocious child and the unscrupulous tailor. The emperor, for all his achievement of an authentic poetic idiom, turns his back on history. Who is to say that he does this out of a neurosis the like of which we will never know? For it is not just that Richard fears history: history really *is* a fearful thing. It tells us, not only that actions and events are irreversible, but that we initiate those actions and events, and must bear their consequences. We are all of us at times aware of having all too much power, aware that our words really do make a difference, though it is assuredly not by magical means that they do. It may be futile to work magic, but, given the continuous pain of historical consciousness, it may not be altogether inexplicable that one in Richard's position should try.

II

It would be in some ways convenient to say that we have done with the emperor and are now at liberty to concentrate on the child and the tailor. But the dialectical process in which the past is continually reassumed in the present, the veering about which so often accompanies political upheaval, makes it a difficult matter to forget the emperor entirely. The name of Richard becomes a rallying cry for faction in the vigorous world of the two parts of *Henry IV*, and the memory of the old order, now at enough of a distance that it may be readily sentimentalized, will continue to fascinate even those who have been most materially involved in pulling it down.

To be sure, the discoveries effected by the usurpation are experienced at first as an enormous liberation. So much energy is, in fact, set loose that the man responsible for its liberation, now Henry IV, seems in certain private moments overwhelmed as he contemplates the huge and unruly rabbit he has plucked from what looked like an ordinary-sized hat. He is a man, and in this he is like most of us, not entirely happy about bearing the consequences of his irreversible historical actions. A king who is in the curious position of having denied that the king's words have any privileged efficacy, who has rightly seen that the power of the word lies in its context and not in itself, will be hard pressed to keep his discovery a secret. Certain implications of the usurpation are not lost on John Falstaff, for instance, and he will not fail to point out some embarrassing correspondences in the scheme of the new order. Here he is, trading lines with Prince Hal, admitting quite frankly that he is a thief; in fact, as he says, thievery is his vocation, and "'tis no sin for a man to labor in his vocation" (1 Henry IV, I.ii.104–5). Under other circumstances we would not allow this outrageous extension of the word's reference; we would argue that the criteria in virtue of which we apply the word "vocation" are simply not present in the area of thievery. But if the man now sitting on the throne has, indeed, stolen his crown, has he not in some sense sanctioned the extension of reference that we would otherwise be prone to disallow? If the king resents being called a thief (and he surely does), must he not buy the silence of thieves by allowing them to call their thievery a vocation? Here is Richard's old problem with Mowbray fantastically compounded, for presumably Richard had a choice about entering into conspiracy with Mowbray, though, as we have seen, once in conspiracy he was powerless to get out again. But in a very real sense, Henry, in choosing to steal the crown, has relinquished his freedom to choose his confederates, for he depends on the silence of all who speak English and have the wit to understand the situation he has created. This is perhaps a historical consequence of the usurpation that he has not foreseen.

As Henry enters, willy-nilly, into uneasy alliance with pickpockets, footpads, and similar unsavory types, he must notice not only the presence of unforeseen consequences, but also the absence of certain institutions of convenience generated by the old order that he has swept away with such apparent ease. Consider, for instance, the oath, that locutionary act by means of which men bind themselves, on pain of personal discomfiture, to carry out specific performances. Here is a sampling of oaths, selected not quite at random from the literally hundreds that stuff the language of 1 Henry IV:

1. By the Lord, and I do not, I am a villain.

(I.ii.96)

2. I'll make one, an' I do not, call me villain and baffle me.

(I.ii.100–101)

3. By God, he shall not have a Scot of them,
No, if a Scot would save his soul, he shall not!

(I.iii.214–15)

Henry IV

4. An' it be not four by the day, I'll be hang'd.

(II.i.1–2)

I choose these because they represent a situation, not at all uncommon in the play, where an oath is given and then immediately contravened. The first two, and the clearest examples, are Falstaff's. With the first he swears to reform his wicked ways; with the second, a mere five lines later, he swears to join Hal in stealing a purse. Falstaff makes the outrageous contradiction highly visible by invoking the same penalty (being reduced to the rank of villain) on two incompatible performances. We should be exceedingly wary of believing (as Hal seems to do here) that Falstaff has been caught out, that the contradiction is inadvertent. He *displays* the contradiction, invites our attention to it, precisely in the way he will later underscore a patent fabrication by multiplying men in buckram suits (II.iv.191 ff.). In that later instance Hal will accuse him with some heat of lying about his exploits. The accusation imprudently overlooks the fact that Falstaff's exaggerations are clearly designed to be seen through. He isn't lying, he claims implicitly, but spinning a yarn, and to accuse a yarn-spinner of lying is to make yourself look something of a sore-headed spoilsport. One of the weakest kinds of triumph is to think you have caught a man in a lie, and then have him show that he was only trying to entertain you. The stakes are perhaps somewhat lower in the matter of Falstaff's contradictory oaths, but the principles are similar: catch him out, and you become a killjoy; let the contradiction pass unremarked, and you seem to connive in degrading the whole institution of promising. This real dilemma, conjured up with a couple of apparently casual oaths, suggests that Falstaff's verbal skill is of a very high order.

Not so with the next oath in our sample, which belongs to Hotspur. He is denying his Scottish prisoners to King Henry, and doing this with some force; but fifty lines later, when Worcester has broached the conspiracy against the King, he agrees without demur to deliver them up unransomed. He is by no means aware of the contradiction; he has simply forgotten, in his characteristically hare-brained way, that he has promised anything at all.

The shrewd man may very well break a promise: this is the case with our last oath, which belongs to the unnamed carrier in II.i. He swears that it is four o'clock in the morning (if it is not, he will be hanged); he even offers supporting astronomical evidence: "Charles' wain is over the new chimney" (l. 1-2). Yet when the thief Gadshill, about whom the carrier has every reason to be suspicious, asks him the time, he says "I think it be two a' clock" (l. 33). He is very wisely denying a potential highjacker information about a time when he may expect to find portable property on the road. This is clearly more important in the circumstances than the very remote possibility that anyone will actually offer to hang him for contravening his initial oath. Perhaps the worst that can happen is that Gadshill will glance at Charles's wain over the new chimney and conclude that the carrier is lying. But that risk is certainly worth taking: if it succeeds, the advantage gained is real; if it fails, the consequences are trivial.

But no such careful calculation informs the promises that Hotspur makes and breaks. It may be argued that genuinely to forget a promise is not the same as to break it, and that the forgetful man enjoys a certain moral superiority over the consciously duplicitous one. But there is, for all that, a very high price to be paid for this moral superiority, for you deliver yourself over, body and soul, to those with a deeper understanding of the institution of promising, to those who are more than willing to suffer your old-fashioned talk about honor and justice and right, and then let you pay, for an hour or so of chivalric masquerading at Shrewsbury, with your life. The day belongs, even as it did in Richard's time, to the man who thinks in and through the language he speaks, and not to the man who allows that language to think in him.

The day belongs, in short, at least in the world of *1 Henry IV*, to Falstaff. He has fully mastered one of the lessons that Richard has to teach, that weakness, properly managed, may result in real power. Another characteristic locutionary act in the play, one closely related to the oath, is the boast, an assertion of personal power peculiarly vulnerable to deflation:

> *Gadshill.* We steal as in a castle, cock-sure; we have the receipt of fern-seed, we walk invisible.
> *Chamberlain.* Nay, by my faith, I think you are more beholding to the night than to fern-seed for your walking invisible.
>
> (II.i.85-90)

Glendower. I can call spirits from the vasty deep.
Hotspur. Why, so can I, or so can any man,
  But will they come when you do call for them?
                                                                            (III.i.52–54)

Falstaff. But, as the devil would have it, three misbegotten
  knaves in Kendal green came at my back and let drive at
  me, for it was so dark, Hal, that thou couldest not see thy
  hand.
Prince. These lies are like their father that begets them, gross
  as a mountain, open, palpable.
                                                                            (II.iv.221–26)

The difference between Falstaff's boast and those of Gadshill and
Glendower is simply that Falstaff offers his in full awareness of
the way in which it renders him vulnerable. Indeed, his vulnerability is so obvious that the prudent man will be wary of it, and
suspect that it conceals a trap.

In *2 Henry IV*, Falstaff will speak of turning "diseases to commodity": "'Tis no matter if I do halt, I have the wars for my color,
and my pension shall seem the more reasonable. A good wit will
make use of any thing" (I.ii.245–48). It is a good description of
Falstaff's strategy in general, for he is continually presenting
himself as weak and vulnerable in order to gain advantage. Asked
to impersonate the king in a play *ex tempore* (and much of Falstaff's
behavior elsewhere might be described as a play *ex tempore*, for
he is above all a brilliant improviser), he elects to do the part "in
King Cambyses' vein," that is, in the patently artificial and old-
fashioned ranting style of Thomas Preston. Falstaff embraces
incompetence (and King Cambyses' vein turns out to sound oddly
like the euphuistic prose of John Lyly) in order to play what is in
fact a deep and complicated game. For in presenting himself as a
clumsy actor, Falstaff manages to insinuate with utter impunity
the very disloyal suggestion not only that the real king is a player-
king (because he has no lineal title to the office of anointed king
which he now fills), but that his monarchical impersonation is
transparent and unconvincing. The style of Thomas Preston (or
John Lyly) is the appropriate one for the part of King Henry
precisely because it *is* artificial and obvious:

That thou art my son I have partly thy mother's word, partly
my own opinion, but chiefly a villainous trick of thine eye,

and a foolish hanging of thy nether lip, that doth warrant
me. If then thou be son to me, here lies the point: why being
son to me, art thou so pointed at? Shall the blessed sun of
heaven prove a micher and eat blackberries? a question not
to be ask'd. Shall the son of England prove a thief and take
purses? a question to be ask'd.

(*1 Henry IV*, II.iv.403–10)

Falstaff avoids any unseemly explicitness, but the nimble play
with the homophones "sun" and "son" is rather dazzling. To the
ear, the phrase "son of England" is indistinguishable from "sun of
England," a well-known locution for the reigning monarch. It is a
question to be asked, since the present sun of England has,
indeed, proved a thief, and not of paltry purses, but of a throne.
Falstaff's pretended vulnerability reveals Henry's very real vulnerability at a deeper level.

To speak effectively in the new world created by the usurpation requires the exploitation of all the figurative resources of
language, of irony, of understatement, of wary hyperbole and
deft paronomasia. The days are gone when simple grandiloquence of the "This land of such dear souls, this dear dear land"
kind will do. When in the deposition scene of *Richard II* Bullingbrook asks Richard if he is contented to resign the crown, Richard's riddling reply, "Ay, no, no ay" (IV.i.201), is something more
than idle play with the homophones "ay" and "I." Richard has
come to realize that a language that can only speak of either/or,
that can generate no discourse governing the in-between, is inadequate to cover the complex of feelings he is now experiencing.
His equivocation is the true expression of his inability to answer
Bullingbrook's bald question with anything like the clarity Bullingbrook seems to require.

The changes of history demand changes of language, and to
survive in the world of the two parts of *Henry IV* is to learn to
speak in ways that are adequate to the occasion. Much of Hal's
"education" in the course of the plays, if that is what it is, may be
described as his attempt to master new languages, to be able to
"drink with any tinker in his own language" (II.iv.19); to be able to
speak like Hotspur ("'Give my roan horse a drench,' says he, and
answers, 'Some fourteen,' an hour after; 'a trifle, a trifle,'"
II.iv.106–8); to speak like a king; or to speak like himself:

> I know you all, and will a while uphold
> The unyok'd humor of your idleness,
> Yet herein will I imitate the sun.
>
> (*1 Henry IV*, I.ii.195–97)

The homophonic play (which at this early stage, when Hal tends to sound a bit smug, may not be fully conscious) suggests "imitate the son." The real task, in the shifting and ambiguous world created by the usurpation, is to be yourself. This is not a matter of the "naturalness" of manner tirelessly recommended in books of etiquette and treatises on how to succeed. It is a rigorous process of learning the languages of others and inventing a language of your own. When in the first reconciliation scene, Hal replies to his father's long sermon on the proper behavior exemplified by his aristocratic ancestors, his reply is anything but casual: "I shall hereafter, my thrice-gracious lord, / *Be more myself*" (III.ii.92–93). And we will not be surprised to find him at the very end of *Henry V* learning yet another language, this time the French of his affianced Kate.

It is those who do not grow in language, who do not submit themselves to its shifting substance and stubborn materiality, who are defeated by history in the world of the Henry IV plays. Hotspur is first in this group, because, for all his eloquence, he has a thoroughly naïve relation to the language he speaks. There is so much in him to remind us of the new order that it is easy to underestimate the extent to which he abandons himself to the aristocratic myths of the old order. Yet his gaze is basically retrospective, and it is in his casualness with language, and particularly in his unreflective relation to the institution of promising, that we can discover his allegiances most clearly. Here is Hotspur in soliloquy, congratulating himself warmly on the excellence of the anti-Lancastrian conspiracy:

> By the Lord, our plot is a good plot as ever was laid, our friends true and constant: a good plot, good friends, and full of expectation; an excellent plot, very good friends. . . . Is there not my father, my uncle, and myself? Lord Edmund Mortimer, my Lord of York, and Owen Glendower? is there not besides the Douglas? have I not all their letters to meet me in arms by the ninth of the next month?
>
> (*1 Henry IV*, II.iii.15–19, 23–28)

We should be suspicious of Hotspur's way of upping the verbal ante here ("a good plot, good friends. . . . an excellent plot, very good friends"), for, as the example of Richard made clear, you can't make a thing so by saying it, nor a friend true by heaping him with honorific adjectives. Wishes are not horses, they are words, and that is why beggars have to walk. Hotspur's touching faith in the written promises of his fellow conspirators, in the letters he has in hand, is rather cruelly rewarded when, of the good friends he mentions here, all but two fail to show up and do battle.

III

I do not want to leave the impression that in Richard's day (or any other) no one broke promises. We have seen that a man's word is never in fact a magical guarantee of anything, and that men keep promises because, for whatever reasons, they choose to keep them. We have been concerned with the institution of promising, a matter of consensus, not a matter of some mysterious power actually present in words. It is doubtful that any society can securely maintain for long the collective fiction that words bind when men choose not to be bound. Too much happens to contradict it: divine vengeance invoked will fail to materialize, men under oath will continue to renege after consulting private interest. But this sensible and hard-headed view should not obscure the fact that there are in every society a few people who believe the myth of verbal magic some of the time, and still others who would like to believe it. There is often a very fine line between wishing something were so and believing you can bring it about by wishing. We are all liable at times to confuse imagination with power, which is one reason why words must be discounted if they are to have any real power at all. Perhaps kings are particularly vulnerable, since they tend to be surrounded by flatterers, by men who see it as their job to support the confusion. If the king does not smell them out, as Lear finally does on the heath, he may come to believe that he really is everything. But we know that this is a lie; the king is not ague-proof.

King Henry, shrewd man of the new order that he is, is yet

not immune to this danger. He is certainly capable of wishing, and his wishes are revealing. He wishes, for instance, that his eldest son would behave better, be an old-fashioned gentleman like Northumberland's son Hotspur:

> O that it could be prov'd
> That some night-tripping fairy had exchang'd
> In cradle-clothes our children where they lay,
> And call'd mine Percy, his Plantagenet!
>
> (*I Henry IV*, I.i.86–89)

Henry is perfectly in possession of himself here, and we shall hardly credit him with a belief in fairies on the basis of these lines. They hint, however, at a genuinely dialectical phenomenon in which a process begins to veer back on itself, in which the man who succeeded in pulling down the old consensus now looks back on its ruins in search of those consolations mere history refuses to provide. In his first reconciliation with Hal, Henry will speak a language which on one level is designed to scold a wayward boy, but which is nonetheless obliquely eloquent of Henry's own longings for order and clarity, for an unambiguous world where good and evil are readily identifiable and rewards and punishments are symmetrically distributed. There is a conundrum implicit in the lines that follow, which turns out to be as pertinent to the relationship between kings and their subjects as it is to the relationship between parents and their children: who will scold the scolder?

> I know not whether God will have it so
> For some displeasing service I have done,
> That in his secret doom, out of my blood
> He'll breed revengement and a scourge for me;
> But thou dost in thy passages of life
> Make me believe that thou art only mark'd
> For the hot vengeance, and the rod of heaven,
> To punish my mistreadings. Tell me else,
> Could such inordinate and low desires,
> Such poor, such bare, such lewd, such mean attempts,
> Such barren pleasures, rude society,
> As thou art match'd withal and grafted to,
> Accompany the greatness of thy blood,
> And hold their level with thy princely heart?
>
> (*1 Henry IV*, III.ii.4–17)

This language, on careful examination, proves to be full of odd displacements and skewed emphases. Henry calls his own misdoings "mistreadings"; he speaks vaguely of "some displeasing service" for which God must be angry with him. But these misdoings he so evasively names were once called usurpation and regicide, and still would be if some were empowered to speak freely. Henry's language thus reduces what are (by some standards) enormities to mere misdemeanors, at the same time that it takes Hal's misdemeanors (which amount, after all, to some youthful pranks and a couple of drinks with the boys) and promotes them to enormities—"such poor, such bare, such lewd, such mean attempts." We recognize in Henry's catalogue the same technique of repetition and adjectival onslaught that we remarked in Gaunt's deathbed speech and in Hotspur's soliloquy. And those features are here, as elsewhere, the surest sign that words are at odds with a reality the speaker has no *real* power to control.

In the heady days of the usurpation, Henry certainly did not behave like a man who believed that transgression would be punished swiftly by the efficient operation of the cosmic machine. Yet here he speaks of God breeding "revengement and a scourge," of "hot vengeance, and the rod of heaven," terms which are, by the way, oddly out of proportion to the kinds of sins one can legitimately call "mistreadings." The return of the repressed, which no political revolution ever succeeds in doing away with, operates with full force in these lines, for even as Henry struggles to mitigate his sense of sinfulness by calling usurpation and regicide "mistreadings," his conviction of guilt is bound upon him afresh with the inflated terms he chooses for divine vengeance. It is further remarkable that not once does Henry suggest that God might punish *Hal* for Hal's misdoings—remarkable because, after all, Hal is the one who incurs blame for his own actions, whether we choose to call them sins or the youthful sowing of wild oats. The reasonable expectation that Henry is warning *Hal* of divine displeasure is so powerful that it is something of a struggle for us to see what Henry's lines are really saying. Henry speaks of his own punishment, and in so doing betrays a wish for the moral order he has in another sense denied.

It is understandable that a man who begins by discovering an intoxicating freedom—even *thrones* are there for the taking— should come to long, deep in his soul, for the very sanctions he

has daffed aside. Historical consciousness is painful precisely because it cannot generate a stable and symmetrical world. In the
new order Henry is nominally the most powerful man in the land,
yet he can not even control the behavior of his own flesh and
blood. Meanwhile, he has relinquished the consolations of the old
order, among them a language that seemed to enable men to
speak with authority and conviction about a symmetry of crime
and punishment. Henry is perhaps not the only man who
would—even at the price of his *own* punishment—buy back that
symmetry if only the balefulness of history would allow.

The tinge of nostalgia in Henry's speech, which becomes
much more than a tinge as he sickens throughout the second part
of *Henry IV*, is indicative of a general inertia in language. On
account of this inertia, language tends to lag behind the rapid
changes of historical movement; it tends to continue to be governed, in the face of massive upheaval, by a previous harmony.
This retrograde character of language is particularly in evidence
in the second part of *Henry IV*, where it afflicts even the verbally
nimble Falstaff. It puts visible strain on certain words whose
meanings are beginning to be placed in doubt by history, words so
common that they seem, without question, to designate a readily
distinguishable segment of reality. "Gentleman" is such a word,
and when the Lord Bardolph arrives at Northumberland's castle
with a glowing report of rebel victory, he does not hesitate to
guarantee the truth of his report by invoking the breeding of the
gentleman from whom he has had it:

> I spake with one, my lord, who came from thence,
> A gentleman well bred and of good name,
> That freely rend'red me these news for true.
>
> (I.i.25–27)

That the good news proves utterly false is an early indication that
the word "gentleman" is no longer the powerful guarantee that it
once was.

The second part of *Henry IV*, even more than the first, shows
us a world in which the old aristocrat no longer finds himself
alone. There is an extremely vital and energetic underclass in the
plays, and it makes itself increasingly known to the higher orders.
The petit bourgeois merchant, the tradesman, the seller of var-

ious commodities (a word very much in the process of changing
its meaning in this historical watershed) are all jostling for position and asserting their rights.[6] This cast of characters is largely
invisible, hardly more than a succession of names and occupations
cropping up here and there in the speeches of the main characters, yet they are somehow more real than the country folk with
label-names (Mouldy, Wart, Shadow, Feeble) who actually appear
on stage. There is, for instance, the witty physician who says of
Falstaff's urine sample that "the water itself was a good healthy
water, but for the party that ow'd it, he might have moe diseases
than he knew for" (I.ii.3–5). There is Master Tisick, the deputy,
and Master Dumbe, the minister, impressive men in the eyes of
the Hostess. There is, above all, Master Dommelton, the independent mercer, who refuses Falstaff credit:

> Let him be damn'd like the glutton! Pray God his tongue be
> hotter! A whoreson Achitophel! a [rascally] yea-forsooth
> knave, to bear a gentleman in hand, and then stand upon
> security! The whoreson smoothy-pates do now wear noth-
> ing but high shoes, and bunches of keys at their girdles, and
> if a man is through with them in honest taking up, then they
> must stand upon security. I had as live they would put
> ratsbane in my mouth as offer to stop it with security. I
> look'd 'a should have sent me two and twenty yards of satin
> (as I am a true knight), and he sends me security!
>
> (I.ii.34–45)

Falstaff encounters here a stubborn reality, which refuses to
credit an older language (the words "gentleman" and "true
knight") with the power to guarantee that it once had. Falstaff
encounters increasing difficulty, even with the gullible Hostess:

> *Falstaff.* As I am a gentleman!
> *Hostess.* Faith, you said so before.
> *Falstaff.* As I am a gentleman! Come, no more words of it.
>
> (II.i.136–38)

It is not a little ironic that Falstaff should find himself using a
language that has become partly obsolete, for he has been active
in discrediting it. Not only have his escapades put the integrity of
knighthood in doubt; his profound playing with language has
suggested the very transformations that here inconvenience him.

When, as in the first part, "squires of the knight's body" become "squires of the night's body" (I.ii.24), it is not certain whether thieves shall be taken for knights, or knights for thieves. In some sense Falstaff's attempt to give thievery a good name has gone awry in the second part, and succeeded only in giving knighthood a bad one. But what is of real interest is the extent to which Falstaff clings to an idiom whose power has been substantially reduced in the face of historical change. The world of the first part is concerned with a transitional period in between two consolidated orders, a time when the vocabulary of the vanished order still has a certain power, even though the system on which it rested has been virtually dismantled. But such a situation must be inherently unstable. The old appraisive terms are increasingly met with a healthy skepticism on the part of the newly independent underclass, and are in the process of being discarded or redefined. The period when the man skilled in language can seem to rule the world is necessarily short-lived. Language cannot be appropriated permanently, because it is not, finally, property. It is "vulgar" in the literal sense, held in common, and Falstaff's dwindling power in the second part is largely due to the public's decreasing willingness to credit his vocabulary with the power conferred upon it by the vanished order.

We see the tendency to cling to the idiom of the old order nowhere more clearly than in the private moments of Henry IV himself, the very man who has been most practically involved in bringing the old order down. In his first reconciliation with Hal in the first part (III.ii), the fact that he invokes the old standard of aristocratic blood and speaks of Hal's "affections, which hold a wing / Quite from the flight of all thy ancestors" (l. 30–31) is remarkable, but not ultimately surprising. The king's nostalgia for the very order that his actions have so profoundly denied is simply a measure of the historically generated divisions within the man, divisions that are close to the surface in his famous soliloquy in the second part:

> How many thousands of my poorest subjects
> Are at this hour asleep! O sleep! O gentle sleep!
> Nature's soft nurse, how have I frighted thee,
> That thou no more wilt weigh my eyelids down,
> And steep my senses in forgetfulness?

Why rather, sleep, liest thou in smoky cribs,
Upon uneasy pallets stretching thee,
And hush'd with buzzing night-flies to thy slumber,
Than in the perfum'd chambers of the great,
Under the canopies of costly state,
And lull'd with sound of sweetest melody?
O thou dull god, why li'st thou with the vile
In loathsome beds, and leavest the kingly couch
A watch-case or a common 'larum bell?

                                                    (III.i.4–17)

We detect here a rather sentimental portrayal of the lower
orders, some members of which we have just seen in anything
but peaceful repose. The thrust behind Henry's speech is a pastoral longing, and we suspect that his emergent "nostalgia for the
bottom" comes not from his sense of the responsibilities attendant upon high station, but from the guilt of having acquired that
high station in the first place. Envying the lower orders is a
pastoral alibi for the guilt of continuing to possess things got by
doubtful means. Pastoral is an aristocratic myth aimed at covering
up the real character of a longing for the bottom, and the surest
sign of this is that pastoral always wants to have it both ways: it
wills a simple life *and* the perquisites that go with high station.
Shakespeare elsewhere pokes a good deal of fun at this willed
contradiction in pastoral,[7] but here Henry's embracing of the
contradiction is simply the sign of his divided allegiance. He would
like to go on speaking the language of the old order, while enjoying the advantages of the new.

"Uneasy lies the head that wears a crown": this familiar,
sententious utterance contains a telling pun, one that we have
already seen Falstaff exploiting adeptly at Shrewsbury in part
one: "Lord, Lord, how this world is given to lying! I grant you I
was down and out of breath, and so was he, but we rose both at
an instant and fought a long hour by Shrewsbury clock"
(V.iv.145–48). In the world after the usurpation, the head that
wears a crown will always lie, however uneasily, for possession of
the crown depends upon a fabrication. That this has always been
the case is made clear by the example of Richard, but in the old
order perhaps the lie of anointed kingship was not always an

uneasy one. At least it had the tacit support of a consensus. In sweeping away that consensus, Henry acquires an uneasiness that will hereafter be part of the business of ruling.

NOTES

1. At the outset I should like to make clear my debt to Sigurd Burckhardt in much of what follows. His "Swoll'n with Some Other Grief: Shakespeare's Prince Hal Trilogy" in *Shakespearean Meanings* (Princeton: Princeton Univ. Press, 1968), pp. 144–205, takes much the same view of history as the one propounded here. Joseph Porter's *The Drama of Speech Acts: Shakespeare's Lancastrian Tetralogy* (Berkeley: University of California Press, 1979) came to my attention after I had written this article, but I note that we agree about a number of points about speech acts in the Lancastrian plays.

2. Mircea Eliade remarked, "In this total adherence, on the part of archaic man, to archetypes and repetition, modern man would be justified in seeing not only the primitives' amazement at their own first spontaneous and creative free gestures and their veneration, repeated *ad infinitum*, but also a feeling of guilt on the part of man hardly emerged from the paradise of animality (i.e., from nature), a feeling that urges him to reidentify with nature's eternal repetition the few primordial, creative, and spontaneous gestures that had signalized the appearance of freedom." See *The Myth of the Eternal Return, or Cosmos and History* (1949), tr. Willard R. Trask, Bollingen Series XLVI (Princeton: Princeton Univ. Press, 1971), p. 155.

3. *The Riverside Shakespeare*, ed. G. Blakemore Evans, et al. (Boston: Houghton Mifflin, 1974). All subsequent quotations from Shakespeare's plays are taken from this edition.

4. For a succinct statement of this duality in monarchy see Otto Gierke, *Political Theories of the Middle Age*, tr. Frederic William Maitland (Boston: Beacon Press, 1958), pp. 30–37.

5. One such paradox is the doctrine of the king's two bodies, thoroughly discussed by Ernst Kantorowicz in *The King's Two Bodies: A Study in Mediaeval Political Theology* (Princeton: Princeton Univ. Press, 1957). See especially chap. 2, "Shakespeare: King Richard II," pp. 24–41.

6. For an excellent discussion of the shifting meanings of words in history, and specifically of the word "commodity," see Quentin Skinner, "Language and Social Change" in *The State of the Language*, ed. Leonard Michaels and Christopher Ricks (Berkeley: Univ. of California Press, 1980), pp. 562–78.

7. C. L. Barber remarked in discussing *As You Like It* that Touchstone's discussion of the shepherd's life (III.ii.13–22) "mocks the contradictory nature of the desires ideally resolved by pastoral life, to be at once in the court and in the fields, to enjoy both the fat advantages of rank and the spare advantages of the mean and sure estate." See *Shakespeare's Festive Comedy: A Study of Dramatic Form and Its Relation to Social Custom* (1959; rpt. Princeton: Princeton Univ. Press, 1972), p. 227.

Robert N. Watson

The *Henry IV* Plays (1984)

At the end of *Richard II*, Shakespeare's ambitious figures become versions of primal criminals such as Oedipus and Cronus, whose myths associate father/son rivalry with political rebellion. The Henry IV plays use this association to study the evolution of filial identity, the individual's imperative and dangerous growth toward sovereignty. Here, even more elaborately than in *The Tempest*, Shakespeare offers a sort of morality play about an individual's moral and psychological development; but while it may be helpful to make that allegory explicit in a systematic, Freudian way, it is crucial to remember that the playwright uses it as a merely subliminal resonance to his analysis of ambition. Shakespeare exploits his deterministic power over his play-world to simulate a divinely determined world in which ambition is limited by the constitution of the individual as well as the universe. The psychoanalytic allegory which seems to arise naturally from the narrative events is one more way in which Shakespeare makes us feel that there are deep moral imperatives, not only in the universe but also in its human microcosm, for ambition's rise and fall. A coherent pattern attaches to ambition, which may be experienced in similar ways by an individual psyche at one phase in its development, and by English society at a crisis in its historical evolution. In the Henry IV plays, the private and public experiences of ambition are not only congruent, they are simultaneous, and mutually causal.

The rebels in the Henry IV plays suffer their own versions of the ambitious syndrome when they try to replace the reigning king. In *1 Henry IV*, Hotspur and Worcester discuss in suggestive terms the news that Northumberland will not appear for the battle. Hotspur argues that his father will therefore provide

> A rendezvous, a home to fly unto,
> If that the devil and mischance look big
> Upon the maidenhead of our affairs.
> *Worcester.* But yet I would your father had been here.
> The quality and hair of our attempt
> Brooks no division.
>
> (4.1.57–62)

Worcester's fear makes practical sense, but it also reminds us that Northumberland's absence constitutes the sort of bodily division that generally disables Shakespeare's rebels: It is "a very limb lopp'd off" (4.1.43), as Hotspur momentarily admits. When Hotspur subsequently boasts that "our joints are whole," and Douglas rejoins, "As heart can think," the statement is as self-contradictory as Douglas's restatement of the idea: "There is not such a word / Spoke of in Scotland as this term of fear" (4.1.83–85). The Scot has just spoken the word, and the notion of joints as whole as heart can think suggests an unhealthy jumbling of limbs, breast, and brains. The threat to this rebellion's birth is all the greater because Northumberland is figuratively the father of rebellion in these plays, and literally the father of Hotspur, who embodies the rebellious spirit. Without the father's presence at "the maidenhead," the insurrection seems doomed to a sinister, unnatural sort of birth.

In *2 Henry IV*, the implication that rebellion is born only through a dangerous distortion of the procreative process becomes more explicit. Lord Bardolph worries that unless Northumberland's forces arrive, the rebellion will resemble a man's "part-created" construction that must be left "A naked subject to the weeping clouds" of "churlish winter's tyranny." Though the analogy is to the building of an over-ambitious house, the lines immediately following encourage us to recognize the suggestion, on a secondary level, of an infant exposed to the winter by a paternal tyrant, as Oedipus was by Laius, or Perdita by Leontes. Hastings answers:

> Grant that our hopes (yet likely of fair birth)
> Should be still-born, and that we now possess'd
> The utmost man of expectation,
> I think we are so a body strong enough,
> Even as we are, to equal with the King.
>
> (1.3.60–67)

In the same speech, Lord Bardolph also worries about the empty naming and the vegetative death that often accompany rebellion: an insurrection that uses "the names of men in stead of men," he argues,

> Lives so in hope, as in an early spring
> We see th' appearing buds, which to prove fruit
> Hope gives not so much warrant, as despair
> That frosts will bite them.
>
> (1.3.57, 38–41)

The abnormal and premature birth of this uprising generates a nemesis consisting of stillbirth, paternal vengeance, diseased nature, disconnected names, and discordant bodies.

In *1 Henry IV* Glendower portrays his birth as another archetypal perversion of procreation. The archetype here is not a bodily rivalry with the father that must end in stillbirth or infant exposure, but rather the self-induced Caesarean birth by which the father may be overcome. Such a birth—though, significantly, it is merely a boast in Glendower's case—sometimes signals a classical or Renaissance hero's determination to conquer his natural limitations, to surpass his hereditary constraints. When Glendower claims that various disturbances of nature "mark'd me extraordinary" and above "the common roll of men" at his birth, Hotspur replies with a sarcastic, degraded version of Glendower's personal myth:

> Diseased nature oftentimes breaks forth
> In strange eruptions; oft the teeming earth
> Is with a kind of colic pinch'd and vex'd
> By the imprisoning of unruly wind
> Within her womb, which, for enlargement striving,
> Shakes the old beldame earth, and topples down
> Steeples and moss-grown towers. At your birth
> Our grandam earth, having this distemp'rature,
> In passion shook.
>
> (3.1.26–34)

Hotspur has twisted Glendower's analogy between his mother's
labor and the world's eruptions, which carries with it an implicit
claim to autochthonic birth, into its least appealing form—a form
which also allows Hotspur to dismiss Glendower's boast, by metaphor as well as tone, as merely hot air, of a particularly unattractive sort.

Figures in English Renaissance literature whose ambitions
compel them to claim autogenous or autochthonic status often
claim this sort of birth: they carve their own way out of mother-
earth in an eruption of air, and in doing so they topple down the
old towers or trees of paternal sexual authority. Such births, or
rebirths, are in both senses Caesarean.[1] Tamburlaine makes a new
self by martial assertion, disdaining his "parentage" in order to
command a thunderous army who "make the mountains quake, /
Even as when windy exhalations, / Fighting for passage, tilt
within the earth."[2] Spenser's autochthonic giant Orgoglio, the
embodiment of pride and partner of the sexually sinister Duessa,
performs a figuratively Oedipal attack to permit his own Caesarean rebirth:

> The greatest Earth his uncouth mother was,
> And blustring Aeolus his boasted sire,
> Who with his breath, which through the world doth pas,
> Her hollow womb did secretly inspire,
> And fild her hidden caves with stormie yre,
> That she conceiv'd.

This derivation makes it all the more suggestive that "all the earth
for terrour seemd to shake, / And trees did tremble" when Orgoglio advances on Redcrosse. The giant tears "a snaggy
Oke . . . Out of his mothers bowelles," and swings it so hard
that he could strike down "a stony towre"; the wind from that
"thundring" swing, clearly analogous to the force that originally
conceived him, strikes down his rival for Duessa (I.vii.7–14)[3]
When "his dreadfull club" reaches his mother-earth, he seems to
be planting himself to reenact his birth by his own power:

> The idle stroke, enforcing furious way,
> . . . . .
> So deepely dinted in the driven clay,
> That three yardes deepe a furrow up did throw:

> The sad earth wounded with so sore assay,
> Did grone full grievous underneath the blow,
> And trembling with strange feare, did like an
> earthquake show.
>
> (I.viii.8)

The next stanza compares this blow to Jove's lightning—an impregnating force in myth—which "making way, / Both loftie towres and highest trees hath rent, / And all that might his angrie passage stay, / And shooting in the earth, casts up a mound of clay." But Orgoglio's club becomes stuck there, permitting Redcrosse to cut off the arm of the giant, whose resulting howls suggest sexual suffering (I.viii.10-11). Toppled towers and severed arms are still towers and arms in the poem, of course, as cigars in dreams may represent cigars. But the close coincidence of these Oedipal and Caesarean motifs strikes me as significant, particularly because it occurs so consistently in the context of ambitious quests for heroic rebirth.

Milton's Satan is evidence that this archetype survives through Shakespeare's lifetime, and again the creature boasting of rebirth is a creature determined to claim that his own energies have conquered the derivativeness, and hence the fatedness, that limited his aspirations. By his incestuous conspiracy with the parthenogenetic Sin, and with their son Death who so resembles his father, Satan has made an open highway in the windy space beneath the earth, where he himself

> Toil'd out my uncouth passage, forc't to ride
> Th' untractable Abyss, plung'd in the womb
> Of unoriginal *Night* and *Chaos* wild,
> That jealous of thir secrets fiercely oppos'd
> My journey strange, with clamorous uproar
> Protesting Fate supreme.
>
> (Book X, 475-80)[4]

The birth of the rebel Glendower, which Shakespeare revises from Holinshed's account toward this archetype, associates him with a tradition of windy, ambitious, and self-induced rebirths; the efforts of Richard III, Henry IV, Macbeth, and Coriolanus to carve out their own passages to glory may be associated with, and moralized by, the same sexually fraught tradition.

Other symptoms of the ambitious ailment afflict these rebels. When he hears of his son's death in the failed insurrection, Northumberland himself becomes a furious rebel, calling for an end to natural order, individual identity, and family harmony, in a world that has become merely a stage (2 Henry IV, 1.1.153–59). His allies urge him to eradicate rather than exaggerate those characteristic ailments of their cause. If he will join forces with the Archbishop of York, the instinct against rebellion that rendered his son's troops divided creatures and lifeless shadows can be reversed:

> *Morton.* My lord your son had only but the corpse,
> But shadows and the shows of men, to fight;
> For that same word, rebellion, did divide
> The action of their bodies from their souls.
>
> (1.1.192–95)

The archbishop would prefer to blame the ambitious syndrome— the disruption of time's normal order and humanity's normal form—on Henry's bad fatherhood. In repressing his subjects' pleas, Henry has bred a multiheaded and sleepless son in their place:

> The time misord'red doth, in common sense,
> Crowd us and crush us to this monstrous form
> To hold our safety up. I sent your Grace
> The parcels and particulars of our grief,
> The which hath been with scorn shov'd from the court,
> Whereon his Hydra son of war is born,
> Whose dangerous eyes may well be charm'd asleep
> With grant of our most just and right desires.
>
> (4.2.32–40)

Unless the bad son Henry becomes the good father Henry by such concessions, Hastings adds, this unnatural procreation of Hydras through death will permanently replace England's life-giving process of generational succession: "And so success of mischief shall be born, / And heir from heir shall hold his quarrel up / Whiles England shall have generation" (4.2.47–49). Inheritance thus becomes a blight on birth, a doubling and redoubling of miscarriages.

The rebels revealingly describe Henry's violation of his own heritage and Richard's as an archetypal parricide, with themselves in the role of abused parent rather than abusive child:

> *Worcester.* . . . being fed by us you us'd us so
> As that ungentle gull, the cuckoo's bird,
> Useth the sparrow; did oppress our nest,
> Grew by our feeding to so great a bulk
> That even our love durst not come near your sight
> For fear of swallowing.
>
> (*1 Henry IV*, 5.1.59-64)

The simile uses Henry's warlike approach to confirm his identity as an unlineal child, and even implies that he acts this way precisely because he knows he is not a natural heir. Worcester concludes by telling Henry that he and his fellow-rebels "stand opposed by such means / As you yourself have forg'd against yourself," and when Henry compares himself to a father-bee murdered by the child (Prince Hal) he has fed to strength, we recognize that Worcester was speaking more wisely than he was aware of.

Henry answers by dismissing these accusations as merely "the garment of rebellion" and the "water-colors" that "impaint" their excuse for insurrection; he thus locates the rebellion in the realms of costuming and painting that so often characterize ambitious identity in Shakespeare. This accusation, too, rebounds on Henry, without losing its validity as an accusation, when the king becomes a thing of costumes and colors at Shrewsbury:

> *Hotspur.* A gallant knight he was, his name was Blunt,
> Semblably furnish'd like the King himself.
> *Douglas.* A fool go with thy soul, whither it goes!
> A borrowed title hast thou bought too dear.
> Why didst thou tell me that thou wert a king?
> *Hotspur.* The King hath many marching in his coats.
> *Douglas.* Now, by my sword, I will kill all his coats;
> I'll murder all his wardrop, piece by piece,
> Until I meet the King.
>
> (5.3.20-28)

Douglas's remarks carry several unpleasant implications for Henry: first, that his own "borrowed title" of king may prove as costly an acquisition as it was for Blunt, and second, that the kingship may itself be only a wardrobe, clothes with no emperor, since his own act of usurpation has made the royal identity so easy to transfer and divide. When Douglas finally discovers King Henry beneath the colors that have become a disguise rather than a proclamation of identity, he finds him only by a process of elimination that is easily mistaken for a process of multiplication:

> *Douglas.* Another king? they grow like Hydra's heads.
> I am the Douglas, fatal to all those
> That wear those colors on them. What art thou
> That counterfeit'st the person of a king?
> *King.* The King himself, who, Douglas, grieves at heart
> So many of his shadows thou hast met
> And not the very King.
>
> (5.4.25–31)

Again Douglas raises troubling questions for King Henry. Is there actually any "very King" to be met, in the aftermath of a usurpation, or is there merely an assemblage of borrowed robes, painted colors, and two-dimensional shadows? Is "The King himself" yet one more ordinary mortal "That counterfeit'st the person of a king," as Henry's answer can be taken to imply?

Douglas alludes to Hydra merely to express his exasperation at the fact that each time he beheads a king, two new kings seem to appear. But this allusion may also serve to remind us that Henry has pitted himself against the same sort of unbeatable foe. By causing the assassination of the one rightful king, he has created two heads (as the factions are often called) that are vying for the throne; if the kingship has Hydra's heads, it is because Henry has initiated a splitting of identity that his counterfeits at Shrewsbury nicely symbolize. The myth of Hydra, at least in the Henry IV plays, seems to be a cautionary myth about inheritance: Hydra resembles a gruesome family tree, and the monster that must be quelled is the fraternal strife that would arise over the division of property each time a person died, were there no system of legacies. Civilization successfully represses this monster until Richard and Henry unleash it by violating that system, leaving each legacy open to deadly contention. Shakespeare reveals an England resembling the primal societies described in Freud's *Totem and Taboo* and Girard's *Violence and the Sacred*, societies whose rituals are essential to prevent an endless competition for patrimonies and an endless reciprocity of violence.[5] Some seventy lines before the archbishop blames Henry's misdeeds for generating "this Hydra son of war," Shakespeare prepares us to understand the allusion's larger implications by having the archbishop argue that Henry will not dare to execute the rebels after a negotiated peace, "For he hath found to end one doubt by death / Revives two greater in the heirs of life" (4.1.197–98). As Henry's "buried fear . . . Richard of Burdeaux" (*Richard II*, 5.6.31–33) produces the warring heads of Henry and Mortimer, and as Henry's death is expected to produce a war between Hal and some rival, so will the heirs of the archbishop's rebels second their fathers' rebellion, and their heirs will second the seconding, and so on through eternity (4.2.45–49). That is precisely what we see in Shakespeare's version of the War of the Roses, until Richmond cauterizes the wound in God's order (as Hercules cauterized Hydra's severed neck), and thus turns the two heads—the two Houses—miraculously into one.

Henry V's succession provides an interim solution by setting legacies back on a lineal track. That may help explain why Shakespeare has Canterbury describe the miraculous transmigration of Henry IV's solemn virtue into his son, concurrent with the transfer of the royal body politic, as a glorious conquest of "Hydra-headed willfulness" (*Henry V*, 1.1.24–37). Until his glorious transformation, though, Hal is the unnatural "Hydra son" who threatens to become simultaneously the royal heir and the enemy of royal heritage at his father's death. Hal vacillates repeatedly between his disobedient Eastcheap identity and a noble filial identity. When Hal inherits the unlineal crown, he faces the Herculean task of uniting those conflicting identities, as good and bad son, and as subject and monarch, into a single natural successor. Two crucial scenes, in which Henry's conflict with Hal parallels Hal's conflict with himself, prepare us to recognize the ethical imperatives of that task.

Act three, scene two, of *1 Henry IV* begins with Henry's interpreting Hal's misbehavior as a divine punishment for his own misdeeds. Though Henry, as usual, pretends to be slightly uncertain what his own crime might have been, a son's rebellious refusal to rise to the level of his royal blood would be an entirely

appropriate rebuke to his father's rebellious insistence on rising
to claim that royal heritage. The psychoanalytic maxim that the
bad son has bad sons, and the physical maxim that what goes up
must come down, both work to subvert Henry's hopes for a royal
heir:

> I know not whether God will have it so
> For some displeasing service I have done,
> That in his secret doom, out of my blood,
> He'll breed revengement and a scourge for me;
> But thou dost in thy passages of life
> Make me believe that thou art only mark'd
> For the hot vengeance, and the rod of heaven,
> To punish my mistreadings. Tell me else,
> Could such inordinate and low desires,
> Such poor, such bare, such lewd, such mean attempts,
> Such barren pleasures, rude society,
> As thou art match'd withal and grafted to,
> Accompany the greatness of thy blood,
> And hold their level with thy princely heart?
>
> (3.2.4–17)

This insistence on blood finding its own level may be Henry's
effort to bluster away the fact that "his blood was poor" until he
stepped "a little higher than his vow" and usurped Richard's
throne (4.3.75–76). Hal's "affections" may indeed "hold a wing /
Quite from the flight of all thy ancestors," making him "almost an
alien to the hearts / Of all the court and princes of my blood"
(3.2.29–35), but Henry is also on an errant flight from his hereditary place. The system rights itself from within: in the very act of
being a punitively bad son to Henry, Hal is said to resemble
Richard, to stand "in that very line" of the man whose right it was
to place his likeness on the throne (3.2.85–94).[6]

As Henry becomes caught up in the excitement of scolding his
son, his language reveals a recognition that this throne is actually
founded on such externalities as costume rather than such inter-
nalities as blood. He boasts of clothing himself in the simulation
of an inward virtue, and of maintaining his person as if it were a
borrowed garment: he won the people's affection when he
"dress'd myself in such humility / That I did pluck allegiance from
men's hearts," yet retained their respect by keeping "my person

fresh and new, / My presence like a robe pontifical . . ." (3.2.51-
56).⁷ Marvell's warning to Cromwell in the "Horatian Ode" that
"The same arts that did gain / A power must it maintain"
(lines 119–20) seems applicable to Henry here: he discovers that
the kingship gained by replacing a natural identity with an artificial one, replacing a person with a garment, can only be maintained by his remaining a polished costume rather than an authentic human being.

The redefinition of kingship implicit in Henry's usurpation is
inextricably linked to a redefinition of identity, and one result is
that not only Hal, but Sir Walter Blunt, and even Jack Falstaff, can
play the role of King Henry IV with some success (2.4, 5.3). If Hal
is what his father here calls him abusively, "the shadow of succession," there is good reason for it (3.2.99). Even Hal's promise that
he "shall hereafter . . . / Be more myself" (3.2.93) has ironic overtones as a response to his father's criticisms, since Henry has just
finished arguing that he won the throne by retaining an artificial
self, or at least an artificial distance from himself. Whether it is
Hal's irony or Shakespeare's, Henry's effort to define a true heir
is trapped in a contradiction of his own making.

Finally the king manages to express his ultimate fear, the fear
that uncivil disobedience (such as defying a banishment) will
become outright murderous rebellion (such as killing a king). The
way Henry expresses this fear suggests that he is projecting his
own guilty deeds onto Hal, and thus conflating the roles of bad
son and bad subject:

> But wherefore do I tell these news to thee?
> Why, Harry, do I tell thee of my foes,
> Which art my nearest and dearest enemy?
> Thou that art like enough, through vassal fear,
> Base inclination, and the start of spleen,
> To fight against me under Percy's pay,
> To dog his heels and curtsy at his frowns,
> To show how much thou art degenerate.
>   (3.2.121–28)

One of the psychoanalytic tenets about this play is that "Hotspur's rebellion represents also Prince Hal's unconscious parricidal
impulses. Hotspur is the Prince's double."⁸ If this is so, then Hal's

denial of his father's accusation represents a classic Freudian compensation-mechanism: the son's avowed wish to protect the father is really a response to his forbidden desire to destroy that father.[9] But whether events at Shrewsbury simply demonstrate Hal's filial loyalty, or whether they allegorically anatomize the psychological struggle that precedes and permits such loyalty, the crucial fact is that Hal re-establishes his identity as a true son by defeating Hotspur. He does so, on the figurative level, by retreating with that patricidal alter ego to an earlier developmental phase. There they both struggle for Caesarean rebirth with their swords, both seeking glory, but seeking opposite sorts of glory. Separated from his father, rebelling, "this Hotspur, Mars in swathling clothes, / This infant warrior" (3.2.112–13), is doomed to stillbirth in his own blood with his noble name revoked. Hal, in contrast, reverses the usual dangerous pattern of Caesarean rebirth, since his rebirth entails reclaiming, not evading, his lineage:

> I will redeem all this on Percy's head,
> And in the closing of some glorious day
> Be bold to tell you that I am your son,
> When I will wear a garment all of blood,
> And stain my favors in a bloody mask,
> Which wash'd away shall scour my shame with it.
>   (3.2.132–37)

The king is right to take this as a complete answer to the indictment at hand. Hal has discovered a way to prove his royal merit while reconciling blood with garments, and the hereditary self with the adopted self. By drawing the battle back to that quasi-infantile stage, Hal can undo his status as an inferior changeling for "this same child of honor and renown, / This gallant Hotspur" (3.2.139–40). Now it is Hotspur who is abandoned by his father, and Hal who has recovered a healthy lineal identity. The son who was, in several senses, "degenerate," is now, in the same senses, regenerate.

The same pair of intermingled confrontations—Henry against Hal, and Hal's loyalty against a representation of his rebelliousness—appears again in 2 Henry IV, during the crown-stealing sequence (4.5). Shakespeare's willingness to resurrect the doubts that were apparently put to rest by the end of Part One, and to retain so many elements of the first confrontation, suggests that he considered the psycho-symbolic situation very fruitful for exploring his theme. Again the Oedipal threat arises to punish Henry's usurpation, and again the suppression of that threat, by re-enlisting Hal in a healthy filial role, prepares for the martial victory that will affirm the new royal family's place on the throne.

Through most of Part Two, Hal's filial identity is badly in doubt. He is right, both on a personal and a symbolic level, to break Falstaff's head "for liking his father to a singing-man of Windsor" (2.1.89–90): the comparison implies that Henry is a eunuch,[10] his procreative powers ruined like those of Shakespeare's other usurpers, and that Hal therefore cannot be his authentic son or a legitimate successor. In the next scene Hal is reminded that the world still thinks his ambitions and rebelliousness preclude his mourning his father's illness (2.2.39–57). This observation grows out of banter about the ways "kindreds are mightily strengthen'd" by illegitimate births, and leads into two discussions about the ambitious ways people distort their kinship. First, Poins mocks people who seize every conceivable occasion to mention some distant consanguinity with the royal family (2.2.110–18); then Hal mocks Poins for his rumored plan to marry Hal to Poins's sister (2.2.127–41). These ambitious claims to royal kinship are recognizable versions, and hence recognizably symptoms, of Henry's unlineal usurpation and the national disease it caused. Hal, in Eastcheap, is trying to cure that disease by actions precisely opposite to the ambitious claims: he evades his close kinship with Henry, and avoids close contact with the seat of royal power. Naturally his father is unable to recognize the corrective character of this conduct, and the misunderstanding over this paradox sets the stage for the crown-stealing confrontation.

As the scene begins, Henry's visage reveals the ambitious man's emptiness and mutability: "His eye is hollow, and he changes much" (4.5.6). Hal is greeted with the information that "The King your father is dispos'd to sleep," but he soon reminds his father that sleep is forbidden to the ambitious, and reminds us why it is forbidden. Slumber in an unnaturally elevated position—whether literally, as a boy on a masthead (3.1.18–20; cf. *Richard III*, 3.4.99), or figuratively, as a man wrongfully on a throne—is both difficult and dangerous. As soon as Henry lets go, yields to that natural urge to relax, he also implicitly yields to his natural self, and the crown is taken from him. Hal describes the crown as "so troublesome a bedfellow" (4.5.22), as if it were a restless spouse in the king's bed, then steals that spouse from the king's pillow where it was supposed to remain until death did them part. Again the Oedipal overtones are clear, and again they serve a broader purpose than providing a fragmentary psychoanalysis of a character. The fact that Hal must steal his father's "bedfellow" in order to create his royal new self is the most incisive condemnation of his self-promoting impulse.[11]

Henry's response when he awakens sharpens our awareness of an Oedipal pattern, adding to the hint of mother-son incest a clear accusation of patricidal impulses (4.5.63–79) and the suggestion that these impulses have been abetted by a subconsciously chosen error of recognition: "Is he so hasty that he doth suppose / My sleep my death?" (4.5.60–61). The patricidal implications would doubtless have been strengthened for much of the audience by the precedent of *The Famous Victories of Henry V*, in which Hal comes to the brink of actually murdering his father for the crown. Henry's first words to his returning son verify that the mechanisms described in Freud's theories about errors and about the Oedipal impulse are both at work here:

> *Hal.* I never thought to hear you speak again.
> *Henry.* Thy wish was father, Harry, to that thought:
>   I stay too long by thee, I weary thee.
>   Dost thou so hunger for mine empty chair
>   That thou wilt needs invest thee with my honors
>   Before thy hour be ripe? O foolish youth,
>   Thou seek'st the greatness that will overwhelm thee.
>   (4.5.91–97)

The wording of this reproach points to all the symptoms of overreaching in Shakespeare, and as Henry points out, Hal's overhasty seizure of the crown would indeed convert what could be a natural inheritance into another usurpation. Hal would, in taking the bedfellow-crown, be fathering his own wishes into substance; he would therefore, like his father, be a sort of ghost or void while seated in that royal place, as a secondary reading of line 94 suggests. He might eventually have to ask, as Richard III does after battling and seducing his way to the throne, "is the chair empty?" (4.4.469). Hal's acquisition of these honors under such circumstances would be, again like his father's, a mere investiture, an act of costuming; and it would preclude Hal's ever becoming fully "ripe" for the throne, since Shakespeare generally suggests that a life forcibly cut off from its source cannot be given vital growth again (see *Othello*, 5.2.13–15; *King Lear*, 4.2.34–36). Whether Shakespeare is merely using Henry's speech to remind us of these hazards, or whether he intends us to believe that Henry is at least subliminally aware and expressive of them, the cluster of suggestive wordings at such a crucial moment in the transfer of identities seems significant.

Hal, for his part, hastens to re-establish his position as a natural successor, combining his answer to the charge of ambition with an answer to the charge of patricidal intentions:

> Accusing it, I put it on my head,
> To try with it, as with an enemy
> That had before my face murdered my father,
> The quarrel of a true inheritor.
>
> (4.5.165–68)

Again, a Freudian might argue that the son who imagines avenging his father's murder derives his pleasure from the premise of the fantasy, and adds the vengeance as a compensatory cover. But Henry is well satisfied with this answer, and asserts that Hal, because he is "a true inheritor," will be spared the unrest and mere theatricality of his father's reign:

> All these bold fears
> Thou seest with peril I have answered;
> For all my reign hath been but as a scene
> Acting that argument. And now my death
> Changes the mood, for what in me was purchas'd
> Falls upon thee in a more fairer sort;
> So thou the garland wear'st successively.
>
> (4.5.195–201)

Even this formulation, of course, depicts kingship as a garment, rather than an immanence, to be inherited; and Hal enjoys only a partial immunity to the ambitious disease as a lineal heir to an unlineal throne. His very first lines as king indicate that, as in

Macbeth (5.2.20–22), the giant robes of majesty hang incongru-
ously on a successor of questionable legitimacy: "This new and
gorgeous garment, majesty, / Sits not so easy on me as you think"
(5.2.44–45). Even his heart and its inmost filial sorrow are tainted
by the theatrical world his father's role as player-king created:

> Yet be sad, good brothers,
> For by my faith it very well becomes you.
> Sorrow so royally in you appears
> That I will deeply put the fashion on
> And wear it in my heart.
>
>   (5.2.49–53)

The difficulty in discerning what is sincere feeling here and what
is acting alerts us to the fact that this world has only been partly
redeemed from its artificialities, and that it will be virtually impossible to return it to a Golden Age. The nation's loss of innocence
about identity, like the ambitious man's loss of self that often
causes it in Shakespeare, is extremely difficult to reverse.

Perhaps the terrible difficulties that critics have in agreeing on
who Hal really is provide a good measure of Shakespeare's success in portraying a world where moral distinctions and distinct
identities have clouded simultaneously.[12] Is Hal entirely a cynical
manipulator of his Eastcheap companions, or does he truly enjoy
their kind of life and their version of friendship until the time
comes when he must abandon them? Is he a ruthless king, or
merely a king who must avoid thinking sentimentally about individuals so that he can be kind to his kingdom as a whole? Significantly, these questions about Hal's personality are intimately
connected with questions about his legitimacy as a king (over
France as well as England) and as a son (to Falstaff as well as
Henry). The problems of kingship and kinship remain as deeply
interwoven as they were in *Richard III*.

One index to the elusiveness of Hal's identity is the number of
different names he is given; one indication of his peculiar genius is
the way he converts this multiplicity, which shatters Richard II,
Henry IV, and Macbeth, into a political advantage.[13] From his
famous first soliloquy onward (*1 Henry IV*, 1.2.195–217), Hal
seems conscious of an opportunity that his father grasps only
sporadically. Henry makes use of theatrical identity in wooing the

common people (3.2.39–59) and in sending counterfeits into the field at Shrewsbury, but nearly all of Hal's actions are based on the theory that, if identity must be merely role-playing, he should make the most of it. He wins a new set of adherents to his reign by befriending "a leash of drawers" who "take it already upon their salvation, that though I be but Prince of Wales, yet I am the king of courtesy, and tell me flatly I am no proud Jack like Falstaff, but a Corinthian, a lad of mettle, a good boy (by the Lord, so they call me!)" (2.4.6–13). By letting them choose his names, he becomes their master. In France, he uses the name Harry le Roy for another strategic incursion into the lower ranks of his subjects.

In his confrontation with Hotspur, Hal's quest for an ideal name becomes deeply interwoven with his quest for a filial identity. Hal fights Hotspur to regain his good name—we may think of Edgar whose "name is lost" until he proves himself a loyal rather than a patricidal son (*King Lear*, 5.3.121)—and wins "proud titles" by defeating him (5.4.79). But the process of winning back those noble names involves not only a superficial act of loyalty to the father, but also a deep, quasi-allegorical acceptance of the father's role in forming Hal's selfhood. Hal's encounter with Hotspur—like the returning Henry's first encounter with Richard's lieutenants (*Richard II*, 2.3.69–75)—begins with a dispute over names:

> *Hotspur.* If I mistake not, thou art Harry Monmouth.
> *Hal.* Thou speak'st as if I would deny my name.
> *Hotspur.* My name is Harry Percy.
> *Hal.*   Why then I see
>   A very valiant rebel of the name.
>   I am the Prince of Wales.
>
>   (5.4.59–63)

There is something archetypal in this combat, where "Harry to Harry shall, hot horse to horse, / Meet and ne'er part till one drop down a corse" (4.1.122–23): it recalls the symmetrical mythic combats, the desperately serious shadow-boxing between the hero and his Doppelgänger, in which the hero's survival is rewarded with a name.[14] England cannot "brook a double reign," as Hal here tells Hotspur, and a name cannot brook a double occupant; only one of them can be Harry the Fourth's royal heir. In

seeking to win the "name in arms" that Hotspur acknowledges is
at stake (5.4.70), Hal is actually trying to recapture the names
Harry Monmouth and Prince of Wales—in other words, the identities as his father's son and his king's rightful heir. Both were
nearly forfeit to Hotspur, as King Henry warned: Hal's relative
dishonor left his political succession uncertain, and made his
father wish,

> that it could be prov'd
> That some night-tripping fairy had exchang'd
> In cradle-clothes our children where they lay,
> And call'd mine Percy, his Plantagenet!
> Then would I have his Harry and he mine.
>
> (1.1.86–90)

Hal's roles as bad prince and bad son, by jeopardizing his name,
have nearly dislodged him from his political and familial patrimonies; to retrieve them he must retrieve the name along with his
royal father's love, and become the Harry who succeeds a Harry
(*2 Henry IV*, 5.2.48–49).

Shakespeare emphasizes that Hal's victory over Hotspur is
essentially an incorporation rather than an obliteration of the
vanquished man's identity. Hal promised to "make this northren
youth exchange / His glorious deeds for my indignities" (3.2.145–
46), and that is what he has done; Hotspur, like Henry IV later,
must have "gone wild into his grave" (*2 Henry IV*, 5.2.123), because all Hal's faults went with him, while his glories revert to
Hal. Those glories consist of all the noble public virtues, all the
things Hal knows his society and his father admire and expect
him to embrace—in Freudian terms, they are the superego. The
argument by analogy, especially an anachronistic analogy, is very
risky, but in this case it suggests some intriguing possibilities,
some deep resonances to Shakespeare's study of a conflict over
filial identity. Freud argues that the superego is shaped in the
renunciation of the Oedipal desires, and consists essentially of the
father's censorious will within the son's psyche; the construction
of the superego is at base the son's incorporation of the father.[15]
Such a superego triumphs on several complementary levels at
once when Hal promises to become the glorious Hotspur of the

world and simultaneously vows not to rebel murderously against his father.

The standard psychoanalytic interpretation that makes Hotspur the embodiment of Hal's patricidal impulses therefore needs revision. Until Shrewsbury, only Shakespeare, and not Hal, could create such a displaced self; but the battle allows Hal to alienate his own rebellious spirit by both destroying and incorporating the opponent who is both rebel and noble son. When he retreats to a figuratively infantile level to compete with Hotspur for his filial identity, Hal may be retreating to a point prior to the Oedipal struggle and its shaping of the superego. In taking over Hotspur's glories while defending his father, what Hal really appropriates is a loyal filial posture. The fact that Hal can fully incorporate his father's nominal identity only by seizing Hotspur's glories corresponds strikingly to Freud's suggestion that the acquisition of a superego and the incorporation of the father are inseparable transactions.

In *1 Henry IV* Hal must defeat Hotspur for possession of his names and the accompanying hereditary roles; to reclaim his hereditary identity in *2 Henry IV*, Hal must similarly overcome his base rebellious impulses in order to reject the names Falstaff offers him. Hal accepts the many playful epithets his Eastcheap companions apply to him in place of his actual name, but only in the way that he accepts their clouding of his royal light in general: temporarily, strategically. A king's name, to twist Richard II's phrase, must not be twenty thousand names, and when Falstaff renews the epithets after the coronation, Hal rejects them and him simultaneously (5.5.41–47).

Several critics have observed that the repudiation of Falstaff is the repudiation of an alternative father.[16] The names that Falstaff bestows on Hal compromise his transformation into Henry's heir. Rejecting them is a forceful and fitting way of rejecting Falstaff's claim to paternity, which was already rendered dubious by procreative powers so badly abused that Falstaff, not Henry, deserves to be slandered as a eunuch. He spends those powers on prostitutes and "begets" only "lies" (*1 Henry IV*, 2.4.225). Even the children that his pillow-stuffed whore claims to be carrying are mocked or willed to miscarriage from all sides (*2 Henry IV*, 5.4.7–

15). He taints Hal with a degrading patrimony, claiming credit for making Hal somehow no longer consanguineous with his father or his brother, Prince John:

> Good faith, this same young sober-blooded boy doth not love me, nor a man cannot make him laugh, but that's no marvel, he drinks no wine . . . Hereof comes it that Prince Henry is valiant, for the cold blood he did naturally inherit of his father, he hath, like lean, sterile, and bare land, manur'd, husbanded, and till'd with excellent endeavor of drinking good and good store of fertile sherris, that he is become very hot and valiant. If I had a thousand sons, the first humane principle I would teach them should be, to forswear thin potations and to addict themselves to sack.
>
> (2 Henry IV, 4.3.87-125)

We are invited to recognize that Falstaff does indeed have thousands of such sons, all of whom have belatedly become consanguineous with him. They are what they drink. He is the father of the appetitive id, and those who give themselves over to that force incorporate him and become his more-than-adopted children. With the filial id as with the filial superego, the father is in the son as the son was in the father.

Of course, in claiming that Hotspur and Falstaff correspond suggestively to Freud's superego and id, I do not mean to imply that Shakespeare set out to write a psychoanalytic allegory in the Henry IV plays. Several critics have become understandably testy about the tendency to read literature as if it were secretly a series of morality plays that have lain inert awaiting a Freudian key to the characters.[17] But the history these plays describe was made by complex human minds, and the plays themselves were made by and for such minds. Characters who exist as words on a page do not have a superego and an id, but the historical person they are designed to evoke presumably did, and the reader or listener presumably does too. What would be absurd to attribute to Shakespeare's characters may nonetheless be relevant to the responses of his audience. As we watch Hal struggle with his alter egos, "we are made to experience a kind of psychomachia or internal civil war."[18]

If Falstaff bears a strong resemblance to what we call the id, then we may legitimately ask what deep associations he might have aroused in Shakespeare's mind and might be capable, whether Shakespeare was conscious of it or not, of arousing in ours. Several of the play's eminent critics have flirted with this issue. Jonas Barish argues that "To banish plump Jack is to banish what is free and vital and pleasurable in life, as well as much that is selfish and unruly," and that there is therefore an "element of *self*-rejection in the new king's action."[19] Franz Alexander calls Falstaff a "pleasure-seeking principle" that "the prince must master in himself."[20] W. H. Auden makes it more explicit: "Once upon a time we were all Falstaffs: then we became social beings with superegos."[21] Most other readings of Falstaff's allegorical identity are compatible with the idea that he represents the id. E. M. W. Tillyard lists several such readings: Satan's assistant since the Fall, youthful vitality, incorrigibility, the fool, the adventurer, the Vice, the epitome of the Seven Deadly Sins, the lord of misrule, and "a perpetual and accepted human principle" resembling Orwell's "principle of man's perpetual revolt against both his moral self and the official forces of law and order" which we may love but must banish from within ourselves.[22] If we accept the contention of J. Dover Wilson and Bernard Spivack that Falstaff is a version of the medieval Vice, we may still inquire what the medieval Vice was supposed to represent, and how it was intended to engage and rebalance the audience's psychic forces.[23] The combination of universality and elusiveness in Falstaff's character invites us to anachronism: we may call him the id if that is the name by which we most effectively understand the force he represents. When some new system for explaining the human psyche emerges, critics will doubtless find another name for Falstaff within it, and another reading of the Henry IV plays arising from it.

The identification of Falstaff with the id provides its most valuable insights at the moment when Hal banishes him, just as the identification of Hotspur with the superego became most valuable at the moment when Hal defeated him. Hal's visible act of loyalty to his father in defeating the rebel Hotspur complements the psychological transaction implicit in that conquest, namely the incorporation of the paternal superego. In the same way, Hal's actual banishment of Falstaff is an act of obedience to, and imitation of, his father, as its precedent in the tavern suggested (*1 Henry IV*, 2.4.481); simultaneously, on the level of the psychological allegory, Hal is banishing his own id, which urges him to resist the demands of his father and of his social role. The outward and the inward transactions in Hal's moments of crisis are equally real; they are absolutely necessary concomitants to each other under the circumstances. Shakespeare has again shaped a situation where the political and the psycho-symbolic imperatives coincide, giving us the impression of a deep moral truth in a morally resonant universe.

This striking coincidence also encourages us to accept one of the stranger implications in Shakespeare's treatment of ambition: the notion that refashioning one's identity constitutes an Oedipal crime. The theft of Hotspur's honor and the banishment of Falstaff establish Hal as a loyal son and a rightful heir; they represent at the same time his incorporation of the paternal superego and his willingness to suppress his id in accepting the hereditary royal role. The establishment of the superego, according to Freud, is necessary to intercept the Oedipal desires put forward by the boy's id, which might lead to castration or death if they were obeyed.[24] The correspondence in Hal between granting the superego power to repress the id, and accepting the hereditary identity, may suggest that an Oedipal desire has been forestalled in both cases, whether it is the literal desire to kill the father and sleep with the mother, or its figurative counterpart in the desire to suppress the self the father made and to let one's deepest wishes conceive a replacement, perhaps in some version of the original womb.

What interests me especially about the banishment of Falstaff, in terms of the psychological allegory, is Hal's use of the Lord Chief Justice as the enforcer of that edict. The notion that this corresponds to the superego's assignment of suppressing the id has been suggested, but its implications have not been fully explored.[25] In *1 Henry IV* Hal faces the ego's usual problems in dealing with the id and the superego. He must conceal the criminal Falstaff from the sheriff in the tavern, worrying at the same time about the political rebellion taking place in the nation as a whole (2.4.500–45); this recalls Freud's description of the ego as "a poor creature owing service to three masters and consequently menaced by three dangers: from the external world, from the libido of the id, and from the severity of the super-ego."²⁶ When Hal stands between the dead Hotspur and the supposedly dead Falstaff at Shrewsbury, he has apparently solved that ego's problems. Unfortunately for him, fortunately for admirers of *2 Henry IV*, Falstaff simply rises back up from his latency, as the id tends to do, and the superego must be reinvigorated to deal with him. The Lord Chief Justice is essentially a reincarnation of the paternal conscience, and his confrontations with Falstaff early in *2 Henry IV* resemble the evasions and encounters of the psyche's mighty opposites. Falstaff declares himself blind and deaf to the Justice's existence, and the Justice replies that Falstaff is indeed insensible or uncomprehending of any moral consideration (1.2.55–69). In their next encounter, the Justice tells Falstaff that "You should have been well on your way to York," and that he should "Pay [Hostess Quickly] the debt you owe her, and unpay the villainy you have done with her" (2.1.67, 118–20). He tells Falstaff, in other words, to meet his unpleasant social obligations in war, money, and marriage—the standard message of the superego.

Falstaff expects to be fully indulged when Hal becomes king, and Henry IV fears that Hal's id will know no restraint once he acquires the power to indulge it:

> For when his headstrong riot hath no curb,
> When rage and hot blood are his counsellors,
> When means and lavish manners meet together,
> O, with what wings shall his affections fly
> Towards fronting peril and oppos'd decay!
>
> (4.4.62–66)

The metaphor portrays Hal as an unruly horse, which is a symbol of the id from Plato's *Phaedrus* up through Freud himself, and which here associates Hal with Phaethon, the Renaissance archetype of the disastrously disobedient son.²⁷ Falstaff's response, on hearing that Hal has gained such power, is "woe to my Lord Chief Justice" (5.3.138). But Hal refuses to accept either the name or the role of Falstaff's "sweet boy" (5.5.43); he turns instead to the father of the superego, or more accurately, the superego of his father, embodied in the Justice. We may not enjoy watching this

choice, but no one says the suppression of instinctual desires is a
pleasant, generous act, only that it becomes a necessary one at
maturity. When Hal, feigning indignation, asks how the Lord
Chief Justice earlier dared arrest and imprison "Th' immediate
heir of England," the man replies that he dared as the one who
gave the heritage:

> I then did use the person of your father,
> The image of his power lay then in me,
> . . . . .
> Your Highness pleased to forget my place,
> The majesty and power of law and justice,
> The image of the King whom I presented,
> And strook me in the very seat of judgment;
> Whereon (as an offender to your father)
> I gave bold way to my authority.
>
> (5.2.70–82)

The emphasis on the Oedipal overtones of Hal's deed could hardly
be stronger; but the surrogate father against whom he has done
violence also offers himself as a surrogate father to whom Hal
may submissively return. The Lord Chief Justice warns quite
clearly what the consequences might be of not submitting. In this
confrontation as in all of Hal's dealings with his actual father,
Shakespeare's cautionary pattern looms ominously. The son who
disdains his father, the subject who disdains his sovereign, invite
similarly violent disobedience from their own sons or subjects:

> Be you contented, now you wear the garland,
> To have a son set your decrees at nought?
> . . . . .
> Nay more, to spurn at your most royal image,
> And mock your workings in a second body?
> Question your royal thoughts, make the case yours:
> Be now the father and propose a son,
> Hear your own dignity so much profan'd,
> See your most dreadful laws so loosely slighted,
> Behold yourself so by a son disdained;
> And then imagine me taking your part.
>
> (5.2.84–96)

This exchange, it seems to me, looks all the way back to the
birth of civilization. This decisive moment in the re-formation of

English society involves the same forces and choices that, according to Freud's furthest-reaching speculations, led to the formation of the first human society: we are watching the superego evolve its authority from the compelling need to prevent endless strife. According to *Civilization and Its Discontents*, the sons in the Primal Horde suffered an ambivalence much like Hal's, and with like consequences. Their hatred yielded guiltily to love, whether or not they actually committed the patricide they fantasized, when they saw their wish fulfilled by their father's death. That love "set up the super-ego by identification with the father; it gave that agency the father's power, as though as a punishment for the deed of aggression they had carried out against him, and it created the restrictions which were intended to prevent a repetition of the deed."[28] The description of this transaction in *Totem and Taboo* bears an equally suggestive resemblance to Hal's submission to the Lord Chief Justice. As penance for a patricidal impulse, even one that was never acted on, the son bows in worship to the dead father's surrogate: "Totemic religion arose from the filial sense of guilt, in an attempt to allay that feeling and to appease the father by deferred obedience to him. . . . They revoked their deed by forbidding the killing of the totem, the substitute for their father."[29] The superego originates from this totemic conversion, Freud argues, and always takes the form of a surrogate father,[30] as the Lord Chief Justice does here: Hal urges him to "be as a father to my youth," then calls him simply "father" (5.2.118, 140).

Freud adds that we re-enact such a transaction in each of our lives: we form the superego by incorporating idealized versions of the self that have been lost as external objects—a dead rival, or, especially, a dead father.[31] Hal announces:

> My father is gone wild into his grave;
> For in his tomb lie my affections,
> And with his spirits sadly I survive,
> To mock the expectation of the world.
>
> (5.2.123–26)

This is an unnatural sort of succession, more the transmigration of a soul than the procreation of a body; but as at Hotspur's death, Hal becomes ideally filial by absorbing the ideal father in his superego. The opportunistic revival of the appetitive impulses embodied by Falstaff has, as I suggested, compelled a reincarnation of the conscience to cope with those impulses. The best part of Henry lives on in his repressive actions, which the Lord Chief Justice both symbolizes and performs; this new father becomes a part of the royal Hal, becomes the new king's censorious agent against Falstaff's pleas, the id's pleas, for special consideration. "The first requisite of civilization," Freud writes, "is that of justice—that is, the assurance that a law once made will not be broken in favour of an individual."[32] The laws of England are not at Falstaff's commandment, as he claims (5.3.136–37), because Hal has installed a new father within his own sovereignty. Such a substitution is possible, however, here as in Freud's analysis, only when the threatening real father is dead, and a surrogate, understood as protective rather than repressive, has taken his place by the son's own will. The Lord Chief Justice says he will now protect Hal (5.2.96), rather than restrain him on behalf of the previous royal father; the same shift occurs from the repressive father in the horde to the protective totem-animal that takes his place, a shift on which Freud comments extensively.

This intricate correspondence between Hal's psychological events and his nation's political events helps to justify the notion that both correspond to the events of human society as a whole. The psychomachia allows Hal's struggle to resemble the struggle of every human mind; its political counterpart may therefore allow us to generalize to the struggle of every human society. Freud argues repeatedly that the individual psyche relives metaphorically the experience of the sons in the Primal Horde, as if phylogeny were recapitulating ontogeny in psychological development, as it was once supposed to do in physical development.[33] Societies established throughout history, he also argues, have all experienced their own versions of the Primal Horde's formative trauma.[34] Nor is the notion wholly anachronistic. In medieval morality plays, the central figure in psychomachia of the sort Hal clearly undergoes was Humanam Genus; "Mankynde" is the name of an entire species. Shakespeare himself, in the Prologue to Henry V, asks us to "Into a thousand parts divide one man," and freely to jump

> o'er times,
> Turning th' accomplishment of many years
> Into an hour-glass: for the which supply,
> Admit me Chorus to this history.
>
> (lines 24, 29–32)

At the end of 2 *Henry IV*, Shakespeare has already tacitly requested admission as such a Chorus.

What the Lord Chief Justice offers to Hal is precisely what the institutionalization of the superego offered to the liberated sons in Freud's Primal Horde: prophylaxis against an eternal cycle of rebellion. Without a surrender of the id to the totemic father-surrogate, the result in virtually any society would be "an ever-recurring violent succession to the solitary paternal tyrant, by sons whose patricidal hands were so soon again clenched in fratricidal strife."[35] The only solution is a law, embodied in the totemic father-surrogate, that distributes rights fairly among the brothers and becomes internalized by each of them as the superego; both this creation of the surrogate, and its internalization, are clearly outlined in Hal's submission to the Justice who promises to end rebellion by even-handedness. Hal has learned the bitter lesson of his father's usurpation, which loosed "this Hydra son of war" not only by the violent precedent it set, but also by Henry's refusal to share the royal privileges among those who helped him overthrow the previous tyrant (2 *Henry IV*, 4.2.35–40). The Percies resemble the younger brothers in the Primal Horde, who, having assisted in killing the repressive father, find they have no choice (and no qualms) about attacking the repressive new father-figure as well. The dying Henry IV seems to recognize the problem, urging Hal's favorite brother Thomas to nurture their affection so that "noble offices thou mayst effect / Of mediation, after I am dead, / Between his greatness and thy other brethren," and thereby provide, as if he were an Anglo-Saxon ring-giver,

> A hoop of gold to bind thy brothers in,
> That the united vessel of their blood,
> Mingled with venom of suggestion
> (As, force perforce, the age will pour it in),
> Shall never leak.
>
> (4.4.19–47)

Three scenes later, when Hal actually succeeds his father, his first words to his brothers are a defense against this danger: he encourages them to continue in their communal mourning for the dead father, but assures them that "Not Amurath an Amurath succeeds," that he will not be like the man who murdered all his brothers when he took power (5.2.46–50). Instead, he has taken into himself the protective (and therefore protected) qualities of the totemic father whom the brothers now mourn and reverence unitedly. For England, as (Freud argues) for societies in all times and places, this is the only way to break the violent cycle. Shakespeare has again grounded his English history in the history of all human societies.

Hal thus becomes a sort of St. George, or perhaps a sort of Beowulf, defending England against the monster of fratricide that his predecessors have awakened, whether that primal dragon takes the name of Hydra or Amurath or Cain. Bullingbrook first appears before Richard II to avenge the spilt blood of the Duke of Gloucester, "Which blood, like sacrificing Abel's, cries, / Even from the tongueless caverns of the earth, / To me for justice and rough chastisement" (1.1.98–106). The lurking accusation, apparently well founded, is that Richard (through Mowbray) played the role of Cain against his kinsman; this accusation starts in motion the horrible fratricidal struggle that dominates both of Shakespeare's tetralogies. Perhaps the worst thing about this moral ailment is that it is contagious, and that it is paradoxically congenital to any *unlineal* inheritance of the throne. When Henry completes the promised vengeance by an indirect murder of his own, he desperately tries to displace his primal culpability onto his agent Exton, whom he sends to wander through the dark world "With Cain" (5.6.43). But the circle cannot so easily be broken. Henry must war with Northumberland, his son Hal with Northumberland's son Hotspur, and when the word of Hotspur's death arrives, Northumberland states the danger only too plainly in bitterly endorsing it:

> But let one spirit of the first-born Cain
> Reign in all bosoms, that each heart being set
> On bloody courses, the rude scene may end,
> And darkness be the burier of the dead!
>
> (*2 Henry IV*, 1.1.157–60)[36]

The crime that "hath the primal eldest curse upon't," in the Henry IV plays as in *Hamlet* (3.3.37), combines patricide, fratricide, and usurpation, in an invitation to endless bloodshed. The same sort of conflation appears in *Gorboduc*, and in the Elizabethan "Homily against Disobedience and wilful Rebellion," which warns that insurrection can only lead "the brother to seek and often to work the death of his brother, the son of the father."[37] Half a century after Shakespeare wrote the Henry IV plays, Thomas Hobbes expressed similar fears in terms that anticipate Freud's interpretation of the primal murder.[38] So the danger Freud perceived was at least partly visible to Shakespeare's contemporaries, and therefore a plausible subject for Shakespeare's stage.

In forbidding Falstaff (and therefore his own id) from using royal power to gratify his appetites at the expense of others, Hal is reenacting society's first triumph over the force that threatened to destroy it, and renewing English society's will to resist that force. It is natural enough, given the respective occupations of Falstaff and the Lord Chief Justice and the relations between the two men, that accepting one as a surrogate father would entail excluding the other; but that natural situation carries a sharp allegorical import. On a realistic level, Hal's suppression of his own unruly impulses allows him to accept the Lord Chief Justice, and that acceptance leads to the rejection of Falstaff. On the level of the psychomachia, the rejection of Falstaff is merely the acting-out of the suppression of the id that we have seen moments earlier in the acceptance of the Justice. We are on shifting levels of allegory that disguise themselves as chronological sequence, as for example when the Redcrosse Knight's battle with Error is essentially an acting-out of a battle he has already fought in traveling through the Wood of Error with Una to reach that dragon, or when Christian and his companions fall into the net of Flatterer only after being coaxed out of the rightful path by flattery and led some distance, in *The Pilgrim's Progress*.[39] Hal's embrace of the Justice and his casting-out of Falstaff can be viewed as a single psychological moment. Time yields to allegory in that archetypal situation, even as that moment in the history of English society becomes suddenly synchronous with the formative moment of all human societies.

The psychomachia lends metaphorical richness to Hal's comparison of his experience of Falstaff to the experience of a wicked dream, in which the appetites of the id run rampant. The self-transformation Hal claims to have accomplished in the rejection speech becomes a slightly presumptuous exclusion of one side of his human heritage, one half of his divided father-figure. The speech shows clear traces of the self-alienation and the wakefulness that characterize the ambitious syndrome, but this is an alienation only from the id, and an awakening only from the dreams of the id:

> I have long dreamt of such a kind of man,
> So surfeit-swell'd, so old, and so profane;
> But, being awak'd, I do despise my dream.
> . . . . .
> Reply not to me with a fool-born jest,
> Presume not that I am the thing I was,
> For God doth know, so shall the world perceive,
> That I have turn'd away my former self;
> So will I those that kept me company.
> When thou dost hear I am as I have been,
> Approach me, and thou shalt be as thou wast,
> The tutor and the feeder of my riots.
>
> (5.5.49–62)

The precedents of this announcement are not promising: other Shakespearean characters who use such phrases are unhealthily at war with their own natures and with nature itself. Richard III asks Queen Elizabeth to "Plead what I will be, not what I have been; / Not my deserts, but what I will deserve" (4.4.414–15); Richard II struggles to "forget what I have been! / Or not remember what I must be now!" (3.3.138–39). Hal's proclamation may even anticipate Iago's "I am not what I am" (1.1.65). From these moments through his last plays, Shakespeare persistently asks whether we can leave a degrading but natural part of ourselves behind, kill the heart of its father, without inviting a devastating nemesis. He refuses to adopt the notion, offered by most of his sources, that Hal simply underwent a miraculous transformation at his coronation; the problems of identity are too important and too complex for him to accept such an evasion.[40] The psychomachia invites us to recognize Hal's self-*askesis*, his amputation of the facets of his identity that do not fit with his royal role. What I am raising again, from a different perspective, is the vexed question of whether Hal's humanity survives the task of assuming a kingship that is only partly lineal, only partly legitimate in its birth.

If *Richard II* ends with Henry being brought "Thy buried fear" (5.6.41), *2 Henry IV* ends with Hal confronting his buried id; and both cases invite our fear that the triumph may prove Pyrrhic, that the king may have buried an essential part of himself in burying his supposed enemy and assuming the crown. Hal's manipulation of his former companions and his wording of grief for his father seem to lack human grace, and may betoken a lack of human feeling. But this apparent heartlessness, and his bloodless mode of inheritance, unattractive and unhealthy as they may be, represent a plausible way for Hal to fulfill his role as the nemesis generated by Henry's violations, without incurring a similar nemesis of his own. Shakespeare and Hal virtually conspire to find an escape from the vicious cycle of Oedipal justice. Hal's political strategy of imitating the sun by hiding his glory temporarily in Eastcheap corresponds, in timing and symbolic form, to the psychological strategy whereby he merely imitates the rebellious son. He plays the disobedient and potentially patricidal part long enough to punish his father and fulfill the general expectation, meanwhile retaining an identity as a temporarily loyal son to Falstaff, against whom he can later carry out the patricidal violence that Shakespeare's pattern insists he must have inherited. Falstaff, like Richard III, becomes a scapegoat in his dramatic creator's system of poetic justice. Like the Lords of Misrule to whom he is often compared, Falstaff is placed in his exalted role only to allow an outlet for hostilities that would be dangerous to express against the actual sovereign. Then, at Henry's death, Hal reclaims his lineal virtues metempsychotically, with the Lord Chief Justice as the visible father of this immaculately conceived new royal self. Hal proves himself his father's natural son by coming to the royal identity as unnaturally as his father had, without committing his father's crimes against lineage in the process.

But if Hal's genius is his ability to live constantly in the familial and political roles his world demands of him, that is also his torment. The unity of his character must always be its capacity for multiplicity, including an unappealing talent (like his brother John's) for duplicity. His innermost self may be so difficult for critics to locate and define because it is equally elusive for Hal himself. The difference between Hal and other victims of the ambitious pattern is not that he retains a vital inner self—it is not clear that he does—but rather that his theatrical self is hereditary, and that he has the *sprezzatura*, the art of disguising his artfulness, to make it viable. To inherit his father's role as king, as Henry had warned him (*1 Henry IV*, 3.2.46–59), he must inherit first his father's theatrical use of his "person," the arm's-length manipulation of the self. Hal learns this lesson and betters the instruction.

NOTES

1. The analogy between births such as Glendower's and Tamburlaine's, and eruptions of trapped air, recalls Lucan's description of Julius Caesar's martial energies: "As lightning by the wind forc'd from a cloud / Breakes through the wounded aire with thunder loud." James M. Swan, "History, Pastoral, and Desire: A Psychoanalytic Study of English Renaissance Literature and Society" (Ph.D. diss. Stanford University, 1974), pp. 300–302, has interpreted this passage as the source for images of self-induced Caesarean birth in Philemon Holland's *Historie of the World* (translated from Pliny in 1601) and in Marvell's "The Unfortunate Lover"; he also confirms my longstanding suspicion that the much-debated lines 13–24 of Marvell's "Horatian Ode" allude to a similar action, complete with a pun on Caesar's name. See also C. A. Patrides, "'Till Prepared for Longer Flight,'" in *Approaches to Marvell* (London: Routledge and Kegan Paul, 1978), p. 35.
2. Christopher Marlowe, *Tamburlaine, Part One*, in *The Complete Plays of Christopher Marlowe*, ed. J. B. Steane (Harmondsworth, Middlesex: Penguin, 1969), 1.2.49–51.
3. Edmund Spenser, *The Faerie Queene*, in *Spenser: Poetical Works*, ed. J. C. Smith and E. De Selincourt (New York: Oxford University Press, 1970). For the impregnating power of Jove's lightning, see Plutarch, *Lives of the Noble Grecians and Romans*, trans. Thomas North (1579), ed. W. E. Henley (London, 1895), IV, 299, 330–331; here again such a conception generates a suggestively Oedipal hero.
4. John Milton, *Paradise Lost*, ed. Merritt Y. Hughes (Indianapolis, Ind.: Odyssey-Bobbs Merrill, 1962); subsequent citations are from this edition.

5. Sigmund Freud, *Totem and Taboo*, trans. James Strachey (New York: Norton, 1950), pp. 142–144. In chapter 6 of his *Violence and the Sacred*, Girard examines the Hydra-like threat presented by twins or doubles, which raise the danger of fraternal rivalry over legacies and even identity.

6. Norman Sanders, "The True Prince and the False Thief: Prince Hal and the Shift of Identity," *Shakespeare Survey* 30 (1977), 30, remarks on the propriety of this resemblance.

7. Ronald Berman, "The Nature of Guilt in the Henry IV Plays," *Shakespeare Studies* 1 (1965), 27, discusses Henry's use of disguise to gain the throne. See also Righter, *Shakespeare and Idea of Play*, pp. 126–127.

8. Ernst Kris, "Prince Hal's Conflict," in Faber, *Design Within*, p. 395.

9. Dreams of saving the father from an assailant, however one wishes to interpret them, are apparently common among young men. Freud, in *Totem and Taboo* (p. 72), speculates about a mechanism whereby "the original *wish* that the loved person may die is replaced by a *fear* that he may die. So that when the neurosis appears to be so tenderly altruistic, it is merely *compensating* for an underlying contrary attitude of brutal egoism."

10. Derek Traversi, *Shakespeare from Richard II to Henry V* (Stanford: Stanford University Press, 1957), p. 125.

11. The parallel is of course imperfect: marrying one's mother does not become appropriate at one's father's death, as inheriting his title might. John W. Blanpied, "'Unfathered heirs and loathly births of nature': Bringing History to Crisis in *2 Henry IV*," *English Literary Renaissance* 5 (1975), 228–229, discusses the displacement of the parricide into the crown; Freud argues that the Oedipal impulse is often displaced into the mother, who is here equated with the crown.

12. Norman Rabkin, *Shakespeare and the Problem of Meaning* (Chicago: University of Chicago Press, 1981), pp. 33–62, argues eloquently and convincingly that our ambivalence toward Hal is not only permissible, it is essential to understanding Shakespeare's sort of meaning.

13. Warren J. Macisaac, "'A Commodity of Good Names' in the *Henry IV* Plays," *Shakespeare Quarterly* 29 (1978), 417–419, comments on the meaningful modulations of Hal's name.

14. George Steiner, in a conversation in 1978, reported finding such stories in many mythologies, stories of a hero battling through the night against a Doppelgänger, and receiving a name from him in the morning.

15. Sigmund Freud, *The Ego and the Id*, trans. Joan Riviere, rev. and ed. James Strachey (New York: Norton, 1962), pp. 21–29; in *Totem and Taboo*, this incorporation of the father takes the literal form of a ritual meal in which the patricidal sons consume the father or his

totem-surrogate as part of a penitential renunciation of their common deed (p. 142). See similarly Freud's *Civilization and Its Discontents*, trans. James Strachey (New York: Norton, 1961), p. 76. An interesting sidelight here is Jacques Lacan's theory that the Oedipal conflict resides essentially in a boy's relation to the name (*nom*, with a pun on *non*) of the father; see Monique David-Menard, "Lacanians Against Lacan," trans. Brian Massumi, in *Social Text* (Fall 1982), p. 90.

16. Kris, "Prince Hal," in Faber, *Design Within*, p. 399, is an early example; see also Faber, pp. 421–422.

17. Meredith Skura, *The Literary Use of the Psychoanalytic Process* (New Haven: Yale University Press, 1981), p. 16, cites several such objections.

18. Edward Pechter, "Falsifying Men's Hopes: The Ending of *1 Henry IV*," *Modern Language Quarterly* 41 (1980), 216.

19. Jonas Barish, "The Turning Away of Prince Hal," *Shakespeare Studies* 1 (1965), 15 and 10.

20. Franz Alexander, "A Note on Falstaff," *Psychoanalytic Quarterly* 2 (1933), 592–606; cited by Barish, *Shakespeare Studies* 1:16 n. 5.

21. W. H. Auden, *The Dyer's Hand and Other Essays* (New York: Random House, 1948; rpt. 1962), p. 195.

22. Tillyard, *Shakespeare's History Plays*, pp. 285–291; the quotations are from p. 289. S. C. Sen Gupta, *Shakespeare's History Plays* (London: Oxford University Press, 1964), p. 127, calls Falstaff "a symbol of the unrepressed instincts of humanity, which thirst for fulfillment, rebel against repression"; cited by Sidney Shanker, *Shakespeare and the Uses of Ideology*, Studies in English Literature, vol. 105 (The Hague: Mouton, 1975), p. 65 n. 19. We may add to Tillyard's list the figure of the *picaro*, cited as an element of Falstaff by H. B. Rothschild Jr., "Falstaff and the Picaresque Tradition," *Modern Language Review* 68 (1972), 14–21.

23. J. Dover Wilson, *The Fortunes of Falstaff* (New York: Macmillan, 1944), pp. 18–28; Bernard Spivack, *Shakespeare and the Allegory of Evil* (New York: Columbia University Press, 1958), pp. 87–91.

24. Freud, *Ego and Id*, p. 26, is one of many statements of this theory.

25. Skura, *Literary Use*, p. 36, mentions "the obvious psychomachia in the triple world of *Henry IV, Part Two*, where Hal has to choose between the id (Falstaff) and the superego (the Lord Chief Justice)." Danby, *Doctrine of Nature*, p. 95, asserts that "In the rejection scene Hal and my Lord Chief Justice stand for Authority; Falstaff is Appetite." Traversi, *Richard II to Henry V*, p. 108, sees Hal in *2 Henry IV* as "engaged in the more arduous and sober pursuit of self-conquest, externally manifested in his submission to the Lord Chief-Justice";

but on p. 158 he doubts that the Justice is "a sufficient counterpart to the 'riot' incarnated in Falstaff."

26. Freud, *Ego and Id*, p. 46.
27. Sigmund Freud, "The Anatomy of the Mental Personality," in *New Introductory Lectures on Psychoanalysis*, trans. W. J. H. Sprott (New York: Norton, 1933), p. 108.
28. Freud, *Civilization*, p. 79. For the sufficiency of a fantasy patricide, see *Totem*, p. 160, and "Moses and Monotheism" in the Standard Edition of Freud's *Works*, trans. James Strachey, XXIII (London: Hogarth, 1964), 87.
29. Freud, *Totem*, p. 145 and p. 143.
30. Freud, *Ego and Id*, p. 28 and p. 38.
31. Freud, *Ego and Id*, pp. 18-21; see also p. 44, and his "Mourning and Melancholia," passim, in *Works*, XIV (London: Hogarth, 1957); see also Hans Loewald, *Papers on Psychoanalysis* (New Haven: Yale University Press, 1980), pp. 270-271.
32. Freud, *Civilization*, p. 42.
33. Ibid., p. 44: "At this point we cannot fail to be struck by the similarity between the process of civilization and the libidinal development of the individual," and goes on, pp. 44-45, to suggest "that the development of civilization is a special process, comparable to the normal maturation of the individual." Further, "The analogy between the process of civilization and the path of individual development may be extended . . . The super-ego of an epoch of civilization has an origin similar to that of an individual" (p. 88). However, we must also heed Freud's warning, on p. 91, that "we are only dealing with analogies and that it is dangerous, not only with men but also with concepts, to tear them from the sphere in which they have originated and been evolved."
34. Freud, "The Group and the Primal Horde," in *Works*, XVIII (London: Hogarth, 1955) 123.
35. J. J. Atkinson, *Primal Law* (London, 1903), p. 228; quoted by Freud, *Totem*, p. 142 n. 1, as the characteristic problem that the totemic law must solve. See also Freud's "Postscript" in *Works*, XVIII, 135, on the necessity of this fraternal pact as a preventative to civil war.
36. For another perspective on these Cain allusions, see Berman, in *Shakespeare Studies* 1:20.
37. Thomas Sackville and Thomas Norton, *Gorboduc* or *Ferrex and Porrex*, Regents Renaissance Drama Series, ed. Irby B. Cauthen, Jr. (Lincoln: University of Nebraska Press, 1970), 2.1.172-75, 5.2.212-14, and passim, shows this combination of crimes plunging the nation out of civilization and into a welter of bloodshed. Intriguingly, these

themes are combined here, as they are in Shakespeare, with occasional suggestions of unnatural birth and the dangers of a usurper's
sleep: see 4.1.65-75 and 4.2.181-90. The Homily is quoted by Tillyard, *Shakespeare's History Plays*, p. 70.

38. In *Leviathan*, part I, chapter 13, Hobbes, discusses the difficulty of
holding any sort of sovereign privileges in a world where "the
weakest has strength enough to kill the strongest, either by secret
machination, or by confederacy with others, that are in the same
danger with himself." This parallels Freud's observation that the
brothers, though individually weaker, manage to overthrow the
father and seize his privileges by conspiring together. A few paragraphs later Hobbes points out the same danger that Freud saw
arising from such a conspiracy. In the absence of the father, or a just
totemic law that takes his place, the brothers will inevitably continue
to battle each other to their deaths: "Hereby it is manifest, that
during the time men live without a common power to keep them all
in awe, they are in that condition which is called war; and such a war,
as is of every man, against every man."

39. Edmund Spenser, *The Faerie Queene*, I.i; John Bunyan, *The Pilgrim's
Progress*, ed. Roger Sharrock (Harmondsworth, Middlesex: Penguin,
1965), pp. 172-173.

40. Tillyard, *Shakespeare's History Plays*, p. 305, makes note of this deviation
from Walsingham and the *Famous Victories of Henry V*.

R. L. Smallwood

Henry IV, Parts 1 and 2 at the Barbican Theatre (1982)

At the beginning of Trevor Nunn's production of the first part of *Henry IV* at the new Barbican Theatre, the stage lights go down at the same time as the house lights and in darkness we hear the opening notes of Guy Wolfenden's solemn, haunting music as a scattered host of twinkling candles advances slowly from every nook and on every level of the black recesses and cells of the honeycomb of a set. It is a breathtaking moment, and, when I first saw it, was greeted by a stunned silence followed by excited cheering. That was, it has to be admitted, on the occasion of the official first performance of the RSCs opening production in its new London home, so some of the applause was no doubt to wish the Company well at the beginning of this new phase of its history. But some, too, was certainly for the moment itself, a piece of pure theatrical magic, and one which, significantly, involved the whole company—actors, musicians, and designers.

Henry IV is a particularly appropriate play to show off the communal talents of a company. Its large cast, the big sweep of history it presents, the great variety, social as well as geographical, of its locations, demand strength in depth if they are to be realised effectively. Trevor Nunn's players respond impressively to the challenge.

John Napier's set of three enormous tower-like structures of beams and spars, crossbows and spears, even a crucifix, all forming cells and spaces, recesses and rooms, ropeways and platforms,

From *Critical Quarterly*, 25 (1983). Reprinted by permission of Manchester University Press.

is the medieval ancestor of his Victorian bric-à-brac construction for *Nicholas Nickleby*. Easily moved on their hydraulic trucks, they come together to present the narrow streets of medieval London, the shadows of Gaultree Forest, or, at their most effective, the catacomb of snugs and parlours and chambers of the Eastcheap tavern. When withdrawn altogether they reveal the empty vastness of the Barbican stage for Shrewsbury Field where they can be used, as they loom menacingly forward from the darkened wings, to suggest huge siege engines in the battle. They seem to have less relevance in the court scenes, where they linger a little obtrusively while council tables, or, for Henry IV's death scene, a plank-like, far from horizontal, bed of obviously excruciating discomfort, are portered on in more traditional fashion.

It is a big set, on a very big stage, and it is one of the great successes of the production that one never feels that the company is failing to fill it. This is particularly true of the tavern scenes, where a marvellous sense of teeming life is created for us with an almost Dickensian atmosphere, apprentice tapsters struggling to carry brimming jugs through rooms crowded with sprawling customers, the boys in the back room, and the girls upstairs, providing a vivid context for the unfolding relationship between Hal and Falstaff, without ever distracting attention from it. The way in which these assorted and disparate groups are drawn together as by a magnet to watch the playacting of Hal and Falstaff in *Part 1* suggests that such impromptu histrionics from these performers are not unknown at the Boar's Head, and that their likely interest makes it worth forgetting other activities. The sense of bustling, crowded life projected in the Eastcheap scenes, with their warmth and cheerful haphazardness quite different from the ordered coldness of the court, is tellingly evoked and is important in suggesting the contrast which attracts Hal to the tavern and repels him from the palace. And it is economically achieved, without a large cast of extras, by dexterous and, on the whole, unobtrusive doubling, though the presence of the production's Bolingbroke, Patrick Stewart, rather thinly disguised, in one of the *Part 1* tavern scenes does make one wonder whether the idea of frustrated fatherly love, subtly explored elsewhere, is here emerging heavy-handedly as the reason for a king going slumming incognito among his subjects, rather like Henry V before Agincourt.

This sharply realised contrast between the bustling crowdedness of Eastcheap and the sparsely populated austerity of the court is epitomized in the performances of Patrick Stewart as Bolingbroke and Joss Ackland as Falstaff, father and surrogate father in conflict for the loyalty of Prince Hal. Patrick Stewart emerges at the beginning of *Part 1* from the candle-bearing procession of chanting monks in a massively embroidered cope, a ceremonial, indeed rather episcopal, garment of symbolically crushing weight, to speak the opening lines: "So shaken as we are, so wan with care." The same cope will engulf his son in the coronation procession at the end of *Part 2*, linking father and son, beginning and ending, in an arcing image of the inescapable burden of kingship. For the rest of the two parts Bolingbroke appears somewhat priest-like in black and white, an austere, clean, neat, fastidious figure with short-trimmed hair and crisp (and splendidly clear) articulation, attempting (not quite successfully) by dutifully governing the realm he has acquired, to atone for his sense of guilt at the acquisition. A machine of a man, one at first falsely assumes, until the undercurrent of possessive paternal emotions is betrayed, initially seeking fulfillment in Hotspur, but soon revealing their true motive whenever he speaks of, or with, Hal. These feelings are made to seem all the more powerful by Patrick Stewart's ability to suggest the self-consciousness and fear of rebuff which is responsible for the attempt to keep them hidden. The timid confession of affection in the first interview with Hal in *Part 1*—"Not an eye / But is a-weary of thy common sight, / Save mine, which hath desired to see thee more"—looks forward to the remarkable emotional release as he clasps Hal to him in the deathbed scene of *Part 2*: "My son."

In the parley scene before the Battle of Shrewsbury Trevor Nunn has contrived a moment in which Hal finds himself between his father and Falstaff, with Bolingbroke's look of envious contempt at Sir John and silent appeal for his son's affection answered by Hal's following his friend's insistent call: "Hal, if thou seest me down in the battle. . . ." The King turns away, apparently defeated, an interesting explanation for what in the text is the curious continuation of the estrangement of Hal and his father in *Part 2* in spite of the outcome of the battle. Not until he sees his father dying is this Hal ready to demonstrate any emotional commitment to him.

The emotional commitment to Falstaff, on the other hand, in the early stages of *Part 1*, is overt, even flamboyant, with hair-rufflings and hugs, and, in their first scene together, Hal actually jumping on to Falstaff's lap and cradling himself in his arms, before getting on to his hands and knees to mop up the mess his friend has made eating his breakfast. Joss Ackland's Falstaff responds rather guardedly to these outbursts of boyish affection. He is obviously flattered by them and, like Bolingbroke, is hungry for filial affection: "If I had a thousand sons," he says in his sherris-sack soliloquy, and the long pause before he completes his putative plans for this numerous tribe resonates wistful longing. This Falstaff is certainly a man of powerful emotions, genuine (from moment to moment at least) in his expressions of affection for Hal, for Mistress Quickly, for Doll. He is envious of Poins's intimacy with the prince, and afraid of it—and could be forgiven for remarking "O my prophetic soul" to himself as Poins flaunts past him in the coronation procession at the end of *Part 2* while he stands bewildered and humiliated by Hal's rejection. But Mr Ackland's is not a sentimental Falstaff: the hard edge of the man is there too, the ambition, the intelligence and agility of mind. His accent suggests a lost, but not forgotten, gentility, which makes of his relations with the denizens of Eastcheap a curious mixture of affection and patronising contempt. He is shocked at the execution of the palpably harmless Coleville of the Dale and assiduous and inventive in the pursuit of his own ease and comfort (ends towards which Hal's affection may be exploited), so that it is hardly surprising that he makes an unforgettable moment of his discovery of the corpse of Sir Walter Blunt on Shrewsbury Field: "I like not such grinning honour as Sir Walter hath. Give me *life*." The same conviction obviously lies behind the deliciously ironic contempt with which he greets Hal's sudden onset of enthusiasm for military activity: "Rare words! Brave world! Hostess, my breakfast!" But such ironic detachment is not all; there is a fearsome glint of the quest for power in his eye that prepares us for the rejection as he shouts exultantly to his cronies on receiving the news that his "tender lambkin now is King!" "Let us take any man's horses—the laws of England are at my commandment."

The filial loyalties for which these two men compete are those of Gerard Murphy's Hal. Mr Murphy has many striking qualities as an actor and the casting decision here has obviously been very deliberate. In a production where so much is splendidly right one therefore pauses before succumbing to one's initial impulse that this is altogether wrong. Big, raw-boned and rather shambling, bare-chested, with a toothy grin and a mop of greasy blond hair, this Hal is physically at the opposite extreme from his father, his rebellion from parental authority epitomised in his appearance, with its vague overtones of modern punkishness. All this is effective enough in suggesting his disaffection with everything the court represents. What the performance seems altogether to miss, however, is Hal's intelligence. "I know you all" he says at the end of his first scene, and the role surely demands a sense of an incisive mind, quick to assess the capabilities and weaknesses of others, ahead of the game and unlikely to be surprised. This Hal lacked these qualities, a fact reinforced by his little scene with Francis the drawer and his "anon, anon, sir." What in any unforced reading is a somewhat tasteless exercise in the revelation of mental superiority became just the opposite as Francis, well aware of what was going on and of the role required of him, put up with these princely pranks with a patient shrug and tried to get on with his tasks. With the dimension of intelligence thus missing from Hal, the thoughtful, probing poetry of his soliloquies, and of his contemplation of his father's imminent death and its implications for himself, seemed misplaced in the young man before us and a good deal was thus lost at the political centre of the play. The puppyish dependence on Falstaff early on, shaken by the first interview with his father and knocked out of him by the brutal experience of Shrewsbury and the discovery that in the end he has to fend for himself, led, in *Part 2*, to a somewhat bored submission to the inevitable reconciliation with Bolingbroke and the inexorable doom of kingly power symbolised in that weighty cope. The sentence of banishment on Falstaff was dutifully uttered with a not uninteresting sense of emotional numbness, of the rebel reclaimed by the establishment. But any sense that the Eastcheap experience might be relevant to the demands of kingship, or that Hal was developing intellectually as well as emotionally, was missing. There were compensations, of course, in the increased concentration on the tension of the relationships with his father and Falstaff, but in the exploration of personal psychology at the expense of broader political issues something of the play's scope was undoubtedly diminished.

Around this central trio of King, Prince, and Falstaff, the director and his performers provide a marvellously rich series of characterisations, above all in the Eastcheap scenes. Mike Gwilym presents a manic Pistol, for once brandishing the weapon that provides his name, obviously mad, and dangerously so, very likely to shoot you if you fail to attend with patience to his raving recitation of the dregs of dramatic twaddle he has picked up in the playhouses. He is chased, hilariously and excitingly, over the rooftops of the set (à la Mantalini in *Nickleby*) by a Falstaff who can finally take no more. Miles Anderson gives us a Poins who is handsome and pleased with himself, a young man who fits Falstaff's enviously apprehensive assessment of "a weak mind and an able body" who "plays at quoits well . . . and wears his boots very smooth like unto the sign of the leg," qualities that in this production earn him a place in Henry V's coronation retinue. Gemma Jones's Doll Tearsheet, frowsy, rouged, and unashamed, brings to her scene with Falstaff a poignant sense of affection which gives it a touch of grace in spite of its vulgar decadence. The Cockney Mistress Quickly of Miriam Karlin, peaky and fretful, is a potent mixture of nagging, resilient self-interest and tearful, emotional dependence on Falstaff. Her solicitous enquiry, on Sir John's return from the fracas with Pistol, "are you not hurt i' th' groin," accompanied by a soothing and affectionate rub of the endangered part, leaves little doubt that she is showing considerable generosity of spirit in allowing Doll to serve her friend's sexual needs. Around all these Eastcheap roles there is ample support in the smaller parts, from the splendidly impassive, lugubrious Bardolph of John Rogan down to the little scene of the carriers at Rochester, often cut but here so tellingly played that the search for fleas seems likely to spread to the auditorium, and adding its significant contribution to the marvellous breadth of the play's social spectrum.

At the other end of that spectrum is Timothy Dalton's youthful, rather starry-eyed, Hotspur, romantically handsome, dashing and impetuous, vibrant with pent-up energy and enthusiastic conviction for his cause. His anger with the "certain lord, neat and trimly dressed" who came to demand the prisoners is wittily, and infectiously, described, while his scene with Glendower, excellently played in all his determined Welsh pomposity by Bernard Lloyd, proves a rich source of comedy, with Hotspur's mischievous goading of the tenacious self-esteem and impenetrable smugness of his ally. The battle between Hotspur and Hal begins as a chivalrous confrontation of adversaries (though as a description of this Hal Vernon's reference to "feathered Mercury" may seem a little excessive), but ends in exhaustion as strength ebbs and heavy bodies wrestle and blunder together in a horrible quest for the killer blow, at last achieved, desperately and meanly, with a dagger.

Finally, there is the Shallow of Robert Eddison, who also provides a canny, rather impressive, and perhaps finally somewhat too sympathetic Northumberland. His Shallow dithers and quavers, both physically and verbally, an amiably forgetful and apparently futile figure who yet rules his household, and no doubt his magisterial district, with autocratic, if sometimes rather pettish, determination. In the late afternoon sunlight of Gloucestershire, as he impatiently instructs Davy to sow the headland with red wheat and agrees to countenance the knave William Visor, or in his orchard, in "the sweet o' th' night," when his cousin Silence (played by David Lloyd Meredith) finds what turns out to be a most powerful, and comically unsilenceable, singing voice, he is harmless enough, but though his alliance with Falstaff may in one sense only be the coming together of a pair of has-beens, there is still a submerged sense of threat about the desire of them both to assert themselves. That threat is crushed in the play's final scene as the solemn music of the coronation procession is interrupted, and the stately dignity of Griffith Jones's patriarchal Lord Chief Justice appalled, by the embarrassing shouts of Falstaff's greeting to his King and Jove. Joss Ackland's Falstaff takes the rejection standing, rooted to the spot, astonished, but dignified, not cowed or broken until the King has gone, and the smirking Poins, and the order comes to carry Sir John Falstaff to the Fleet. Then he crumbles. It is a powerful and a moving scene, and in its presentation of the crushing of the individual by the panoply of the regal and political organisation, it again uses the whole company, actors and musicians, *Part 2* thus ending as *Part 1* began.

This is, then, as impressive a first production at the RSCs new London home as one could reasonably wish for, an exciting exploration of a great deal of the immense variety of these plays, and a striking demonstration of the depth and breadth of the Company's talents.

T. F. Wharton

Henry the Fourth Parts I and II: Text and Performance (1983)

Introduction

The following four widely different productions have been chosen for description and comparison, as contributing most to our understanding of key themes of *Henry IV*, and of the range of possibility in the interpretation of character and staging.

1. The RSC production of 1964 at Stratford-upon-Avon, directed by Peter Hall, John Barton and Clifford Williams; designed by John Bury and with music by Guy Wolfenden; Eric Porter as Henry IV, Ian Holm as Hal, Roy Dotrice as Hotspur and as Justice Shallow, Janet Suzman as Lady Percy, Patience Collier as Mistress Quickly, Susan Engel as Doll Tearsheet, Hugh Griffith as Falstaff.

2. The RSC production of 1975 at Stratford-upon-Avon, directed by Terry Hands; designed by Farrah, lighting by Stewart Leviton, and with music by Guy Wolfenden; Emrys James as Henry IV, Alan Howard as Hal, Stuart Wilson as Hotspur, Ann Hasson as Lady Percy, Maureen Pryor as Mistress Quickly, Mikel Lambert as Doll Tearsheet, Sydney Bromley as Justice Shallow, Brewster Mason as Falstaff.

3. The RSC production of 1982 at the Barbican Theatre, London, directed by Trevor Nunn; designed by John Napier, lighting by David Hersey, and with music by Guy Wolfenden; Patrick Stewart as Henry IV, Gerard Murphy as Hal, Timothy Dalton as Hotspur, Harriet Walter as Lady Percy, Miriam Karlin as Mistress

From *"Henry the Fourth Parts I and II." Text and Performance*, by T. F. Wharton. Reprinted by permission of Macmillan Publishers, Ltd.

Quickly, Gemma Jones as Doll Tearsheet, Robert Eddison as Justice Shallow, Joss Ackland as Falstaff.

4. The BBC TV production, first broadcast in December 1979, directed by David Giles; designed by Don Homfrey, and with make-up by Elizabeth Moss; Jon Finch as Henry IV, David Gwillim as Hal, Tim Piggott-Smith as Hotspur, Michele Dotrice as Lady Percy, Brenda Bruce as Mistress Quickly, Frances Cuka as Doll Tearsheet, Robert Eddison as Justice Shallow, Anthony Quayle as Falstaff. (This version has had international release, with repeat showings.)

A word about the choice of productions: with three Royal Shakespeare Company productions and a BBC production, my choice is more "institutional" than I would have preferred. The reason is simply the absence of suitable alternatives. Since *Henry IV* is in two parts, each a full-length play in its own right, productions of it are comparatively rare—except, that is, by the two institutions committed to making the whole of Shakespeare available. Although there were alternatives, these proved on the whole unilluminating. In the end, I have preferred, whatever the incidental disadvantages, to use a good production rather than a bad one.

Henry and Hal: "A Father to My Youth"

The traditional portrayal of Henry IV has been in terms of anguished guilt. John Gielgud's performance in the Orson Welles film *The Chimes at Midnight* (1967) might be called the classic example. Here the king seemed at once ennobled and soured by his burden of conscience. The voice was majestic, but the face betrayed the dyspeptic sufferings of a man for whom life had turned bitter.

"Uneasy lies the head that wears a crown"—Stratford 1964

In the 1964 RSC production (directed jointly by Peter Hall, John Barton and Clifford Williams), Henry was played by Eric Porter. In his interpretation, the king was less bilious than stricken. Dignified—even graceful—in movement and voice, his eyes were haunted by the past. At times, with a characteristic gesture of raising his hands, he seemed to be trying to ward off his ghosts. Even at the beginning there was the aura of the penitential. The stage, in John Bury's design, had massive metal-plated walls as a set; a high-stepped throne; a vast pentangular metal council table; but also, at the back, a narrow stained-glass window. Priests haunted the scene. By Part 2, Henry had assumed a costume of monkish simplicity: a thick coarse robe, tied at the waist with a rope.

Increasingly, the king's energies seemed spent. Doctors were constantly in attendance. At the battle of Shrewsbury he tottered almost helpless under the onslaught of the Douglas. At the end of Part 2, he summed up his victories: how "everything lies level with our wish"; then, sitting at the edge of his narrow bed, he sighed. There was a long pause before his next words: "Only we want a little personal strength."

Yet, in the vital matter of his relationship with Hal there seemed not even the contact of pity between father and son. Their meeting in Part 1 was played with great physical and emotional distance between the two men. When the time came for Hal (Ian Holm) to declare his loyalty, he first went over and closed the door: a telling gesture with its suggestion of guarded secrecy. He remained inaccessible to his father.

"This vile politician, Bolingbroke"—Stratford 1975

Other directors have taken widely differing approaches. The most innovative was certainly Terry Hands's 1975 RSC production at Stratford, with Emrys James cast as Henry.

In this revolutionary interpretation, Henry was presented as being far from inert. This was an abrasive self-made man: contemptuous, possessive, domineering. He was a man who courted aggression. In his first brush with the Northern lords, over the issue of Mortimer's ransom (1, I.iii), he followed Hotspur across the stage to stab a blunt finger at his face on "he never did encounter with Glendower." Openly laughing at Hotspur, he turned to give Blunt his cue to join in the laugh, which he dutifully did. Returning to the throne, Henry peremptorily beckoned Northumberland across to him, only to dismiss him with another stab of the finger: "We license your departure with your son."

A particularly striking detail in this scene—one which reinforced the impression of Henry as a ruthless business-man—involved the use of a coin. Arguing that Mortimer would have to be ransomed from Wales at the Percy family's own cost, with not "one penny" of the crown's money spent on rescuing a "traitor," Henry flung down a coin at Hotspur's feet. Yet as if to reinforce the idea of "not one penny," he checked his exit at the end of the interview and came back to retrieve the coin from the stage.

With such a man as this, one could well understand the hatred the Percy faction bore him. He was insufferable; his aggression made friendship, even compromise, impossible.

Interestingly, Emrys James's Henry clearly alienated his own son, played by Alan Howard. Here, of course, the king wished to inspire love rather than hate. His affection, however, was just as aggressive as his hatred. He seemed to need to possess Hal: seizing him, dragging him down into his lap, kissing him resoundingly, even on the lips. It was small wonder that Hal recoiled with some revulsion. When, before the battle of Shrewsbury, the prince stepped forward to give defiance to Worcester, his father brusquely pulled him back, and took over.

The reaction of Hal is clearly a vital component of Henry's own uneasiness. As already seen, the king interprets his son's behaviour in terms of a divine punishment for his own misdeeds (1, III.ii). With the king occupying only a relatively minor portion of the plays which bear his name, the scenes with his son assume a proportionately greater significance.

The problem with the 1975 RSC interpretation of Henry is that the father's unattractiveness explains all too easily the son's antipathy. The question of a punishment for Henry's sins in the past becomes irrelevant in the face of his behaviour in the present. Nevertheless, the 1975 production enjoyed the considerable advantage of signalling very clearly the idea of Hal's "two fathers." As Hal recoiled from his natural father, his adopted home was in Eastcheap, with Falstaff. There he seemed completely at ease. This was illustrated in Part 1, III.ii and the following scene.

First, however, it should be explained that Terry Hands's production used a technique of the "overlapping" of stage-sets.

Often, the stage-furniture used for one scene was left on-stage during the next, even though that might be located in a quite different place. And often, even the characters who had appeared in the previous scene would hang about at the end of it and silently look on at the next. So, at the end of II.iv—a tavern scene—some barrels and tankards were left on-stage during the first two scenes of Act III. The second scene of the Act is that of Henry's reprimand of his son and, at the end of it, of their reconciliation. As already mentioned, Henry marked his satisfaction over the reconciliation by seizing and kissing Hal. The prince's recoil was exemplified, in Alan Howard's performance, by his breaking free on Blunt's entry, crossing to one of the barrels left on-stage, picking up a tankard by it, and beginning to drink. This very small detail, which does not go unnoticed by the king, is characteristic of Hal's instinctive recoil from the court, and his equally instinctive recourse to the tavern-world as his home and refuge.

Yet undoubtedly the emotional centre of Terry Hands's production was the second reconciliation of father and son, in Part 2. If, in the greater part of the plays, Hal had seemed emotionally regressive—swishing a stick like a small boy, even sucking a thumb, always retreating to Falstaff for comfort—the second reconciliation scene (IV.iv) marked his growing-up.

Given the aggressiveness with which Emrys James played the king, the scene predictably started in near-hysteria. Awaking to find the crown gone (removed by Hal), Henry rose from his bed of terminal illness to jump on a chair and rant at his son. Snatching the crown, he rammed it back on Hal's head; falling to his knees, he crawled around the bed before collapsing on to it. His prophecy of the ruin of his kingdom was a howl of pain. Yet the audience had already seen from Alan Howard's performance that this was a different Hal. When he first placed the crown on his own head, his face registered anguish as well as wonderment. He blinked as if subjected to a blinding light, but immediately his voice seemed to take on a new authority. When therefore he realised his father was still alive, and that he had robbed him of his crown, he reacted with a quite new moral sensibility. When the king jammed the crown back on his head, Hal cried out in protest. His self-abasement in making his apology was painful to watch, and the reconciliation of father and son intensely moving.

For the remainder of the scene, Hal acted almost as the attentive nurse of his father: supporting him, making him comfortable, retrieving the crown and giving it to him—and finally carrying him out in his arms. The lines at the end of the scene (where other characters should enter) were cut in this production so that this highly emotional reunion should be undiluted.

"His temper therefore must be well observed"—Barbican 1982

Another production making good use of Hal's youth in interpreting his character is that of Trevor Nunn in 1982 at the Barbican Theatre, London. Perhaps even more than the RSC's 1975 production at Stratford, this one performed by the same national company sought to explain Hal's truancy in terms of adolescent rebellion.

In the 1982 production, however, the impulse seemed to come very much from Hal himself, as played by Gerard Murphy. There was much less obvious reason for his behaviour, largely because the king was far less obviously obnoxious as a man.

In fact, in Patrick Stewart's interpretation of the role, the king emerged almost as a nobody. Neither as sick as Eric Porter's Henry IV nor as aggressive as Emrys James's, he is a man in whom almost everything is clamped down under control and neutralised. His costume is the plainest imaginable: a simple white tunic, buttoned high at the neck; black trousers, just visible, tucked into black knee-boots. This was the costume—reminiscent of a Russian kulak—which was revealed beneath his golden cloak of office in the first scene of Part 1; and he wore it throughout, except during the battle. It indicated cleanliness and fastidiousness—an impression reinforced by his short-cut hair, his extreme economy of movement, and the characteristic habit of taking a refined sip of cordial from a goblet that was always at hand for him when he entered and sat.

During the quarrel scene with the Percy leaders (1, I.iii), all the men at the council table were won over by Hotspur's impulsive speech of excuse for the refusal to yield his prisoners' ransoms—all save the king. At one point, as Hotspur bent down at Henry's side, "beseeching" his tolerance, he leaned his arm on the table. Henry moved his hand forward. For an instant, as the hand hesitated, it seemed as if he was going to lay it on Hotspur's arm. But he then reached past him for his goblet, and the moment—and the opportunity for peace that it offered—was gone for ever.

In the first reconciliation scene with Hal (1, III.ii), the same tightly inhibited Henry was evident. There was the same almost prim fastidiousness about the set. The king sat in a sparsely furnished room, with only a table, a chair and a ewer for washing his hands. The table and the ewer-stand were covered with purple cloths, each with a small gold emblem of the crown. Henry kept his son standing. He yielded nothing. Rather, he actually produced, from a drawer in the table, the bags which had been stolen at Gadshill, slamming them down on the table. Crossing to Hal and carrying a cushion, he perched it on his son's head, making him both feel and look a fool, wearing his mock-crown as he had done in the earlier tavern-scene. Returning to his seat, as Hal began his apology in earnest, the king hardly looked at him. He wore, in fact, his most characteristic facial expression: eyes screwed up tight, mouth twisted into an ambiguous ironic smile. Only at the very end of the prince's speech did Henry's expression seem less sardonic, and the son was permitted, for a few seconds, an expression of genuine pleasure on "A hundred thousand rebels die in this." Then, immediately, he tidied the bags back into the drawer of his table and bent back to his paper-work, hardly raising his eyes to his son again. The pattern was repeated again and again. The tight quiet manner very occasionally broke down—as when Henry shouted at his son or at Worcester—to betray the force of feeling inside the man. But whenever a genuine impulse seemed about to escape, he choked it back. When Worcester came to present the dissidents' grievances and Hal made his offer of single combat against Hotspur (1, V.i), the idea seemed momentarily to seize the king's imagination. Patrick Stewart almost ran down from his balcony position to the main stage. On the instant he reached it, however, he checked. The sober control returned, and Henry's next words came out almost stiffly: "Albeit considerations infinite / Do make against it."

In Part 2, Henry became even less expressive. The "book of fate" speech (III.i) seemed deliberately underplayed. When his collapse finally came (IV.iv), he was laid to rest on a bed (tilted forward in a wedge-shape, for visibility), where he lingered for the remainder of his "life." His by-now customary demeanour of a man suffering absurd injuries was merely a little heightened in the second crisis with his son. Warwick's disclosure that Hal had been found in tears over the "stolen" crown was received with a harsh laugh. The king's recriminations to his son were delivered with violent sarcasm. Throughout Hal's long apology, Henry twisted his face away, his true reaction veiled in a sardonic grimace of a smile. It was not clear until his loud cry "O my son," and his embrace of Hal, how he was responding. Then all his remaining energies were summoned to rattle out his last desperate advice to his successor: a political homily which Hal, thinking more of his father's death than of his own succession, seemed hardly to hear.

When told that his death-chamber was called "Jerusalem," Henry alone saw the bitter joke of having been assured that he would die in Jerusalem, and of having thought it meant the Holy Land. Altogether, in Part 2, King Henry in Trevor Nunn's production became a figure who realised the sour jest that life had played on him and his ambitions. He became a man obsessively working himself to death with papers and state-business, knowing that everything he did was pointless.

It was to this man that his son finally responded. For the bulk of the two plays, Gerard Murphy's Hal had been a young man whose feelings and responses to most other men had been confused and contradictory. Suddenly, everything became simple. He responded to his father's imminent death with a complete abandonment to grief: his nose blocked and his voice choked with tears, knuckles in his eyes, his whole body shaking with sobs. Since Gerard Murphy was a stocky well-built Hal, this came over with great theatrical force. The prince who had suffered from such an uncertain and fluctuating temper, who had been such a creature of moods, had finally discovered in himself an uncomplicated and unsullied emotion. He had suddenly found that he had loved his father.

As with Terry Hands's production at Stratford in 1975, this of Trevor Nunn at the Barbican in 1982 was again an interpretation of "growing up." Earlier in the performance, Hal had seemed a particularly loutish, awkward youth. He had so often moved or stood awkwardly, his face contorted into improbable grimaces, violently shaking his head and his shock of fair hair. Hereafter, all these gauche mannerisms were gone. His father's death had taught him how to be a man.

"How came I by the crown, O God forgive"—Television 1979

In all three of the interpretations we have been discussing, one common factor is detectable in regard to the relationship of father and son, among widely differing emphases. It is that, however Hal responds to his father, the king emerges as a figure who is tightly bound up in his own obsessions. He need not be exactly withdrawn. Emrys James's extrovert King Henry in Terry Hands's production shows this. Yet he gives very little to his son. If understanding can be achieved between them, it falls to Hal to penetrate the barriers, not only in himself, but also in his father.

In this respect, the production of the *Henry IV* plays in the BBC's televised "complete Shakespeare" series ran entirely true to form. Directed by David Giles and first broadcast in December 1979, it presented the king, again, as a figure of harsh remoteness. In the end, whatever contact was established between him and his son was made to seem both odd and unsatisfactory.

From the beginning of Part 1, Jon Finch as Henry adopted a highly stylised and stagey delivery of his lines. The words were chanted out, mostly in pedantic monotone. The technique was at its most idiosyncratic in the first reconciliation scene (1, III.ii), with the words perversely chopped up into separate syllables ("pro-phet-ic-all-y"), and the lines desiccated into a sing-song iambic "tune" ("Of év-rỹ béard-lĕss váin cŏm-párătīve"). Only the occasional soar in register broke the pattern.

But then, the director had evidently intended that this scene between father and son should be played very "dead." Jon Finch delivered his complaints moving forward to the camera to ¾-shot, leaving David Gwillim's Hal in long-shot behind him. Hal watched his father with a face absolutely neutral and lifeless. Whenever his father turned to look at him, Hal looked down, avoiding his eyes, raising his own again only when his father had turned away. He seemed locked in a kind of numbness, until stirred by the

king's wilder allegations (that Hal was as much his father's enemy
as Hotspur) into self-defence. Yet even here, the scene avoided
any sense of real contact. Hal's promises of reform were delivered
with a smug half-smile, conveying a sense of secrecy and private
knowledge. He remained as immobile as before, giving nothing to
his father.

In the corresponding scene in Part 2 (IV.iv), the camera was
located beyond the king's bed, catching Hal's approach, and behind him, through an open doorway, the nobles of the court
watching him. Hal's reaction to what seemed to be his father's
death was carefully registered, and the grief seemed strong. Yet,
as he bent over to kiss his father, he was stopped by sight of the
crown on the pillow. The crown seemed to inspire the greater
emotion. He lifted it reverently, wonderingly, up to his own head,
his voice trembling with feeling. The kiss for his father was
forgotten.

Similarly, when the king then awoke to find the crown gone,
its loss revealed tremendous energy still in him, carrying over into
his reproaches on Hal's return. Jon Finch was by turns plaintive,
bitter, angry, mocking and hysterical in his well-shaped long
speech. In the reconciliation it was again the crown which played
a central part in the emotions evoked and experienced. David
Giles's production stressed strongly that what pacified the king
was Hal's little charade of how, thinking his father was indeed
dead, he had taken the crown to reproach it. David Gwillim
played the charade in an extremely broad and stylised way; and as
he established the imaginary relationship with the crown, the
camera registered the incredulity on the king's face giving way to
tentative belief. Finally, the two men crouched at the foot of the
sick-bed as Henry gave his dying advice. Again, it was the crown
which seemed to draw the scene's emotions to itself. It was placed
prominently between them on the bed; and the final camera shot,
before the two men were rejoined by others, was of the king, full-
face, pushing the crown across to his son on "How came I by the
crown, O God forgive, / And grant it may with thee in true peace
live!"

Using the resources of the camera, to zoom and pan and track,
and home-in on the *visual* focus of a scene, the director had given
the crown a physical centrality impossible on a large stage. The
effect was to establish in our minds the distortion of emotion in

Hal and Henry. There were emotions, but they were passed from one to the other only through the crown and its magnetic power to attract avid feeling. Consequently, there was no final understanding between father and son: only a shared obsession.

Hal and Others: "I Know You All"

"Thus we play the fools with the time"—Stratford 1964

The interpretation of the play which has been most committed to the idea of a "cold-blooded" Hal was the RSC 1964 version. Hal was played by Ian Holm, a physically ideal choice. Small, tidy, economical in his acting, everything about him contrasted with Hugh Griffith's Falstaff. Our first view of the two men was of them emerging from sleep from under the straw in a wagon. They went across to a pump, to douse each other with water. Falstaff was in a nightshirt the size of a bell-tent. Hal wore a neat dark doublet and hose. His physical appearance suggested Hamlet rather than a prodigal son.

Holm played the part neither primly nor censoriously. There were moments when his Hal seemed entirely at ease in the world of Eastcheap: the moments when he would lay an arm on Falstaff's shoulder, or allow himself to be picked up and hugged by the fat knight. Yet the impression was always of self-containment. In the great tavern scene of Part 1 (II.iv), there was a good deal of laughter, but the joke was clearly on Falstaff rather than shared with him. One remembers Hal's turning his back on Falstaff's gouty tirade on cowardice, to shake with silent giggles; his assuming an expression of mock wonderment at Falstaff's Gadshill exploits; his bending over the fat knight in the chair, eyebrows raised, gleefully open-mouthed, his head giving little sharp nods, as he issued his challenge for Falstaff to wriggle out of the truth. It was all good fun, but the overwhelming impression of Hal's brand of humour was its stress on the ironic and the preposterous in what he saw around him. When Falstaff claimed, "I knew ye," Hal turned away in disgust. When he "deposed" Falstaff in the role of King Henry, in the "mock reprimand," his expression became much tighter, and with Falstaff groping for comfort—"banish not him thy Harry's company"—looked at him pitilessly as he said, "I do, I will."

Earlier, when Falstaff went to the door to investigate what the nobleman there wanted, Hal, in his absence, had already shown more than a hint of steely authority. As Falstaff disappeared up the stairs, Hal gave a little laugh, and then stopped. He looked at the others. They gave a little laugh, and stopped. Hal laughed again. They laughed again. Then, they clustered round him, to curry favour by excusing their own part in the cowardice and by ratting on Falstaff. Hal heard them with a mocking insolent smile.

Every other detail of Ian Holm's performance reinforced the impression of self-containment and control. His final interview with his father (2, IV.iv) disclosed that he was capable of tears; but he gripped his father's hand tightly, at the bedside, choking them back. Always secretive, he rose at the end of this scene when he heard the others returning, so that nobody should see him in his father's arms. Earlier, when he took away the crown and placed it on his head, he moved slowly, staring into space like a sleep-walker. His face was absolutely neutral. When he actually ascended the throne legitimately (V.ii), his quiet icy authority had finally found the role for which it was suited. His brothers, as one man, sank to their knees. As he walked through them, and away towards the exit, he made no attempt to encourage them to rise. As for Eastcheap, he had, until then, at best condescended to tolerate the company of his inferiors. On his coronation, he rejected Falstaff with exactly the same pitiless sadness anticipated so long before in the "mock-reprimand" scene, as he looked down on the portly kneeling figure.

In the 1966 revival of this production (in fact, Ian Holm was one of only a very few survivors), the character of Hal had been pushed further down the same road. He seemed actively to enjoy giving pain. Yet the pain of others gave him no pleasure, no zest. Even in 1964, however, he had emerged as a joyless figure.

The point was made all the clearer by the carefully contrasted figure of Hotspur, lovingly portrayed by Roy Dotrice. This was a kilted, wild Hotspur, yet everything about him was full of warmth and exuberance.

The major scene with his wife Lady Percy is often played as knockabout (1, II.iii). In the Roy Dotrice/Janet Suzman version, it was still rough, but also very intimate, with a good deal of the scene played on the floor—husband and wife pushing over, kissing, tumbling, wrapping-up, kneeling astride or lying on top. Although Roy Dotrice is not physically large, everything about him seemed impressive. His accent was notably thicker than that of his kinsmen. Where every other warrior was content with a normal sword, Hotspur's was a huge two-handed cleaver.

In war, he was in his element. In anticipation of it, he had "ridden" his saddle which his servant brought in on a saddle-stand. When the event arrived, he seemed on fire. All his restless energy, so evident from the very beginning, found its fulfilment as he leaped to do battle with Hal, laughing aloud as he swung the huge sword clanging against Hal's crossed sword and dagger, or forcing him to draw in his stomach like a hoop to escape it. Battles were an RSC specialty at this period. There were always hordes of extras, gun-smoke, cannon-fire and well-choreographed skirmishing. This fight, though, was exceptional. The audience feared for the physical safety of the two actors. And when finally, as they fought around a long horse-trough, and Hotspur's great sword thudded into the side of it, allowing Hal to get in and stab him under the ribs and lower him, dying, into the trough, there was what can only be described as a collective sigh from the audience. He had won the audience's love by his joy in life. Now he was dead; and curiously, the man who remained alive seemed to have no zest for life at all.

"A most princely hypocrite"—Television 1979

Not too far away from Ian Holm's interpretation was the 1979 television version, with David Gwillim as Hal. It was a more ambiguous performance than Holm's. David Gwillim seemed to have been cast as a fun-loving prince. His dimpled face seemed made for this kind of interpretation. In fact, it never really materialised. His laughter tended to have a scoffing quality. The scene with Poins in Part 2 (II.ii), set in a grimy little wood-panelled room of an inn, was distinctly an edgy one, with Hal's confession of his distaste for his companions done as a calculated insult.

Above all, though, his relationship with Falstaff revealed a similar vein of detachment and distaste. In the great tavern scene of Part 1 (II.iv), Hal was the one man among Falstaff's audience who was not won over by his performance. As Quayle's Falstaff prepared for the play of reprimand, Hal goaded him on the subject of his cowardly "instinct." His comments raised a laugh, trading as they did on Falstaff's own jokes and phrases, but Hal himself did not smile. When, during the reprimand-play, the roles were reversed, Hal as King Henry described Falstaff in a list of insults which were also delivered straight faced. The company began by laughing at these, willingly enough, still buoyed up by Falstaff's own performance as King Henry. Gradually, however, the laughter petered out. The scene became very still, and the only sound was of Hal's voice. The camera, moving in ½-shot between the two men, registered the intentness in Hal, and the injured feelings in Falstaff. For Falstaff to keep up the pretence of good humour ("I would your grace would take me with you. Whom means your grace?") required a distinct effort. In his speech of self-defence, his habitual anxiety assumed the proportion of near-desperation. With the bustle of Bardolph noisily running in, and drawing everyone's attention, Hal's words "I do, I will" were spoken quietly and meaningfully, and heard by Falstaff alone. He opened his mouth to speak, but no words came, as Hal still stared him down.

We have already seen how, in the television version, the relationship of Hal with his father, even in the final reconciliation, seemed depleted and distorted. Again, the production offered—as had the 1964 RSC version—the kind of Hotspur to make the point even clearer by contrast. As with the 1964 version, this Hotspur (in Tim Piggott-Smith's interpretation) was full of affection as well as vitality. With his fellow-conspirators he seemed perhaps no more than the mad-cap young lord, set off against the splendid laconic playing of his uncle Worcester by Clive Swift. With his wife Lady Percy, however, there was a great deal of coarse tenderness. In their major scene together (1, II.iii), Piggott-Smith and Michele Dotrice played it with a smile, with lightness and humour. Hotspur's talk of love was scornful, yet done as boisterous teasing. His wife, not knowing whether to believe him, beat his chest with her tiny fists in frustration. The same tone was sustained in their farewell scene (1, III.i), where their physical contact was a constant rhythm of playful repulses and tender capture. Theirs seemed to have been a long and intimate friendship. When he tried to make her sing, like the Welsh lady, she betrayed in the surprising violence of her reply ("I will NOT sing") all the pent-up force of her anxiety at his departure.

The most memorable scene in either part of the play in this production was Lady Percy's lament for the death of her husband (2, II.iii). Elizabeth Moss's make-up scheme had achieved the difficult feat of making Michele Dotrice look dreadful. She walked a little aside from her parents-in-law for the speech, and the camera tightened in to close-up on her. It held that shot throughout the whole of her lament, except for one brief reaction-shot of a horror-struck Northumberland. She was barely able to begin speaking, managing to do so only by talking with deliberate slowness, one phrase at a time, pulling down her head, fighting off the tears. As the speech proceeded, her agonised face and voice went to the very edge of control. In her anguish, we had the final testimony to the kind of love Hotspur could inspire.

David Gwillim's Hal was a much better-looking man than Hotspur, yet the face which contained the boyish smile and the athletically-working mouth remained totally opaque. There was nothing behind it. When he assumed the role of kingship, he did so with a likable modesty. His rejection of Falstaff was with a look of affecting pity. And yet, here as elsewhere, the skin-deep attractiveness was designed to convey a man almost without strong identity, whose every impulse was pallid. At the very end, his voice subtly changed and took on something of the stilted rhetorical air of his father's, again enhancing the sense that there was almost no such person, no such identity as "Hal." It was a very deeply studied playing, by David Gwillim, of a very shallow man.

"Riot and dishonour stain the brow of my young Harry"—Stratford 1975

Perhaps the great divide, amongst the different types of Hal available, is between those who drink and those who do not. In neither the 1964 nor the television production can it be recalled that Hal actually drank any wine. Perhaps another test is how the director responds to a line of Falstaff's, spoken to Doll with Hal present, in the tavern scene of Part 2: "His grace [the prince] says that which his flesh rebels against." Some productions suggest at this point that Hal is experiencing the stirrings of desire for Doll. Again, the 1964 and television Hals are not guilty. In both the 1975 and 1982 productions, however, Hal both drank and felt desire. These very minor distinctions indicate a quite different emphasis. In neither of these cases do we have a "cold" Hal, but rather a creature of strong impulse.

As to the 1975 RSC version, Hal's relationship with his father and with Falstaff—the triangular relationship which links them— has already been explained. The other, earlier Hals had been— however shallow—fully formed. This Hal of Alan Howard was younger, and in the process of growing up. His speech, "I know you all" was delivered as a vague good intention, not as a meticulous life-plan. His first real rebuff of Falstaff—"I do, I will" (1, II.iv)—was produced when he had been badly stung by a comment of Falstaff's own. The latter's line, on the subject of Hal's enemies, "Art thou not horribly afeared?" had produced a long and awkward silence. Falstaff had evidently struck a nerve, and had to suffer the consequences: discovering, in Hal's sharp promise of banishment, that playing with even the cub of a lion was not without its risks. Yet, the moment was a local collision, not a master-plan. It became increasingly clear that Hal was actually growing away from Falstaff, but the impulse never hardened into a scheme for his rejection. When, before the battle of Shrewsbury, Falstaff, sitting in a cart, tried to detain a now-brisk Hal from rushing away to battle by wrapping his legs around him, Hal wrenched free. Yet the prince seemed to be at pains almost to apologise for his escape, and did so in terms of the horse-play which typified their relationship, lobbing him an apple in a wave of farewell.

At the end of the plays, the emotional climax of the reconciliation with his father marked Hal's final growing-up. It was therefore a new man who, as Henry V, banished his old companion. The banishment began with a tremendously effective theatrical stroke. Farrah's set for the production had been until now very stark and bare. But, before the coronation-procession entered, stage-hands ran down from the back to the front of the stage, drawing down a huge white cloth over the stage behind them. Gold rushes were strewn on the white cloth. The lighting was suddenly brilliant. The bell that had tolled for the death of Henry IV now gave way to trumpets at the coronation of his son. The group of Falstaff's friends formed a ragged line from back to front down the stage-left depth of the stage. The new king's close family and allies entered, forming a similar line, stage-right. The contrast between the resulting two parallel lines was very strong. On the one side, there were the quaint cut-off smocks and wrinkled leggings of the rustics, the thonged-leather ballad-singer-like costume of Pistol, the curious Sinbad-like clothes of Bardolph. On the other were the pure white cloaks and scarlet St. George's crosses of the crowned nobility, and the scarlet robe and golden chain of the Lord Chief Justice. The contrast was very considerably to the disadvantage of the first group. They looked a ragged mob. When therefore the king, in his coronation march, walked down the centre of the alleyway formed by the two lines, clad completely in golden armour from head to toe, a double-winged gold cape behind him, only to be halted by the kneeling figure of Falstaff in his carpet-bag-design coat, red hose and baggy boots, there could be no possible surprise at the rejection.

Henry V's was not only a new régime. It was to be a brilliant one. The dazzling splendour of the court party confirmed that. While we felt for Falstaff's pathetic blindness, there could be no doubt which choice Henry V must now make.

"Presume not that I am the thing I was"—Barbican 1982

By far the subtlest treatment of the role of Hal, however, was in the 1982 RSC production. If the actual standard of acting seemed at first unpromising in general in this production (compared, say, with the exceptionally gifted cast of 1964), there were marvellous compensations in the thoughtfulness of the interpretation.

As already mentioned, Gerard Murphy's Hal was a creature of impulse rather than of calculation. His version of "I know you all" seemed surprisingly bitter. He appeared to snarl out the words, as he sat hunched on a barrel, loutishly picking his feet. The tone of the speech seemed to be, "I'll show you," as if what he had in mind was scoring a point against his enemies. In the "mock-reprimand," his dissatisfaction with a life of waste and pointlessness was evident. What began as a convincing impersonation of his father's stiff manner, complete with sips of cordial, became personally vituperative and savage as he spoke of Falstaff's vices. In this production, however, Joss Ackland's Falstaff remained uncrushed. His, "I would your grace would take me with you. Whom means your grace?" got a laugh that deflated Hal's urgency and irritated him still more. Falstaff's subsequent defence of tavern life was done with confidence, winning growls of approval from the stage-audience of drinkers. This too added to Hal's ill-temper, and when the promised rejection was spoken, it was thrown at Falstaff in the tone of a childish "Yah," and with a nasty coarse laugh. As often happened in the inn-scenes of Trevor Nunn's production, nobody laughed with Hal.

Yet the same man was capable of great spontaneous affection for his fat friend. Immediately after the promise of rejection he gave Falstaff an ardent hug around the neck. When in Part 1 (IV.ii), Falstaff with his cannon-fodder recruits met Hal on the road—or when, rather, Hal almost fell over him, since Falstaff was stretched out for a nap—the director altered the text so that Westmoreland's entry was not with Hal but delayed. By the time he did arrive, Hal and Falstaff were not only enjoying a good laugh together, but actually rolling on the floor, in tavern rough-and-tumble. They both scrambled guiltily to their feet when he entered. At the end of the great Tavern scene in Part 2 (II.iv), Hal concluded his remarkably mild protests to Falstaff about being abusive to Doll and Quickly by gently kissing the old man on the cheek. It was a kind of fond farewell.

Again, the figure of Hotspur helped to form our response to Hal. Here, most unusually, he emerged (in Timothy Dalton's interpretation) not as a contrast but as a parallel. The warm-hearted side of him was played down, and replaced by moodiness. Many of his more "poetic" lines were cut. His impulsiveness was much like Hal's own. In the first scene with his wife (1, II.iii), he knelt, reading, as his wife came creeping downstairs. Played by Harriet Walter as a very submissive lady, she crouched beside him. The two figures became, suddenly, two people talking about their marriage. They looked grim and lugubrious. Hotspur jumped up, to call for his horse. Lady Percy followed, attempting playfully to wheedle his secrets out of him. Quite suddenly he turned on her. The line, "Away, you trifler" was delivered with ferocious force. When he said, "I care not for thee, Kate," there was no doubt that he meant it. If at the end he relented, holding out a hand to her which eventually she took, the patching-up of their marriage was only temporary. In their only other scene together (1, III.i)—a scene which is usually nothing more than a piece of pleasant domestic nonsense, with the Welsh lady's song—Hotspur's declared fancy for the Welsh lady's bed looked all too probably true. When his wife took offence and refused to sing as requested, he seemed deliberately to pick a quarrel on this trivial matter in order to break away and leave her.

Earlier in that scene, listening to Worcester's lecture on good manners, Hotspur again produced an unexpected and unusual emphasis on "Well, I am *schooled*," sarcastically slapping his own wrist. Throughout this scene he had sulked at Glendower, the silken Celtic diplomat. Again, he was trying to pick a fight. Like Hal, he was a difficult man. Trevor Nunn's direction gave particular emphasis to their various envious speeches about each other. They were alike; and this made much more sense than usual of their rivalry.

Yet the most intriguing point of all in this production was that Hotspur was not really Hal's worst enemy.

If Hal emerged, in Gerard Murphy's interpretation, as a deeply unhappy man, it was not merely because he was unhappy and unsettled with tavern life. Far more disturbing to him was the divided response he felt towards his own family. This division of feeling was something particularly concentrated on a pair of figures who emerged almost as the villains of the production: Hal's brother, Prince John, and his nearest friend and ally, Westmoreland (played, respectively, by Kevin Wallace and Bernard Brown).

The production gave full weight to the idea which Hal expressed during the battle of Shrewsbury: that his father's mind had been poisoned against him. In the very first scene, we saw Westmoreland at work, doing the poisoning. The king was speaking of the "gallant" prowess of Hotspur. Westmoreland responded very pointedly: "In faith, / It is a conquest for a *prince* to boast of." The loaded emphasis, and the significant look which accompanied it, transformed an innocent speech into a veiled insinuation, hinting at the deficiencies of the king's own son. When Hal finally appeared at court (1, III.ii) and approached his father, the nobles who left the chamber brushed past him, looking him up and down and snubbing him. At the end of Part 1 Prince John evidently resented Hal's reconciliation with his father. When Hal offered his brother the "gift" of the honour of releasing the Douglas without ransom, Kevin Wallace interpreted the lines, "I thank your grace for this high courtesy, / Which I shall give away immediately," as, "thanks for nothing: I can't wait to get rid of *that* gift."

By Part 2 it became clear that Hal's dislike of his younger brother was well-founded. It was Prince John, not Hal, who seemed to be faking grief on the death of their father. The Gaultree Forest scenes, difficult to condone at the best of times, were so directed as to give full weight to the unpleasantest side of Prince John and Westmoreland. Both became sour-faced sermonisers in their speeches to the rebels, so that their show of piety made their own deviousness all the more repellent. It clearly came hard to Westmoreland to have to kiss the archbishop's hand. Prince John made a much better job of it, emerging as a supersmooth hypocrite, with a glittering smile, which slipped when he was not seen, but was carefully replaced whenever a rebel turned to him. It was clearly, for John, a moment of revenge for having earlier been forced to kiss the archbishop's hand, when he seized it to arrest him, made a mock-gesture of raising it to his lips, but then tore from the hand its ring of office.

The equation was made very clear: of the zeal and clean-living of Hal's young brother, and the operation of politics at its most cynical and inhumane. Slightly against the text, the archbishop's faction came over by contrast as well-meaning innocents.

Even Falstaff was used to reinforce this impression. In Joss Ackland's interpretation, there was no great stress on Falstaff as predator. Rather, he turned out finally to seem to vindicate the claims he had made in Part 1, that his real affinity was with whatever was humane. On the one occasion when Prince John met Falstaff (2, IV.iii), the latter had just captured a prisoner, one Coleville. He was much inclined to gloat over the fact, oblivious to the agonies of embarrassment this inflicted on Coleville. Yet when Prince John smirkingly sentenced Coleville to death, Falstaff registered horror. There was an interesting repeat of these two contrasted reactions at the very end of Part 2, with Prince John enthralled at the prospect of Hal's launching a foreign war, but the Lord Chief Justice clearly deeply disturbed at the thought. The inhumanity of the pious and of their agents was again shown in the brief scene (2, V.iv) featuring the purge of the brothels and the arrest of Doll, in which her captors tried to rape her.

With brutality and ruthlessness so clearly personified in John and Westmoreland, Hal's truancy in Eastcheap finally fell very clearly into place. It was a matter of his instinctive recoil from the tainted politics of his father's reign. Turning from the "respectable" world, he made his gesture of rejection as pointed as possible by keeping the vilest company he could find. Of course, he could never be at ease in Eastcheap. He too clearly despised his own waste and riot, and was all too inclined to take it out on his companions. A neat detail here was the way in which the boy-waiter Francis, about to curl up asleep on the floor at the end of Part 2, II.iv, warily circled around Hal, keeping well out of reach. At this stage, Hal's only profit from Eastcheap was to pick up the trick of fighting dirty (Bardolph in battle was an expert groin-kicker!) which he put to good use in killing Hotspur with a knife under the ribs and across the throat.

Yet Eastcheap was Hal's only outlet for his undoubted capacity to love and to give affection. In Part 2, with the sub-plot so clearly identified with harmlessness, fun and humanity—at least, as much of them as was possible in the edgy and destructive régime of a usurper—Hal's choice of low-life made complete human sense. When, prematurely taking the crown, he placed it on his own head, he did so with no appearance of pleasure or awe. Rather, with a clumsy ugly gesture, he jammed it on his thatch of hair. Its advent brought only grief: partly for the death of his father, but more for the loss of his own treasured escape-route from the contamination of politics. At his coronation procession, in his new public role, he seemed like a man in a daze. When he rejected Falstaff, he deliberately stepped outside the line of the coronation procession, and for those few lines, regained expressiveness, delivering his verdict with a strained smile, choking off a sob. When he resumed his place in the procession, his face was again a blank. The moment symbolised the loss of humanity which his new role entailed, and the extent that humanity had been represented by his old companion.

Intriguingly, at the end of the procession walked the figure of Poins. Against the indications in the text, it seemed that Poins had survived where Falstaff had not. Beautifully played as a cool cynic by Miles Anderson, he had throughout enjoyed a slightly different kind of intimacy with Hal from the others in the tavern: the relationship perhaps of two ex-public-schoolboys. Incapable of being provoked, and with the happy knack of not provoking Hal overmuch, Poins had made himself indispensable. The new king desperately needed human contact, consigned as he now was to the loveless world of the court. Poins, respectable enough to be salvaged from Eastcheap, was the one friend Hal had left.

Conclusions

The performing theatre arts have an extraordinarily broad license in interpreting the plays they perform. In effect, the very marked differences of emphasis from production to production represent the working evidence of widely disparate critical interpretations. Opinions will always continue to shift, and new productions will continue to disclose new resources in the plays.

The key figure is inevitably Hal. Whatever a production does with other key figures matters less than what it does with Hal. Versions of Falstaff might differ widely, as these four have; but his status in the play will always be basically the same, as the chosen focus of Hal's truancy. A new interpretation of King Henry as, say, an abrasive self-made man (as in the 1975 RSC production) may be inventive and pleasing. Yet still, his basic function in the play will likewise be the same: as suffering usurper, and inadequate father.

Yet the chosen nature of Hal in any given production will necessarily condition and entail so much else. If Hal is shallow (as in the TV production) or cold and withdrawn (as in 1964), the corollary is automatically that Hotspur or Falstaff or the Gloucestershire scenes will and must emerge as "warm." If Hal is, on the other hand, played as impulsive or immature (as in 1982 and 1975), then the Hotspur contrast tends to be obliterated entirely. Far more significantly, so does the contrast with Eastcheap.

Both approaches have support in the text, and the 1964 and 1982 versions particularly vividly represent the possibilities of each. Notably, in both versions, Hal is trapped between court and tavern; though in one case nothing at all touches the Prince, while in the other he is racked with conflicting emotions towards both worlds. The second interpretation is more humanly comprehensible. The first makes more sense of the idea of a man awaiting a national destiny, which the plays undoubtedly contain. Inevitably, the most recent of the productions we have discussed tends to seem the most persuasive. Fortunately the play is big enough to accommodate both interpretations.

Bibliography

Auden, W. H. "The Prince's Dog." *"The Dyer's Hand" and Other Essays.* New York: Random House, 1948, pp. 182–208.

Barber, C. L. "Rule and Misrule in *Henry IV.*" *Shakespeare's Festive Comedy: A Study of Dramatic Form and Its Relation to Social Custom.* Princeton: Princeton University Press, 1959, pp. 192–221.

Barish, Jonas A. "The Turning Away of Prince Hal." *Shakespeare Studies* 1 (1965), 9–17.

Bradley, A. C. "The Rejection of Falstaff." *Oxford Lectures on Poetry.* London: Macmillan, 1909, pp. 247–73.

Burckhardt, Sigurd. "'Swoll'n with Some Other Grief': Shakespeare's Prince Hal Trilogy." *Shakespearean Meanings.* Princeton: Princeton University Press, 1968, pp. 144–68, 183–89.

Coleridge, Samuel Taylor. "*Henry IV*: The Character of Falstaff," in conversation as reported by J. P. Collier, c. 1811. From Collier's Preface to his edition of *Seven Lectures on Shakespeare and Milton*, 1856, xiv–1. *Coleridge on Shakespeare*, ed. R. A. Foakes. London: Routledge & Kegan Paul, 1971, p. 130.

Cumberland, Richard. "Remarks Upon the Characters of Falstaff and His Group." *The Observer.* London, 1786, no. 86.

Dorius, R. J. "A Little More Than a Little." *Shakespeare Quarterly* 11 (1960), 13–26.

Dowden, Edward. "The English Historical Plays." *Shakespeare: A Critical Study of His Mind and Art.* London: Kegan Paul, 1875. American and Colonial ed., n. d., pp. 209–17.

Frye, Northrop. "The Argument of Comedy." *English Institute Essays 1948.* New York: Columbia University Press, 1949, pp. 66–73.

Gottschalk, Paul A. "Hal and the 'Play Extempore' in *1 Henry IV.*" *Texas Studies in Literature and Language* 4.4 (1974), 605–14.

Hazlitt, William. *"Henry IV* in Two Parts." *Characters of Shakespeare's Plays*. London: C. H. Reynell for R. Hunter, 1817, pp. 188–202.

Hunter, G. K. "Shakespeare's Politics and the Rejection of Falstaff." *Critical Quarterly* 8 (1959), 229–36.

Hunter, Robert G. "Shakespeare's Comic Sense As It Strikes Us Today: Falstaff and the Protestant Ethic." *Shakespeare, Pattern of Excelling Nature*, ed. David Bevington and Jay L. Halio. Newark: University of Delaware Press, 1978, pp. 125–32.

Johnson, Samuel. *The Plays of William Shakespeare*. London, 1765.

Langbaum, Robert. "Character versus Action in Shakespeare." *The Poetry of Experience*. New York: Random House, 1957, pp. 168–81.

Macdonald, Ronald R. "Uneasy Lies: Language and History in Shakespeare's Lancastrian Tetralogy." *Shakespeare Quarterly*. 35 (1984), 22–39.

Mackenzie, Henry. "Remarks on the Character of Falstaff." *The Lounger*. London, no. 68, Saturday, May 20, 1786, and no. 69, Saturday, May 27, 1786.

Montagu, Elizabeth. *An Essay on the Writings and Genius of Shakespeare, Compared with the Greek and French Dramatic Poets*. London, published for J. Dodsley, 1769, pp. 100–08, 121–24.

Morgann, Maurice. *An Essay on the Dramatic Character of Sir John Falstaff*. London, published for T. Davies, 1777, pp. 1–6, 29–39, 93–107, 113–48.

Morris, Corbyn. *An Essay Towards Fixing the True Standards of Wit, Humor, Raillery, Satire, and Ridicule*. London, published for J. Roberts, 1744, pp. 23–31.

Palmer, D. J. "Casting Off the Old Man: History and St. Paul in *Henry IV*." *Critical Quarterly* 12 (1970), 267–83.

Shaw, George Bernard. *Dramatic Opinions and Essays*. New York: Brentano's, 1909, I, 428–30.

Smallwood, R. L. *"Henry IV, Parts 1 and 2* at the Barbican Theatre." A Review. *Critical Quarterly* 25 (1983), 15–20.

Spivack, Bernard. "Moral Metaphor and Dramatic Image." *Shakespeare and the Allegory of Evil*. New York: Columbia University Press, 1958, pp. 204–05.

Sprague, Arthur Colby. "Gadshill Revisited." *Shakespeare Quarterly* 4 (1953), 125–37.

Tillyard, E. M. W. *"Henry IV." Shakespeare's History Plays.* London: Chatto & Windus, 1944, pp. 264–80.

Van Doren, Mark. *"Henry IV." Shakespeare.* New York: Henry Holt, 1939, rpt. Doubleday, n.d., pp. 97–114.

Watson, Robert N. "The *Henry IV* Plays." *Shakespeare and the Hazards of Ambition.* Cambridge, Mass.: Harvard University Press, 1984, pp. 47–75.

Wharton, T. F. *"Henry the Fourth Parts I and II": Text and Performance.* London: Macmillan, 1983, pp. 44–54, 67–80.

Wilson, John Dover. "The Falstaff Myth." *The Fortunes of Falstaff.* Cambridge: Cambridge University Press, 1943, pp. 17–35, 130–33.

Other Works Cited in the Introduction but Not Included in the Collection

Alexander, Franz. "A Note on Falstaff." *Psychoanalytic Quarterly* 3 (1933), 592–606.

Empson, William. *Some Versions of Pastoral.* London: Chatto & Windus, 1935.

Jenkins, Harold. *The Structural Problem in Shakespeare's "Henry the Fourth."* London: Methuen, 1956.

Kelly, Henry Ansgar. *Divine Providence in the England of Shakespeare's Histories.* Cambridge, Mass.: Harvard University Press, 1970.

Kris, Ernst. "Prince Hal's Conflict." *Psychoanalytic Quarterly* 17 (1948), 487–506.

Schücking, Levin L. *Character Problems in Shakespeare's Plays.* London: Harrap and Co., 1922.

Stoll, E. E. *Shakespeare Studies: Historical and Comparative in Method.* New York: Macmillan, 1927.